The Moving Form of Film

The Moving Form of Film

Historicising the Medium through Other Media

Edited by

Lúcia Nagib and Stefan Solomon

OXFORD
UNIVERSITY PRESS

Oxford University Press is a department of the University of Oxford. It furthers
the University's objective of excellence in research, scholarship, and education
by publishing worldwide. Oxford is a registered trade mark of Oxford University
Press in the UK and certain other countries.

Published in the United States of America by Oxford University Press
198 Madison Avenue, New York, NY 10016, United States of America.

© Oxford University Press 2023

All rights reserved. No part of this publication may be reproduced, stored in
a retrieval system, or transmitted, in any form or by any means, without the
prior permission in writing of Oxford University Press, or as expressly permitted
by law, by license, or under terms agreed with the appropriate reproduction
rights organization. Inquiries concerning reproduction outside the scope of the
above should be sent to the Rights Department, Oxford University Press, at the
address above.

You must not circulate this work in any other form
and you must impose this same condition on any acquirer.

CIP data is on file at the Library of Congress

ISBN 978-0-19-762171-4 (pbk.)
ISBN 978-0-19-762170-7 (hbk.)

DOI: 10.1093/oso/9780197621707.001.0001

Paperback printed by Marquis Book Printing, Canada
Hardback printed by Bridgeport National Bindery, Inc., United States of America

Contents

List of Illustrations   *vii*
Acknowledgements   *xi*
Contributors   *xiii*

Introduction   1
Stefan Solomon and Lúcia Nagib

PART I METHODOLOGIES

1. **Hegel, Cinema, and the Other Arts**   15
   Alain Badiou

2. **One-Dimensional Man? A Reply to Alain Badiou**   21
   James Hellings

3. **Hybrid Variations on an Intermedial Theme**   29
   Robert Stam

4. **Parallax Historiography and Metareference: The Intramedial Case of Nagasaki Shun'ichi's *Heart, Beating in the Dark***   47
   Mark Player

PART II TECHNOLOGIES AND ENVIRONMENTS

5. **Intermediality and the Carousel Slide Projector**   65
   Julian Ross

6. ***Up the Junction*, Intermediality, and Social Change**   81
   Sarah Street

7. **When the Past Is Present: Digital Cinema and the Philosophical Toys of Pre-Cinema**   97
   Ismail Xavier

8. **Panoramic Views, Planetary Visions: An Intermedial Analysis of *Medium Earth* and *Walden***   113
   Tiago de Luca

9. Elemental Intermedia 131
   Stefan Solomon

PART III NATIONAL AND REGIONAL PHENOMENA

10. Cinema from the Perspective of the Stage: For an Integrated History of Theatrical Entertainment in Brazil 151
    Luciana Corrêa de Araújo

11. Flamenco on Screen: The Intermedial Legacy of Carmen Amaya in *Bajarí* 168
    Albert Elduque

12. Impurity and Identification: Historicising Chinese Cinema through Opera 185
    Cecília Mello

13. Historicising the Story through Film and Music: An Intermedial Reading of *Heimat 2* 202
    Lúcia Nagib

PART IV INTERMEDIAL ARTISTS

14. Stephen Dwoskin, an Intermedial Artist 225
    Rachel Garfield, Jenny Chamarette, and Darragh O'Donoghue

15. Intermedial Voices: Intersections in Feminist Sound and Moving Image 247
    Claire M. Holdsworth

16. Entanglements of Intermediality: Polanski, Pinter, *Steptoe and Son* 267
    Jonathan Bignell

17. The Intermedial Reworking of History in Peter Greenaway's *The Tulse Luper Suitcases* Trilogy 281
    Fátima Chinita

Index *301*

Illustrations

4.1 to 4.4	The four storytelling strands of *Heart, Beating in the Dark—New Version*.	56
4.5 and 4.6	Comparison of the original *Heart, Beating in the Dark* and how it appears in the *New Version*.	58
5.1	The slide projectors for *Non-chronological History* (2013) by Prapat Jiwarangsan.	75
6.1	Susan Benson's line drawing for *Up the Junction* (1963).	84
6.2	Ken Loach's TV play adaptation of *Up the Junction* (1965).	85
6.3	Colour and widescreen aesthetics in Peter Collinson's *Up the Junction* (1968).	90
7.1 and 7.2	Dumont turning his hand and extended finger in *Santoscópio = Dumontagem* (2010), by Carlos Adriano.	101
7.3	The mutoscope system in *Santoscópio = Dumontagem* (2010), by Carlos Adriano.	102
7.4 and 7.5	The conversation between Dumont and Rolls in *Santoscópio = Dumontagem* (2010), by Carlos Adriano.	103
7.6	Dumont and Rolls shown upside down in a negative print in *Santoscópio = Dumontagem* (2010), by Carlos.	104
7.7 and 7.8	The kaleidoscopic dynamics in *Santoscópio = Dumontagem* (2010), by Carlos Adriano.	105
7.9	The pixels that form digital images in *Santoscópio = Dumontagem* (2010), by Carlos Adriano.	109
7.10	A large white sheet takes the form of moving wings in *Santoscópio = Dumontagem* (2010), by Carlos Adriano.	110
8.1	A panoramic explanation (1717) of the "view" of Rome.	115
8.2 and 8.3	Forest-seeing in *Walden* (2018), by Daniel Zimmermann.	125
8.4	The cover of *Walden*'s (Daniel Zimmermann, 2018) "visual screenplay."	127
8.5	The installation version of Daniel Zimmermann's *Walden* (2018).	128

9.1	The Brocken spectre in *Umbra* (Florian Fischer and Johannes Krell, 2019).	138
9.2	Monument Valley in *EASY RIDER* (James Benning, 2012).	140
9.3	Dialogue from *Zabriskie Point* (Michelangelo Antonioni, 1970) reverberating in the Californian landscapes of *Victoria* (Lukas Marxt, 2018).	141
9.4	The screen outside the theatre in *A Proposal to Project in Scope* (Viktoria Schmid, 2020).	142
11.1	Carmen Amaya dancing in *María de la O* (Francisco Elías, 1936).	171
11.2 and 11.3	Carmen Amaya singing *bulerías* and tapping on a table with her fingers in *Los Tarantos* (Francisco Rovira Beleta, 1963).	173
11.4 and 11.5	Juanito watching *Los Tarantos* and imitating Carmen Amaya's gestures in *Bajarí* (Eva Vila, 2013).	177
11.6	Karime's feet on stage in *Bajarí* (Eva Vila, 2013).	179
11.7	Juanito's bare feet in *Bajarí* (Eva Vila, 2013).	180
11.8	Karime practises in *Bajarí* (Eva Vila, 2013).	181
12.1	A poster for China's first colour film, *Remorse at Death* (Fei Mu, 1948).	190
12.2	Douzi cries during the opera performance in *Farewell My Concubine* (Chen Kaige, 1993).	196
12.3	"I am by nature a girl": Douzi's painful transformation into a *dan* in *Farewell My Concubine* (Chen Kaige, 1993).	196
12.4	Burning the opera wardrobe in *Farewell My Concubine* (Chen Kaige, 1993).	197
13.1	Nikos Mamangakis in a cameo in *Heimat 2* (Edgar Reitz, 1992).	212
13.2	Clarissa receives a cello lesson in *Heimat 2* (Edgar Reitz, 1992).	213
13.3	Hermann marks Clarissa's absence in *Heimat 2* (Edgar Reitz, 1992).	215
14.1	An image from *Trixi* (1969) is superimposed on *Trying to Kiss the Moon* (Stephen Dwoskin, 1994).	233
14.2	Young Dwoskin in *Trying to Kiss the Moon* (Stephen Dwoskin, 1994).	235
14.3	Young Dwoskin becomes golden-coloured lens flare in *Trying to Kiss the Moon* (Stephen Dwoskin, 1994).	236
14.4	Close-up of young Dwoskin in *Trying to Kiss the Moon* (Stephen Dwoskin, 1994).	237
14.5	Abstracted image of Dwoskin's torso in *Trying to Kiss the Moon* (Stephen Dwoskin, 1994).	238
14.6 and 14.7	Refilmed, slowed-down footage in *Trying to Kiss the Moon* (Stephen Dwoskin, 1994).	239

14.8	Stephen Dwoskin, *Six Figures*, oil on canvas, mid-1960s.	240
15.1	Photo of the Feminist Improvising Group (FIG).	248
15.2	Still from Laura Mulvey and Peter Wollen, *AMY!* (1980).	250
15.3	Poster for FIG performance.	253
15.4	Still from Laura Mulvey and Peter Wollen, *AMY!* (1980).	256
15.5	Still from Laura Mulvey and Peter Wollen, *AMY!* (1980).	258
16.1	Goldberg and McCann terrorise Stanley in Harold Pinter's *The Birthday Party*, 1958.	269
16.2	A gangster invades the couple's domestic space in Roman Polanski's *Cul de Sac* (1966).	272
16.3	The convicts with Harold Steptoe and his father in *Steptoe and Son*.	275
17.1	J. J. Feild auditioning in Peter Greenaway's *Part 1: The Moab Story*.	283
17.2	Timeline in Peter Greenaway's *Part 2: Vaux to the Sea*.	284
17.3	Photo shoot in the Moab desert jailhouse in Peter Greenaway's *Part 1: The Moab Story*.	285
17.4	Maria Falconetti in Carl Dreyer's film in Peter Greenaway's *Part 2: Vaux to the Sea*.	286
17.5	Ingres's deconstructed painting in Peter Greenaway's *Part 2: Vaux to the Sea*.	289
17.6	Roger Rees in Peter Greenaway's *Part 3: From Sark to the Finish*.	290
17.7	A Greenaway lookalike in Peter Greenaway's *Part 2: Vaux to the Sea*.	292
17.8	Auditioning for the roles of Beckett and Kafka in Peter Greenaway's *Part 1: The Moab Story*.	295

Acknowledgements

At the origin of this book is the conference The Moving Form of Film: Exploring Intermediality as a Historiographic Method, held at the University of Reading on 6–8 November 2017. This conference, as much as its ensuing book, are outputs of the project Towards an Intermedial History of Brazilian Cinema: Exploring Intermediality as a Historiographic Method (short title: IntermIdia), 2015–2019, funded by the Arts and Humanities Research Council (AHRC) in the United Kingdom (AH/M008363/1) and the São Paulo Research Foundation (FAPESP) in Brazil (2014/50821-3). We are deeply indebted to these agencies, as well as to the University of Reading, its Heritage & Creativity Research Theme and Department of Film, Theatre & Television, whose unstinting organisational and managerial support, as well as further funding, were decisive for the project's full fruition.

The editors of this book owe a personal debt to the enthusiasm, insight, and comradeship of our colleagues on the IntermIdia Project: Luciana Corrêa de Araújo, Flávia Cesarino Costa, Samuel Paiva, Suzana Reck Miranda, Margarida Adamatti, Alison Butler, John Gibbs, Lisa Purse, Albert Elduque, Richard McKay, Tamara Courage, Debora Taño, Sancler Ebert, and Danielle Ribeiro, without whom none of our hundred-plus outputs would have been possible. Throughout its life, the IntermIdia Project was blessed with the engagement of a brilliant advisory board, including Ágnes Pethő, Julian Ross, Lisa Shaw, and Deborah Shaw. We owe them our heartfelt thanks. Thanks to Hsin Hsieh for her last-minute heroics in copyediting the volume, which were very much appreciated. Special thanks are due to Peter Greenaway for granting us free use of a still of *The Tulse Luper Suitcases* project on the book cover. Thanks, too, to Judith Acevedo, for her terrific work in compiling the index.

Stefan would like to thank Monica O'Brien and Vincent Solomon O'Brien for their forbearance, understanding, and support over the past two years. Lúcia has a debt, as always, to Stephen Shennan for his enthusiasm and readiness to read and discuss her work.

Finally, thanks are due to our editors at Oxford University Press, Norman Hirschy and Lauralee Yeary, for their patience and care, as well as to our anonymous reviewers for their helpful advice.

Contributors

Luciana Corrêa de Araújo is an assistant professor at the Federal University of São Carlos. Her research on Brazilian silent cinema focuses mainly on intermedial relations, women's activities, and cinema in the state of Pernambuco. She is the author of *A crônica de cinema no Recife dos anos 50* (1997) and *Joaquim Pedro de Andrade: Primeiros tempos* (2013), co-editor with Lúcia Nagib and Tiago de Luca of *Towards an Intermedial History of Brazilian Cinema* (2022), and has published in journals and edited collections, including *Nova história do cinema brasileiro* (Sheila Schvarzman and Fernão Pessoa Ramos, eds., 2018) and *Stars and Stardom in Brazilian Cinema* (Tim Bergfelder, Lisa Shaw, and João Luiz Vieira, eds., 2016).

Alain Badiou, a French philosopher, is one of the world's most influential thinkers. He is former chair of philosophy at the Ecole Normale Supérieure and founder of the Faculty of Philosophy of the Université de Paris VIII with Gilles Deleuze, Michel Foucault, and Jean-François Lyotard. His oeuvre spans philosophy, literary fiction, theatre, opera, and journalism. He has published a number of major philosophical works, including *Theory of the Subject* (2009), *Being and Event* (2005), *Manifesto for Philosophy* (1999), and *Deleuze: The Clamor of Being* (1999). Other books include *The Meaning of Sarkozy, Ethics, Metapolitics, Polemics, The Communist Hypothesis, Five Lessons on Wagner, Wittgenstein's Anti-Philosophy, Handbook of Inaesthetics*, and *In Praise of Love*. His incursions into cinema include his book *Cinema*, a collection of articles dating between 1958 and 2010. Badiou was politically active very early on and continues to figure regularly in public political debates. Together with journalist Aude Lancelin, he holds monthly online discussions called *Contre-courant* (https://qg.media/programme/contre-courant/). At eighty-six years of age, he has just published the third and last volume of the saga *Being and Event*, titled *The Immanence of Truths* (2022) (the second volume being *Logiques des mondes*).

Jonathan Bignell is a professor of television and film at the University of Reading. His books include the monographs *Beckett on Screen* (2009), *Postmodern Media Culture* (2000), three editions of *An Introduction to Television Studies* (2004, 2008, 2013), two editions of *British Television Drama: Past Present and Future* (edited with Stephen Lacey, 2000, 2014), *A European Television History* (edited with Andreas Fickers, 2008), and the collection *Writing and Cinema* (1999). His articles include contributions to the journals *Screen, Critical Studies in Television*, the *Historical Journal of Film, Radio and Television*, and *Media History*. His recent work includes research into science fiction TV of the 1960s and the history of transatlantic television drama. He has managed teams of researchers on a series of large-scale collaborative projects, most recently a three-year study funded by the British Arts and Humanities Research Council about Harold Pinter's work for television, cinema, radio, and theatre.

Contributors

Jenny Chamarette is a senior research fellow at Reading School of Art. Co-editor of *Guilt and Shame: Essays in French Literature, Thought and Visual Culture* (with Jennifer Higgins, 2010) and author of *Phenomenology and the Future of Film* (2012), her next monograph, *Museums and the Moving Image: Cinemuseology, Cultural Politics, Film*, is forthcoming with Bloomsbury in 2024. From 2018–2022 she was co-investigator on the interdisciplinary AHRC-funded project *The Legacies of Stephen Dwoskin's Personal Cinema*. She sits on the editorial boards of the Film Section for *Modern Languages Open*, on the advisory board for *MAI: Journal of Feminism and Visual Culture*, and is commissioning co-editor for MAI Press, an open access, experimental scholarly imprint of Punctum.

Fátima Chinita is an associate professor at the Theatre and Film School of the Polytechnic Institute of Lisbon, and a researcher at ICNOVA. She completed her postdoctoral research partly at the Intermediality and Multimodality Centre of the University of Linnaeus under the supervision of Professor Lars Elleström. She is the author of the book *O Espectador (In)visível–Reflexividade na Óptica do Espectador em INLAND EMPIRE* (2013), and is currently preparing a monograph on symbiotic cinema. She publishes on intermediality and interarts, metanarrative, metacinema, authorship, and the essay film, and has recently guest-edited journal issues for *Ekphrasis* and *Interfaces*.

Tiago de Luca is a reader in film studies at the University of Warwick. He is the author of *Planetary Cinema: Film, Media and the Earth* (2022) and *Realism of the Senses in World Cinema: The Experience of Physical Reality* (2014) and the co-editor (with Nuno Barradas Jorge) of *Slow Cinema* (2016) and (with Lúcia Nagib and Luciana Corrêa de Araújo) *Towards an Intermedial History of Brazilian Cinema* (2022). He is the co-editor, with Lúcia Nagib, of the Bloomsbury Film Thinks series.

Albert Elduque is a lecturer in film studies at Universitat Pompeu Fabra, Barcelona. His research areas are intermediality and film, political cinema, and music documentaries, with a focus on Spanish and Brazilian cinemas. He has published widely on intermediality and filmmakers such as Pier Paolo Pasolini, Rainer Werner Fassbinder, Werner Herzog, and Marta Rodríguez. Between 2016 and 2019 he was a postdoctoral researcher in Brazilian cinema at the University of Reading, attached to the major AHRC-FAPESP-funded project Towards an Intermedial History of Brazilian Cinema: Exploring Intermediality as a Historiographic Method, and since 2016 he is co-editor of the peer-reviewed academic journal *Comparative Cinema*, published by Universitat Pompeu Fabra.

Rachel Garfield is an artist and a professor of fine art at the Royal College of Art (RCA). She is the author of *Experimental Film-making and Punk: Feminist Audio Visual Culture of the 1970s and 1980s* (2022), co-editor with Henry K. Miller of *Dwoskino: The Gaze of Stephen Dwoskin* (LUX Publishing, 2022) and the principal investigator of a large AHRC-funded project (2019–2022), *The Legacies of Stephen Dwoskin's Personal Cinema*. Exhibitions and screenings of her work in the United Kingdom have been hosted by The Whitechapel Gallery, The Hatton Gallery, Wolverhampton Art Gallery, Focal Point, London Short Film Festival, and Open City Doc Festival, and abroad in the Galerie du Presbytère, Saint-Briac, CCA Santa Fe, Arizona State University Museum, and Aqua Art Fair Miami. Garfield's work has featured in Amelia Jones's "An 'Other' History: Feminist Art in Britain since 1970" in *Contemporary Art in the United Kingdom* (2015).

Contributors xv

James Hellings is a lecturer in art at the University of Reading School of Art. He has published numerous essays and a book on modern and contemporary art and aesthetics, with an emphasis on the Frankfurt School of critical theory. His first monograph, *Adorno and Art: Aesthetic Theory Contra Critical Theory* (2014), is soon to be followed by his second monograph, *Adorno and Film: Thinking in Images*.

Claire M. Holdsworth is an independent archivist and writer based in London. With a specialist interest in sound, their work reexamines histories of artists' moving image (from the late 1960s to the late 1980s). They currently lecture at the University of the Arts London, had an Early Career Research Fellowship at Kingston School of Art (Kingston University London), and completed an AHRC-funded PhD based in the British Artists' Film and Video Study Collection, Central Saint Martins (UAL). Holdsworth has written for a number of journals and books and is currently writing a monograph on the overlaps between experimental feminist moving image and sound practices in London in the late 1970s/early 1980s.

Cecília Mello is a professor of film and audiovisual media at the Department of Film, Radio and Television, University of São Paulo. Her research focuses on issues of audiovisual realism, cinema and urban spaces, and intermediality, with an emphasis on Chinese and British cinemas. She is the author of, among others, *The Cinema of Jia Zhangke: Realism and Memory in Chinese Film* (2019), which received Honourable Mention for the 2020 Award for Best Monograph, British Association of Film, Television and Screen Studies.

Lúcia Nagib is a professor of film at the University of Reading. Her research has focused on polycentric approaches to world cinema, new waves and new cinemas, cinematic realism, and intermediality, among other subjects. She is the author of many books, including *Realist Cinema as World Cinema: Non-cinema, Intermedial Passages, Total Cinema* (2020), *World Cinema and the Ethics of Realism* (2011), and *Brazil on Screen: Cinema Novo, New Cinema, Utopia* (2007). Her edited and co-edited books include *Towards an Intermedial History of Brazilian Cinema* (with Luciana Corrêa de Araújo and Tiago de Luca, 2022), *Impure Cinema: Intermedial and Intercultural Approaches to Film* (with Anne Jerslev, 2014), *Theorizing World Cinema* (with Chris Perriam and Rajinder Dudrah, 2011), *Realism and the Audiovisual Media* (with Cecília Mello, 2009), and *The New Brazilian Cinema* (2003). She is the writer and director, with Samuel Paiva, of the award-winning feature-length documentary, *Passages* (UK, 2019).

Darragh O'Donoghue works as an archivist at Tate. He completed a PhD on Stephen Dwoskin at the Department of Art, University of Reading, for which he compiled a catalogue raisonné. He is a contributing writer for *Cineaste*, and a regular writer for *Senses of Cinema*, for whom he co-edited a special dossier on popular Hindi film in May 2022. He has also written for *ARC*, *The Irish Journal of French Studies*, *MIRAJ (Moving Image Review & Art Journal)*, and *Radio Journal*, wrote on the British reception of Andrzej Wajda for the anthology *Polish Cinema in a Transnational Context* (2014) and won the inaugural Pete Walsh Critical Writing Award, Irish Film Institute (2014). He has lectured in Ireland and the UK on film and art history, literature, and archives. He is contemplating a book on auteurism and "Bollywood."

Mark Player is a lecturer in film at the University of Reading. His PhD thesis investigated the intermediality of Japanese film production during the punk era of the 1970s and 1980s. His research has been published in such journals as *Japan Forum*, *Punk & Post Punk*, and *Acta Universitatis Sapientiae, Film and Media Studies*. He has also contributed chapters to *Punk Identities, Punk Utopias: Global Punk and Media* (2021) and *Fifty Key Figures in Cyberpunk Culture* (2022).

Julian Ross is a researcher, curator, and writer based in Amsterdam. He is an assistant professor at Leiden University Centre for the Arts in Society and is co-organising Doc Fortnight 2023 at The Museum of Modern Art (MoMA). He co-edited *Japanese Expanded Cinema and Intermedia: Critical Texts of the 1960s* (2020).

Stefan Solomon is senior lecturer in media studies at Macquarie University and writes on the intersections of cinema and other media. He is the author of *William Faulkner in Hollywood: Screenwriting for the Studios* (2017), editor of *Tropicália and Beyond: Dialogues in Brazilian Film History* (2017), and co-editor (with Alix Beeston) of *Incomplete: The Feminist Possibilities of the Unfinished Film* (2023).

Robert Stam is a university professor at New York University. He has authored, co-authored, and edited some nineteen books on film and cultural theory, national cinema (French and Brazilian), comparative race and postcolonial studies. His books include *François Truffaut and Friends* (2006), *Literature through Film* (2005), *Film Theory: An Introduction* (2000), *Tropical Multiculturalism* (1997), *Subversive Pleasures* (1989), *Reflexivity in Film and Literature* (1995), and *Brazilian Cinema* (1982). He is co-author (with Ella Shohat) of *Unthinking Eurocentrism* (1994, and 2014 with a new afterword) and *Race in Translation: Culture Wars around the Postcolonial Atlantic* (2012). His most recent books are *Keywords in Subversive Film/Media Aesthetics* (2015) and *World Literature, Transnational Cinema, Global Media: Towards a Transartistic Commons* (2019). His *Indigeneity and the Decolonial Gaze: Transnational "Indians," Media Aesthetics, and Social Thought* has just been published. His books have been translated into French, Spanish, German, Portuguese, Italian, Greek, Farsi, Korean, Japanese, Chinese, Hebrew, Estonian, Turkish, Serbo-Croatian, and Arabic.

Sarah Street is professor of film at the University of Bristol, UK. She has published extensively on British film history. Her publications on colour film technologies and aesthetics include *Colour Films in Britain: The Negotiation of Innovation, 1900–55* (2012) and two co-edited collections (with Simon Brown and Liz Watkins), *Color and the Moving Image: History, Theory, Aesthetics, Archive* (2012), and *British Colour Cinema: Practices and Theories* (2013). Her most recent books are *Deborah Kerr* (2018), *Chromatic Modernity: Color, Cinema, and Media of the 1920s* (2019, co-authored with Joshua Yumibe) and *Colour Films in Britain: The Eastmancolor Revolution* (2021). She is Principal Investigator on the European Research Council Advanced Grant STUDIOTEC: Film Studios: Infrastructure, Culture, Innovation in Britain, France, Germany and Italy, 1930–60.

Ismail Xavier is an emeritus professor in the School of Communications and Arts, University of São Paulo. He has been a visiting professor at New York University and the University of Iowa; Leverhulme Visiting Professor at the University of Leeds; and

Tinker Foundation Visiting Professor at the University of Chicago. His many books include *Alegorias do subdesenvolvimento: Cinema Novo, Tropicalismo, Cinema Marginal* (1993 and 2012), *Sertão Mar: Glauber Rocha e a estética da* fome (1983 and 2007), *O Discurso Cinematográfico: A opacidade e a transparência.*(1977 and 2014), *O olhar e a cena: Melodrama, Hollywood, Cinema Novo, Nelson Rodrigues* (2003), *O cinema brasileiro moderno* (2001), and *Allegories of Underdevelopment: Aesthetics and Politics in Brazilian Modern Cinema* (1997).

Introduction

Stefan Solomon and Lúcia Nagib

Writing in New York in 1960, Siegfried Kracauer (1997: 33–34) famously defined film according to two basic kinds of movement: "objective motion," or the movement of objects in front of the camera, and "subjective motion," which aligns the spectator's point of view with the movements of the camera. Subjective motion is further compounded, in Kracauer's view, by editing, which "rush[es] the audience through vast expanses of time and/or space" (34). Additional to this basic scheme, film scholarship has devoted a great amount of attention to film's unrivalled power to "move" the viewer through its unique mimetic properties, which are conducive to immersive, haptic, illusionistic, and, in some cases, interactive spectatorship. Taking an ambitious step forward with relation to these theories, this book places its bet on a hitherto little-explored kind of cinematic movement: the fluid quality of the film form itself. Histories of film as a technological medium have focused on its specificity as it gradually separated from the other art and medial forms at its base: theatre, dance, fairground spectacle, painting, literature, still photography, and other pre-cinematic expressions. Instead, this collection takes to heart Alain Badiou's (2005: 79) claim that cinema does not add itself to preexisting art forms but draws on them all in a permanent movement "that subtracts them from themselves." By observing the ebb and flow of film's contours within the bounds of an array of other artistic and medial expressions, this collection aspires to establish a flexible historical platform for the moving form of film, posited, from production to consumption, as a transforming and transformative medium.

At the origin of this book is the November 2017 conference at the University of Reading that spawned its title, as part of the larger AHRC/FAPESP-funded project Towards an Intermedial History of Brazilian Cinema: Exploring Intermediality as a Historiographic Method (2015–2019). The wager of that collaborative project was that the history of Brazilian cinema in particular—given the nation's rich cultural associations with various musical, performative, and visual traditions—is one perceptibly marked by the interweaving of film with other forms, and as such would present a compelling case study for testing the possibilities of the intermedial method (see Nagib and Solomon 2019; Courage and Elduque 2020; Nagib, Araújo, and de Luca 2022). However, the IntermIdia Project's broader ambition was to test intermediality as a historiographic method applicable to cinema as a whole. This is not to say that the national approach would lose its appeal in the international arena, and in fact many of the chapters in this book consider their chosen examples within a particular national film industry or culture: Sarah Street in Chapter 6 and Jonathan Bignell in Chapter 16 demonstrate the particular entanglement of theatre and television practices within British cinema, while in Chapter 12 Cecília Mello unveils the indelible mark of operatic traditions in Chinese cinema of all times. However, while cinema has often been understood with recourse to the nation-state as an organising principle, its potential for global circulation and its early claims to speak a "universal" language suggest that intermedial connections are equally at work beyond national borders. It is not by accident that films have often been approached via literature and treated as a kind of universal "language," as per Christian Metz's (1991) foundational semiology of the cinema. Likewise, Vachel Lindsay's (1998) early vision of a "hieroglyphics" of the cinema presents us with an intermedial form, which would make of moving images and sounds a usable linguistic system.

That cinema was born of mixed artistic and medial parentage and continues to develop with and against other cultural forms is by now quite clear; indeed, while the contributions of the many collaborators and participants in our project attest to this fact, the assertion that cinema is in and of itself an intermedial art form is nothing new. From the vantage point of today—when "hybridity" seems to have all but worn out its welcome as a radical concept (Nagib 2014) and the convergence of all media in the infinitude of the digital seems complete—it is not only uncontroversial but nigh on tautological to argue that film studies must look outside of cinema as a discrete entity if it is to understand the medium and its place in the world. To illustrate the point: almost twenty years ago now, when Janet Staiger (2004: 127) called for a more capacious approach to film history and cautioned that "being sheltered by studying only film is to work with blinders on," David Bordwell (2005) rejected the very idea that film scholars study "only film" and argued that were such a blinkered formalist approach possible it would still not necessarily amount to the full embrace of medium specificity.

In recent years, intermediality has appeared particularly apt to approach film's moving form. The term "intermedia" derives principally from the artist Dick Higgins (Higgins and Higgins 2001), who was writing in the United States in the 1960s during what would be dubbed the "Paleocybernetic Age"

(Youngblood 1970: 41), an era of expanded cross-pollinations of cinema, performance, and the visual arts that were perceived as being matched by the utopian possibility of an expanding consciousness. But the notion of an intermedial cinema has been touched upon, if not always by name, by a wide variety of observers expressing in one way or another the value of approaching the audiovisual medium from a place beyond the screen. We might consider immediately a few specific suggestions of cinema's borrowings from its sister media: Sergei Eisenstein's (1977) assertion that the parallel action and cross-cutting of D. W. Griffith's body of work was to an extent presupposed by a kind of novelistic montage dreamed up long before by Charles Dickens; the fact that celluloid film's base is still photography, whose distinctiveness is lost in the illusion of motion dispensed by the projector (Stewart 1999); and the way that more recent digital cinema harbours a relation to pixels which is similar to that of previous supports with photography, both of which form its "extrusive" substrate (Stewart 2020: 44).

Cinema contains multitudes, to be sure, but on and off the screen it digests and interacts with other art forms and media differently over the course of history, and is itself transformed through these encounters. Viewed intermedially, cinema was apprehended in its early decades of existence variously as a deficient "artistic composite" that was once imperilled by the blunt invasion of sound to accompany its silent moving images (Arnheim 1957) or as a kind of summative parvenu, as in Ricciotto Canudo's 1911 assessment of it as "the Art of total synthesis" that "reconciles all the others" (Canudo 1975: 253, 254). But against the centrifugal power of the cinema screen, which serves as the meeting point of the other arts and media, indeed of all reality outside of it, for much of its lifespan film has also moved away from the traditional theatrical setting itself. In 1981, Serge Daney (1998) followed cinema to the television set and back and found that, like an old couple, the two had come to resemble one another; in the twenty-first century, television has itself accepted the plaudits originally reserved for the big screen, with its quality dramatic offerings regularly referred to as "cinematic TV." More recently, in what Raymond Bellour (2018) has denoted as the "quarrel of the dispositifs," moving images shown in the black box of the movie theatre and as installations in the white cube of the gallery reveal both affinities and irreconcilable differences. And today it seems clear that cinema is in a constant process of "relocation" to an array of different devices and screens that call for a reassessment of its singularity (see Casetti 2015).

Aside from these and many other observations of cinema's affiliations with the other arts, intermediality, a byproduct notably of the digital epoch, has catalysed a wealth of scholarly undertakings. (For surveys of the field, see

Pethő 2010, 2020.) Indeed, several decades now of concerted and detailed research into intermediality has carved out a place for the concept to the extent that a whole host of monographs, edited collections, journals (the Canadian *Intermédialités* and the Romanian *Acta Universitatis Sapientiae, Film and Media Studies*), and book series (Rodopi's "Studies in Intermediality"; Edinburgh University Press's "Studies in Film and Intermediality") all either bear its name or are guided by its spirit. More specifically, intermediality has come to designate in a positivist sense the "in between" of cinema and other media, as the prefix "inter-" suggests (Rajewsky 2005) and which at times defines itself against a congeries of other cognate terms, such as "semiotics," "intertextuality," "transmediality," "multimodality" (Elleström 2010), "interart," "transartistic" (Stam 2019; this volume), and "remediation" (Bolter and Grusin 1999), while at other times drawing on such coinages to explore the relations between cinema and that from which it is qualitatively distinct. We certainly owe a debt to such scholarship, and particularly to its efflorescence in film studies, where it has been put to particularly productive use (see Mack 2017; Houwen 2017; Bruhn and Gjelsvik 2018; Durcan 2020).

However, while we remain aware of the complicated taxonomies of intermedial research, it will become clear upon surveying the chapters of this collection that nothing like a "uniform" intermedial approach is adopted throughout, with contributors drawing on the reserves of wildly different persuasions, generating lively debates. Film's moving form starts, here, as a theme for philosophical enquiry, framed in terms of a resurrected totality drawing on Hegel's classification of the arts, in Alain Badiou's fascinating Chapter 1, which is, however, fiercely contested by James Hellings in Chapter 2, by recourse to Theodor Adorno's negative dialectics and cultural-industry theory. Intermediality is then brought into dialogue with media archaeology by Ismail Xavier (in Chapter 7) and Tiago de Luca (in Chapter 8), both of whom excavate pre-cinematic forms from within contemporary experimental practices. Elsewhere, moreover, "media" refers to a number of unsuspected innovative enactments, such as environmental phenomena (Stefan Solomon in Chapter 9), body language (Albert Elduque in Chapter 11), the human voice (Claire Holdsworth in Chapter 15), and even artists' lives (such as that of experimental filmmaker Stephen Dwoskin, explored by Rachel Garfield, Jenny Chamarette, and Darragh O'Donoghue in Chapter 14).

Nevertheless, the overarching aim of this collection is to show how film's structural hybridity might be conceived of and employed specifically as a *method* that alters our perceptions of dominant historiographies of cinema and demonstrates how a willingness to think around and beyond cinema might return us to the medium with new insights about a historical trajectory we think we know so well. Visions of the "evolution" of cinema have traditionally hinged on the axis of World War II that separates so-called classical Hollywood cinema from a purported modern European-style production. Though embraced under various guises by scholars of the caliber of André Bazin (2009b), Giles Deleuze (2005), and David Bordwell et al. (2006), as well as contested by Jacques Rancière (2006) and others, this scheme subjects the entire world to the cinematic history of two hegemonic centres. By offering alternative, democratic, and nonlinear narratives of film-historical phenomena, the chapters gathered together here attend to cinema's imbrication within wider ecologies of cultural production to interrogate its supposedly "discrete" existence, effectively seeking to retell its history in tune with the likes of Müller (2010), who has offered a vision of how an intermedial historiographic method might operate. This means that the variety of approaches included here ask questions of their case studies that draw them out of themselves, either by locating within established film histories the incursions or parallel tracks of other media or by finding that cinema has taken leave of the screen altogether and has made its presence felt in unexpected places and times. As such, the thing we call "cinema" in this book might emerge from a recognisable source—the darkened film theatre, the elaborate home entertainment setup—but equally from the theatre stage itself (as demonstrated by Luciana Corrêa de Araújo in Chapter 10) or the carousel slide projector (as analysed by Julian Ross in Chapter 5). Not to mention that film, with all its nonfilmic expressions, can equally serve as a means of history-telling, as argued by Fátima Chinita in Chapter 17 with regards to Peter Greenaway's *Tulse Luper Suitcases* trilogy, and by Lúcia Nagib in Chapter 13, focusing on the monumental *Heimat* project.

In making our collective advance on cinema and its history from such angles, we heed Bazin's (2009c) call, whose defence of cinema's "impure" admixture has informed our work elsewhere (Nagib and Jerslev 2014). Two connected concepts from Bazin's body of work have been particularly inspirational to this collection. First, Bazin saw in cinema's evolution the residual effect of other media; cinema was born as a "mixed" or "impure" medium, the seventh art beginning and continuing its trajectory perpetually in relation to the art forms that preceded it: literature, theatre, painting, dance, music and photography, among others. The second Bazinian idea that informs this collection is the notion that cinema need not exfoliate all of these other influences, but indeed might see in them forms of reality itself, that might be captured wholesale by the camera just as the profilmic world could also enter the lens without undue interference. This is why he can say, for instance, that Robert Bresson's adaptation of *The Diary of a Country Priest* (1948) is not simply an approximation of the Georges Bernanos source text, but that it "*is* the novel*"* (Bazin 2009a: 159).

Even if we can agree that the "evolution" of the medium does not necessarily entail its journey "toward a predetermined essence" (Rodowick 2007: 37), cinema might be seen conventionally as a medium that has drifted from its intermedial roots, morphing from its earliest instances as a kind of "filmed theatre" to become the technically proficient and wondrous art form we have today. But for Bazin, writing in the late 1940s, it was already clear that the medium would not easily shake its associations with a wide variety of non-cinematic and proto-cinematic forebears, which persisted even as motion pictures continued to beat a path away from their own origins. Bazin recognised this in his oft-cited critical review of Georges Sadoul's encyclopedic *Histoire générale du cinéma* (1946), noting that with every technological advancement, cinema was not moving forward but was returning to its roots: "Every new development added to the cinema must, paradoxically, take it nearer and nearer to its origins," he wrote. "In short, cinema has not yet been invented!" (Bazin 2009d: 17).

A range of scholars have explored such a sentiment by retracing the steps of cinema but have resisted the temptation to find at the dawn of cinema only the "machine for telling stories" (Metz 1991: 93) that we are familiar with today. Much of the work undertaken in the so-called new film history, as has been well-documented, returns us to cinema's origins so as to discover the conditions for the medium's emergent self-sufficiency and stabilisation in the early 1900s (Musser 2004). And indeed, several of the chapters in this collection look to the innovations of media archaeology (see Elsaesser 2016) to explore what those technologies that predated cinema properly speaking might tell us about the history of the moving image. But of course, the intermedial condition of cinema continues today, with the proliferation of newer media— themselves often derived from motion picture technologies—also making their presence felt on film screens in both content and form. The chapters assembled here find in the moving form of film a medium for which its early interlocutors in the arts do not provide a necessarily teleological blueprint for its future, nor one that is anywhere near "finished" today, even as it seems subsumed within the digital sameness of our present.

Collection Overview

The collection is divided into four sections, each of which explores the use of intermediality as a historiographic method by way of a particular prism within its overarching sphere of influence; the array of different approaches here itself suggests not one but many ways of understanding intermediality's capacity to reframe film history. The first section, "Methodologies," lays out some of the theoretical possibilities of intermediality, surveying the range of historical debates over how cinema might be considered in relation to the other arts and media. It begins with a daringly speculative piece by the French philosopher Alain Badiou, who presents a kind of counterfactual: if Hegel had been alive to witness the arrival of cinema, how would the "newcomer" medium have entered into his aesthetic system? For Hegel, modern comedy, as the culmination of its preceding forms, would ultimately lead to the dissolution of all arts. Badiou, however, asks: Would cinema, with its combination of architecture, sculpture, painting, and dramatic poetry, be able to cause "the dissolution of this dissolution," that is, the end of art history, not through the negative pirouettes of comedy but by the seriousness and anxiety combined in its redemptive totalisation? In Chapter 2, James Hellings offers a spirited response to this interrogation, contrasting Badiou's vision of cinema as dialectical endpoint with the work of Theodor Adorno, for whom cinema rendered as the seventh art suggests only a "suspect synthesis" of those forms that preceded it.

In the third chapter, Robert Stam offers a broad historical and theoretical overview, both as regards questions of terminology—the distinctions and similarities between "intermedial" and "transmedial" in particular—and with respect to the recurring tendencies of medial cross-pollination across millennia. In Stam's longue durée perspective on the topic, Aristotle commingles with Janelle Monáe, and the affordances of the digital draw cinema out of itself and into the era of Web 2.0, where it now shares the stage with music videos, YouTube shorts, and all manner of social media ephemera. The infinite possibilities of interactive spectatorial response, in turn, lead to a number of questions regarding authorship, appropriation, and copyright that future scholarship would do well to address. Mark Player focuses more squarely on one of the many possible uses of the intermedial method in Chapter 4, where he attends to the concept of "parallax historiography" as a way of understanding the coexistence of the emergent, dominant, and residual media forms that orbit about cinema as we know it. More specifically, he applies this idea to Nagasaki Shunichi's *Heart, Beating in the Dark*, a project that morphed from its first iteration on Super 8 in 1982 into a metareferential remake or sequel of the same name in 2005, and into which the first film was absorbed "intramedially."

The chapters of the second section, "Technologies and Environments," take up this historical thread of the changing tools associated with film production and exhibition but also expand outwards to factor in other non-cinematic media and milieux that have anticipated or shadowed cinema's emergence as a supposedly discrete, identifiable medium. In Chapter 5, Julian Ross addresses the contemporary significance of a seemingly outmoded medium—the carousel slide projector—that continues to inform the practice of a number of artists today, including his two case studies: the Brazilian Dutch artist Pablo Pijnappel and the Thai installation artist and filmmaker Prapat Jiwarangsan. By teasing out the tensions between stillness and movement conjured by the technology, Ross contends that the sphere of influence of projected slides might extend outside the gallery space and into our very understanding of cinema as a moving image form. Such a comparative approach also occupies Sarah Street, in Chapter 6, although here it is cinema's bête noire, television, that forms the point of contrast. In her analysis of two near-contemporary adaptations of Nell Dunn's kitchen-sink short story collection *Up the Junction* (1963)—Ken Loach's 1965 black-and-white version for BBC and Peter Collinson's 1968 reimagining of the work in widescreen and in Technicolor—Street examines how two rival forms of screen media in 1960s Britain might seek to distinguish their respective capacities for realism and entertainment while dealing with the same source text.

In Chapter 7, Ismail Xavier adopts an archaeological approach in his analysis of *Santoscopio = Dumontagem* (2010), an experimental work by the Brazilian filmmaker Carlos Adriano. While the film itself was shot on 35mm and edited digitally, it appropriates a scene that unfolded in an earlier time and from an older medium: a one-shot film featuring a 1901 meeting between one of the earliest aviators, Albert Santos Dumont, and motoring pioneer Charles Rolls and intended for viewing in the proto-cinematic device known as a Mutoscope. Xavier's reading of this confluence of media in Adriano's work demonstrates some of the commonalities between early and contemporary film, but also points to the way that the "toys" of pre-cinema might inform our understanding of its history. Though focusing on recent phenomena, the experimental documentary works *Medium Earth* (The Otolith Group, 2013) and *Walden* (Daniel Zimmerman, 2018), Chapter 8 also resorts to media archaeology when comparing the use of the circular panorama in these films to the nineteenth-century panorama, an immersive medial form that provided its audiences with a novel mode of large-scale "Earth-seeing." For Tiago de Luca, this is the beginning of the longer-lasting panoramic shot, still employed in a wide range of films in which the rotating camera is "an attempt to grasp elusive global and geophysical processes," taking cinema outside the theatre space and into the world. Stefan Solomon also looks beyond film technology and traditional anthropogenic media in Chapter 9, which advances a case for what he calls cinema's "elemental intermedia." Locating in the natural world various approximations of the camera and the screen, Solomon argues that artists' cinema in particular has represented such non-technical forms of cinema in its depictions of eclipses, camera obscuras, and other environmental phenomena, suggesting radically new ways of understanding media today.

The book's third section, "National and Regional Phenomena," apprehends some of the ways in which intermediality might account for the diverse and uneven flows of media forms across global cinema, recasting national and regional film histories in the process. In Chapter 10, Luciana Corrêa de Araújo offers us a reverse shot by focusing on cinema from the perspective of the stage. She demonstrates not only how the Brazilian *teatro de revista* (revue theatre) was forged in the context of silent cinema but also how films imported from the United States and Europe were instrumental in facilitating, rather than hindering, the rise of this theatrical form. By paying attention to such understudied forms as the movie prologues—short theatrical sketches that preceded film screenings in the 1920s—Araújo uncovers a means of reframing early Brazilian cinema and theatre as co-constitutive globally oriented forms. In Chapter 11, Albert Elduque explores the overlapping histories of flamenco and the arts of the Roma people of Spain by looking at the international dance star Carmen Amaya. Starting from Amaya's appearances on screen, Elduque uncovers the diachronic reverberations of dance as a form of gesture, which reaches across time and media in Barcelona before finally arriving in *Bajarí* (Eva Vila, 2011), a documentary about the dancer closely analysed in the chapter.

Incorporating dance, music, and theatre, opera is itself a mode that invites intermedial analysis, especially given its tendencies toward totalisation as the Wagnerian *Gesamtkunstwerk*. In Chapter 12, Cecília Mello explores how Chinese opera has made itself felt across the history of the country's cinema, and how an intermedial reading of the landmark *Farewell My Concubine* (*Bawang Bie Ji*, Chen Kaige, 1993) can demonstrate the artificiality of historical binaries: operatic and realist modes, old and new media, socialist and postsocialist arts. In Chapter 13, Lúcia Nagib turns to Edgar Reitz's monumental *Heimat* film cycle, with a particular focus on its second instalment (1984–2013), as part of a "total-history" project, that is, the retelling of the history of Germany from the nineteenth century to today. While the series is invested in the country's political and cultural history, Nagib locates its most significant intermedial dimension in the way that it "presents history in the making" through the use of music as theme and diegetic performance, as well as the organisational principle of all episodes.

The fourth and final section, "Intermedial Artists," explores the function of artists and filmmakers as living crucibles for the meeting of different art forms on screen, raising questions of intentionality and authorship within the increasingly vast media ecology in which cinema is embedded. In Chapter 14, Rachel Garfield, Jenny Chamarette, and Darragh O'Donoghue argue that the experimental filmmaker Stephen Dwoskin provides an exemplary case study in this regard, not only due to his avowedly intermedial creative praxis but also because intermediality as a method offers "a way of acknowledging the integration of artistic self-expression within a wider sphere of cultural influence." By attending to Dwoskin's outsider status as a working-class, disabled Jewish man, the authors of this chapter contend that intermediality was nothing less than "an aesthetic underpinning" of the artist's life. The British underground film scene also provided fertile ground for interchanges between music and cinema in the 1970s. In Chapter 15, Claire Holdsworth follows some of these connections as they emerge in *AMY!* (Laura Mulvey and Peter Wollen, 1980), a short experimental re-creation of aspects of the life of the aviator Amy Johnson, who was the first woman to fly solo from England to Australia. In analysing this film, Holdsworth uncovers how Johnson as a subject is conjured in particular by the voice, a medium that echoes here from the 1930s but which is also expressed through the avant-garde vocalisations of the Feminist Improvising Group.

Jonathan Bignell also draws his case study from the United Kingdom, but looks to the way that intermediality as a method exhorts us to seek out the transnational connections emerging from our objects of study. In Chapter 16, Bignell adopts an *histoire croisée* approach to investigate the place of Harold Pinter among a coterie of films, plays, and television programs in the 1960s and 1970s, but also sounds a note of caution about the potentially infinite expansiveness that an intermedial focus seems to offer. Finally, in Chapter 17, Fátima Chinita offers a close analysis of Peter Greenaway's *Tulse Luper Suitcases* trilogy (2003–2004), a complex series of films that interweave history, cinema, and other art forms. Seeing Greenaway as a kind of media archaeologist, Chinita explores the way that neither history nor media are presented as stable integers in the films, but are co-constitutive and constantly in flux.

Needless to say, this wide-ranging coverage, in both historical and geographical terms, is only a modest sample of all the possible intermedial phenomena that have marked the moving form of film throughout its existence. Nonetheless, we are confident that the lover of the arts and media will find in these contributions a wealth of fascinating material, which will hopefully spark the imagination of future researchers in their pursuit of new avenues within this inexhaustible theme.

References

Arnheim, Rudolf. 1957. "A New Laocoön: Artistic Composites and the Talking Film." In *Film as Art*, 199–230. Berkeley: University of California Press.
Badiou, Alain. 2005. *Handbook of Inaesthetics*. Translated by Alberto Toscano. Stanford, CA: Stanford University Press.
Bazin, André. 2009a. "*Diary of a Country Priest* and the Robert Bresson Style." In *What Is Cinema?*, translated by Timothy Barnard, 139–160. Montreal: Caboose.
Bazin, André. 2009b. "The Evolution of Film Language." In *What Is Cinema?*, translated by Timothy Barnard, 87–106. Montreal: Caboose.
Bazin, André. 2009c. "For an Impure Cinema: In Defence of Adaptation." In *What Is Cinema?*, translated by Timothy Barnard, 107–138. Montreal: Caboose.
Bazin, André. 2009d. "The Myth of Total Cinema." In *What Is Cinema?*, translated by Timothy Barnard, 13–20. Montreal: Caboose.
Bellour, Raymond. 2018. "The Quarrel of the *Dispositifs*: Reprise." Translated by Danny Fairfax. *Senses of Cinema* 86 (March). https://www.sensesofcinema.com/2018/cinema-and-the-museum/the-quarrel-of-the-dispositifs/#fnref-34283-2.
Bolter, Jay, and Richard Grusin. 1999. *Remediation: Understanding New Media*. Cambridge, MA: MIT Press.
Bordwell, David. 2005. "Film and the Historical Return." March. https://www.davidbordwell.net/essays/return.php.
Bordwell, David, Janet Staiger, and Kristin Thompson. 2006. *The Classical Hollywood Cinema: Film Style and Mode of Production to 1960*. London: Routledge.
Bruhn, Jorgen, and Anne Gjelsvik. 2018. *Cinema between Media: An Intermediality Approach*. Edinburgh: Edinburgh University Press.
Canudo, Ricciotto. 1975. "Manifesto of the Seven Arts." Translated by Steven Kramer. *Literature Film Quarterly* 3, no. 3 (Summer): 252–254.
Casetti, Francesco. 2015. *The Lumière Galaxy: Seven Key Words for the Cinema to Come*. New York: Columbia University Press.
Courage, Tamara, and Albert Elduque. 2020. "Performing the Intermedial across Brazilian Cinema." *Alphaville: Journal of Film and Screen Media* 19, no. 1: 3–12. https://doi.org/10.33178/alpha.19.01.
Daney, Serge. 1998. "Comme tous les vieux couples, cinéma et télévision ont fini par se ressembler." In *Ciné journal, vol. 1: 1981–1982*, 104–112. Paris: Cahiers du cinéma.
Deleuze, Giles. 2005. *Cinema 1: Movement-Image*. New York: Continuum.
Durcan, Sarah. 2020. *Memory and Intermediality in Artists' Moving Image*. Cham, Switzerland: Palgrave Macmillan.
Eisenstein, Sergei. 1977. "Dickens, Griffith, and the Film Today." In *Film Form: Essays in Film Theory*, edited and translated by Jay Leyda, 195–255. New York: Harcourt Brace.
Elleström, Lars, ed. 2010. *Media Borders, Multimodality, and Intermediality*. Basingstoke: Palgrave Macmillan.
Elsaesser, Thomas. 2016. *Film History as Media Archaeology: Tracking Digital Cinema*. Amsterdam: Amsterdam University Press.
Higgins, Dick, and Hannah Higgins. 2001. "Intermedia." *Leonardo* 34, no. 1 (February): 49–54.

Houwen, Janna. 2017. *Film and Video Intermediality: The Question of Medium Specificity in Contemporary Moving Images*. London: Bloomsbury.
Kracauer, Siegfried. 1997. *Theory of Film: The Redemption of Physical Reality*. Princeton, NJ: Princeton University Press.
Lindsay, Vachel. 1998. *The Art of the Moving Picture*. New York: Random House.
Mack, Jonathan. 2017. "Finding Borderland: Intermediality in the Films of Marc Foster." *Cinema Journal* 56, no. 3 (Spring): 24–46.
Metz, Christian. 1991. *Film Language: A Semiotics of the Cinema*. Translated by Michael Taylor. Chicago: University of Chicago Press.
Müller, Jürgen E. 2010. "Intermediality and Media Historiography in the Digital Era." *Acta Universitatis Sapientiae, Film and Media Studies* 2: 15–38.
Musser, Charles. 2004. "Historiographic Method and the Study of Early Cinema." *Cinema Journal* 44, no. 1 (Autumn): 101–107.
Nagib, Lúcia. 2014. "The Politics of Impurity." In *Impure Cinema: Intermedial and Intercultural Approaches to Film*, edited by Lúcia Nagib and Anne Jerslev, 21–39. London: I. B. Tauris.
Nagib, Lúcia, Luciana Corrêa de Araújo, and Tiago de Luca, eds. 2022. *Towards an Intermedial History of Brazilian Cinema*. Edinburgh: Edinburgh University Press.
Nagib, Lúcia, and Anne Jerslev. 2014. "Introduction." In *Impure Cinema: Intermedial and Intercultural Approaches to Film*, edited by Lúcia Nagib and Anne Jerslev, xviii–xxxi. London: I. B. Tauris.
Nagib, Lúcia, and Stefan Solomon. 2019. "Intermediality in Brazilian Cinema: The Case of Tropicália: Introduction." *Screen* 60, no. 1 (Spring): 122–127.
Pethő, Ágnes. 2010. "Intermediality in Film: A Historiography of Methodologies." *Acta Universitatis Sapientiae, Film and Media Studies* 2: 39–72.
Pethő, Ágnes. 2020. *Cinema and Intermediality: The Passion for the In-Between*. 2nd enlarged edition. Newcastle upon Tyne: Cambridge Scholars Publishing.
Rajewsky, Irina O. 2005. "Intermediality, Intertextuality, and Remediation: A Literary Perspective on Intermediality." *Intermédialités: Histoire et théorie des arts, des lettres et des techniques*, no. 6: 43–64.
Rancière, Jacques. 2006. *Film Fables*. Oxford: Berg.
Rodowick, D. N. 2007. *The Virtual Life of Film*. Cambridge, MA: Harvard University Press.
Staiger, Janet. 2004. "The Future of the Past." *Cinema Journal* 44, no. 1 (Autumn): 126–129.
Stam, Robert. 2019. *World Literature, Transnational Cinema and Global Media: Towards a Transartistic Commons*. Oxford: Routledge.
Stewart, Garrett. 1999. *Between Film and Screen: Modernism's Photo Synthesis*. Chicago: University of Chicago Press.
Stewart, Garrett. 2020. *Cinemachines: An Essay on Media and Method*. Chicago: University of Chicago Press.
Youngblood, Gene. 1970. *Expanded Cinema*. New York: P. Dutton.

PART I
METHODOLOGIES

1
Hegel, Cinema, and the Other Arts

Alain Badiou

About sixty years after Hegel's death there appeared what would come to be called the "seventh art." Indeed, the traditional list of the earlier arts contained six forms: architecture, sculpture, painting and the other visual arts, music, literature, and theatre and the other scenic arts.

Had Hegel experienced this newcomer, he would have called it, if we stick to his own lists, either the sixth art (after architecture, sculpture, painting, music, and poetry) or the fourth romantic art (after painting, music, and poetry) or the fourth form of poetry (perhaps under the name "visual poetry" after epic, lyric, and dramatic poetry) or—if cinema by itself represented a totally new dimension of art—the fourth type of art (after symbolic, classical, and romantic art). Modern art? Contemporary art (but not contemporary with Hegel . . .)? The definitive art? We will see later on.

From the strict point of view of Hegel's text in his *Aesthetics*, the question as to whether it is conceivable that a new, hitherto unknown art can emerge from within the Hegelian system makes little sense. Indeed, for Hegel, modern comedy is the final form of dramatic poetry, which is itself the final form of the development of the poetic arts, which are themselves the final form of romantic art, which is itself the culmination of the general system of the arts, concentrated in the dialectical trilogy of symbolic, classical, and romantic art. The idea that modern comedy can be surpassed by a new art is strictly out of the question. Hegel thinks he has shown that modern comedy is the last of the arts, the one with which art becomes "a thing of the past." Hegel's text is categorical: "[Modern] comedy leads . . . to the dissolution of art altogether."

Let's take a close look, however, at the central argument underpinning this thesis, which, in the process, will allow us to encounter a definition of art in general:

> All art aims at the identity, produced by the spirit, in which eternal things, God, and absolute truth are revealed in real appearance and shape to our contemplation, to

our hearts and minds. But if comedy presents this unity only as its self-destruction because the Absolute, which wants to realize itself, sees its self-actualization destroyed by interests that have now become explicitly free in the real world and are directed only on what is accidental and subjective, then the presence and agency of the Absolute no longer appears positively unified with the characters and aims of the real world but asserts itself only in the negative form of cancelling everything not correspondent with it, and subjective personality alone shows itself self-confident and self-assured at the same time in this dissolution. (Hegel 2010: 1236)

The question we can ask is this: Why does Hegel rule out an additional dialectical twist, which would be the dissolution of this dissolution in a new figure? This new and final figure of art could be *the full deployment of its already existing resources*. We would have a figure of representation whose essence would be to unfold the henceforth timeless destiny of an as it were absolute art. This art would then be the last one, not because the Absolute would appear only in a negative form in it, not because art would be dissolved, but, on the contrary, because art would appear in the total mobilisation of the different types of representation. It would be architecture, sculpture, painting, and dramatic poetry all at once. This new art would bring the history of art to an end, not through the negative twists and turns of comedy but through the combined seriousness and concern of a salutary totalisation.

Actually, there was at least one attempt, two decades after Hegel's death, to engage in the project of a total art: the project that Richard Wagner formulated and attempted to achieve. It was a totalisation in the form of a work of art, that is, in the format of an opera. For Wagner, poetry was in the libretto, painting was in the stage sets, tragedy (the first act of *The Valkyries*, say) and comedy (*The Meistersingers*) belonged to the theatre, and ultimately music blended them all together. The only thing missing was architecture, and by persuading King Louis II of Bavaria to build him a theatre with a new design, tailored specifically to him, Wagner plugged that hole.

So let's say that, prior to Wagner, Hegel might have conceived of, if not achieved, a final art, beyond modern comedy, as the redemptive future of destroyed art, in the form of a total art that would have repudiated comic negativity in a positive way.

But would it be cinema, then? Many champions of our "seventh art" have asserted that cinema was, far better than anything Wagner could imagine and achieve, a total art. Let's take a close look at this.

Cinema is architecture because of its final arrangement, editing, which organises into a coherent whole "bits of images," now transformed into the materials of the whole. This aspect is evident in the work of the greatest artists of the era of silent movies: Eisenstein, especially in *Battleship Potemkin*, made the temporal architecture of the shots a fundamental resource of—let's say, to be Hegelians—the Absolute as it is expressed in the film work.

Cinema is in the process of becoming sculpture through experimentation with 3D. That the effect of a natural object, observed in its three dimensions, artistically reconstructed as at once tangible, immobile, and absolute, can be produced in this way was recently proved by Godard in his *Goodbye to Language* (*Adieu au langage*, 2014). He discovered the poetic power of concealment of the "flat" background, hidden by the sculptural figure of a simple tree, as if it were in front of the screen.

Cinema is painting, and has been so, in my opinion, right from the days of black-and-white. For one of cinema's basic resources is the creation, by its general movement, of subtle freeze-frames in which the arrangement of the sets and the actors is expressed as an artistic combination of landscape and portrait painting. Just think, for example, of the shots that Murnau, in *The Last Laugh*, also known as *The Last Man* (*Der letzte Mann*, 1924), devoted to his hero's return to the poor, bleak, working-class neighbourhood where he lives. This return, after work, is fictionally magnificent. We envy the man who will become "the last man" simply because he wears his hotel doorman's uniform so proudly. It is immediately apparent that black-and-white, in this genre painting, is by no means defined as a lack of colours but on the contrary as the very type of colours that the subject imposes.

Of course, the advent of colour was to make the relationship between cinema and painting both richer and more complex. The height of sophistication in this regard is Gustav Deutsch's film *Shirley* (2013), whose original visual material is made up entirely of paintings by the brilliant American artist Edward Hopper, which are essentially re-created filmically by real sets and actors. The cinematic artwork here is both a tribute to painting and its mimetic retotalisation in the temporal movement of the film. This is a Hegelian synthesis: the spatial immobility of painting re-created in the temporal movement of music. Only cinema is capable of such a dialectical tour de force. *Shirley*'s French subtitle, translated as "A Trip through the Paintings of Edward Hopper," underscores the dimension of homage to the painter. But the original subtitle is "Visions of Reality." It underscores almost ironically that the filmic replacement of painting may well constitute its dialectical truth because it would indicate its reality-in-motion.

Cinema is music, not primarily because it makes use, heavy-handedly at times, of musical excerpts but because it is an art of time. The emotion it arouses, intense like the emotion we feel during a concert, is also created from inherently musical effects. Who cannot see that, in Ozu, say, there is an extremely subtle handling of the melancholy adagio? Or that in a given Ford Western there can be sudden accelerations similar in every respect to those found in Beethoven's symphonies? Or that one of cinema's, like any musician's, primary concerns is how to end, how to *set up the ending*, in the time of the work itself? Consider the last-minute miracle of the reconciliation of the couple, whose relationship has been strained throughout the film, at the end of Rossellini's *Voyage to Italy* (*Viaggio in Italia*, 1954): this miracle is actually set up by the sequence in the ruins of Pompeii of the restoration of a couple from antiquity, in the form of a plaster cast. This couple's immortality will unconsciously create the ultimate need for the modern couple's reunion.

For an unequivocal musical element to occasionally be so deeply embedded in a film that it becomes a symbol of it, as is the case with the adagio from Mahler's Fifth Symphony in Visconti's film *Death in Venice* (*Morte a Venezia*, 1971), wouldn't be possible if the musicality specific to cinematic time didn't exist.

Last but not least, cinema is dramatic poetry: the plot, the actors, the text (renamed the script, dialogues)—nothing is missing. This is obviously a crucial point, because in this way cinema enacts its connection to/separation from the final form of art, according to Hegel, namely, theatre (modern comedy). The actor, whom Hegel praises lavishly, has attained his complete sovereignty, his social existence as a star, only because a film's timelessness and omnipresence go beyond theatrical performance, which is trapped in a particular moment, in a particular place. Who would deny that Mankiewicz's *Julius Caesar* (1953) is like a glorious, timeless capturing of Shakespeare's tragedy? You'll say: It owes everything to Shakespeare. But that's not so! The play has been dialectically re-treated by the film inasmuch as it is an enduring interpretation, at once constantly changing and eternal, henceforth connecting actors, sets, images, and music in a temporal order that cannot be reduced to that of the stage.

But cinema is also attuned to poetry. What is Kurosawa's film *The Seven Samurai* (*Shichinin no samurai*, 1954) if not a perfect epic poem? Cinema is attuned, of course, to lyric poetry. Everyone here can choose their own favourite example: the synthesis of a place, a love story, and two sublime actors, with the whole thing given a rhythm, a cadence, by the way the shots are organised, has been an important part of cinema's emotional grandeur. I, for my part, would choose Mizoguchi's *The Crucified Lovers* (*Chikamatsu monogatari*, 1954).

So there was more than enough for Hegel to have recognised, in cinema, the totalising overcoming of the negative impasse of modern comedy. He could have crowned cinema quite simply as the absolute art.

That leaves the final argument. Cinema, of course, offers imaginatively a totalisation of the arts, but it is unable to achieve this totalisation in the form of a true artistic singularity. It is less an art than a retrospective nostalgia for the time when real arts existed.

This thesis is actually contained in the famous conclusion of a text by André Malraux, who was himself the author of a remarkable epic film adapted from his no less essential novel *L'Espoir*, or *Man's Hope*. After laying out one argument after another in support of a genuinely artistic baptism of the seventh art, Malraux (1940: 53) abruptly concluded, "Also, we must never forget—the cinema is an industry."

That's all too true. Cinema is undeniably industrial, corrupt, at the service of destructive politics, a lackey of the established order, a seller of subjective junk.

Nevertheless, can cinema and its offspring, television and the internet, be reduced to an artistic-industrial complex of Capital? Yes, undoubtedly. But in the absolute movement of art, in the artistic truth procedure embodied by cinema, it is also a question of what, subjectively, transcends its industrial essence and, in the political realm, will ultimately end up destroying that of which Hollywood is the divided emblem. One of the most striking contemporary signs of this dialectical function of cinema is its contemporary striving to become critical documentary, or what is awkwardly called "docufiction." It is actually a sort of quest, blind at times but stubborn, for a simultaneous grasp of the working-class and activist real and the underlying structure of oppression. In many cases, cinema is alone in attempting this. It's significant, for example, that a whole swath of Israeli cinema testifies to the fact that the political invention of a new equality between Jews and Palestinians can and must be everyone's task in the future. It is just as significant that great and terrible pieces of the situation in South Sudan and the overwhelming shared responsibility of the Chinese and Westerners in the horrendous crimes committed there are known to us only thanks to the Austrian director Hubert Sauper's remarkable film *We Come as Friends* (2014). Even great "classic" feature films, big, extremely expensive industrial blockbusters, like some of Clint Eastwood's movies, deal with the dialectical ambiguity of the contemporary real, just as some TV series, a genre usually devoted to the more or less racy intimacy of social entertainment, now rise to the level of serious subject matter that shows that the honour of the world today is what is an exception to its laws. This is the case with David Simon's magnificent series *Treme* (2010–2013) and *The Wire* (2002–2008).

Hegelian through and through, or, in other words, dialectical, cinema also helps pave the way for the elimination of the corrupt financial world of which it is both a product and an example.

References

Hegel, Georg Wilhelm Friedrich. 2010. *Aesthetics: Lectures on Fine Art.* Vol. 2. Translated by T. M. Knox. Oxford: Oxford University Press.
Malraux, André. 1940. "Sketch for a Psychology of the Moving Pictures." *Verve* 8, no. 2: 69–73.

2
One-Dimensional Man?

A Reply to Alain Badiou

James Hellings

> No film, strictly speaking, is controlled by artistic thinking from beginning to end. (Badiou 2003: 84)

The End of the Dialectic

In his latest theory of film, "Hegel, Cinema, and the Other Arts," published in this book, Alain Badiou constructs a dialectic... of sorts:

> Cinema, of course, offers imaginatively a totalisation of the arts, but it is unable to achieve this totalisation in the form of a true artistic singularity. It is less an art than a retrospective nostalgia for the time when real arts existed....
>
> Cinema is undeniably industrial, corrupt, at the service of destructive politics, a lackey of the established order, a seller of subjective junk....
>
> But in the absolute movement of art, in the artistic truth procedure embodied by cinema, it is also a question of what, subjectively, transcends its industrial essence, and, in the political realm, will ultimately end up destroying that of which Hollywood is the divided emblem.

On the one hand, cinema *offers a totalisation of the arts* (albeit *imaginatively*). On the other hand, cinema expresses the impossibility of *true* or *real* art in the contemporary (*a retrospective nostalgia*). There ends Hegel's *visitation,* and the dialectic. For Badiou collapses these positions as soon as he has constructed them: cinema is prima facie "the seventh art."[1] And, as *the seventh art*, cinema *transcends its industrial essence*, albeit *subjectively*, via *the absolute movement of art, in the artistic truth procedure embodied by cinema.* To put it another way, a one-dimensional way: some cinema is both artistic and, of necessity, a touch industrial (e.g., "critical documentary, or what is awkwardly called 'docufiction'"), and some cinema isn't artistic at all (e.g., film as a mere industrial "complex of Capital"). For all of his talk about a totalisation of the arts, the absolute, truth procedures, Hegel and his *Aesthetics*, Badiou's theory of film rests on a one-dimensional, extreme form of subjectivism: some film is good (artistic-yet-industrial, anticapitalist), and some film is bad (merely industrial, capitalist). Artistic-yet-industrial film might "pave the way for the elimination" of the commercial racket that is the culture industry, and such a cinema, *in the political realm* (presumably exhibiting the right kind of political commitment), *will ultimately end up destroying* "the corrupt financial world." Badiou's description of cinema's coup de grâce on capitalism is so staggeringly romantic and positively naïve it is, perhaps, worth asking how he understands *the absolute movement of art* and its relation to the other arts, including cinema.

A Dialectical Twist

Badiou asks why Hegel's *Aesthetics* rules out "an additional dialectical twist, which would be the dissolution of this dissolution [of art] in a new figure." Why no seventh art? Why no seventh art that brings together and/or supersedes the other six forms of art? Cinema, for Badiou, in synthesising "the other arts" (i.e., architecture, sculpture, painting, music, literature, and theatre) *is* this *new figure*. "All the arts," according to Badiou-the-cinephile, "flow through cinema" (Badiou [2010] 2013: 7). With cinema, then, as *the seventh art*, "[w]e would have a figure of representation whose essence would be to unfold the henceforth timeless destiny of an as it were absolute art. This art would then be the last one, not because the Absolute would only appear in a negative form in it, not because art would be dissolved, but, on the contrary, because art would appear in the total mobilisation of the different types of representation." Certainly, cinema as *the seventh art*, as a *new figure of representation*, as *a totalisation of the arts* in an end without end, is Badiou's *additional dialectical twist*. There may well be something in this particular twisting of the Hegelian dialectic, that is, the dissolution of this dissolution ad infinitum—*an as it were absolute art*. To put it another way, an ~~absolute~~ art. But that would be a resolutely negative dialectic, historical through and through, which would not be so bold as to crown cinema as *the* seventh art. It would not be so bold as to claim that cinema, *the* seventh art, "*opens up* all the [other] arts, strips them of their aristocratic value and delivers them over to the image of life" (Badiou [2003] 2013: 210). It would not be so bold as to claim that cinema, *the* seventh art, "does not add itself to the other six while remaining on the same level as them. Rather, it implies them—cinema is the 'plus-one' of the arts. It operates on the other arts, using them as its starting point, in a movement that subtracts them from themselves" (Badiou [1998] 2005: 79). To cancel absolute art does not necessitate the cancelling of art and the other arts, as seems to be Badiou's endeavour. Unless, of course, cinema is positioned as *the* highest form of *representation*. But who would seriously claim such a thing today?

The conclusion that Badiou draws from all this *movement*, his twisting, that is, *art would appear in the total mobilisation of the different types of representation,* is neither new nor original. Badiou's *proper name* for such a *total mobilisation* or *a totalisation of the arts* is Richard Wagner, whose *Gesamtkunstwerk* acts as something of a precursor to Badiou's own preferred form of art or figure of representation, the last art, the seventh art, the synthesising art par excellence: cinema. And yet, one can usefully look elsewhere for another conclusion, another, additional twist of the dialectic.

Let's Twist Again

In 1967, Theodor W. Adorno published an essay entitled "Art and the Arts," which addresses a similar topic albeit with a different conclusion (and without the Hegelian grandeur or the Wagnerian bombast of Badiou, that is, *the total mobilisation,* "the combined seriousness and concern of a salutary totalization"). Taken together with his essay "Transparencies on Film," published concurrently, Adorno ([1967] 2003: 386) argued for the boundary-blurring, interfraying, infringing (*Verfransung*), and intermedial[2] potentialities of film—as the "newest form" of the arts—vis-à-vis art, which may well act as a critical rejoinder to Badiou's (absolutely Wagnerian, pseudo-Hegelian) "suspect synthesis" of cinema as the seventh art (369).[3]

"In recent times," Adorno ([1967] 2003: 368) observed, "the boundaries between the different arts have become fluid, or, more accurately, their demarcation lines have been eroded." Unlike Badiou, or Hegel, Adorno felt no need "to classify them" or synthesise them, constructing and/or deconstructing a normative hierarchy of the forms of art—but he did feel compelled to "try to understand... this process of erosion" (369). He also felt compelled to defend the *fluid boundaries* and *eroded demarcation lines between the different arts* because "[a]ttempts to give a definitive answer to the priority of art or the arts come mainly from cultural conservatives. For it is in their interest to reduce art to unchanging factors that are openly or covertly based on the past and that can be used to defame the present and the future" (377). Adorno's response to the erosion of art or fluidity of the arts is clear enough, and it is *genuinely* Hegelian *with a twist*: "Whatever tears down the boundary markers is motivated by historical forces that sprang into life inside the existing boundaries and then ended up overwhelming them" (370). In "progressive, contemporary art" "boundaries are violated" and "hybridity" becomes commonplace, which unsettles "the so-called wider public" (370). Adorno, as he was wont to do, and with reason, cites in this regard the "pathological dimensions in the National Socialist cult of pure race and the denigration of hybridity" (370). The Nazis had a keen interest in keeping the forms of art *pure*, normative, disciplinary-specific, hierarchically organised and classified—so-called *degenerative art* must be made by and for so-called *degenerates*. *Progressive, contemporary* art that rebuked such nonsense, that blurred such boundaries, that played with them, that improvised, rejoicing in its alleged impurity, was "held to be licentious and decadent" (370). "Today, however, the avant-garde, when confronted by the philistine question 'Is that still . . .?,' takes it quite literally. It sometimes responds with a kind of music that really no longer aspires to be music any more. . . . The artistic genres appear to revel in a kind of promiscuity that violates some of the taboos of civilization" (370–371).

It is entirely possible to substitute any form of art for Adorno's favoured music; for instance, *sometimes* avant-garde cinema responds with a kind of cinema that really no longer aspires to be cinema any more. Take, for example, the cinema of Alexander Kluge, Edgar Reitz, and Volker Schlöndorff, about which Adorno ([1967] 1981–1982: 199) has this to say: "In this comparatively awkward and unprofessional cinema, uncertain of its effects, is inscribed the hope that the so-called mass media might eventually become something qualitatively different." New forms of art, such as this type of cinema, "which have not completely mastered their technique, conveying as a result something consolingly uncontrolled and accidental, have a liberating quality" (199). "Film," for Adorno, "must search for other means of conveying immediacy: improvisation which systematically surrenders itself to unguided chance should rank high among possible alternatives" (200). Who said *artistic thinking* couldn't direct film?

This critical nonconformism, this "resistance" to cultural conservatism, together with this reaching out to an "element of alterity" (Adorno [1967] 2003: 375), has been an ongoing artistic pursuit since the earliest days of the so-called historical avant-gardes. What was true then, that *one cannot have a new and advanced art without anti-art*,[4] still holds true for all forms of art, and aesthetics. It follows, therefore, that in Adorno's ([1967] 1981–1982: 200) theory of film, *contemporary, progressive* cinema requires anti-cinema (or "[w]hatever is 'uncinematic'"). Indeed, the "original example of the erosion of art," according to Adorno ([1967] 2003: 385), "was the principle of montage," which owes as much to early cinema as it does to cubism, dada, and surrealism. "Art needs something heterogeneous in order to become art" (375). Cinema needs something heterogeneous in order to become cinema.

In a certain sense, avant-garde art (and cinema) devours itself so that no one else can take a bite:[5]

> "My music is not lovely," grumbled Schoenberg in Hollywood when a film mogul unfamiliar with his work tried to pay him a complement. Art renounces its culinary side.... But now that the culinary element, sensuous charm, has split itself off and become an end in itself and the object of rational planning, art rebels against every sort of dependency upon pre-existing materials that are reflected in the classification of art according to different art forms and that resist shaping by the autonomous artist. For the scattered materials correspond to the diffuse stimuli of the senses. The great philosophers, Hegel and Schopenhauer among them, have laboured, each in his own way, at the question of heterogeneous multiplicity and have attempted to provide a theoretical synthesis.... Hegel's attempt took the form of a historical, dialectical system that was supposed to culminate in poetry. Neither attempt was adequate. It was obvious that the ranking of works of art did not coincide with the ranking of the different arts. They depended neither on the position of one art in the hierarchy of the arts nor—as indeed the classicist Hegel was careful not to assert—on their historical position in the sense that the later work was the superior one. Such a general assumption would have been as false as its opposite. A philosophical synthesis in the idea of art that would strive to go beyond the simple coexistence of the various arts condemns itself by judgements of the kind made by Hegel about music. (Adorno [1967] 2003: 371–372)

Or, for that matter, judgements of the kind made by one-dimensional, great philosophers about cinema as *the seventh art*. As Adorno ([1967] 2003: 372) makes clear, contra Hegel, Schopenhauer, and Wagner—and also in contrast to Badiou's contemporary theory of film—"the actual historical development of art does not move toward such a synthesis." For what results is all too often an "aesthetic hodgepodge" (375) and/or an extreme form of subjectivism. There is, then, an alternative conclusion, another twist—against the *total mobilisation* of such a suspect synthesis, against such an extreme form of subjectivism:[6]

> No work of art, not even the most subjective, can be completely identical with the subject that constitutes it and its substantial content. Every work possesses materials that are distinct from the subject, procedures that are derived from the

materials of art, as well as from human subjectivity. Its truth content is not exhausted by subjectivity but owes its existence to the process of objectification. That process does indeed require the subject as an executor, but points beyond it to that objective Other. This introduces an element of irreducible, qualitative plurality. It is incompatible with every principle of unity, even that of the genres of art, by virtue of what they express. (Adorno [1967] 2003: 375)

The ongoing boundary blurring, interfraying, infringing, and intermediality of *contemporary, progressive* art (and cinema) *is* this *element of irreducible, qualitative plurality* that *points beyond it to that objective Other.* It is an open, licentious, scattered plurality, a *heterogeneous multiplicity,* without synthesis, without end, without dissolution. It is in the process of formation; that is, spontaneity, luck, and play are all essential to it. It is dialectical, but twisted negatively—a great refusal of all that counts. In the context of the *newest form* of the arts, cinema, this means that "[f]ilm is faced with the dilemma of finding a procedure which neither lapses into arts-and-crafts nor slips into a mere documentary mode" (Adorno [1967] 1981–1982: 202–203). In this regard, the *plus-one* of *docufiction* remains *suspect.*

Art, naïvely understood as the essentially differing expressive elements of the arts, does not—contra Badiou—*appear in the total mobilisation of the different types of representation.* Art and the arts are "neither encapsulated in an image nor bluntly uttered," and they resist theoretical synthesis—even as a *plus-one.*[7] Rather, they may be experienced, aesthetically, "in a momentary flash only to disappear a moment later" (Adorno [1967] 2003: 377). For art "can be distilled neither into the pure multiplicity of the different arts nor into a pure unity" (382). Art is neither the one nor the many. "Its dialectical nature consists in the fact that it can carry out its movement toward unity simply and solely by passing through multiplicity" (383). A blurring without end . . . "It is as if the end of art threatens the end of mankind, a mankind whose sufferings cry out for art, for an art that does not smooth and mitigate. Art presents humanity with the dream of its doom so that humanity may awaken, remain in control of itself, and survive" (385).

Notes

1. In his *Aesthetics* (actually penned by one of his students), Hegel ([1835] 1975) divides art accordingly: Symbolic art (e.g., architecture), Classical art (e.g., sculpture), and Romantic art (e.g., painting and the other visual arts, music, poetry and literature, and theatre and the other scenic arts). As Badiou notes in his chapter in this book, "From the strict point of

view of Hegel's text in his *Aesthetics*, the question as to whether it is conceivable that a new, hitherto unknown art can emerge from within the Hegelian system makes little sense.... Hegel thinks he has shown that modern comedy is the last of the arts, the one with which art becomes 'a thing of the past.' Hegel's text is categorical: '[Modern] comedy leads . . . to the dissolution of art altogether.'"

2. "For the time being, evidently, film's most promising potential lies in its interaction with other media, themselves merging into film, such as certain kinds of music. One of the most powerful examples of such interaction is the television film *Antithèse* by composer Mauricio Kagel" (Adorno [1967] 1981–1982: 203). "In the overall context of the dynamization of intermedial relations, film comes to exemplify art's rebellion against art and the reach toward extra-aesthetic reality that Adorno considers part of such intermediality. Ultimately, Adorno concludes, the interfraying or 'mutual cannibalism' of the arts, by unwittingly surrendering to a historical reality that has itself compromised all artistic imaging and nonetheless requires it, makes for a 'false demise' of art" (Hansen 2012: 245).

3. The "eroding tendency is evidence of something more than flattery or the suspect synthesis whose traces frighten the beholder when they appear in the name of the *Gesamtkunstwerk*" (Adorno [1967] 2003: 369).

4. "In the formal crises of early twentieth century art, inaugurated by the so-called 'historical' avant-gardes—that is, the construction of new forms and, even, formlessness—(anti-)art challenged the authority, tradition and institution of Art. Anti-art provoked and intervened, often destructively and almost always negatively (adjectives pejoratively associated with Adorno's critical theory). But this challenge and ensuing crisis did not bring art to an end. Rather the crises of art, fuelled by the new forms and formlessness of avant-garde (anti-)art, which defined themselves in opposition to what they were not (i.e., forms of traditional academic art), was, for Adorno, actually generative for new art's continued autonomy from the aestheticized society" (Hellings 2014: 13–14).

5. "It is as if the artistic genres, by denying their own firm boundaries, were gnawing away at the concept of art itself" (Adorno [1967] 2003: 385).

6. "The entire output of Stockhausen can be regarded as an attempt to test musical coherence in a multidimensional continuum. Such sovereign mastery, which makes it possible to establish coherence even in an incalculable variety of dimensions, creates from the inside the link between music and the visual arts, architecture, sculpture, and painting. The more the coherence creating methods of the individual arts spread their tentacles over the traditional stock of forms and become formalized, as it were, the more the different arts are subjected to a principle of uniformity" (Adorno [1967] 2003: 374).

7. One might argue, following Adorno ([1967] 2003: 378), that Badiou's cinematic synthesis does to Hegel what Croce once did to Hegel: "Croce had removed the element of true dialectics from Hegel's philosophy, believing that it was dead, and had replaced it with the notion of development . . . which flattened everything out to a peaceful juxtaposition of different phenomena." Badiou emphasises the cinematic "nature of all art. However, because of that ontologisation, the distinctions between the arts, their relation to specific materials, is elided as a matter of secondary importance" (381). "[W]e must dismiss the naïve, logical view that 'art' is no more than the generic term for the arts, a genus that contains different species within itself.... This generic term 'art' ignores not merely what is accidental but rather what is essential to the arts.... Differences like these [between images, music, and literature] have their own profound implications, but at all events they demonstrate that the so-called arts do

not form a continuum that would allow us to provide the entire complex of phenomena with a single unifying label" (382). "Without doing violence to either of them, we may compare the relation of art to the arts with that of the orchestra to its instruments. Art is no more the concept embracing the arts than the orchestra contains the spectrum of all possible timbres. Notwithstanding this, the concept of art has its truth—and the orchestra likewise contains the idea of totality of timbres as the goal of its development. In contrast to the arts, art is in the process of formation, it is potentially contained in each art form, just as each must strive to liberate itself from the chance nature of its quasi-natural aspects. *However, such an idea of art in the arts is not positive, it is not anything simply present in them, but must be thought of exclusively as negation.* . . . [A]ll recoil from empirical reality: historically, they secularize the magic and sacred realms. All require elements taken from the empirical reality from which they distance themselves, yet their products are part of that reality" (383).

References

Adorno, Theodor W. (1967) 1981–1982. "Transparencies on Film." Translated by Thomas Y. Levin. In "Special Double Issue on New German Cinema," *New German Critique*, nos. 24–25 (Autumn–Winter): 199–205.

Adorno, Theodor W. (1967) 2003. "Art and the Arts." In *Can One Live after Auschwitz? A Philosophical Reader*, edited by Rolf Tiedemann, translated by Rodney Livingstone, 368–390. Stanford, CA: Stanford University Press.

Badiou, Alain. (1998) 2005. "The False Movements of Cinema." In *Handbook of Inaesthetics*, translated by Alberto Toscano, 78–88. Stanford, CA: Stanford University Press.

Badiou, Alain. 2003. *Infinite Thought: Truth and the Return to Philosophy*. Translated and edited by Oliver Feltham and Justin Clemens. London: Continuum.

Badiou, Alain. (2003) 2013. "Cinema as Philosophical Experimentation." In *Cinema*, translated by Susan Spitzer, edited by Antoine de Baecque, 202–232. Cambridge, UK: Polity Press.

Badiou, Alain. (2010) 2013. "Cinema Has Given Me So Much: An Interview with Alain Badiou and Antoine de Baecque." In *Cinema*, translated by Susan Spitzer, edited by Antoine de Baecque, 1–20. Cambridge, UK: Polity Press.

Hansen, Miriam. 2012. *Cinema and Experience: Siegfried Kracauer, Walter Benjamin, and Theodor W. Adorno*. Berkeley: University of California Press.

Hegel, Georg Wihelm Friedrich. (1835) 1975. *Aesthetics: Lectures on Fine Art*. Vols. 1 and 2. Translated by T. M. Knox. Oxford: Oxford University Press.

Hellings, James. 2014. *Adorno and Art: Aesthetic Theory Contra Critical Theory*. Hampshire: Palgrave.

3
Hybrid Variations on an Intermedial Theme

Robert Stam

From Aristotle to Hollywood

In this chapter, I would like to explore some of the terminology and grids that have been deployed with regard to the interrelations between different media, arts, and texts, while also giving examples of how interlaced these issues have become in the age of the internet.[1] It is not always easy to separate an art form from a medium. The cinema, for example, is both an art form and a medium, as is painting. The terminology for defining the multilateral relations between media—that is, intermedia—has gone through myriad transformations over the centuries, going back to the classical Greek period. Aristotle's analysis of tragedy already invoked categories that reference various arts and media: *mythos* (story) involves both the storytelling of narrative and the performative representation of theatre; *ethos* (character) evokes both diegetic personae and embodied theatrical performance; *dianoia* (thought, reasoning, concepts) evokes all the thought processes involved in creating, staging, and understanding a work of art; *lexis* evokes all the verbal and discursive arts activated in a play; *melopoeia* explicitly references music, reminding us that the tragedies were alternately spoken and sung; *opsis*, finally, evokes visual spectacle, art direction, and costumes.

It is no coincidence that Aristotle's (1967) *Poetics* is often called "The Bible of Hollywood producers," while a standard guidebook is called *Aristotle's Poetics for Screenwriters: Storytelling Secrets from the Greatest Mind in Western Civilization* (Tierno 2002). Thus manuals advise prospective screenwriters to start a story at the beginning, proceed to the middle, and climax with the end—an orthodox sequencing famously scrambled by Jean-Luc Godard's addendum "but not necessarily in that order" (quoted in Tynan 1966: 24). The well-disciplined screenwriter should also clarify the primary cause triggering the action: follow a three-act structure and build the story around a character's desires, opposed by an antagonist individual or group, all within an organically complete story which moves logically toward a climactic finale generative of emotional release. Nor is it an accident that many film journalists, presumably unknowingly, follow the Aristotelian sequence of categories of analysis. Journalistic and TV film reviews are often structured as follows: "X film is a story" (*mythos*) "about a character" (*ethos*), "which shows that love will always triumph over fear" (*dianoia*), usually followed by observations about performance (*lexis*), music, such as "with a lush symphonic score" (*melopoeia*), and spectacle, such as "garishly decorated by the art director" (*opsis*, spectacle). We see the kernel of intermediality theory, then, already in Aristotle's *Poetics*.

In India, meanwhile, the *rasa* aesthetic (Sanskrit for "flavour" or "taste" or "savour"), articulated in the *Natyashastra* and usually attributed to the sage Bharata, is often compared in its historical positionality to Aristotle's *Poetics*, in that it too established a foundational matrix for a theory of performance arts which held sway over vast regions and over a long period, generating an endless series of revisions and commentaries. Unlike the *Poetics*, *Natyashastra* was based not on *mimesis* (representation) or *mythos* (story) or character (*ethos*), but on the subtle "culinary" orchestration of feelings and tastes. At once mystical and practical, the *Natyashastra* points to the emotional architectonics of artistic creation and spectatorship. It combines spirituality—each *rasa* has a presiding deity—with practical recommendations about stagecraft, makeup, costumes, music, and dance. Rather than discuss dramatic structure, the treatise elaborates eight (later nine) *rasas*, such as love, pity, anger, heroism, terror, and comedy. For many scholars, the *rasa* aesthetic shaped not only the forms of classical Indian music and dance but also the modalities of Indian cinema. Indeed, Indian director Shyam Benegal has spoken of a pan-Asian *rasa* aesthetic that he himself had been practicing unawares, one shared, in his view, by the popular entertainment cinemas of much of Asia.[2]

The dramaturgical theories of the explicitly anti-Aristotelian Bertolt Brecht, millennia later, can be seen as simply taking a reflexively contrarian approach to these same Aristotelian categories by foregrounding, rather than naturalising, the construction of the story (*mythos*), deconstructing character (*ethos*) by calling attention to character construction and the protocols of acting as verbal performance (*lexis*), while foregrounding dialectical concepts (*dianoia*) and the separation of the elements of music (*melopoeia*) from style (*opsis*) (see Brecht's 1964 writings on theatre). The modern period brings many refashioned theories relevant to the transtextual relations between arts, media, and texts: the historical avant-garde's penchant for Cubist collage and *papiers collés*, Oswald de Andrade's "anthropophagy" (intertextuality as cannibalistic devoration in a neocolonial context; Brecht's "refunctioning"; and the

Situationists' *detournement*. The "transtextual turn," which has implications for the "inter/transmedial turn," gained momentum with the advent of structuralism and semiotics in literary and film studies, and with the dissemination of Bakhtin's (1981) ideas about "dialogism" and "embeddedness"; Derrida's (1972) ideas about dissemination and *différance*; and Henry Louis Gates's (1988) Afro-diasporic "Signifying," all of which help illuminate the multifaceted relations between the arts, media, and texts, even when those arts and media were not directly referenced. The Internet Age, meanwhile, generates a proliferation of related terms, such as "sampling," "remix," "mashup," "culture jamming," "memes," and "media jiujitsu" (deploying the power of the dominant media against domination). Jay David Bolter and Richard Grusin (1999) proposed the term "remediation" as part of their argument that the so-called new digital media actually gain their cultural significance by absorbing and refashioning earlier media and artistic practices.

The Provenance of Terms

One way to look at terminology is through the issue of provenance. Where do the terms that have to do with relations between arts, media, and texts come from? Some are long-consecrated terms from literary genre study, such as "parody," "satire," "pastiche," and "burlesque." Others emerge from the twentieth-century concern with self-reflexivity in philosophy and the arts, generating terms like "self-consciousness," "self-referentiality," "metafiction," "anti-illusionism," "breaking the frame," "collapsing the fourth wall." Others come from artistic modernism and the avant-garde: "collage" in Cubist painting, "dislocation" in surrealist film, William Burroughs's "cut-ups" in literature, "serialism" in music. Dramaturg/theorist Brecht (1964) by himself created scores of terms related to artistic transformation of preexisting materials: *Verfremdungseffekt*, "alienation," "gestus," "tableaux effect." At times, terms initiated in relation to one art form (like collage in painting) get extrapolated for other art forms; "objets trouvés" become "images trouvées." Multimedia artist Amir Baradaran resuscitated futurism, in a more progressive version called "FutARism," where the "AR" refers to "Augmented Reality," as a project aiming at the subversive artistic incorporation of downloadable "applications." Other terms come from anthropology: Claude Lévi-Strauss's (1966) "bricolage" and "poaching," an ancient practice theorised by transdisciplinary philosopher Michel de Certeau (1984), remediated by Henry Jenkins (1992) and cinematised by Agnès Varda. The cluster of "re-" words like *re*functioning, *re*purposing, *re*mediating, and *re*cycling, meanwhile, spotlighted the ways that art reinvents itself through repetition and variation. Brazilian multiartist Gilberto Gil, an advocate of the Creative Commons, offered his free contribution to the movement by releasing his "Re" trilogy—consisting of albums with recombinant titles starting in "re-": *Refazenda* (1975), *Refavela* (1977), and *Realce* (1979)—as an homage to the centrality of anthropophagic remodelling and reincarnating in the arts. Meanwhile, the many "-isation" formulations—actualisation, relocalisation, indigenisation, Africanisation, feminisation—perform a similar function, pointing to variant forms of transforming and transmogrifying preexisting texts.

Here I will concentrate on the trans/intermediatic and the trans/interartistic aspects of the media. Cinema, for example, is inherently, definitionally, transartistic. The term "the seventh art" implies the incorporation of the other six preexisting arts and the simultaneous embrace of the temporal arts like music and the spatial arts like painting, even if on a deeper level all the arts and all texts are spatial and temporal, or "chronotopic," in Bakhtinian terminology, mingling *chronos* and *topos*. Unlike single-track media like literature, which has only words to play with, audiovisual media have the advantage of being multitrack, consisting, at least prior to the advent of the digital, in Christian Metz's (1974: 16) "five tracks," allowing for the orchestration of various intertexts, as each track had potentially available the arts affiliated with that track: the music track potentially inherits the entire history of music; the image track embeds and rearticulates the history of visual representation and the pictorial arts; and both image and sound tracks potentially absorb the history of theatre, speech, and performance. One of Deleuze's (1986, 1989) signal contributions has been to show that cinema, like philosophy, generates concepts, not through words but through image and movement. I would extend Deleuze's insight to other realms. Not only does cinema generate concepts, including through words, but so do all the arts and cultural practices that enter into or are in parallel with the cinema: music video, stand-up comedy, painting, carnival samba pageants; every cultural activity can embed and generate concepts.

The methodology of which I am speaking is also "transartistic" in that it welcomes a number of arts, such as literature, cinema, painting, theatre, and music. But this "transartistry" already forms part of the already "impure" (Nagib 2014) individual arts. Through a theorised practice of mutual embeddedness and reciprocal impact, we can explore the rhizomatic interfaces across arts, media, and disciplines, to suggest that they are invested in one another, that literature is "in" the cinema (and vice versa), that philosophy is "in" literature. All the arts are "in bed with" all the other arts, generating what can become a fruitful *ménage à mille*. Any art can serve as a gateway drug into the ecstasies of the other arts and the jouissance of their intercourse. More broadly, time and space are chronotopically mingled; the past is in the present (and vice versa), the transnational is in the national (and vice versa), the Global South is in the Global North. Film and the media, in this sense, have been endlessly enriched by their dialogue with other arts and media. For Alain Badiou (2005: 79), the cinema does not add itself to preexisting art forms, but draws on them all in a permanent movement "that subtracts them from themselves." In the era of transartistic convergence, all the arts are mutually invaginated in a regenerative remix. The fact that the maxim "Good artists copy. Great artists steal" has been variously attributed to the poet T. S. Eliot, to the painter Pablo Picasso, to the dramatist Bertolt Brecht, and to the composer Igor Stravinsky suggests that borrowing and alchemising the old to create the new have long been common practices in the arts.

Cross-art comparisons and analogies proliferate in artistic discourses and commentary, reflected in generic rubrics like the "chamber" film (modelled on "chamber music") or in definitions of cinema as "sculpture in motion," or the play of light (in German, *Lichtspiel*), or in cross-art characterisations of artists—"Godard as the Picasso of the Cinema" or "Proust as the Debussy of literature"—or when a novel is titled a "portrait" (of a Lady, for example) or a "scene" (of Provincial Life, for example) or when a written text is said to "aspire to the condition of music" or when the films of Lucrecia Martel are described as "Faulknerian" or when James Baldwin aspired to write the way Aretha Franklin sang[3] or when Stuart Hall claims, in John Akomfrah's (2013) film *The Stuart Hall Project*, that Miles Davis was "playing what I was thinking." Thus many texts deploy a supposedly "alien" art to define and refine and reenergise their own aesthetic practice. Think, for example, of the cross-art impact of painting on music videos: Kanye West's "Famous," inspired by Vincent Desiderio's painting *Sleep*; or David Bowie's "Look Back in Anger," inspired by Oscar Wilde's *The Picture of Dorian Gray*; or the video of Kate Bush's "Wuthering Heights," which performs transgenerational female identification by proclaiming solidarity with the character Catherine Earnshaw. The audio-visual-digital arts are ontologically, irrevocably, "impure," arguably transartistic and transmedial all the way down. What are music videos if not transmedial adaptations of music and lyrics? Many are mini-films with aesthetic ambitions, replete with homages to well-known films and filmmakers in their visuals and mise-en-scène. The video of the Smashing Pumpkins' "Tonight, Tonight" consists of a playful pastiche of Méliès's *Voyage to the Moon* (*Le Voyage dans la Lune*, 1902), while Janelle Monáe's music videos evoke the android from Fritz Lang's *Metropolis* (1927). In the era of transmedial convergence, all the arts are nested in and cohabit with other media under the larger ambit of digital media convergence.

In the case of intermediality or transmediality, it is not as if a pure medium simply encounters another equally pure medium; most media are to some extent always already "impure," as Lúcia Nagib (2014), building on, elaborating, and complexifying a concept from Bazin (1967), lucidly stresses. The separate media were always already transmedial before their encounter with any new medium. Media studies is intrinsically a form of comparative studies, since "no medium has its meaning or existence alone, but only in constant interplay with other media," as Marshall McLuhan (1994: 26) puts it. In other words, we can define a medium only differentially, in diacritical relation to what it shares or does not share with another medium. Christian Metz (1974), in *Language and Cinema*, carefully maps the overlapping Venn diagrams that reveal the semiotic and institutional similarities and differences between film and television: the two media share performance and two-dimensional image, but only television has direct transmission. In the case of intermediality or transmediality, both media are to some extent always already intermedial before their meeting. Here, we are not far from McLuhan's (McLuhan and Fiore 1967) rearview mirror theory, that the content purveyed by each new medium is drawn from antecedent media, or from the more profound idea of "embeddedness" (Bakhtin 1986), that would suggest all the arts are embedded in all of history per se and in all the history of the arts. Digital media, obviously, greatly expand transmediatic possibilities by facilitating a wide gamut of combinatory configurations.

Richard Wagner (1895), in a hyperbolically romantic reincarnation of Aristotle's theories in the *Poetics*, spoke of the total work of art, the *Gesamtkunstwerk*, which encompassed all genres and arts: music, poetry, dance, architecture, and painting. But the "total work of art" need not take such grandiose and elite forms. Spectacularisation can also take nonoperatic forms reminiscent of Brecht's dream of a "popular opera." One thinks of the "street opera" of Brazilian carnival pageantry in Rio de Janeiro, which also embraces the arts of story/*mythos* (*samba-enredo* or "samba plot") and *ethos* (in that the pageants are often dedicated to revered historical figures, many of them artists), all combined with elaborate costumes (*fantasias*), floats (*alegorias*), and music, all potentially spread and refiltered and processed through other media, such as radio, television, film, and the internet. The notion of the *Gesamtkunstwerk* can also be expanded beyond the Wagnerian conception to apply to religious ceremonies such as a Catholic Mass or to Afro-diasporic spirit ceremonies like those of *candomblé*, which also embrace all the senses and all the arts: narrative, poetry, dance, music, costume, and cuisine. It is not an accident that these religions were so attractive to those

I call the "trance-Modernists," like Wole Soyinka, Maya Deren, Ola Balogun, Haile Gerima, Julie Dash, Jean Rouch, and Glauber Rocha.[4]

The spirit of the *Gesamtkunstwerk* lives again in popular and mass culture, whether in the form of Broadway musicals, Hollywood musicals, Bollywood extravaganzas, or artistically ambitious music-video films. Janelle Monáe's Afro-futurist "cyber soul" songs and videos constitute a pan-artistic extended allegory about Black history. Her short *Many Moons* (2009), for example, features her character Cindi Mayweather as a dancer-entertainer at an Android Auction, in a layered allegory that anachronistically mingles the erudite and the popular, the past of the slave auction and the future of science fiction, the utopian and the apocalyptic, in a spectacular mix of visual arts and musical styles. Music videos have become artistically ambitious, sometimes constituting the equivalent of feature films. We find another example of a total artwork in the multiart productions of The Carters duo (Beyoncé and Jay-Z). The "Apeshit" video which accompanies the *Everything Is Love* (2018) album has the two stars dance and pose with scores of dancers interacting with the Louvre's paintings and sculptures, like the *Mona Lisa*, the *Winged Victory of Samothrace*, the *Venus de Milo*, and *The Raft of the Medusa*. The official music video conflates a series of contraries, mingling the lofty and the vulgar, the high and the low, the subversive and the co-optive, Afro-centrism and Black capitalism, Europe and Africa, social critique and product placement, pop hegemony and artistic resistance. The Carters present themselves as a gender-equal royal couple in parallel to Napoleon and Josephine, while the video becomes an exercise in Black-inflected art history, which locates moments of transcendent Blackness within the canon of Western art. The ode to Black beauty subverts a white institution while also paying complicitous homage to it. The couple's nonchalance as they stand in front of the *Mona Lisa* in their pastel-coloured shirts recalls the irreverence of the casual footrace through the Louvre of Godard's characters in *Band of Outsiders* (*Bande à part*, 1964), while hinting at an inversion of the white colonial gaze; it also recalls the more explicitly anticolonialist film by Chris Marker and Alain Resnais, *Statues Also Die* (*Les statues meurent aussi*, 1953), banned by the French government from March 1953 to October 1964 because of its critique of the theft and appropriation of African art.

Transmediatic Actualisations

Another key trans- word, with nods to André Gaudreault (Gaudreault and Marion 2004), Henry Jenkins (2006), and many other scholars, is *transmediatic*, in that the corpus studied would not be composed only of feature films or even feature documentaries, but rather drawn from the broadest possible spectrum of audio-visual-digital arts and media. Defying all attempts to be corralled into essentialist definitions, the cinema's famed "specificity" consists precisely in its being nonspecific and thus capable of cannibalising the most heterogeneous materials, a trait exacerbated in the period of "media convergence" (Jenkins 2006: 282). Rather than exalt the feature film as the ontological quintessence of cinema over and above all of other forms and genres, we would do well to include television, interactive documentaries, music video, filmed performance, cable TV satire, sketch comedy, internet parodies, online games, web series, and social network activism in our analyses.

The various prolongations of Jane Austen's novels furnish a cornucopia of materials to illustrate concepts of intermedia and transmedia, forming part of a constant process of revising and actualising antecedent texts. As the novels migrate across various media, for example, in literary rewritings such as Seth Grahame-Smith's (Grahame-Smith and Austen 2009) *Pride and Prejudice and Zombies* and P. D. James's (2011) *Death Comes to Pemberley*; fictional biographies like *Jane Bites Back*, a novel by Michael Thomas Ford (2009); transvocalisation like *Pride and Prejudice* from a feline point of view (Austen, Pamela Jane, and Deborah Guyol's 2013 *Pride and Prejudice and Kitties*); plus novelistic transtemporalisations/actualisations like Karen Joy Fowler's (2004) *The Jane Austen Book Club* and Emma Campbell Webster's (2007) *Lost in Austen*. Apart from the multiple film versions of the novels *Emma* and *Pride and Prejudice*, there are films based on Austen's life, along with actualisations such as *Emma*, covertly remediated as *Clueless* (film and then TV series), plus second-degree homages like the Bridget Jones books and films, and even the transmediations in the form of card games (Marrying Mr. Darcy: The Pride and Prejudice Card Game) and Austen-related interactive websites, and finally the inevitable transgeneric mashups such as "Jane Austen's Fight Club." The latest example of the Austen textual diaspora is the Netflix series *Bridgerton* (2020), a remediation of various Julia Quinn novels, which proliferates in allusions to virtually all of Austen's novels, from *Pride and Prejudice* to *Mansfield Park*. The series can also be seen as transtemporal in that it superimposes twenty-first-century songs on an early nineteenth-century (Regency) period piece. The music itself is transtemporal in that it mediates twenty-first-century hits by Billie Eilish ("bad guy") and Ariana Grande ("thank u next") in a kind of chamber (pop) music through the classical musical medium of the string quartet. The series is also transtemporal in its multiracial actualisation of Austen's lily-white world. All these examples reflect what Bakhtin (1986: 170) called the "homecoming festival" of texts over "*great time.*"

We find a different kind of actualisation, this time technological and mediatic, in the web series version of *Pride and Prejudice*, *The Lizzie Bennet Diaries* (2012–2013), the first literary adaptation produced exclusively for the internet platform YouTube. The episodes are filmed as video blogs from Lizzie to her followers, where producers maintain social media accounts for the characters who interact and produce Facebook posts about their lives. The series begins with "Lizzie" directly addressing the audience—a device once associated with avant-garde and Brechtian art films but now a standard feature of vlogs and TV series. She wears a T-shirt on the front of which is inscribed the famous first line of the novel: "It is a truth universally acknowledged that a single man in possession of a good fortune," and then on the back the completion: "must be in want of a wife." The monologue is treated in jump cuts, rather like Antoine's interview with the psychologist in *400 Blows* (*Les Quatre cents coups,* François Truffaut, 1959). Lizzie then explains that her mother gave her the T-shirt, that she never wears it, that she is a twenty-four-year-old grad student living at home and burdened with a mountain of debt yet eagerly preparing for a career. For her, Austen's Mrs. Bennet resembles her own mum; the only thing that matters is that she does not remain single. This media-savvy Lizzie disputes the "universally acknowledged" truth by pointing out that contemporary rich single men are often not looking for wives at all, and that the pool of available males is composed of 22% "sleazeballs and scumbags, 26% of men stuck in dead-end relationships; 18% sailing around the world trying to find themselves." Yet, according to her mother, "every rich man was put on Earth to impregnate her daughter." Lizzie here is not only the actualised Elizabeth from the novel but also, in a way, an actualised transhistorical feminist version of Austen herself.

An especially interesting character is Charlotte Lu (Chinese American actor Julia Cho)—based on Charlotte Lucas in the novel—Lizzie's best friend, an aspiring filmmaker, and the fictive director/editor in more than forty of the episodes, and thus in a way the narrator, of Lizzie's vlog. As Silke Jandl (2015: 180) points out, Charlotte is in Genettian terms "homodiegetic," insofar as "her remarks point to the self-assembly element[s] that go hand-in-hand with vlogging, but they never allude to the fictionality of herself or any other of the characters." She brings in a Godardian reflexive dimension by making cine-literate observations about the techniques of filming a vlog in terms of lighting, freeze-frames, jump cuts, the benefits of low-tech as an authenticating device, the subtleties of avoiding "boob close-ups." Her less-is-more approach is a more pop conventional version of the aesthetics of poverty, hunger, and garbage, or "the DIY look."

As an advanced form of transmedia storytelling (Jenkins 2006), the story is told not only through Lizzie's blog but also through various platforms, such as Twitter, Tumblr, and Lookbook, which complement the development of the characters, who also interact with the viewers through online Q&As. The conversation, then, is between actual people and fictional characters. In the contemporary media environment, all media have become mixed. Political talk shows like Samantha Bee's *Full Frontal*, John Oliver's *Last Week Tonight*, and Trevor Noah's *The Daily Show* typically feature pop-up visuals, photoshopped animations, fictional vignettes, archival footage, and feature film sequences. Such complex and multifaceted texts oblige us to completely rethink the founding question of the cinema studies field, What is cinema?, that is, the question of medium specificity. A text like *The Lizzie Bennet Diaries* opens up an assemblage of inescapably mixed specificities, opening up such questions as Is there such a thing as a Twitter specificity, or Tumblr specificity, or Pinterest specificity, or TikTok specificity, since each app has its technical characteristics which mediate the communication utterance, and then enter into the larger impure mix of the overlapping and interacting specificities?

Overlapping Specificities

A related question that haunts the field is what, within these overlapping and interacting specificities and within a new digital environment, is a film. Is it restricted to celluloid (or celluloid-presenting digital) productions of, to echo Aristotle (1967) on tragedy, a "certain magnitude," shown in movie theatres to an audience? Or does it refer to any audio-visual-digital text manifesting a degree of staging and editing? For example, Amir Baradaran, the proponent of FutARism cited above, made a YouTube mock-news clip called "BBC Breaking News: Mona Lisa Veiled," cleverly superimposing a faux BBC News report about the scandalous "defacing of the *Mona Lisa*" with re-subtitled denunciations by European leaders, taken from preexisting TV footage.[5] The news clip supposedly denounces Baradaran's 2011 AR app *Frenchising Mona Lisa*, which allows users to train their smartphones on Leonardo's mysteriously smiling lady, who then is shown loosening her hair and wrapping a French flag around her head in the form of the officially banned Islamic hijab. While mocking the Islamophobia behind the ban, Baradaran also advances his neofuturist project, but, rather than destroy the museum à la the Marinetti of the manifestoes, he uses AR to alter perceptions while leaving the artifact intact. Another "film" resuscitates the avant-gardism of the 1920s. *Man with a Movie Camera: Global Remake* (launched in 2007 and ongoing) is a crowdsourced re-creation of Vertov's paradigmatically reflexive silent 1929 film, in which Perry Bard broke down the Vertov film shot by shot and made a worldwide call for submission of new shots where participants would re-create or change the original shots in whatever manner they chose. The Global Remake code would then pull shots at random from a database of similar shots, ensuring a shuffling film which would never be exactly the same twice, presumably generating ever-shifting coefficients of transnationality in terms of images, locales, and participants.

The obsession with literary specificity on the part of the Russian Formalists (and the literary New Critics in their wake), and later with modernist artistic specificity (Clement Greenberg), and still later with cinematic specificity with the film semiologists (Metz), has given way to an emphasis on multimedia art and what Jihoon Kim (2016) calls "hybrid moving images in the post-media Age." From the 1990s onward, digitization, Kim points out, has "precipitated the flexibility of media image[s] because they are grounded in numerical codes subject to putatively unlimited manipulations" (3). Every medium, within this perspective, constitutes itself through the appropriation and reworking of other media, leading to the weakening, if not the demise, of the medium-specificity thesis. Nicolas Bourriaud's (2009: 53–54) notion of "relational art," for example, explicitly claims to go beyond the modernist focus on medium specificity. In this context, "intermediality" and "transmediality" become umbrella terms sheltering not only the different media but also the vast repertoire of their mutual interfecundations. Video games, as Kim (2016: 38) points out, "borrow the representational strategies of film," while films reciprocate by adopting digital interfaces and computer graphics.

The age of what Henry Jenkins et al. (2009: 8) call "participatory culture" has generated a sea change in the ways that young people can "archive, annotate, appropriate, and recirculate media content in powerful new ways." These new possibilities have enabled revisionist remixed adaptations of literature like the cartoonisation of the novella *Heart of Darkness* (Joseph Conrad) via the film *Apocalypse Now* (Francis Ford Coppola, 1979) and the stories *Winnie the Pooh* (A. A. Milne) in the mashup *Apocalypse Pooh* (Todd Graham, 2012), and the rap version of *Moby Dick* by MC Lars, featuring a Pequod crew as multiracial as Melville's own.[6] Another entry in the genre of technologically inspired inter/transmedial adaptations is the video game based on Henry David Thoreau's *Walden*. Here we are on the very border of what divides film from its mediatic others. The choice of subject is surprising in that Thoreau is often seen as a Luddite, detoxing from what he saw as the overmechanised modernity of nineteenth-century Boston, choosing the dialogical solitude of his cabin. What could the man who advised us "Simplify, simplify" have to do with the high-tech world of gaming? The game answers these questions by following the rhythms of the seasons, beginning in summer and ending a year later. A kind of subtle reproach to the competitive frenzy of the typical video games, *Walden* stresses quiet contemplation and austere simplicity, coaxing the players into collecting arrowheads and fishing in tranquil ponds. The game's pastoral-intellectual attractions include building cabins, planting beans, sending articles to Horace Greeley, collaborating with the Underground Railroad, and chatting with Transcendentalist philosopher Ralph Waldo Emerson (see Pogrebin 2017).

"The ease of use of creative technologies and the networked organisation of today's communications infrastructure," according to Aram Sinnreich (2010: 71), "ensure that the tools of media configurability are accessible to hundreds of millions of inter-connected individuals." The corporate music world was ill-equipped, however, to deal with the explosive Web 2.0 "software-isation" of the arts. The explosion of the sampling and cut-and-mix aesthetic in hip-hop, which always had a filmic dimension, brings up the issue of copyright and the enclosure of creativity by corporate power. In an early phase, hip-hop authorised freewheeling raids on the musical commons, bypassing the bourgeois proprieties of copyright. Found bits from other songs, political speeches, and advertisements were placed in ironic, mutually relativising relationships. Rap music videos, at least in the 1980s, recycled the voices and images of Black martyrs and ancestors such as Malcolm X and Martin Luther King in a "versioning" or remediation which sets up a direct line to African culture heroes, to the African American intertext, and, as "Black Folks' CNN" (Chuck D's term), to the Afro-diasporic communities. In the documentary *Corporate Criminals* (Benjamin Franzen, 2009), Chuck D, who describes Public Enemy's music as an "assemblage of sounds," asks a basic question about the legitimacy of corporate enclosure: Can anyone "own a beat?" It is perhaps not a coincidence that those who have ancestors whose very lives and bodies were stolen and turned into property should display a certain scepticism about private property and the morality of stealing. How, one wonders, did a situation arise where the infinitely rich tradition of African and Afro-diasporic percussive polyrhythms could come to be "owned" by a corporation, as if one could parcel off or "enclose" a few drops in the ever-churning sea of circumatlantic musicality? Unfortunately, the corporate policing of sampling did manage to partially dam the flood of hip-hop creativity, as corporate predators saw the possibility of new revenue streams derived from musical property rights.

The "remix" phenomenon is transmedial in that it was first associated with practices in popular music but then extended to other arts and cultural practices. Musical remix emerged in the 1970s from a creative environment that used new recording technologies to sample and reconfigure existing pieces from the musical commons, leading to the explosion of phenomena such as sampling and cut-and-mix, along with the corporate attempt to "enclose" such expression. But "remix" as a concept existed long before the digital; Robert Farris Thompson (2011: 7) speaks of the "antiquity of the cool" as a "means of putting innovation and tradition, invention and imitation, into amicable relations with one another."

The term "intermediality" evokes the possible movements from any art or medium to another enclosing medium on an omnivorous internet that easily absorbs every genre, format, and medium. Nina Paley draws on the verbal medium of literature—to wit, the *Ramayana*—but turns it into the 2008 internet feature *Sita Sings the Blues*. Written, directed, produced, and animated by the artist with the help of a computer in her Chicago apartment, the film might be called a digital blockbuster, an epic film created not with millions of dollars and a cast of thousands but only with 2D computer graphics and flash animation. *Sita Sings the Blues* counterpoints a feminist version of the *Ramayana* story, about the relationship between Prince Rama and the endlessly patient and devoted Sita—the Chaucerian equivalent would be "patient Griselda"—and the story of the artist's breakup with her husband, in such a way as to link Sita and the author as two women tormented by the slings and arrows of outrageous male insensitivity. In this transtemporal text, the two stories are then interwoven with a third "series"—the 1920s scorned-love jazz crooning of Annette Hanshaw— "sung" (in the Bollywood "playback" manner) by a simulacral Sita, visually presented, thanks to vector-graphic animation, as a reincarnation of Betty Boop. Paley brings in the art/medium of painting in that the episodes with dialogue are enacted by painted figures of the characters in profile in a manner resembling the eighteenth-century tradition of Rajput brush painting, a tradition historically associated with illuminated manuscripts telling epic stories such as the *Ramayana*. But just as germane as the film's relation to the literary and painterly commons is its quite literal relation to the digital commons. As an artist-activist, Paley made the film available on the internet under the free distribution model so it could be copied, shown, and broadcast legally and for free. The credit to the producer of the film reads "You," and the financier is "Your Money." Thus, the film forms the meeting ground not only of various media but also of the *artistic commons* and the Creative Commons, the nonprofit organisation devoted to expanding the range of creative works available for others to build upon legally and to share.

In a formulation rich in implication for filmic adaptations of novels, Bakhtin (1981: 421) suggested that "every age reaccentuates in its own way the works of [the] past." A high proportion of feature films consists of filmic adaptations drawn from the authorial literary commons of classic texts, some of them in the public domain and therefore not requiring copyright. Artistic remediation is a form of artistic file-sharing that usually takes its source from literature but also draws on all the other arts and media integral to the cinematic medium, resulting in a multiplication and amplification of mediatic intertexts. Henry Fielding, interestingly, referred to the commons in *Tom Jones* when speaking of his own debts to classical writers: "The ancients may be considered as a rich Common, where every Person who hath the smallest tenement in Parnassus hath a free right to fatten his muse" (quoted in Hyde 2010: 46). Adaptation in this sense can be seen as a form of textual poaching, a metaphor redolent of the agricultural commons, described by Michel de Certeau (1984) in *The Practice of Everyday Life* as comparable to the poor poaching their way across fields searching for the leftovers after the harvest, classically portrayed in Jean-François Millet's painting *Des glaneuses*. Henry Jenkins (1992) extended the term to apply to the subcultural appropriation of mass culture, referring to procedures whereby the consumer absorbs the scraps of mass-mediated culture to become a producer. Adaptations borrow from literature but also draw on all the other arts integral to the cinematic medium, resulting in a multiplication and amplification of intertexts, a stretching of the verbal text in keeping with the rich potentialities of a multiartistic medium.

An insistence on strict fidelity in adaptation can constitute a form of hermeneutic "enclosure" that asserts ownership on the meaning of a text, as opposed to a view open to transmedial remodellings of a source text. Film adaptations, in this sense, are almost necessarily "unfaithful" not only because of the passage of time or change of country but also because they transform a single-track literary text—where the only track is verbal—into a multitrack text rooted in a medium which is both syncretic and synesthetic. An updated version of Situationism, with or without the radical politics, has become a kind of norm on the internet. For the Situationists, all the great art had already been produced; the artist's mission was to tweak it and play with it in a subversive manner. Yet copyright quarrels about plagiarism and justified laments about cultural appropriation also have to do with playing with tradition and the "relations between texts." As Lauren Michele Jackson (2019: 1) points out, "The practice of repurposing culture is as old as culture itself, and America has been *making* other cultures *appropriate* to its amusements and ambitions since the very beginning." Artistic and cultural practices, she argues, cannot be closed to outsiders, especially in the Information Age. On the other hand, the key question has to do with entitlement, power, and credit, and the abuses that occur when white musicians and producers profit from appropriations of Black talent and expression, resulting in what she calls "black aesthetics without black people" (6). Appropriation is therefore a historically situated communicative utterance. The question is Who is appropriating whom, to whose benefit, to what end, to whose credit, in what style, to what effect, and in what concrete power situation?

A number of films address the issue of power in a different way of borrowing by taking a radically open stance toward issues of copyright and fair use, the most well-known being *Everything Is a Remix* (2010), a four-part web series documentary by Kirby Ferguson. Jamie King's *Steal This Film* (2006) offers a radical defence of piracy culture against the abuse of copyright and denounces the Hollywood film lobby. The brilliant *A Fair(y) Use Tale* (2007), a collective effort led by Eric Faden from the Stanford University Fair Use project, offers an extreme yet legally authorised example of using the power of the dominant against domination, in this case that of the Walt Disney Company, an imperious extractionist exploiter of the artistic and legendary commons and one of the most litigious of corporations—Disney against Disney. The film performs its own argument by demonstrating the creative possibilities of going to the limits of copyright law. The film consists of very short clips from Disney films, legally permitted, all changed and manipulated in some way—required by law for legitimacy—using the actual words of the Disney "characters" to explain copyright law while simultaneously denouncing Disney-style abuses of the law. Since no Disney film actually uses the word "copyright," the authors simply combined the two components of the word drawn from different films; thus one hears the characters say "Copy" followed by "Right?" In the end, characters drawn from *The Lion King* and *The Jungle Book* are made to say, in the very words from the film, "Fair use is the only defensible position."

In his discussion of Shakespeare as the heir of cumulative artistic bounty, Bakhtin (1986) speaks of artistic "embeddedness." The "semantic treasures Shakespeare embedded in his works," Bakhtin writes, "were created and collected through the centuries and even millennia: they lay hidden in the language, and not only in the literary language, but also in those strata of the popular language that before Shakespeare's time had not entered literature, in the diverse genres and forms of speech communication, in the forms of a mighty national culture (primarily carnival forms) that were shaped through millennia, in theatre-spectacle genres (mystery plays, farces, and so forth) in plots whose roots go back to prehistoric antiquity, and, finally, in forms of thinking" (5). It is noteworthy that Bakhtin addresses questions of relations between texts and media in a way that is both broad and deep, erudite and popular, a longue durée transmediality that operates over millennia. Significantly, Bakhtin does not emphasise Shakespeare's debt to individual authors but rather to transindividual traditions and the anonymous destinies of genres. The media, in a similar sense, are "embedded" in the larger history of the aesthetic commons. Within the history of technology, our smartphones and laptops embed all the technologies that preceded them. The cinema, in this sense, is not a century old; it is, rather, the heir of millennial traditions. The notion of *embeddedness* goes far beyond the literary-historical philological tradition of tracing "sources" and "influences"—roughly T. S. Eliot's (1919) ideas in the essay "Tradition and the Individual Talent"—to embrace a more diffuse dissemination of ideas as they penetrate and interanimate all the "series" generated by what Bakhtin (1986: 3) calls the "powerful deep currents of culture." Film aesthetics in this sense, to paraphrase Bakhtin's words about literature, "is an inseparable part of culture [that] cannot be understood outside the total context of the entire culture of a given epoch" (2). Just as individuals cannot be understood purely as autonomous but only as wrapped in an environing sociality, so art cannot be understood apart from its surrounding social ecology. Twenty-first-century arts and media offer a form of "deep remixability" (Manovich 2007), whereby digital environments become the hosts not only of all the arts but also of all formats and styles, resulting in a systematic hybridisation. Instead of the classical "five tracks" of cinema, we find an infinite *combinatoire* of "variables" susceptible to infinite juxtapositions, interfaces, and cross-fertilisations, whereby a variety of aural and visual materials—live action, motion graphics, musical performance, archival footage, computer animation, composited images—can be woven together in a constantly mutating flow.

Notes

1. While the focus of this book is on "intermediality," and while that term is vitally important, and while I respect the work done under that rubric, and while I myself sometimes slide between the "inter" and the "trans," my theoretical and personal preference is for "trans-" prefixes such as *trans*mediality, *trans*textuality, and *trans*linguistic. To schematise shamelessly, in my view, "multi-" implies mere additive multiplication ("multiculturalism" as a list of separate cultures); "inter-" incorporates multiplicity but adds reciprocity (interculturalism as mutually impacting phenomena); while "trans-" embeds both multiplication and reciprocity while intimating possibilities of transformation and transition from one state to another. But that is a personal choice, and in many cases where I use the word "transmedial," the word "intermedial" would serve as well.

2. In conversation with me when we both attended the Subversive Film Festival in Zagreb in 2011.
3. James Baldwin, letter to David Baldwin, 10 March 1968, *James Baldwin Papers*, box 1, folder 2, Schomburg Center for Research in Black Culture, New York Public Library.
4. For more on "Trance-modernism," see Stam, Porton, and Goldsmith (2015: 246–251).
5. Amir Baradaran, *FutARism Manifesto Performance*, solo show, Benrimon Gallery, New York, 2011. See "BBC Breaking News: Mona Lisa Veiled" at https://www.youtube.com/watch?v=ILzcu6CtGxg.
6. For an illuminating study of new internet-based literary pedagogy, see Jenkins et al. (2013).

References

Akomfrah, John, dir. 2013. *The Stuart Hall Project*. Smoking Dogs Films.
Aristotle. 1967. *Poetics*. Translated by Gerald F. Else. Ann Arbor: University of Michigan Press.
Austen, Jane, Pamela Jane, and Deborah Guyol. 2013. *Pride and Prejudice and Kitties: A Cat-Lover's Romp through Jane Austen's Classic*. New York: Skyhorse.
Badiou, Alain. 2005. *Handbook of Inaesthetic*. Translated by Alberto Toscano. Stanford, CA: Stanford University Press.
Bakhtin, Mikhail. 1981. *The Dialogic Imagination: Four Essays*. Translated by Caryl Emerson and Michael Holquist. Edited by Michael Holquist. Austin: University of Texas Press.
Bakhtin, Mikhail. 1986. *Speech Genres and Other Late Essays*. Translated by Vern W. McGee. Edited by Caryl Emerson and Michael Holquist. Austin: University of Texas Press.
Bazin, André. 1967. "In Defense of Mixed Cinema." In *What Is Cinema?*, translated by Hugh Gray, vol. 1, 53–75. Berkeley: University of California Press.
Bolter, Jay David, and Grusin, Richard. 1999. *Remediation: Understanding New Media*. Cambridge, MA: MIT Press.
Bourriaud, Nicolas. 2009. *The Radicant*. New York: Lukas & Sternberg.
Brecht, Bertolt. 1964. "The Modern Theatre Is the Epic Theatre: Notes to the Opera *Aufstieg und Fall der Stadt Mahagonny*." In *Brecht on Theatre: The Development of an Aesthetic*, edited and translated by John Willett, 33–42. London: Methuen.
Certeau, Michel de. 1984. *The Practice of Everyday Life*. Berkeley: University of California Press.
Debord, Guy, and Gil J. Wolman. (1956) 2007. "A User's Guide to Détournement." *Les Lèvres Nues*, no. 8 (May). In *Situationist International Anthology*, rev. ed., translated and edited by Ken Knabb, 14–20. Berkley, CA: Bureau of Public Secrets.
Deleuze, Gilles. 1986. *Cinema 1: The Movement-Image*. Translated by Hugh Tomlinson and Barbara Habberjam. Minneapolis: University of Minnesota Press.
Deleuze, Gilles. 1989. *Cinema 2: The Time-Image*. Translated by Hugh Tomlinson and Robert Caleta. Minneapolis: University of Minnesota Press.
Derrida, Jacques. 1972. *La Dissémination*. Paris: Editions du Seuil.
Eliot, T. S. 1919. "Tradition and the Individual Talent." *The Egoist* 6, no. 4: 54–55.
Ford, Michael Thomas. 2009. *Jane Bites Back: A Novel*. New York: Ballantine Books.
Fowler, Karen Joy. 2004. *The Jane Austen Book Club*. New York: Plume.
Gates, Henry Louis, Jr. 1988. *The Signifying Monkey: A Theory of African American Literary Criticism*. Oxford: Oxford University Press.
Gaudreault, André, and Philippe Marion. 2004. "Transécriture and Narrative Mediatics: The Stakes of Intermediality." In *A Companion to Literature and Film*, edited by Robert Stam and Alessandra Raengo, 58–70. Malden, MA: Blackwell.

Grahame-Smith, Seth, and Jane Austen. 2009. *Pride and Prejudice and Zombies*. Philadelphia, PA: Quirk Books.

Hyde, Lewis. 2010. *Common as Air*. New York: Farrar, Straus and Giroux.

Jackson, Lauren Michele. 2019. *White Negroes: When Cornrows Were in Vogue . . . and Other Thoughts on Cultural Appropriation*. Boston: Beacon Press.

James, P. D. 2011. *Death Comes to Pemberley*. London: Faber and Faber.

Jandl, Silke. 2015. "The Lizzie Bennet Diaries: Adapting Jane Austen in the Internet Age." *AAA: Arbeiten aus Anglistik und Amerikanistik* 40, nos. 1–2: 167–196.

Jenkins, Henry. 1992. *Textual Poachers: Television Fans and Participatory Culture*. New York: Routledge.

Jenkins, Henry. 2006. *Convergence Culture: Where Old and New Media Collide*. New York: New York University Press.

Jenkins, Henry, Wyn Kelley, Katie Clinton, Jenna McWilliams, Ricardo Pitts-Wiley, and Erin Reilly. 2013. *Reading in a Participatory Culture: Remixing* Moby Dick *in the English Classroom*. New York: Columbia University Teacher College Press.

Jenkins, Henry, Ravi Purushotma, Margaret Weigel, Katie Clinton, and Alice J. Robison. 2009. *Confronting the Challenges of Participatory Culture*. Cambridge, MA: MIT Press.

Kim, Jihoon. 2016. *Between Film, Video, and the Digital: Hybrid Moving Images in the Post-Media Age*. London: Bloomsbury.

Lévi-Strauss, Claude. 1966. *The Savage Mind*. Chicago: University of Chicago Press.

Manovich, Lev. 2007. "Deep Remixability." *Artifact* 1, no. 2: 76–84.

McLuhan, Marshall. 1994. *Understanding Media: The Extensions of Man*. Cambridge, MA: MIT Press.

McLuhan, Marshall, and Quentin Fiore. 1967. *The Medium Is the Massage: An Inventory of Effects*. Corte Madera, CA: Gingko Press.

Metz, Christian. 1974. *Language and Cinema*. Translated by Donna Jean Umiker-Sebeok. The Hague: Mouton.

Nagib, Lúcia. 2014. "The Politics of Impurity." In *Impure Cinema: Intermedial and Intercultural Approaches to Film*, edited by Lúcia Nagib and Anne Jerslev, 21–39. London: I. B. Tauris.

Pogrebin, Robin. 2017. "In Walden Video Game, the Object Is Stillness." *New York Times*, 25 February.

Sinnreich, Aram. 2010. *Mashed Up: Music, Technology, and the Rise of Configurable Culture*. Amherst: University of Massachusetts Press.

Stam, Robert, Richard Porton, and Leo Goldsmith. 2015. *Keywords in Subversive Film/Media Aesthetics*. London: Wiley/Blackwell.

Thompson, Robert Farris. 2011. *Aesthetic of the Cool: Afro-Atlantic Art and Music*. New York: Periscope.

Tierno, Michael. 2002. *Aristotle's Poetics for Screenwriters: Storytelling Secrets from the Greatest Mind in Western Civilization*. New York: Hyperion.

Tynan, Kenneth. 1966. "Verdict on Cannes." *The Observer*, 22 May.

Wagner, Richard. 1895. *Richard Wagner's Prose Works*. Vol. 1: *The Art-work of the Future*, translated by William Ashton Ellis. 2nd edition. London: Kegan Paul, Trench, Trübner.

Webster, Emma Campbell. 2007. *Lost in Austen: Create Your Own Jane Austen Adventure*. New York: Riverhead Books.

4
Parallax Historiography and Metareference

The Intramedial Case of Nagasaki Shun'ichi's *Heart, Beating in the Dark*

Mark Player

In this chapter, I shall consider the extent to which intermediality can be used to read cinema and its complex media-historical development, by drawing on conceptual tools that address the medium's past and present specificities. Doing so makes it possible to view cinema not as a homogeneous monolith but instead as a highly variegated and continually evolving medium, whose aesthetic, technological, and industrial changes throughout its history are capable of manifesting unique interactions with one another. To demonstrate this, I shall look at the work of Japanese film director Nagasaki Shun'ichi,[1] specifically the *Heart, Beating in the Dark* (*Yami utsu shinzō*) diptych produced in 1982 and 2005.

Nagasaki's *Heart, Beating in the Dark* (2005), known internationally as *Heart, Beating in the Dark—New Version,* is a profoundly self-reflexive work, marking a complex return to the director's earlier amateur film of the same name from 1982, which was shot on Super 8 using a nonprofessional cast and crew. Born in 1956, Nagasaki first emerged as a leading figure within Japan's *jishu eiga* (self-made film) scene of the 1970s and 1980s, which saw hundreds of young, aspiring filmmakers self-fund, self-produce, and self-screen amateur narrative films outside the Japanese industrial context. The emergence of this mode of filmmaking in Japan was shaped by two factors: first, the arrival of the sync-sound Super 8 camera in 1973 made it easier for novice filmmakers with minimal resources to shoot dialogue-driven narrative films; second, the demise of Japan's major film studios throughout the 1970s made it very difficult to enter the film industry, as most apprenticeship opportunities disappeared. As such, *jishu* filmmaking became a do-it-yourself alternative for

Mark Player, *Parallax Historiography and Metareference* In: *The Moving Form of Film.* Edited by: Lúcia Nagib and Stefan Solomon, Oxford University Press. © Oxford University Press 2023. DOI: 10.1093/oso/9780197621707.003.0005 a new generation of young filmmakers to develop their craft. It also became a pathway for new talent to be noticed by Japan's emerging post-studio film industry (made up of multiple media, publishing, and leisure companies rather than a handful of studios), thanks in part to *jishu* filmmaking showcases such as the Pia Film Festival, which began in 1977 (see Player 2021). The original *Heart, Beating in the Dark* (1982) was an important work of this *jishu eiga* scene, going on to be screened abroad at the London Film Festival in 1984 (a rarity for this type of film), with Nagasaki in attendance.

Although the opening of the *New Version* reflexively announces itself as a "remake" via voiceover narration, it also functions as a sequel and remediation of the original 1982 film by incorporating its original cast and using excerpts from the original film. It also "documents" its own production through the inclusion of dramatised "behind-the-scenes" sequences, which show the *New Version* taking shape in preproduction meetings, in the rehearsal room, and during principal photography. I argue that, by incorporating various storytelling modes—sequel, remake, documentary—and remediating past work, all of which blur the line between the film's fiction and the reality of its production, the self-reflexive narrative of *Heart, Beating in the Dark—New Version* allows for the study of two newly introduced intermedial concepts: parallax historiography and metareference.

By reflecting on these concepts in relation to *Heart, Beating in the Dark—New Version*, I shall demonstrate how certain self-reflexive or metafictional films can also function "intramedially," especially when incorporating past cinematic artefacts from different technological bases. Intramediality differs from intermediality in that the latter focuses on the relations and fusions that can occur *between* different media, while the former focuses on medial phenomena taking place *within* the same medium. Intramediality in cinema, then, refers to the reading of different modalities and processes of cinema that can occur within a single film. In the case of *Heart, Beating in the Dark—New Version*, which mixes different filmmaking modes that make use of 8mm, 35mm, and video formats, it enables the filmmaker to comment upon how his present work relates to his past and how his past amateur filmmaking has shaped his present. As such, an intramedial approach to this Nagasaki work has the capacity to interweave independent and industrial histories of Japanese cinema through the creation of intramedial passages to the filmmaker's past.

This chapter starts by unpacking the concepts of parallax historiography and metareference. I shall then move on to consider *Heart, Beating in the Dark—New Version*, paying close attention to its metafictional and multilevel narrative, as well as how its remediation of footage from the 8mm original creates intramedial passages to the real and fictional pasts of the actors, director, and industry.

Parallax Historiography and Metareference: "Passages" between Intermedia and Intramedia

The concept of parallax historiography was first proposed by Catherine Russell (2002) as a way to develop "cyberfeminist" insights into early cinema through the use of newer media technologies. For Russell, "new media technologies have created new theoretical 'passages' back to the first decades of film history" (552). These "passages," then, can refer to the ways in which earlier modes of cinema can be revisited and reinterpreted from the perspective of newer cinematic forms and vice versa, drawing our attention to parallel phenomena that occurred at different points in cinema history. For example, scholars have found new ways to reconsider early cinema from the perspective of more recent technological trends. This includes regarding George Méliès as "the father of computer graphics" (Manovich 2001: 200) and arguing that early film actualities such as the Lumière brothers' *Train Pulling into a Station* (*L'Arrivée d'un train en gare de La Ciotat*, 1896) engage with the same "outward aesthetics" as modern 3D cinema (Moulton 2012: 6–7). As such, a parallax historiography of cinema, while linear, can also be folded in on itself, highlighting moments within the medium's history that appear to rhyme and intersect in different ways. Russell (2002: 552) adds, "The term 'parallax' is useful to describe this historiography, because it is a term that invokes a shift in perspective as well as a sense of parallelism," but also stresses that parallax historiography "does not simply involve a rewriting or reversibility of history. Instead, it conceives history as a panorama that shifts according to the gaze of the observer" (565).

Parallax historiography and its ever-shifting perspectives on cinema and (its) history has been picked up by Ágnes Pethő (2010) as one of several possible methods for engaging with cinematic intermediality. While Pethő questions "whether the relation of older and newer forms of moving images should be considered intermediality or a sort of trans-mediality within moving pictures," she ultimately finds the idea of parallax historiography "extremely appropriate at a time of an incredible multiplication of the media forms of moving images and of an ever-widening area of the remediation of cinematic images" (55). For Pethő, the concept also facilitates the idea of "the history of cinema not as a linear progress in time, but as a set of paradigms that can be revisited and refashioned" (55), which resonates with Russell's assertion that parallax historiography treats cinema's history as a "panorama" whose perspective can shift.

A striking commonality between parallax historiography and intermediality is the idea of "passages," which has become an increasingly useful metaphor to explain the movements, traces, fusions, and figurations of different media within intermedial artworks. A "passage," writes Johan Foräs (2002: 90), "is either a movement through, across or past some kind of structure (like a walk through a corridor), or that very structure itself through which such a movement goes (the corridor itself)." He elaborates: "These *passages* give rise to an immense number of different kinds of *meetings*, where people meet people (interaction, identification), media meet media (intermediality, intertextuality) and people meet media (consumption, interpretation, representation)" (Foräs 2004: 128). Elsewhere, Lúcia Nagib (2014) has argued that intermediality can facilitate another kind of "meeting"—one that results in a rupture of the boundaries between art and life. For Nagib, "the will to abolish the schism between art and life" (29) is the ultimate political goal for all intermedial artworks. She has more recently advocated for the presence of "intermedial passages" within cinema, whereby films that incorporate other media can act as "a channel to historical and political reality" (Nagib 2020: 31). As such, Russell's parallax view and Nagib's intermedial view of "passages" within cinema are both predicated on the medium's ability to communicate with media-historical realities, which can bleed into one another beyond their boundaries.

Moreover, parallax historiography has the added potential to cross-examine the evolving realities of cinema's existence in terms of material bases, production processes, economics, infrastructures of production, screening practices, perceptual experiences afforded, and sociopolitical functions. Such an approach, then, can reemphasise cinema's historical reality as a culturally and technologically complex medial entity.

The concept of metareference, in turn, can help facilitate the transition from an intermedial to an *intramedial* approach to cinema, as it fosters a highly self-reflexive view of a given medium and its conventions through a process of "metaisation." Werner Wolf (2009: 3) explains that metaisation refers to any movement "from a first cognitive or communicative level to a higher one on which the first-level thoughts and utterances, and above all the means and media used for such utterances, self-reflexively become objects of reflection and communication in their own right." Notions of metareference and, more specifically, "intramedial reference" have been explored in relation to music by scholars such as Jörg-Peter Mittmann (2009), but less often to visual arts such as cinema. However, Eckart Voigts-Virchow (2009: 146) has made reference to the "*intra*medial meta-film," which he briefly and broadly defines as "a film that addresses the mediality of film-making," suggesting a self-reflexive film that places a heightened level of scrutiny upon its own filmmaking processes.

Additionally, cinema's reproducible nature includes the phenomenon of remakes, which constitutes a privileged site for intramedial readings via both parallax historiography and metareference. As noted by Anat Zanger (2006: 9), "[t]he relationship between original and version [of a film] encapsulates the dialectic of repetition, the dialectic between old and new, before and after, desire and fulfilment." Nagasaki's *Heart, Beating in the Dark—New Version* makes for a particularly fascinating case in this regard, as it is a remake that remediates footage from its original 8mm film, thereby placing "original and version" into direct dialogue. Thus the rest of this chapter seeks to answer two questions: How does *Heart, Beating in the Dark—New Version* use its stacked storytelling strands to dramatise ideas of parallax historiography and metareference? And how does its remediation of the original film create intramedial passages between past and present in a way that also erodes the boundary between art and real life, and between film as fiction and film as artefact?

Heart, Beating in the Dark: Parallel Narratives and Metafictional Stacking

To understand the parallel narratives and their metafictional stacking in *Heart, Beating in the Dark—New Version*, it is first necessary to introduce the original film and the circumstances behind remaking it. Made during the height of Japan's amateur *jishu eiga* phenomenon in the 1970s and 1980s, the original *Heart, Beating in the Dark* is a zero-budget chamber piece about a young couple, Ringō and Inako (played by then-amateur actors Naitō Takashi and Muroi Shigeru), who are on the run after their negligence kills their baby daughter, Yoshiko. Spending the night in a vacant apartment (arranged by Ringō's friend, played by Suwa Tarō), the couple gradually confront each other over the infanticide they committed. Writing for the Japanese film periodical *Image Forum* in 1982, Nagasaki referred to the film as "a drama that has lost its structure" (Rayns and Field 1990: 21). A number of reflexive techniques are used to both set up and undermine the film's dramatic flow. Title cards that read "Ringō's past" and "Ringō and Inako's past" are used to both chapter and signpost the narrative. However, the drama suggested by these title cards is routinely undercut: Naitō and Muroi perform numerous, sometimes lengthy, sex scenes and deliver prosaic monologues directly to camera, sometimes while playing each other's characters; a nonsensical dream sequence, brought about by food poisoning, is constructed from remediated 16mm black-and-white test footage shot previously by Nagasaki and featuring Naitō and Suwa in a number of violent scenarios that lack context;[2] and two prolonged interjections of a social worker being interviewed in a café derail the couple's story completely. The film ends anticlimactically, with the couple leaving the apartment the next morning without receiving any closure or comeuppance for their actions.

The idea to remake *Heart, Beating in the Dark* was suggested to Nagasaki several times by film producer Sasaki Shirō, who was instrumental in launching his career as a professional film director in the early 1980s. As former president of the Art Theatre Guild (Japan's preeminent independent film production and distribution company throughout the 1960s, 1970s, and 1980s), Sasaki gave Nagasaki the opportunity to direct his first professional feature film, *The Lonely Hearts Club Band in September* (*Kugatsu no jōdan kurabu bando*, 1982), a drama involving biker gangs that resulted in Nagasaki being hospitalised following a near-fatal motorcycle accident during the shoot. Despite this, the pair have continued to collaborate, with Nagasaki crediting the accident for pushing his filmmaking towards a more self-reflexive direction. Speaking about the accident to Chuck Stephens and Tom Mes (2006), he recalls, "What I realised is that up to that point I had been imitating the films that I liked, and I felt I should change that." In response, Nagasaki returned to the *jishu* filmmaking underground and effectively started over with the original *Heart, Beating in the Dark*, shooting quickly and cheaply with his filmmaker friends in early 1982, before reworking and completing *The Lonely Hearts Club Band in September* that summer.[3]

Nagasaki was initially reluctant to pursue the idea of remaking *Heart, Beating in the Dark*; indeed, why remake a film that set out to no longer be imitative of past films? Nevertheless, he began to work on a script that focused on a new young couple, Toru and Yuki, who largely repeat the same overnight, apartment-bound scenario of the original film after having killed their baby, Natsumi, in similar negligent circumstances. However, this new project soon grew to be more than just a straightforward remake, as Nagasaki explains: "There was a script, but I felt something was lacking, I wasn't happy with it. Then we came up with the idea of having the lead actors from the original version appear in the film in some kind of documentary style. But they also weren't quite happy with that idea and felt that it still needed something more" (Stephens and Mes 2006). The original actors wanting there to be "something more" is dramatised in an early scene of the *New Version*, which sets into motion not only the film's metareferentiality but also its engagement with parallel histories that connect real and fictional events. As part of a handheld documentary (shot on video), Naitō, now middle-aged and seemingly not in character, enters Office Shirous, Sasaki Shirō's real-life production company (founded in 1993). Naitō meets with Sasaki and another producer, Sato Miyuki (who both play themselves). A poster for *The Lonely Hearts Club Band in September* is partly visible on the wall behind Sasaki, acting as a media-historical waypoint for the careers of Sasaki, Nagasaki, and Naitō (who starred in this film as well) and also as a kind of cryptic citation for the genesis of the original *Heart, Beating in the Dark*. It is during this meeting that Naitō proposes he should also have a role in the remake, playing his character from the original film, Ringō. Naitō's desire to be included is so that he can "punish" Ringō by punching his replacement, Toru. He argues, "The Toru in this script is basically me from 20 years ago, right? So it would be about me 20 years later punching myself of 20 years ago." His rationale for this is that his character (and Muroi's) got away with killing their baby in the original film. "The film sympathises with it," Naitō stresses. "I feel like the crime needs punishment, and I don't think they got it." He rests his case to the producers by stating, "Because, you know, this remake needs to have some meaning."

It is here that the film's metafictional stacking of narrative strands begins to reveal itself, which can be understood as featuring three levels: metafictional, fictional, and archetypal. In accordance with Wolf's definition of metaisation, the metafictional level is the highest level of this stack, consisting exclusively of the "documentary" strand. Although this is also fabricated for the film, the documentary strand dramatises some of the real-life motivations and circumstances behind the making of the *New Version*. Following Naitō's meeting with the producers, the film bifurcates into two further narrative strands that are told in parallel: a sequel strand and a remake strand (both shot on 35mm film), which constitute the fictional level of the stack. The sequel strand reunites Naitō's Ringō and Muroi's Inako; now older, they spend an evening awkwardly catching up over dinner after two decades of estrangement. Meanwhile, the remake strand follows the new couple, Toru (Honda Shōichi) and Yuki (Eguchi Noriko), who replicate several narrative moments from the original version, including its numerous sex scenes and direct-to-camera monologues. Both strands from the fictional level are complemented with remediated excerpts from the original *Heart, Beating in the Dark*, whose status as an 8mm *jishu eiga* is not only preserved but emphasised (as I shall discuss further later). The use of this footage constitutes the lowest level of the metafictional stack: the archetypal level. It is the lowest of the three due to the 8mm film's primordial status as the "original" and therefore the media-historical blueprint from which the *New Version* is working, as well as its presence as a kind of mise-en-abyme: a film within the film.

The narrative function of this archetypal level changes depending on what narrative strand it is complementing on the fictional level. For the sequel strand, the original footage functions as a simple flashback device, showing Ringō and Inako as their younger selves in 1982. For the remake strand, the original footage functions instead as a comparative device in which the viewer is invited to directly cross-examine and scrutinise the minutiae between the original and remake, thereby dramatising within a single film the dialectic between old and new, or between the original and its remake, according to Zanger (2006). As such, intramedial passages begin to open up.

Passages are present between the sequel and remake strands of the fictional level, as well as between the fictional and metafictional levels of the film. The former results in a conflation of parallel pasts, presents, and futures, while the latter results in a blurring between art and (an imitation of) life. Beginning with the fictional level, a motif develops in which both the original couple (Ringō and Inako) and the new couple (Toru and Yuki) are "haunted" by their shared past of infanticide as well as by the presence of their parallel narratives. This parallelism is partly facilitated by the similarity of each couple's apartment setting. Both apartments share similar design features—most notably an open door leading to a darkened room that is never entered, which seemingly act as physical passages to respective fictional pasts. In the remake strand, the sound of Toru and Yuki's baby giggling can be heard as the camera pushes in on this doorway in their vacant apartment; in the sequel strand, Inako's looking over her shoulder and noticing the same door, also ajar, in Ringō's apartment leads to an excerpt from the original 8mm film showing Ringō and Inako, now twenty-three years younger, eating noodles together when they were in the same situation that Toru and Yuki now find themselves. Both couples appear to feel the presence of each other, with Toru and Yuki feeling the presence of their parallel future and Ringō and Inako feeling the presence of their parallel past, all occurring within a slowly conflating present. Their eventual meeting is anticipated in a brief moment of spatial convergence as a slow dolly shot moves away from Ringō and Inako and reveals Toru and Yuki in the next room of the same apartment. Here, a passage is momentarily created between sequel and remake strands through a compression of fictional space within this single camera move.

The convergence of these two narrative strands results in the couples meeting "by chance" after both separately decide to go out driving, finally providing Naitō-Ringō with the opportunity to punch "himself" using the Toru character as a surrogate. Both couples first cross paths at a roadside diner, with Ringō inexplicably following the new couple to a nearby beach. However, just as Ringō grabs Toru and raises his fist, Naitō senses that the moment feels forced and breaks character. Someone yells "Cut," and, in a single edit, the film switches back to its making-of documentary strand, as indicated by the switch to a different camera that pans and zooms out to reveal the crew. Naitō approaches Nagasaki (who also plays himself) for consultation, while the crew wait for whether there will be another take.

At this moment in the *New Version* its metafictional and fictional levels are seemingly at odds, creating passages between the film and the reality that surrounds its making, and, more broadly, between art and life. First, we see actors move in and out of character, making us conscious of both performer and performance. We also see them interact with those behind the camera, who should not exist in the fiction. More profoundly, there is a confusion between the character's and the actor's motivation within the (meta)fiction: it is Naitō (the actor) who wants to punch Toru, not Ringō (his character), which is ultimately the reason why the fictional level breaks down in this moment and reverts to the metafictional. This serves as a reminder of the hierarchy of the stack and is reinforced by a changing of camera format (from 35mm film to video), which draws our attention to cinema's capacity for various aesthetic and technological modalities.

The fictional level of the *New Version* can also be affected by the presence of the original 8mm version, creating another passage between its fiction and its reality. This is best illustrated by an early scene that sees Toru and Yuki waiting at a suburban level crossing on their way to the apartment (a moment that also features in the original film between Ringō and Inako). As Toru watches the train approach, he suddenly senses that a depressed Yuki may try to jump in front of it and preemptively snatches her hand. We are then shown the same scene from the original, where an unprepared Ringō has to suddenly restrain Inako as she tries to throw herself onto the tracks. This moment is indicative of the original film's status as the archetypal "blueprint" for the *New Version* and also suggests that the character and actor of Toru has knowledge of what happened previously in the original film and seeks to counteract it in his version.

The *New Version* thus features three storytelling strands (documentary, sequel, and remake) that are shared across two narrative levels (metafictional and fictional), with the remediated footage of the original film acting as a third level (archetypal) (Figures 4.1 to 4.4). The strands that exist "above" and "below" the fictional level—that is, the making-of documentary (metafictional) and the original film (archetypal)—can intrude and alter the "fiction" of the *New Version*, thereby creating passages between art and different representations of "real life." These include a dramatisation of the filmmakers' desire to give "meaning" to their remake and a self-awareness of a real *jishu*

Figures 4.1 to 4.4 The four storytelling strands of *Heart, Beating in the Dark—New Version*: the sequel and remake strands, both shot on 35mm (Figures 4.1 and 4.2), the making-of documentary strand, shot on video (Figure 4.3), and the remediated original film, shot on Super 8 (Figure 4.4).

Figures 4.1 to 4.4 Continued

film produced in 1982, respectively. However, the passage created by the latter is not just limited to the storytelling strands within the *New Version*. It extends beyond to encompass the original and new versions as separate film artefacts from different periods in Nagasaki's career and of Japanese film history.

Heart to Heart: Intramedial Passages between Original and New Versions

The opening narration of the *New Version* (voiced by Naitō) explains that a Super 8 film called *Heart, Beating in the Dark* was made in 1982 and that a "remake" of this film is about to start. This gesture immediately marks the original version both as a narrative device that interacts with other strands within the *New Version* and as a real and autonomous media artefact that exists within the history of Japanese cinema. Its historical nature is emphasised and shifted through a number of alterations to the footage. The colours and contrast have been manipulated so that excerpts often exhibit garish tones that were not originally present, lending the footage an aged effect. Meanwhile, print scratches, dirt, speckles, and flicker are not only preserved but emphasised, and a prominent whirring sound of an unseen film projector is added, drawing our attention to the original's different and aged material base, as well as its antiquated recording and exhibition apparatus. Finally, the aspect ratio is changed from its original Super 8 ratio of 1.33:1 to the more commonly used modern ratio of 1.85:1, resulting in the top and bottom portions of each shot being cropped to fit the more rectangular frame. A kind of parallax aesthetic emerges from this treatment of the original's footage, with some alterations emphasising and exaggerating its age, thereby pushing it further into the past, while other changes contemporise it, so that it can better integrate into the metafictional stack of the *New Version* (Figures 4.5 and 4.6).

Figures 4.5 and 4.6 Comparison of the original *Heart, Beating in the Dark* (Figure 4.5) and how it appears in the *New Version* (Figure 4.6). Both versions were released on DVD in Japan in 2006.

These changes serve to highlight, through metareference, the technological advancement that has occurred during the intervening years between the original and new versions, as Nagasaki has moved from the 8mm filmmaking of the original to the 35mm filmmaking of the *New Version*, simultaneously evoking the amateur and professional film production modes that are associated with these formats. As per Pethő's (2010) statement cited above, whether this reflexive mixing of film gauges can be considered intermedia or transmedia is, of course, open to debate. But regardless, it remains evocative of a type of intramedial archaeology, with the *New Version* effectively excavating and preserving fragments of the original *jishu eiga* version, which has become difficult to screen over the years due to its 8mm format. When the original *Heart, Beating in the Dark* was screened at the London Film Festival in 1984, it had to do so with a live narration (performed by British film critic Tony Rayns and reminiscent of the Japanese *benshi* who used to narrate films during the silent era), because it was not technically possible to add English subtitles to the 8mm print (Nishimura 2008: 65). This is one more example of a deliberate historiographic manipulation that calls attention to Nagasaki's changing position within the Japanese film industry and the changing nature of the industry itself along with its technologies.

The archival function implicit in bringing the existence of the original version to the attention of modern audiences can represent an instance of "intramedial reference." Jörg-Peter Mittmann (2009: 280) uses this general term "for all types of reference in a given art or medium to objects generated within the same art or medium." Mittmann's intramedial analysis of music argues that cases of "music in music" can be considered "instances of intramedial reference," whether in relation to the "artist who refers" or to the "composition *itself*" (280–281). This principle can also provide insight into cinema, especially for films that incorporate footage from other films. *Heart, Beating in the Dark—New Version* is especially interesting because not only is there a film in a film—the original within its remake—but that original and remake are by the same director. As such, "artist" (i.e., filmmaker) and "composition" (film) become intramedially bound. The purpose of the *New Version*, then, is not just about its characters coming to terms with their fictional past but also Nagasaki coming to terms with his real past by revisiting a key film that developed out of a traumatic yet epochal moment at the start of his career.

It is here that the intramedial reference of the "film in film" in the *New Version* turns into an intramedial passage that folds media history to connect two modes of Japanese film production: *jishu eiga* made by amateur filmmakers during the 1970s and 1980s, and early twenty-first-century post-studio film production, made professionally by a small production company

(Office Shirous). In doing so, to paraphrase Nagib (2020), this intramedial (rather than intermedial) passage becomes a channel to the respective historical realities of these film production modalities. This in turn has the potential to imbue both versions of *Heart, Beating in the Dark* with a renewed sense of media-historical purpose that feed into one another. As I previously argued, the purpose of the *New Version* was to attain some kind of narrative closure in the form of an actor (Naitō) physically punishing his former character through a contemporary surrogate (played by Honda). But this lack of closure in the original film partly stems from the original's lack of dramatic structure, which in turn stemmed from a life-threatening accident on the set of another production intended to be Nagasaki's debut as a "professional" film director. The intramedial passage created between the two *Heart, Beating in the Dark* films, in which their fictions and realities intertwine, retroactively gives the original version a new dramatic structure by serving as the "blueprint" for the *New Version*. The *New Version*, then, attains the "meaning" that Naitō desired in the dramatised production meeting at the start of the film, by giving the original version a new media-historical relevance.

In conclusion, *Heart, Beating in the Dark—New Version* demonstrates that by combining the concepts of parallax historiography and metareference, intramedial passages between present and earlier modes of cinema become visible and fold media history to create interactions and fusions between modalities in a way that is similar to the political goal of intermediality, which is to "abolish the schism" between art (i.e., the films) and life (i.e., the media-historical realities of their production). However, the cinematic intramediality I have attempted to demonstrate here does not need to be thought of as an adversary or an inversion of intermediality. Instead, it should be thought of as a complementary approach that can access and explore the space *in between* that can occur *within* cinema and its different media-historical forms.

Notes

1. This chapter uses the traditional order for Japanese names: family name, then given name.
2. The origin and format of this dream sequence footage was confirmed to me by Nagasaki during a meeting that took place at Office Shirous in Tokyo on 5 July 2018. In a follow-up email dated 17 October 2018, Nagasaki explained that the reason for including this unrelated footage was to add a further "violent element" to Ringō's character, even though Naitō was not playing Ringō when this test footage was shot.
3. Nagasaki made another film during this period, *After That* (*Sonogo*, 1982), which begins as a documentary about the accident that happened during the making of *The Lonely Hearts Club Band in September* (featuring interviews with Sasaki, Naitō, Suwa, and other cast members

and filmmakers). However, the documentary becomes more interested in the "real-life" interpersonal drama occurring during its own production, bleeding into outright fiction that results in Naitō and Suwa gunning each other down in the street over a young woman. As such, *After That* is an important precursor to the self-reflexive metafiction of *Heart, Beating in the Dark—New Version*.

References

Foräs, Johan. 2002. "Passages across Thresholds: Into the Borderlands of Mediation." *Convergence* 8, no. 4: 89–106.
Foräs, Johan. 2004. "Intermedial Passages in Time and Space: Contexts, Currents and Circuits of Media Consumption." *Nordicom Review* 25: 123–136.
Manovich, Lev. 2001. *The Language of New Media*. Cambridge, MA: MIT Press.
Mittmann, Jörg-Peter. 2009. "Intramedial Reference and Metareference in Contemporary Music." In *Metareference across Media: Theory and Case Studies*, edited by Werner Wolf, Katharina Bantleon, and Jeff Thoss, 279–298. Amsterdam: Rodopi.
Moulton, Carter. 2012. "The Future Is a Fairground: Attraction and Absorption in 3D Cinema." *CineAction* 89: 4–13.
Nagib, Lúcia. 2014. "The Politics of Impurity." In *Impure Cinema: Intermedial and Intercultural Approaches to Film*, edited by Lúcia Nagib and Anne Jerslev, 21–39. London: I. B. Tauris.
Nagib, Lúcia. 2020. *Realist Cinema as World Cinema: Non-Cinema, Intermedial Passages, Total Cinema*. Amsterdam: Amsterdam University Press.
Nishimura, Takashi. 2008. "My Ten Years with the Self-Produced Films and PFF, or the Days of Wine and Roses." In *30th Pia Film Festival*, edited by Otake Kumiko, 64–66. Tokyo: Pia Corporation.
Pethő, Ágnes. 2010. "Intermediality in Film: A Historiography of Methodologies." *Acta Universitatis Sapientiae, Film and Media Studies* 2: 39–72.
Player, Mark. 2021. "Uto*Pia*: An Early History of Pia and Its Role in Japan's 'Self-Made' Film Culture." *Japan Forum*. 1–30. http://doi.org/10.1080/09555803.2021.1895283
Rayns, Tony, and Simon Field, eds. 1990. *Young Japanese Cinema*. London: Institute of Contemporary Arts.
Russell, Catherine. 2002. "Parallax Historiography: The Flâneuse as Cyberfeminist." In *A Feminist Reader in Early Cinema*, edited by Jennifer M. Bean and Diane Negra, 552–570. Durham, NC: Duke University Press.
Stephens, Chuck, and Tom Mes. 2006. "Shunichi Nagasaki." *Midnight Eye*, 8 June. http://www.midnighteye.com/interviews/shunichi-nagasaki-2.
Voigts-Virchow, Eckart. 2009. "*Metadaptation*: Adaptation and Intermediality—Cock and Bull." *Journal of Adaptation and Performance* 2, no. 2: 137–152.
Wolf, Werner. 2009. "Metareference across Media: The Concept, Its Transmedial Potentials and Problems, Main Forms and Functions." In *Metareference across Media: Theory and Case Studies*, edited by Werner Wolf, Katharina Bantleon, and Jeff Thoss, 1–87. Amsterdam: Rodopi.
Zanger, Anat. 2006. *Film Remakes as Ritual and Disguise: From Carmen to Ripley*. Amsterdam: Amsterdam University Press.

PART II
TECHNOLOGIES AND ENVIRONMENTS

5
Intermediality and the Carousel Slide Projector

Julian Ross

The 2017 exhibition *Slides: A History of Projected Photography* at Musée de l'Elysée in Lausanne, Switzerland, set out to present the history of projected still images through two overarching methods: first, by showcasing the history of lens-based media and its development through the display of mostly archaic projection apparatuses and other related ephemera; second, through installations of various artworks using the slide medium. As the exhibition title and the list of exhibited works suggest, the curators considered the role of their show to be a survey of a bygone era. With the exception of one recent work, all twenty-one artworks presented in the context of this exhibition were from the 1960s and 1970s, the period in which the slide projector was at the height of its popularity.[1] With Kodak terminating the industrial production of carousel slide projectors in 2004, the omission of contemporary artworks using the now defunct medium is somewhat understandable. Nevertheless, it contributes to the widespread impression that still image projection is a thing of the past, an assumption that the surge of slide-based works made and exhibited since 2004 proves otherwise.

While smartphone apps are certainly now the primary method for photo-sharing, the carousel slide projector, almost two decades since its demise, still holds a prominent place within the field of contemporary art and (audio) visual media. At the 2014 Turner Prize exhibition, two out of four artists presented slide-based works in the annual exhibition of recent works by up-and-coming British artists.[2] Artists have expressed fascination with the characteristics of the slide projector: the rhythmic oscillation between light and darkness; the sculptural quality of the projector apparatus, often visibly present within the exhibition site; the saturated colours and high resolution of the 35mm slide film; and the pulsating sound the machine emits as the slides click in and out of the frame. Yet the key reason for its continuing relevance is arguably its innate intermediality, despite the defining characteristics that have

Julian Ross, *Intermediality and the Carousel Slide Projector* In: *The Moving Form of Film*. Edited by: Lúcia Nagib and Stefan Solomon, Oxford University Press. © Oxford University Press 2023. DOI: 10.1093/oso/9780197621707.003.0006 been outlined. Situated between the still and moving image, the slide projector is known for its ephemerality. Tracing the etymology of "dia" (from Greek, "through"), the prefix used for the term for slides in many languages, reveals that slides intersect with notions like "through" and "between," and as such, one might suggest it is by definition in between.[3] Neither entirely photography nor film, slide projection itself is intermedial, existing in the interstices between the two media. Perhaps because of its effervescence, slide projection also has the ability to interact with other media. In fact, its definitions as a distinct medial form—its engagement with presence and the present—become clearest in the intermedial encounter with other distinct media.

While we have established that slides have a certain elusive quality, this is not their only mode of being. Indeed, this might be the experience of looking at or working with slides, especially for many artists with a background in fine arts; paintings, for example, don't vanish off the wall. For filmmakers working with analogue film, however, slide projectors offer precisely the opposite. Running at twenty-four (or sometimes several fewer) frames per second, individual frames on a filmstrip are invisible to the human eye.[4] Slide projection, on the other hand, with its slower projection speed and the darkness that bookends each slide, makes each frame visible. Each slide is pronounced as if it were a punctuation mark in a sentence. Moreover, the loud clicking sound that the mechanics of the projector makes as it shifts to the subsequent slide is similarly emphatic, particularly in a gallery or museum space where visitors usually take part in a quiet spectatorship, and even more so on the rare occasion slides are presented in the cinema space. Rather than hidden in a projection booth, as we often find in cinematic projection, the carousel slide projector is usually situated in the middle of an exhibition space and visitors cautiously position themselves around it, attempting not to disrupt the projection beam. Calling for our attention through the boldly audible clicks and the oscillation between lightness and darkness, the slide projector captures our attention and demands we notice it. Its presence is assertive. Its survival into the digital age, contrary to expectations, is perhaps due to this factor; rather than adapting to the digital, its stubborn resistance has ensured its enduring relevance.

As a form of media invented in the age of mechanical reproduction, slide film is part of the economy of reproducibles, as it is possible to produce slide duplicates. As such, what it projects is a photographic document of a past event. Yet, unlike print film, reversal film is photochemically processed as a positive image, and therefore it does not undergo the same intermediary process of printing from a negative. Presenting exactly what was captured on film, slide film more directly embodies the Bazinian continuum between the event of reality and the site of a photo image: what the camera saw is what you get.[5] In such ways, the slide image is at an intimate distance from the recorded event. The digital recorded image is also a translation, and arguably even more so than print film, as the captured moment is interpreted into pixels. A close observation of their renditions of "black" highlights the difference between a projected slide and its digital counterpart. While even "black"—as seen in intertitles, for example—is a pixel interpretation in the digital image and its projection, the alternation to "black" for slide projections is a direct result of the projection beam being physically interrupted by the mechanism of the apparatus that allows the switch from one image to the next. In this way, the display of "black" in a slide projection is an act that takes place in the present moment in a way that is unique for the projected analogue image. In its carousel form, slides also offer an alternative to cinema projection, and its fixed sequential succession of images as carousel slide projection has the function of a loop inherent in its form, where it is often impossible to determine a beginning or an end. Unlike cinema, where each image can be placed within the context of a sequence, the carousel slide projection does not have a "first" image and, as such, is always in the present moment, divorced from a sense of progression, narrative or otherwise.

In this chapter, I will propose that key characteristics of the carousel slide projector—namely, its presence and its engagement with the present—are further accentuated, first, by its placement into the contemporary context after it was effectively made redundant by the industry and, second, through its juxtaposition with other media in an intermedial encounter. Despite Kodak's termination of its production in 2004, the carousel slide projector has long outlasted its industrial demise in a way that makes us question whether the user or the industrial producer determines the expiry date of a technological apparatus. In an age of swipe and scroll, technology and media are declared outdated at an accelerated pace. In a show of resistance against such imposed progress and the incessant capitalist promotion of the new, we must take a moment to consider the afterlife of so-called outmoded technology, as the line of scholarly enquiry known as media archaeology has continued to promulgate in recent years.[6] The use of the carousel slide projector in the current context allows us to assess what we mean by progress and what we have lost or gained in the digital evolution. Not only finding relevance but excelling in the contemporary context, the carousel slide projector similarly reveals its unique characteristics through juxtaposition with other distinct media. Embodying features of two fundamentally different media, cinema and photography, the carousel slide projector showcases the porosity of its medial borders that allows for a fluidity in its interactions with other media in ways that also give shape to its key characteristics.

The chapter will examine the role of the carousel slide projector in two contemporary works to consider how the key features of the projector apparatus are highlighted through the gesture of revisiting the machine after its cessation and positioning the object among other distinct media. First, I will examine the carousel slide projector being used within the framework of contemporary performance. Through my analysis of Brazilian artist Pablo Pijnappel's *Casa de Michèle* (2014), a slideshow involving a live telephone conversation, I will discuss how key characteristics of the carousel slide projector are brought to the foreground by placing it in dialogue with other medial modes. Second, I will explore how the specificity of the slide projector is also highlighted in its presentation as an installation. In a close analysis of Thai artist Prapat Jiwarangsan's slide-based installation *Non-chronological History* (2013), I will propose its multiprojection and intermedial formation emphasises its unique characteristics as a form of projection media. Apart from being two contemporary works that present the two different modes of performance and installation, the rationale for choosing these two case studies is twofold. First, being works that emerge out of Brazil and Thailand, they both exemplify the existence of slide-based work outside of the Euro-American circles that most recent studies have confined them to. The history of the slide projector and its use by artists needs to be reexamined beyond its Eurocentric geographical scope to give a fuller picture of the impact of this technology. Much of the academic and curatorial discourse thus far has entirely neglected slide-based activities and artworks produced from countries outside of North America and Europe. *Slides: A History of Projected Photography*, the aforementioned exhibition at Musée de l'Elysée, featured no artworks produced from outside of these two continents despite purporting to survey the history of the medium. Neither did *Slideshow*, curated by Darsie Alexander for the Baltimore Museum of Art in 2005, an exhibition serendipitously offered to audiences across the United States just a year after Kodak decided to terminate production of the projector apparatus.[7] The omission of works outside of these Euro-American circles gives a one-sided history of the slide projector, resulting in narrow understandings of their use within and beyond artistic purposes. Considering slide projectors were used as pedagogical tools in Taiwan and Korea when they were under Japanese colonial rule, for example, nostalgia cannot be the only perspective from which we analyse slide-based works, as not everybody shared the same historical relationship with the technology. As Rosalind Krauss (1997: 5) notes, mediums "acquire histories" and, as such, are in continual negotiation with external factors that determine their existence and development. Second, as both Pablo Pijnappel and Prapat Jiwarangsan also work with analogue film or digital film, their use of slides can be interpreted as a choice that came with a recognition of what other medial forms offer. In both works, the carousel slide projector invites a consideration of time through its (dis)placement into the present, where it allegedly no longer belongs.

Slides as Performance: Pablo Pijnappel's *Casa da Michèle* (2014)

The story of media history is often defined by the advent of technology, so the continued artistic use of an apparatus long after its industrial demise challenges this story.[8] In discussing medium specificity, Rosalind Krauss (1999) proposed to separate "medium" and "technical support" by considering media to be a set of conventions that are recursively made over time. In such ways, the medium can be made, or "invented," while the technical support remains intact.[9] Following this logic, media can evolve when the technological support finds itself in a position of obsolescence; thus, media can find new purpose, meanings, and sets of conventions. A teleological sense of progress is often expected with media, particularly the support for media, where new technological devices would render previous models obsolete by offering something its predecessors were not able to do. Yet, as Krauss (1997: 5) notes, the slide tape "must have been born obsolete," as it arrived into the consumer market when most of its technicalities had already been surpassed by film and video. Invented half a century into the history of cinema and rendered outdated in the midst of cinema's continued dominance, the slide projector nonetheless provided artists with something neither film nor photography gave them, namely, something in between both, which Krauss characterised as a "static seriality" (26). This particular temporality of the carousel slide projector is further emphasised when it is juxtaposed with another medium that possesses an entirely different temporal register, for example, performance. The ease of its use and the ability for a user to control its temporality meant that slide projectors were adopted by artists into slideshows, in other words, live presentations involving a slide projector, which accompanied the prevalence of performance in contemporary art from 1960s onwards. This symbiotic relationship, where one medium influences the development of the other, is in line with Philip Auslander's (1996: 198) suggestion that liveness in performance emerged as its key characteristic only with the arrival of recording technologies. This section will focus on a recent slideshow performance by Pablo Pijnappel to examine the mutual reciprocation between the two mediums.

Born in Paris in 1979, Pablo Pijnappel is an artist based in Rio de Janeiro and Rotterdam with an artistic practice that primarily spans photography and film. His work interrogates memory as a subject but also as an experience for exhibition visitors and audiences that encounter his work. In his exploration of what he appropriately calls the "mechanisms of memory" (Pijnappel 2017: 8), his frequent choices of media are often 16mm analogue film and 35mm slides, both of which are considered obsolete forms of photographic media as their digital equivalents have surpassed them in popular consumption. As such, Pijnappel's choice of old media evokes nostalgia and a tangible sense of history. The use of old media as a historical artefact helps the artist stage an interplay with time, with storytelling as his chosen method, a narrative device that brings about a sense of the present regardless of the content of the story. In his film *Lucas* (2013), for example, Pijnappel films himself in a single take delivering a story accompanied by several images printed on paper that he displays in front of him. Loosely based on the fragmentary novel *A Certain Lucas* (*Un tal Lucas*) by Julio Cortázar, the artist-cum-storyteller shares glimpses of an encounter and stories shared by the titular protagonist Lucas in a manner that evokes the Japanese storytelling tradition of *kamishibai*, where on-street performers would tell stories armed with a stack of paper, each piece with a single drawing, that they would slide one by one out of its frame and put aside as the story progresses. In the case of *Lucas*, however, Pijnappel accentuates the materiality of each page by spinning it around, waving it, and crumbling it into a ball in moments within the story where the gesture would reflect on the described scenario. In this way, the interplay between the image and the story places an emphasis on the present moment in which the story is being shared. Considering storytelling to be a key part of his artistic practice, he describes it as a mode of recollection that involves "always looking back, or at least, to project the past into the future" (2017: 8). Pijnappel expanded on this particular aspect of his artistic practice through storytelling as live performance and brought the carousel slide projector with him.

Carousel slide projectors have always had a strong association with storytelling. As with many iterations in the history of slide projectors, the carousel slide projector was intended as a domestic product for household entertainment. Storytelling took place, albeit in a more private manner between family and friends, when members of a household shared personal accounts accompanied by the projection of family photos taken on holidays. The popularity of the medium beyond this purpose was mostly happenstance, although its ease of use was part of its design, enhancing its accessibility, which certainly contributed to its popularity among artists. Entering the market at a time when small-gauge film and video were both also in their ascendance, the carousel slide projector was affordable, simple to operate even for those without much technical knowhow, and lightweight, relatively speaking, increasing its portability. The carousel slide projector also emerged at a time when performance was becoming popular as a mode of artistic expression, despite its fundamental difficulties in thriving in the art market due to its lack of a purchasable art object. Jack Smith, Dan Graham, and Nan Goldin used the carousel slide projector in their performances, which would often involve storytelling and have various iterations.[10] The performances were often the kind staged in front of intimate audiences who gathered together at alternative spaces, which once again benefitted from the operational simplicity and ease of mobility that the projector apparatus provided. Often also used in lecture theatres in educational environments, the carousel slide projector can be seen as an early precursor to the artist's adoption of the lecture performance, a contemporary mode of artistic expression that often incorporates PowerPoint software, a derivative of slideshows. Preceding the carousel slide projector by centuries, the magic lantern slide, the earliest form of slide projectors, was another instrument for stage performances and entertainment shows where storytelling held a central position. The slide projector thus had an intimate relationship with storytelling as a mode of performance from the outset of its invention.

Pijnappel taps into this history of the projection apparatus in his performance *Casa da Michèle* (2014), a live telephone conversation and slideshow, which the artist staged on 1 March 2014 at the Galerie Juliette Jongma in Amsterdam.[11] Pijnappel invited artist Adaire Reeford to talk to him about a film he was trying to make in Rio de Janeiro while staying in the house of the famous French artist Michèle Gálvez Forst, armed with a carousel full of photographs made during his location scouting. Reeford, however, got stuck in a traffic jam on his way to the airport and missed his flight. Changing plans, Pijnappel and Reeford connected over a phone conversation instead; with the telephone wired into a PA system, audiences, including myself, listened in for close to an hour while watching projected photographs of serene street corners, museum artefacts, and a random assortment of images taken by Reeford while he recounted his days spent as an artist in residence, which mostly involved social occasions like dinner parties and gallery openings. With frequent detours, the story was delivered in a relaxed tone and with a touch of humour. The projected images would at times confirm accounts shared by Pijnappel's faceless conversation partner, attesting to the power of visual affirmation for the experience of the listener. In other moments, however, the projected images would contradict details offered in the story and begin to undermine its authenticity, leading the audience to ask about the veracity of the performance itself: If Reeford was unable to make it, how did the photographic slides arrive in Amsterdam? And why would Pijnappel invite another artist to share his experience as an artist in residence in Rio de Janeiro for the closing event of his exhibition? Though it was never revealed during the performance, Reeford is, in fact, a fictional character, and the entire situation was staged.

While audiences sat listening to the performance, their bodies were comfortably fixed in their seats but their minds were continuously activated as the performance encouraged connections between image and story. As Reeford spoke, the slide images, eighty in total, appeared and disappeared in perpetual rotation; we'd see the same image several times throughout the performance. Occasionally the improvised conversation would sync with the projected slide image, and at other times Reeford's recollections would appear to refer to an image we'd just seen or would see shortly thereafter.[12] These coincidental moments highlight the cross-temporal oscillations that take place in the act of storytelling. For example, an image of the viewing stands at a horse race appeared when Reeford recounted a story of how he gambled on the jockey with the longest nose, boasting that his beginner's luck rewarded him with some profit. In these moments of unrehearsed coincidence, the liveness of the performance would be highlighted because of the tension created between the immediacy of the conversation and the projected image photographed in the distant past. The performance also encouraged its audience to engage in their own process of memory by making spoken references to images they would have encountered while watching the carousel go through its numerous rotations. The cross-temporal condition of storytelling—where the present meets the past or an imagined future—is emphasised even further in the dynamic interplay between live performance and slide projection. Containing photographic records taken from another place and in the past, slides are presented in the context of a live performance with a devotion to the here and now. While the two media are brought together in their concurrent staging, the juxtaposition draws out the essential qualities of both. This intermedial encounter, where the idiosyncrasies of each end up being highlighted, recalls 1960s expanded cinema where the "liveness" of performance is brought together with cinema in a way that highlights the reproducibility of the film medium and its machinic reliance by way of comparison. Historical accounts of expanded cinema have found that artists and filmmakers were using both film and slide projection in their expanded cinema performance.[13] But what is it about slides that offered something distinct? Carolee Schneemann, in conversation with Gene Youngblood (1970: 368), stated, "I like using slides against films because I can start and stop, overlap, black out, manipulate." Again, its mechanical characteristics and relative ease of use allow for carousel slide projectors to offer moment-to-moment shifts for artists and, therefore, to be adopted into the language of performance and the immediacy it requires.

Slides as Installation: Prapat Jiwarangsan's *Non-chronological History* (2013)

Similarly to performance as a mode of expression, installations provide a platform and avenue for an engagement with the present. Art historian and philosopher Juliane Rebentisch (2012: 185), in fact, suggests we should call a work an installation only when there is a "structure of temporal openness." With the loop structure embedded into its very form, the carousel slide projector was quickly adopted into the exhibition context in the 1960s. Arguably, it was the first projector apparatus that offered the installation form as an option for moving image projection, and its early uses in the art context foreshadowed the prevalence of moving image installation that was to take over the artworld in the years to come. Installation remains the preferred format in the artistic use of the carousel slide projector. This section will focus on a slide-based installation by Thai artist Prapat Jiwarangsan to examine how the framework of an installation offers opportunities for contemporary artists using the carousel slide projector to stage an interaction with the present and with other media.

As its title suggests, *Non-chronological History* (2013) by Prapat Jiwarangsan reshuffles the chronology of over two hundred years of Thai political history in its simultaneous multiprojection formation. What is visible on the individual slides is a seemingly endless list of Thai names, which are relevant in one way or another to Thai history, but in this presentation are taken entirely out of context and stripped of individual status; some of the names are well-known and many others are less so, and each name is presented in identical fashion in order to de-emphasise any preestablished hierarchy of importance. The multiprojection creates associations between the names that establish continuity between the names and their associated historical events based not on linearity but on interconnectivity. The random connections that are configured between the names allow for speculation on the emergence of deeper connections between various points in history. For example, Praison Thompson, one of the names presented in the installation, was one of ninety-three people killed in the 2010 military crackdown on protests that took place near the Democracy Monument in the city centre of Bangkok. This name might appear before, after, or together with, for example, Bat Pheungphrakhun, who was a member of the Khana Ratsadon (Peoples' Party), a Siamese group of military civil officers who staged a coup against King

Prajadhipok, which led to the transformation of the country's absolute monarchy into a constitutional monarchy in 1932. Living almost a hundred years apart, the two ostensibly have little to do with one another, but the installation establishes a continuum and situates them together in interconnectivity. In its most recent installation involving nine carousel slide projectors, approximately seven hundred names are displayed as individual slides; because each projector is set at different projection speeds, the potential associations that develop between them are seemingly endless. Most important, these relations are subject to chance rather than predetermined, as they would be if it were a film projection, where the sequentiality would be fixed.

The stipulated duration of *Non-chronological History* at 59 minutes 57 seconds similarly rejects the perfect circle of the hour in a way that proposes reevaluations of history cannot be neatly fit into preestablished experiences of time or understandings of history. Yet, in principle, the work functions as a loop, as its duration is dependent on the viewers' attention, the hours the space is open, and the durability of the projector. Jiwarangsan approaches the installation of his work differently on each occasion: the first iteration was installed at the Bangkok Art & Culture Centre in 2014; its second version was presented in the context of the exhibition *Concept Context Contestation: Art and the Collective in Southeast Asia*, a 2015 touring exhibition in Yogyakarta, where he included names of Southeast Asian citizens who had had a role in Southeast Asian political history since the Cold War era, thus establishing an intraregional set of possible connections. In 2016, at a solo exhibition in Corner Art Space in Seoul, he presented the previous two versions together. Most recently, in 2019, his installation used nine slide projectors, three sets of three projectors stacked on top of each other, all projected against the same wall in a grid-like formation (Figure 5.1).[14] The varying status of the work appears to suggest that Jiwarangsan considers history, the subject of this piece, as something that can and should be endlessly reworked and rethought.

Thailand has experienced an extended period of instability over the past century, only selectively remembered in official state history and in history lessons at school, and marked by twelve coups since the end of direct rule by the kings in 1932. With the latest coup staged in 2014, it is no mistake that Jiwarangsan first presented this project in the same year, another moment of reflection for Thai citizens who have been experiencing history as recurring. Jiwarangsan includes several slides with no names in each carousel, which appear at random in the projections. These slides, for Jiwarangsan, represent two groups of people who are left unaccounted for: actors or victims of history who remain anonymous or unknown and people in the future who will take

Figure 5.1 The slide projectors for *Non-chronological History* (2013) by Prapat Jiwarangsan at group exhibition *Blackout* in Ambika P3, London, March 2019. Photo by David Freeman, University of Westminster.

part in the formation of Thai history.[15] In this way, Jiwarangsan utilises the circularity of the carousel slide projector in his recognition of history as an act in continual development but one that often repeats itself. Newly suggested connections are drawn between different moments in the past, and even possible futures, but each moment in time is pulled into the present. In this regard, it is interesting to note that Jiwarangsan has chosen digital video for his various works that deal with the subject of Thai migration to other parts of the world: to South Korea in *The Wandering Ghost* (2017), to Japan in *Destination Nowhere* (2018), and to Singapore in *Ploy* (2020). In his film *Dok-rak* (*The Asylum*, 2015), one of his documentary subjects is a child from Myanmar seeking refuge in Thailand. Although the decision to migrate is not a choice made out of a sense of freedom but rather one that is forced, Jiwarangsan uses single-channel video when his subjects are in transition; in conveying a sense of his home country being stuck, he chooses to work with the carousel slide format.

As with Pijnappel's performance *Casa de Michèle*, the particularities of the carousel slide projector are highlighted through its juxtaposition with other media in the installation of *Non-chronological History*. Jiwarangsan stages a play of contrasts between photographic media in his most recent installations of the work by presenting the slide installation alongside *Dust under Feet* (2011), his project that involves a pile of photographs the size of dust particles that each depict individual portraits entirely detached from any context or name.[16] In contrast to the ephemerality of the slide projections, the mini-photographs gathered on a tabletop are resolutely material, as they are visible first and foremost as an accumulation of tiny bits of material and only later, with the assistance of magnifying glasses, reveal themselves to be a series of portrait photographs.[17] The anonymous faces represent Thai citizens whose names might not be widely known but who nevertheless are impacted by historical events.[18] While addressing the individual in the broader current of history, the two artworks juxtaposed together, which is currently Jiwarangsan's preferred mode of display, offer a staging of contrasts that highlight the specificities of each. The loud cacophony of mechanical sounds emitted by the nine slide projectors is amplified by the silence of the display of miniature photographs. The physical interactivity expected in the experience of *Dust under Feet* differentiates itself from the automatic rotation of the slides that continue onwards, with the loop as its structural determinant. In such ways, the interaction with other media accentuates the specificities of the carousel slide projector.

In his use of the carousel slide projector, Jiwarangsan also gestures towards its use in education. Alongside overhead projectors, carousel slide projectors were a familiar sight in universities and schools in the past century, until digital beamers were installed in the classroom. The portable and simple apparatus provided a useful way to initiate the collective study of a photograph or an illustration, often to accompany science and art history lessons. Jiwarangsan deals with the subject of education directly in *Aesthetics 101* (2019), a slide-based installation that is an artistic outcome of his sifting through seven thousand slides that he inherited from Somkiat Tangnamo, an art history professor who was also the founder of Midnight University, a Thailand-based free and online educational project and discussion forum for political and social issues. Although Tangnamo passed away in 2010, the online forum he founded continued to be active until 2014, when Thailand's military junta blocked access to its website. Continuing his legacy for education and commitment to social debate, Jiwarangsan presents a selection of Tangnamo's slides that he used for his classes that are made visible to exhibition visitors through carousel slide projectors and lightboxes.[19] Just as it does for *Non-chronological History*, the multiprojection slide installation initiates random connections between different projected images and encourages the exhibition visitor to come up with their own associations.

Conclusion

An artist who has made several digital films, Jiwarangsan's choice of the carousel slide projector is deliberate.[20] Unlike artists in the 1960s and 1970s who found an affinity with the projector at least partially due to its portability and ease of use, the decision by Prapat Jiwarangsan and Pablo Pijnappel to use this antiquated object comes at significant cost in both budgetary and technical limitations. Due to decreasing consumer demand, increasingly few laboratories take on the photochemical development of slide film, and for similar reasons most technicians no longer possess the technical expertise and experience required. At the current state, their digital equivalents would provide contemporary artists with what the carousel slide projectors offered artists in the 1960s. As such, the use of the carousel slide projector comes down to other factors, and it has been the primary undertaking of this chapter to pinpoint some of the artists' motivations.

Reasons contemporary artists may utilise the defunct medium despite its apparent obsolescence are manifold, but can be broadly categorised into two thematic frameworks. First, the carousel slide projector has presence. In the contemporary context, where digital media increasingly seeks to conceal itself and its mechanisms, the carousel slide projector is both physically and sonically assertive. Second, despite its display of reproduced images, the carousel slide projector resists the linearity of progression found in cinematic projection and, with its looped structure, engages with the present. As my analysis of Pablo Pijnappel's and Prapat Jiwarangsan's slide-based works has demonstrated, these key characteristics of the carousel slide projector are given attention in the staging of the projector apparatus in two ways: its use in the contemporary context after the demise of its industrial production and in intermedial dialogue with other distinct media.

An analysis of only the artistic use of the carousel slide projector during the time of its industrial production would be a disservice to the number of artistic projects that continue its legacy beyond its expiry date. In fact, observing its use in the current digital context gives a stronger indication of its specific characteristics that contribute to its excelling in its afterlife. While I hope my analysis of the two case studies in this chapter contributes to internationalising this field of study, there is much work to be done in exploring both historical and contemporary slide-based works on a global scale; achieving this would provide us with a dynamic history of the slide projector which, much like its carousel form, will not offer a clear-cut sense of linear progression.

Notes

This research on contemporary uses of the carousel slide project was undertaken as part of my Leverhulme Early Career Fellowship at the Centre for Research and Education in Arts and Media, University of Westminster, in 2015–2018.

1. The only artwork exhibited was *Sea Grammar* (2015) by Swedish artist Runo Lagomarsino, which involves a series of slides depicting the view of the sea interrupted by perforations that accumulate in number as the carousel rotates.
2. James Richards's *The Screens* (2013) involved four slide projectors positioned adjacently and facing the same wall, and Tris Vona Michell presented several slide-based works, including *Finding Chopin: Dans l'Essex* (2014).
3. Tina Weidner (2011), a conservator at Tate who led the research project Dying Technologies: The End of 35 mm Slide Transparencies (2011–2012), breaks down the etymologies of the words used to describe slides in several languages: "All three terms *slide*, *transparency* and *dia* describe an ephemeral presence, a state in which a picture is formed, lasts and disappears." Weidner references the exhibition catalogue of the German exhibition: Bauer (2000).
4. In the case of flicker films such as *Arnulf Rainer* (Peter Kubelka, 1960) and *The Flicker* (Tony Conrad, 1966), where black film leader and clear film leader oscillate in quick succession, the subject of the films is arguably the individual frames, and as such, viewers are encouraged to be more attentive to them or, at least, the existence of individual frames in the composition of a film.
5. Instant film, most famously produced by the Polaroid Corporation, also establishes a direct continuum between the photographed event and the photograph and has similarly been a subject of a resurgence of interest.
6. Media archaeology, as seen in Zielinski (2006), Parikka (2012), and Huhtamo (2013), maps out a genealogy of media that questions the commonplace trajectory of its development as becoming progressively complex. In this scholarly field, defunct and forgotten forms of media are excavated and their place in the history of media reassessed. I consider my project on carousel slide projectors and their artistic use to be in touch with and in response to this line of enquiry.
7. The exhibition was first presented at the Baltimore Museum of Art between 27 February and 15 May 2005, after which it travelled to Contemporary Arts Center in Cincinnati, Ohio (2 July–11 September 2005) and the Brooklyn Museum in New York (7 October 2005–8 January 2006).
8. Again, the assumed linearity of technological and, in the case of cinema and other artistic media, creative progression can be undermined by such examples that complicate the history of technology as a succession of inventions. Jean-Louis Comolli (2015: 198) points out the issue of the overuse of the "fixed syntagm 'for the first time'" as it alludes to film language as something that is progressively developing as if film history was working towards an unified goal: "Ineluctably, it seems, the decisive operation of these 'histories' is to evoke and give an overview of the greatest possible number of technical, stylistic and formal innovations, each one of which is presented (and sought out) as the initiation of a succession of aesthetic developments (the 'progress' of a 'language') whose finality, endpoint or perfection is the cinema such as it is practised at the moment when each historian writes its history."

Intermediality and Carousel Slide Projector   79

9. Krauss (1999: 289–305) expands on this further.
10. While their slide-based artworks are often exhibited as installations, many of them were originally performances: Nan Goldin's *The Ballad of Sexual Dependency*, for example, was originally a series of improvised live performances with slide projectors prior to its current form as an installation. For example, it was presented at the 1985 Whitney Biennial as a screening.
11. The performance was presented as the closing event for his solo show *Pareciam ser de um cinza translúcido*, held between 11 January and 1 March 2014 at the gallery. The aforementioned film *Lucas* was also installed in 16mm projection as part of the exhibition.
12. The play with synchronisation between audio and image evokes Hollis Frampton's *(nostalgia)* (1971), a film where the audience is shown a series of still photographs placed on an active burner one after another. As the photograph disintegrates, we hear a story that relates to the image that we will see next, an asynchronic pattern that continues throughout the film and similarly expects an active spectatorship from the audience.
13. Andrew V. Uroskie (2014: 167, 240) discusses the works of Stan VanDerBeek and Ken Dewey that combined slides and film projection. In my research on 1960–1970s Japanese expanded cinema, I have come across works that combine film and slide projection by artists such as Hiroshi Manabe, Takahiko Iimura, Toshio Matsumoto, and Kenji Kanesaka and in the collective work *Document 6.15* by Van Film Science Research Centre (see Ross 2014).
14. This version of the installation was presented in the context of *Blackout*, a group exhibition I curated in 2019 that was presented in the following venues: Kunstal, Rotterdam, as part of International Film Festival Rotterdam, 24 January–3 February; Ambika P3, London, 12–17 March; and Greylight Projects, Brussels, 3–14 April, in the context of the multi-university research project B-Magic. While it was previously presented in variations of a triple-projection version, Jiwarangsan always intended for the piece to involve nine projectors and had prepared eight hundred slides, which are in fact enough for sets of carousels. Nonetheless, until his participation in *Blackout*, he had not been able to realise his original intentions due to budgetary and technical limitations. *Non-chronological History* featured alongside nine other installations using the carousel slide projector in various ways, all made after Kodak cancelled its industrial production.
15. Jiwarangsan in conversation with me during the installation of *Non-chronological History* at Kunsthal Rotterdam, 2019.
16. Jiwarangsan presents both works under one title, *Non-chronological History*, on his artist website, http://www.prapat-jiwarangsan.com/.
17. According to 10 Chancery Lane Gallery, Hong Kong, which represents the artist, the artwork comprises three thousand digital prints.
18. The title of the work is an allusion to the Thai phrase "May the power of the dust on the soles and the dust under the soles of your royal feet protect my head and the top of my head," which is a formal address expected to be delivered to the king as a form of subjugation.
19. *Aesthetics 101* was commissioned for the 2019 Singapore Biennale, 22 November 2019–22 March 2020, and installed appropriately for the duration of the show at an educational institution, the LASALLE College of the Arts. At this installation, Jiwarangsan used two carousel slide projectors, four LED video projectors, and two lightboxes that were accompanied by magnifying glasses. According to Jiwarangsan, the analogue and digital hybrid formation was primarily due to technical limitations. An earlier version of *Aesthetics 101* was presented as a digital film at the film festival EXiS in Seoul, South Korea, in 2016.

20. Jiwarangsan's recent digital films include *Parasite Family* (2022), *Ploy* (2020), *Destination Nowhere* (2018), *The Wandering Ghost* (2017), and *The Asylum* (2015). His films have been presented as installations in galleries and museums but also as cinematic projections at international film festivals, including at International Film Festival Rotterdam, Singapore International Film Festival, and Internationale Kurzfilmtage Winterthur.

References

Auslander, Philip. 1996. "Liveness: Performance and the Anxiety of Simulation." In *Performance and Cultural Politics*, edited by Elin Diamond, 196–213. London: Routledge.
Bauer, Stéphane. 2000. *Dia, slide, transparency: Materialien zur Projektionskunst*. Berlin: Neue Gesellschaft für Bildende Kunst (NGBK).
Comolli, Jean-Louis. 2015. *Cinema against Spectacle: Technique and Ideology Revisited*. Edited and translated by Daniel Fairfax. Amsterdam: Amsterdam University Press. Originally published in *Cahiers du cinema*, 1971–72.
Huhtamo, Erkki. 2013. *Illusions in Motion Media Archaeology of the Moving Panorama and Related Specatacles*. Cambridge, MA: MIT Press.
Krauss, Rosalind. 1997. ". . . And Then Turn Away? An Essay on James Coleman." *October* 81 (Summer): 5–33.
Krauss, Rosalind. 1999. "Reinventing the Medium." *Critical Inquiry* 25, no. 2 (Winter): 289–305.
Parikka, Jussi. 2012. *What Is Media Archaeology?* Cambridge, UK: Polity.
Pijnappel, Pablo. 2017. *Works*. Berlin: Pineapple Tree Press.
Rebentisch, Juliane. 2012. *Aesthetics of Installation Art*. Translated by Daniel Hendrickson with Gerrit Jackson. Berlin: Sternberg Press.
Ross, Julian. 2014. "Beyond the Frame: Intermedia and Expanded Cinema in 1960–70s Japan." PhD thesis, University of Leeds.
Uroskie, Andrew V. 2014. *Between the Black Box and the White Cube: Expanded Cinema and Postwar Art*. Chicago: University of Chicago Press.
Weidner, Tina. 2011. "35 mm Slide Medium." Tate. https://www.tate.org.uk/about-us/projects/dying-technologies-end-35-mm-slide-transparencies/35-mm-slide-medium.
Youngblood, Gene. 1970. *Expanded Cinema*. New York: P. Dutton.
Zielinski, Siegfired. 2006. *Deep Time of the Media: Toward an Archaeology of Hearing and Seeing by Technical Means*. Translated by Gloria Custance. Cambridge, MA: MIT Press. Originally published as *Archäologie der Medien: Zur Tiefenzeit des technischen Hörens und Sehens*, 2002.

6
Up the Junction, Intermediality, and Social Change

Sarah Street

> Escaping my unpeopled background to the energy of the city.
> (Dunn [1963] 2013: x)

This chapter examines adaptations of Nell Dunn's *Up the Junction*, a collection of sixteen observational stories published in 1963.[1] These were based on the author's cross-class experiences of living and working in Battersea in the late 1950s and take the form of reported conversations and descriptive prose. On first publication they were considered controversial for their candid depiction of female sexuality and as an uninhibited, vibrant record of working-class women's struggles for survival on the edge of poverty and social deprivation in South London. Poet Adrian Henri (1988: loc 94) described the stories as recording "a particular moment in English social history: the destruction of large areas of inner-city terraced housing, and with it a whole way of life." In 1965 Ken Loach directed *Up the Junction* in the pioneering BBC *Wednesday Play* series of controversial, socially conscious dramas which aired between 1964 and 1970. Dunn wrote the screenplay, the story editor was Tony Garnett, and *Up the Junction* is widely acknowledged as "the play that took television drama out of the studio and into the real world" (Cooke 2015: 71). Then, in 1968 a feature film version directed by Peter Collinson was released; this time Dunn was not involved, but the film retains many elements of her book and, as this chapter will demonstrate, can be related to the TV play despite its very different formal design as a widescreen film shot in colour. In terms of establishing a web of media connections, these two screen versions are profoundly intermedial, forging connections which accumulate and resonate across texts, particularly concerning the establishment of space and place,

Sarah Street, Up the Junction, *Intermediality, and Social Change* In: *The Moving Form of Film.* Edited by: Lúcia Nagib and Stefan Solomon, Oxford University Press. © Oxford University Press 2023. DOI: 10.1093/oso/9780197621707.003.0007 while maintaining a foundational relationship and engagement with Dunn's original stories. I argue that the TV play nevertheless remains closest to Dunn's original narrative and affective sensibility, with its resonant, televisual development of her core themes and style. The text's intermedial journey is illustrative of the complex interrelations and tensions between media during a period when film was reacting to the advance of television as the most popular entertainment medium.

Dunn's interest in other media continued in her later career: her novel *Poor Cow* (1967) was adapted for film by Ken Loach, with whom Dunn co-wrote the screenplay, and she collaborated with Patricia Losey on the screenplay for *Steaming*, the 1985 film directed by Joseph Losey that was based on Dunn's play (1981). While openness to a variety of forms of creative expression could be a pragmatic strategy which might increase a writer's income, Dunn's consistent engagement with different media suggests that *Up the Junction* was a formative experience that had a profound influence on the rest of her career. Her direct involvement in Loach's TV play resulted in a particularly resonant adaptation that captured the source text's energetic flow through an evolutionary, intermedial process which complemented her literary vision. Her lack of direct involvement in Collinson's film demonstrates that more than authorship is at stake when a creative work is adapted to different media forms. *Up the Junction* illuminates the experience of the media involved in its appropriation and how these were preoccupied with their own identities and strategies for survival.

The particular set of textual interconnections arising from *Up the Junction* will be explored through the lens of intermedial theory, which suggests insights into their origins, nature, and consequences. The conception of intermediality that is most appropriate to this case study refers in particular to outward-facing aspects, such as performativity and dialogue, as well as inward dimensions, including self-reflexivity. Ágnes Pethő (2011: 40) describes this approach as "[t]he repetition or the re-inscription of a medium as a form in the form of another medium, where the procedure of intermediality itself is also figurated, that is: it becomes observable and it refers reflexively to itself." As Jonathan Mack (2017: 30) argues in their reading of Pethő's "re-inscription," this conception presents intermediality as highly performative: "It is often an action, part of a dialogue between media and arts in which influences and even rivalries are recognized." The liminal hybridity of such fluid formations usefully deploys Rodowick's (2001) idea of the "figural," a critical space that reveals the "deep imbrication" of media boundaries, inviting us to think of intermediality as "an ever-changing aesthetic configuration, and a sensuously perceivable excess" (Pethő 2018: 169). Dunn's *Up the Junction* certainly generated "sensuously perceivable excess" that resonated across the three articulations of her vivid stories.

Dunn's book had potential for intermedial dialogue because it was conceived as an open text in form and genre; when published it was considered unconventional in form and content. As Stephen Brooke (2012: 430–431) observes, Dunn's submersion in the world of working-class Battersea permitted her to "explore new subjectivities, particularly in terms of gender and sexuality," while class is conveyed "as an active and dynamic social identity." This exploratory spirit also pervaded the book's literary techniques. John Hill (2011: 37) refers to *Up the Junction* as "hybrid . . . partly literature, partly sociology" since the stories are told primarily through direct speech "that we are led to understand has been spoken to, or overheard by, the narrator. The descriptive prose, linking the speech, is also restricted to external observation and deliberately avoids overt authorial commentary or speculation on the characters' inner thoughts and feelings." Tony Garnett said the TV version was "not a play, a documentary, or a musical. It is all of these at once," indicating the richness of its hybrid form that indeed captures the stories' exuberant frankness about sexuality, the women's working lives, and socialising in pubs and clubs (quoted in Hill 2011: 38). This can be related to Rodowick's (2001: 33) ideas of the figural in which distinctions between the textual and visual, in this case Dunn's combination of dialogue and sparse prose and the dynamic visual energy of Loach's drama, are collapsed.

Susan Benson's line drawings that illustrated the book's first edition add a visual, pictorial quality that was needed because of its lack of prose descriptions of place, space, and characters and its concentration on speech. The drawings can be thought of quite literally as figurations that are mostly evocative of locations such as the corner shop, a street where scrap metal is collected, and a yard where children play amidst dilapidated, discarded cars. Although they provide points of visualisation, the drawings are executed relatively sparsely, and there are only a few faces. Line drawings, also known as contour drawings, use clean, simple lines which can nevertheless be very evocative in relation to their source. As John Elderfield (1971: 13, 15) explains, drawing "becomes the assimilation of mental and environmental data," and "line is the engineer's straight-edge but also the magician's wand." Although similar in approach to the economy of Dunn's prose, the drawings provide a visual topography that recalls her memories of Battersea through the suggestiveness of line. We can see how this process of partial visualisation gave Loach graphic potential in the TV play; the drawings invite a dialogue between the

Figure 6.1 Cars for scrap: Susan Benson's line drawing for *Up the Junction* (1963).

two texts, and several shots were clearly inspired by Benson's drawings, for example, the row of terraced houses with the chimneys of a factory silhouetted in the background (Dunn [1963] 2013: 42), and children playing on an abandoned car ready to be scrapped (114) (Figures 6.1 and 6.2). Dunn advised Loach when he was looking for suitable London locations, so her authorial input was crucial. The TV play's documentary elements include establishing a strong sense of the urban locale and the realist authenticity of place. This avoidance of clutter, as it were, in terms of writing and drawing, allowed a space for imaginative responses to the subject matter, a challenge both Loach and Collinson exploited in interesting ways which made the most of their respective media while also engaging in an interactive dialogue. The affective similarities between the writing and the drawings created a foundational intermedial symbiosis for *Up the Junction* as a text that readily lent itself to rearticulation in a range of other media forms.

Figure 6.2 Cars for scrap: a scene from Ken Loach's TV play adaptation of *Up the Junction* (1965).

For many critics, Loach's *Up the Junction* is a milestone in television drama, a foretaste of his groundbreaking Wednesday Play *Cathy Come Home* (BBC, 1966).[2] His celebrated improvisational techniques were first deployed, however, in *Up the Junction*, an approach that was at the heart of Dunn's writing. In this way the stories and TV version were already integrated through form, gesture, performance, and style. The TV play is indebted to Dunn's improvisatory approach in Loach's replication of the book's episodic interludes instead of imposing a conventional three-act structure. Drawing on Julia Hallam and Margaret Marshment's (2000: 101) terminology, this can be related to "expositional realism" in popular cultural forms in which "an episodic or picaresque narrative structure aims to explicate the relationship between characters and their environment." "Up the Junction" is the title of only one of the stories; the others involve the same characters—Rube, Sylvie, and Lily, who work in a sweet factory—covering different experiences in their lives, many of which feature in the TV play. Loach preserves a sense of aural realism by including snippets of snatched, sometimes overlapping conversations that capture the book's communication of the women's lively communal banter and quick-witted humour. The fragmentation of sound reinforces a sense of communal, interactive pleasure that spreads attention across characters rather than directing the viewer towards any one in particular. The unpolished camerawork style also gives the impression of filming real events and people, using black-and-white cinematography, which readily identifies it with a realist aesthetic.

In addition, elliptical editing is a dominant mode, giving the drama an energetic quality as well as the ability to juxtapose conversational fragments and images. This was made possible by shooting on 16mm film plus "the use of a 16mm back-up print for the post-recording editing of material shot in the studio" (Hill 2011: 41). Ten percent had to be shot in the studio as a consequence of Equity[3] rulings, but with this footage Loach preserved the same edgy, modernist stylistic approach to filming on location. Music also features prominently in the TV play, picking up on Dunn's quotation of lines from popular songs that the women sing along to, often to lighten the drudgery of their working day. These add another layer of intermedial complexity, enabling a different kind of aural commentary that highlights the songs' centrality to the women's everyday lives. The American songs, such as "Sweet Little Sixteen" (Chuck Berry, 1958), with lyrics about desire, romance, dancing, and coming-of-age scenarios, provide a utopian sensibility to the women's enjoyment of them, much in the sense of Richard Dyer's (2002: 20) ideas about popular entertainment forms as offering "the image of 'something better' to escape into, or something we want deeply that our day-to-day lives don't provide. Alternatives, hopes, wishes, these are the stuff of utopia." By having the women sing along to the songs they somehow make them their own, combining the rough-sounding liveness we now associate with karaoke with the familiar recorded voices of pop singers. This produces a kind of aural intermediality within the text, while gesturing to the transnational appeal of popular music in the mid-1960s.

Dunn's engagement with popular music is also evidenced by her lyrics for the play's title song, "Bad Girl," co-written with film and television composer Stanley Myers. The lyrics express a man's playful sentiments to "a good little girl," saying she'll be "glad" when he makes her a "bad girl." In opening the drama, the song is part of the diegesis. The singer is first focused on in close-up before the lyrics are heard as soundtrack to a series of images which establish the drama's iconic locations and three main characters walking down a street. We then return to the singer, who is performing in a pub where the women enjoy a night out, perhaps exhibiting some of the "bad girl" freedoms and sexual assertiveness to which the song gestures and which characterises their banter for much of the drama.

Technology and Social Change

Collinson's 1968 feature film has a more conventional approach to narrative and maintains a rather different relationship with Dunn's stories, filling the gaps, if you like, while showing self-reflexive awareness of Loach's version as well as the film's own technical capabilities. Whereas the imbrication between the book and TV play is almost seamless, demonstrating strong aesthetic interconnections producing the very essence of "sensuously perceivable excess," the film relates much more to notions of intermediality in which media rivalries are self-reflexively performed. A big difference with the film of *Up the Junction* is that we see the "narrator," who is not referenced as such in Loach's version. The film follows Dunn's personal history by featuring an upper-middle-class character, with accent to match, called Polly, who, like Dunn herself, moves from Chelsea to Battersea in London. Polly's viewpoint is sustained throughout the film as we follow her leaving Chelsea; getting a factory job; making friends with Rube and Sylvie, working-class characters who feature in the book and TV play; getting a flat; and meeting a man called Peter, a character created for the film that expands the spasmodic appearance of Dave, the narrator's love interest in Dunn's stories. The narrative is conscious about conveying her impressions of a new lifestyle, "slumming it" while experiencing a greater sense of personal freedom, friendship, and love than in her former life. When Polly shows Rube and Sylvie her rented bed-sit room, they say it looks "old-fashioned" and that they prefer "modern" furnishings. This contrast between Polly's background and the working-class women's desire to escape the cramped housing conditions they grew up in touches on the text's engagement with the transitional historical moment Henri identified as at the core of *Up the Junction*'s social commentary. While Polly finds the older housing refreshing, her new friends cannot understand her choice. The feature film's greater length also invites the viewer to identify with Polly's personal journey from the perspective of an outsider. While this references Dunn's own experience, it nevertheless seems more obviously staged and removed from her impressions of Battersea as captured in the stories. The film's approach to character differs from the more communal, immersive experience conveyed by Loach's version, which celebrated the women's ensemble, collective relationship.

The film is also different in terms of form because it was shot in colour using a widescreen aspect ratio (2.35:1; the TV play is 1.33:1). Just as Loach was experimenting with new approaches to technologies in television drama, Collinson's film was released at a key moment of technological change for the film industry. It was somewhat ironic that television's aspect ratio was the same as the "academy" ratio that had been the standard for film until into the 1950s. Most widescreen films were incompatible with television exhibition, which accelerated the perception of media differentiation in the 1960s. Both colour and widescreen were relatively new technologies to British cinema. The tipping point was 1965, when colour films exceeded for the first time the annual number of black-and-white productions in the sound era (Street et al. 2021: 8–9). Cheaper, faster colour film stocks were increasingly used beginning in the mid-1960s, and by the end of the decade the vast majority of films were made in colour. Whereas in the silent era most films were coloured using applied techniques, and from the mid-1930s a few sound films a year were made in Technicolor, by 1968 Eastmancolor was fast becoming the default stock for all filmmakers. Technicolor was an expensive technology that required the use of a special three-strip camera; because Eastmancolor was cheaper and could be used in any camera, Technicolor was forced to sustain its commercial viability by concentrating on film processing and developing a new, economical technology called Techniscope. This used a two-film-perforation negative pull-down per frame instead of the standard four-perforation frame usually exposed in 35mm film photography. This enabled widescreen films to be shot more cheaply and quickly than usual, using lighter cameras and lenses. More than one camera could also be used for certain shots. Using this technology enabled the film in places to replicate the TV play's vérité, documentary-style aesthetic that would not have been so easy had more conventional widescreen technology been used. This had an interesting formal impact on Collinson's film since it included a few shots and scenes that resemble the TV play, while also making use of the more static, breathtaking framing capabilities of widescreen. Collinson exploited the technology to suggest an homage to Loach, creating an intermedial connection between the texts. This process of technological mediation supports scholarship foregrounding cinema's dialogic and at times competitive relationships with emergent media such as television (Young 2006). As Jay David Bolter and Richard Grusin (1999: 65) observe, a medium never operates in isolation because "it must enter into relationships of respect and rivalry with other media."

In this sense the film is self-reflexive, using new technologies in Mack's (2017: 30) sense as "part of a dialogue between media and arts in which influences and even rivalries are recognized." At a time when watching television was becoming more popular than going to the cinema, and the BBC broadcast its first colour programmes in the summer of 1967, *Up the Junction* can be seen as an attempt to assert the superiority of film as a medium that could deliver more, especially in terms of widescreen formats. Yet the profoundly intermedial history of *Up the Junction* as a text results in a liminal, hybrid, "figural" film version that also plays with the legacy of Dunn and Loach's symbiotic articulations of and creative responses to a transitional moment in British social history. While Collinson's film celebrates Eastmancolor widescreen cinema, it is also a visual homage to the iconicity of Loach's version and the innovative televisual style it represented. Collinson selectively appropriated Loach's verité approach, which conveyed a spontaneous "liveness" in the performances often associated with television as a medium (Young 2006: xiii, xxi). In the film, however, this gesture to realism is far less pronounced in a text that is also concerned to project its own unique features. The tensions between these positions contributes to the idea that all three versions form integrated yet evolving aesthetic configurations of *Up the Junction* that reflect their respective production in key moments of technological change and aesthetic experiment.

This can be seen in particular through the television and film texts' shared concerns to document the transformation of the urban landscape. As noted by Brooke (2012: 435), Dunn's work documents how "the new society of affluence and popular culture is imbricated in a much older landscape" of "hybrid modernity" that characterised London's development in the mid-1960s. London's tenements were knocked down by the end of the decade, and both versions show the changing urban topography in which shambling, dilapidated Victorian terraced houses and piles of rubble appear in the same frame as new, high-rise blocks of flats. In Loach's version the new flats and detritus of urban development are framed to suit television's aspect ratio of 4:3 (1.33:1). The shots are composed as documentary photographs from which, like Benson's drawings, the characters are generally absent, such as a shot of a block of flats taking up much of the image and the roofs of terraced houses visible in the foreground. The images are designed centripetally, as in a shot of a street with four chimney stacks in the background which, however, dominate the frame and draw the eye because of their central positioning. Loach wanted to achieve a filmic look that was in the verité style of direct cinema by using 16mm film. This made exterior locations convey an immediate effect, much like news reportage, in order to reinforce the authenticity that gave *Up the Junction* its reputation as marking "a quantum leap in the development of British television drama" (Cooke 2015: 78). The shots also resemble photojournalism's realist photographic conventions, as established by magazines such as *Picture Post*.

Collinson's film, by contrast, uses colour and widescreen for a different graphic effect as part of its social commentary, as in one shot when Peter takes Polly to the derelict house where he used to live. The urban landscape is shown to be intertwined with the characters' lives, so the film's narrative

Figure 6.3 Colour and widescreen aesthetics in Peter Collinson's *Up the Junction* (1968).

is never far from being perceived as integral to the image composition. The screen shows Peter in the dark on one side and Polly on the other framed in front of a window beyond which is the orange-blue glow of the dusk light, which appears to underscore her more "rosy" view of Battersea. This view forms a frame within the frame, inviting the viewer to look through it, to the horizon that reinforces the image's centrifugal effect (Figure 6.3). Peter's working-class origins give him a different, perhaps more realistic experience of the older houses which upper-middle-class Polly has romanticised. In this way the film incorporates the TV play's commentary on the changing urban topography that was such a striking feature of Dunn's stories, while using colour and an expansive frame as additional sources of commentary. As "in-between" texts, both reflect a moment of social history that was similarly in transition, with class continuing to be a social referent in "affluent" postwar Britain (Brooke 2012).

The "Gold Blouse" Incident

To illuminate the "in-between" nature and intermediality of these texts in more detail, the rest of this chapter will examine an incident that features in the TV and film versions of *Up the Junction*. It is based on a chapter of Dunn's ([1963] 2013: 19–26) book collection titled "The Gold Blouse," when the women turn a factory tea-break into an impromptu dance. The differences between the renditions of this episode are telling in terms of how each offers a "reinscription" which illuminates many of the creative, resonating qualities of intermediality highlighted by this case study. In Dunn's story, the sweet factory is established as the locale where the women wrap and pack fake liqueur chocolates in two cramped rooms. Like much of the book, the perspective is on the women's interlinked experiences of work, leisure, and desire. Occasionally, when prose is used rather than dialogue, a sense of place is established quite literally with how it feels to be in a particular environment, such as the cramped factory. In a rare instance of prose description Dunn writes, "My eyes began to ache in the cold electric light. There are no windows in the room where we have been sitting since eight in the morning earning our two-and-five pence an hour" (21). A siren hoots to signal a tea break; the women gather in the cloakroom to chat, drink their tea, and the urn is then emptied down a toilet. They find a box of cigarettes at the bottom, which has made the tea taste bitter. The focus of the episode is to convey the spontaneous intimacy and animated camaraderie of the women's exchanges about their families and relationships, communicated during a brief moment of release from the drudgery of their manual work.

The radio is on and the women sing to the pop song "Twistin' the Night Away" (Sam Cooke, 1962). One of them, described as a "hunch-back," is nicknamed "Bent Sheila," the character who then assumes importance in the vignette. Dunn ([1963] 2013: 25) writes, "Sheila opens her mouth, swaying desperately. As the music reaches its climax she flings off her coat revealing a gold damask blouse." We learn that her mother bought it for her, and Rube, one of her co-workers, cuts off its sleeves and cuts the back so that it has a V-shape. Dunn continues: "The blouse had large armholes, and now Sheila's grubby bra was exposed. . . . The blouse slid sideways revealing a torn vest" (26). This strange scene is interrupted by the end of the tea break, abruptly announced by the foreman: "Back to work you women" (26). In a scene that might otherwise have appeared disturbing, Sheila does not seem to mind the women's drastic intervention: "Sheila, still grinning, sat down hugging her arms to her chest till someone threw her a worn cardigan. On the brown lino, amid discarded sweet papers and cigarette ends, the gold sleeves lay gleaming in the raw electric light" (26). "The Gold Blouse" ends where it began, but with the electric light transformed from being a "cold," harsh workspace light to the key illuminant for the glistening, gold-spangled damask blouse that has briefly held centre stage. Why Sheila was wearing it underneath her coat is not addressed, but its transformation serves as a symbolic means of glimpsing the women's desire for glamour amidst the drabness of their working environment. Its placement between a coat and "grubby," torn underwear creates a surprise reveal, enabling the scene to shift in register. The blouse's initial association with an older generation (Sheila's mother), with its unfashionable long sleeves and covering of the flesh (it is described as Victorian and "richly embroidered"), is displaced by Rube's attempt to update it and to sexualise its meaning as clothing. This small instance of transformation resonates with Benson's drawings of Battersea's similar process of redevelopment. Benson did not illustrate the gold blouse in the book, presumably because a line drawing would not have captured its colour or spectacle.

In Loach's *Up the Junction* the scene begins with the tea being poured down a toilet. The next shots are vérité style, a jumble of close-ups and low camera angles of the women dancing. Conversations are heard, but nothing really of note is picked out on the soundtrack as the women's animated chatter overlaps. The montage is cut to the rhythm of the music and uses "Sweet Little Sixteen" rather than "Twistin' the Night Away." This change is interesting for the songs' rather different inflections. "Twistin' the Night Away" is about communality, "everybody's feelin' great," as young and old dance together. It also references clothes: "the man in the evenin' clothes" who is "dancin' with the chick in slacks." "Sweet Little Sixteen" has a more sexualised edge; its lyrics describe a young girl with "the grown-up blues" who wears "a tight dress and lipstick," though tomorrow "she'll be in class again." This sentiment underscores the scene's suggestion of two locations and affective sensibilities simultaneously: the literal setting of the factory where the women are regimented ("in class"), and the "grown-up" freedoms experienced in environments such as clubs and dance halls, which are suggested by the carnivalesque transformation of the women's tea break and Sheila's appearance. In black-and-white the blouse's shimmering gold simply glistens in the light, but the blouse otherwise appears dark. The cutting of the already short sleeves is done quickly, and Sheila clearly enjoys the transformation. The whole incident is quite short, concluding with the music being turned up, followed by the foreman's abrupt interruption of the impromptu dance. In bringing together literature, radio, and television the scene's intermedial energy captures the improvisatory strategies at the heart of the women's physical and emotional survival; they make pop songs their own by singing them out loud, just as they ingeniously "adapt" Sheila's blouse, bringing it up to date.

Sheila's brief backstory is not used by Loach to introduce pathos into this scene, which, as noted above, is over quickly and with little sense of exposition. In Dunn's account, Sheila implies she is exploited by the local boys, who "take me upstairs where it's dark" when she visits the local café. This sparse information about Sheila's life, including her mother's gift of an old-fashioned blouse that is worn to work and hidden between outer and inner clothing, is unsettling compared with Loach's rather literal representation of the incident, which appears to eschew character development. For Loach, Sheila's story is not the centre of the scene, which instead has a more collective function of showing the women's resilience, how they find pleasure in short tea breaks, while communicating the transformative, dynamic impact of popular music. The blouse and its transformation are symbolic of a carnivalesque spirit that pervades the scene; the women can be resourceful and survive, turning their tea break into a spectacle of communality. Sheila is simply an incidental character in the vignette that serves as a symbolic means of achieving this aim. In addition, as a black-and-white drama the gold blouse itself cannot occupy the spectacular position it is accorded in Collinson's film.

Collinson's film has a very different interpretation of the "Gold Blouse" incident; it lasts longer and is tied to the film's more conventional narrative. It begins with the "Tea up" call; the women queue for tea and comment that it tastes "orrible." A brief shot in the lavatories shows one of the women being sick, and the contents of the tea urn are poured down the toilet. This is shot from inside the toilet, with Rube and Sylvie looking into the bowl to find that cigarettes have contaminated the tea, making it taste foul. This provides a clear explanation for the problem with the tea compared to Loach's more economical, fleeting treatment of the incident. The women dancing are introduced by a zoom shot, and colour enhances the contrast between the women's blue overalls and the glistening of the gold on Sheila's blouse as she dances in the centre. The use of a zoom constitutes an assertive change of style within the scene as the conventions of shooting a dance hall are applied. The arrangement of the figures appears to be more formal than in the TV version, the women's blue overalls forming a kind of pattern around Sheila, who looks awkward; she is wearing a scarf and placed in the centre; more of a spectacle is made of her when the sleeves are cut. Unlike the TV version, she looks a little anxious and bewildered as her co-worker taunts her, saying, "Who's gonna look sexy?" The cutting of the sleeves is laborious; one woman can be heard saying "Leave her alone," and for a moment the incident borders on being cruel. Another difference is that the music is blander in the film version, just a jazzy soundtrack in the background rather than a popular song to which the women sing along. This means that more of the women's conversations can be heard; there is less overlapping of dialogue. The moment when Sheila's blouse is cut is emphasised by the camera being more static and the scene more obviously staged. The incident also concludes with the foreman's interruption of the dancing, but then Rube faints, which links to the next steps of the narrative, which deal with her pregnancy and subsequent abortion. In this way Collinson's rendition of "The Gold Blouse" is more overtly "filmic" through the deployment of colour and shots such as the zoom that were typically used in widescreen films. The more conventional approach to characterisation has the effect of making Sheila more awkward and exploited, tying the function of an incidental character to the expository conventions of narrative cinema.

Conclusion

This chapter has shown how, as reinscriptions of Dunn's original text, the TV and film versions of *Up the Junction* demonstrate high degrees of reflexivity concerning their various media forms. The co-presence of different kinds of transition, or border-crossings in terms of generic hybridity, experimental techniques, and narrative about social change make *Up the Junction* a productive case study of how a foundational creative idea can be elaborated across texts, media, and time. Just as "The Gold Blouse" begins and ends in broadly the same way in all three versions, what happens in between—the resonances, similarities, and differences between and within texts—is best understood through the perspective of intermediality. The hybrid form of Dunn's sparse prose invited practitioners in other media to respond to its openness while investing each iteration with its own medial sensibility. As we have seen, the visual sense of place provided by Benson's drawings had a profound effect on the TV play and the film. Dunn's authorship was never a closed notion; her collaboration with Benson and Loach invited her work to be subject to, and indeed enriched by, different forms of creative expression. The "sensuously perceivable excess" of the incidents and conversations Dunn recorded resulted in Loach's recurrent visual and aural strategies that retain their own impression of freshness and authenticity, of witnessing people as they are in vérité style. Loach and Collinson filmed the changing physical spaces of Battersea as urban regeneration was transforming the landscape, engaging with and developing Dunn's documentation of a key historical moment of social change. Their work also reflects changes being experienced in the film and television industries. Loach's use of 16mm film and preference for exterior locations was unconventional, as was Collinson's exploitation of colour and Techniscope. Techniscope enabled the film to pay homage to Loach's version in some scenes, while it also used a widescreen aspect ratio to contrast different views and impressions of the city within a single frame. The decision to feature Polly as a character was a way to include implicit reference to Dunn, but this tended to reduce the multiperspectival elements of the book and TV play, thus distancing the film from their evocative modes of direct, communal address. The use of colour in the film was in some scenes very vivid and occasionally extended what Loach had achieved with black-and-white, a point that relates to how intermedial dialogue can touch upon competition between media. But despite these differences, there is a sense of circularity and productive exchange between the three texts as expressive of Dunn's memories, as she put it, of "the excitement of escaping my unpeopled background to the energy of the city" (preface to 2013 edition: x).

Each medial expression of *Up the Junction* looked backwards and forwards, much in the spirit of present-day multi-iterative performances in which a central idea is "worked through" as a cumulative process in dialogue with its constituent parts. *Up the Junction*'s generative spirit eloquently demonstrates a predisposition to intermedial exchange, a process with which Dunn was clearly fascinated and continued to draw upon in subsequent work, including screenwriting and further collaboration with Loach. As I have argued, this was expressed most strongly in the symbiotic interactivity between her book, Benson's line drawings, and Loach's TV play. While the film drew on these iterations to some extent, its exploitation of relatively novel technical innovations and approach to character and narrative meant it became further removed from Dunn's original vision. The medial and temporal shift to film did not necessarily result in a superior development of Dunn's original narrative but offered something less improvisatory or immediate in its emotive impact. In this way *Up the Junction*'s intermedial journeys into "the energy of the city" took Dunn's work to both familiar and unexpected places while reflecting a complex reinscription of competing media forms.

Notes

1. Dunn moved to Battersea in 1959 and began writing short stories which were published in the *New Statesman*. These were collected in a book and published in 1963 as *Up the Junction*.
2. *The Wednesday Play* was an anthology series of BBC British television dramas broadcast in 1964–1970. They were often controversial in terms of subject matter and varied in their formal styles (Bignell 2014).
3. Equity is the UK trade union for creative practitioners.

References

Bignell, Jonathan. 2014. "The Spaces of *The Wednesday Play* (BBC TV 1964–70): Production, Technology and Style." *Historical Journal of Film, Radio and Television* 34, no. 3: 369–389.

Bolter, Jay David, and Richard Grusin. 1999. *Remediation: Understanding New Media*. Cambridge, MA: MIT Press.

Brooke, Stephen. 2012. "'Slumming' in Swinging London? Class, Gender and the Post-war City in Nell Dunn's *Up the Junction* (1963)." *Cultural and Social History* 9, no. 3: 429–449.

Cooke, Lez. 2015. *British Television Drama: A History*. London: Palgrave.
Dunn, Nell. (1963) 2013. *Up the Junction*. London: Virago Modern Classic.
Dyer, Richard. 2002. *Only Entertainment*. London: Routledge.
Elderfield, John. 1971. "Drawing as Suspended Narrative." *Leonardo* 4, no. 1: 13–22.
Hallam, Julia, and Margaret Marshment. 2000. *Realism and Popular Cinema*. Manchester: Manchester University Press.
Henri, Adrian. (1987) 2013. "Introduction." In Nell Dunn, *Up the Junction*, 59–150. London: Virago Modern Classic.
Hill, John. 2011. *Ken Loach and the Politics of Film and Television*. London: Bloomsbury.
Mack, Jonathan. 2017. "Finding Borderland: Intermediality and the Films of Marc Forster." *Cinema Journal* 56, no. 3 (Spring): 24–46.
Pethő, Ágnes. 2011. *Cinema and Intermediality: The Passion for the In-Between*. Newcastle-on-Tyne: Cambridge Scholars.
Pethő, Ágnes. 2018. "Approaches to Studying Intermediality in Contemporary Cinema." *Acta Universitatis Sapientiae, Film and Media Studies* 15: 165–187.
Rodowick, David N. 2001. *Reading the Figural*. Durham, NC: Duke University Press.
Street, Sarah, Keith M. Johnston, Paul Frith, and Carolyn Rickards. 2021. *Colour Films in Britain: The Eastmancolor Revolution*. London: British Film Institute/Bloomsbury.
Young, Paul. 2006. *The Cinema Dreams Its Rivals: Media Fantasy Films from Radio to the Internet*. Minneapolis: University of Minnesota Press.

7
When the Past Is Present
Digital Cinema and the Philosophical Toys of Pre-Cinema

Ismail Xavier

The experimental film *Santoscópio = Dumontagem* (2010), by Carlos Adriano, belongs to a constellation of works whose emphasis on a process of repetition and difference becomes a structural key presiding over the spectator's interaction with the material. On the flat surface of the image, we find the re-editing and animation of fragments taken from a fifty-five-second single-shot film showing a simple conversation between two renowned figures: Alberto Santos Dumont, the Brazilian who played a central role in the invention of the airplane, and Charles Stewart Rolls, founder, alongside Frederick Henry Royce, of the pioneering automobile enterprise Rolls-Royce Limited, established in 1906. The exchange between the two was filmed in London on 3 December 1901 for the American Mutoscope and Biograph Company as *Santos Dumont Explaining His Air Ship to the Honorable Charles Stewart Rolls*.

Over a century later, Carlos Adriano worked with this material to produce a fifteen-minute found-footage digital film that re-edited the original images and performed a series of operations inspired by nineteenth-century inventions ranging from proto-cinematic toys to the cinematograph. The work makes the media of the past present in its orchestration of images: while it revels in the affordances of the digital by zooming in on Santos Dumont's gestures and by evoking both the grain of celluloid and the pixels of the digital image, it also uses digital animation and editing techniques to approximate the movements and sounds of the very visual technology upon which the original film was designed to be viewed. Through Adriano's process of appropriation, *Santoscópio = Dumontagem* thus stands as a paradigm of remediation and intermediality, linking digital cinema to examples of proto-cinematic devices that led to the invention of cinema, and also harking back more broadly to the era of industrial advance and the dawn of mechanical transportation.

More specifically, Adriano's film devises an image track inspired both by the 1901 film and by the nineteenth-century experience of playing with proto-cinematic devices of home entertainment, such "philosophical toys" (Oubiña 2009) as the phenakistiscope (1833), the zoetrope (1867), and the praxinoscope (1877), among others. Each device produced moving images derived from series of drawings of the same animal or object carefully disposed in a rotating circular structure that allowed for each minimal change in image to produce a sense of movement provided by their fast substitution. These artefacts, which resulted from a series of connected inventions prior to the creation of the cinematograph, provided the experience of watching moving images while concealing the means of their production. As we will see, the *Santos Dumont* film was destined for viewing in the slightly more advanced device known as the Mutoscope, and Adriano's reimagining of this film pays particular homage to the workings of that toy of the pre-cinema era.

In this chapter, I argue that the connection between proto-cinematic devices and digital cinema established by the formal composition of Adriano's experimental film provides a means of looking anew at film history. I begin by retracing his research process, before analysing the formal structure of his film in connection with both structural filmmaking and digital cinema and considering the diachronic possibilities of intermediality in quoting other media and in bringing together technologies from the past and present.

From Philosophical Toys to Digital Montage: An Intermedial Experiment

The short 1901 film was uncovered by Adriano in his research, which began in São Paulo and was completed in New York. In 2002, he came across a curious device during a visit to the Museu Paulista at the University of São Paulo, placed very discreetly in the room dedicated to the museum's Santos Dumont Collection. Intrigued by it, he asked staff about its provenance. All they could say was that it had come from Santos Dumont's private collection and that they knew very little about its function. With the museum's permission, Adriano examined the artefact and was particularly attracted by the material he found inside it: 658 cards with photographs and 664 blank cards.[1] These were arranged alternately and mounted on a reel, activated by a human-powered crank. The curious device was in fact the Mutoscope, patented by Herman Casler in 1894 and marketed by the New York–based American Mutoscope and Biograph Company from 1896 onwards. This was the same

New York company that would become one of the most important producers of the one-reel films that dominated the film market until 1912–1913, and where D. W. Griffith carried out most of the work that was central to the development of the classical narrative cinema from 1908 onwards.

The Mutoscope became a type of domestic entertainment around the same time that cinema became the major form of mass entertainment. Both worked with photographic images and created their effects from the very fast replacement of successive lighted photos passing in front of a window. But only cinema, which projected its images onto a screen at a distance, could be shared by large audiences. The Mutoscope had a viewer adjusted for a single spectator, which meant that its images could be seen by only one person at a time. Besides, its reels could not operate with a large number of cards, and as such could usually offer only around one minute of viewing time. The Mutoscope, as a gadget available only to the wealthier classes, was more advanced than any other of its kind, but it involved the same principle of photographic succession as cinema. To produce its moving images, the Mutoscope used an existing thirty- to sixty-second film, enlarging its frames as independent photographic cards. These frames were then arranged in the same order in a reel placed inside its central body, ready to be activated by the movement of a hand-crank operated by its user.

Although (like Adriano's film itself) it depended on the preexistence of a short filmed scene, the Mutoscope shared with other devices developed in the second half of the nineteenth century the status of home entertainment typical of the pre-cinema period. The fact that it allowed for an individual to project images at the viewer's desired pace meant that it shared the charm of older prestigious devices considered rather "magical" in their effects. These devices produced moving images from drawings, and more rarely from photographs, and were very attractive due to their illusionist power and their combination of entertainment and technological advance. In other words, their value came first from the immediate (and desired) sense of the device's prodigious effect, and second from the knowledge—sometimes kept a secret by its owners—of the technology that generated its effects, and prompted the question "How is this movement produced?"

Based on information he was able to gather through his research, Adriano used the cards from the Mutoscope unit he examined at the Museu Paulista and restored the original *Santos Dumont* film. He then employed digital strategies of fragmentation and recomposition of the single scene and its frames to create a new choreography for the conversation between Santos Dumont and Rolls, using the found footage material not to make a compilation film—a kind of documentary portrait of a historical moment—but to explore the moving image in its formal and material malleability. In his film, the aesthetic dimension of the original photographic images is foregrounded, intertwined with the innovations made possible by advances in digital imaging that had begun long before with those nineteenth-century visual technologies.

In this experiment, Adriano poses questions regarding the relationship between pre-cinema and digital cinema precisely through different methods of audiovisual manipulation. The possibilities available to him allowed for the reanimation of the images in such a way that not only the speed and the order but the very configuration of the sequential frames could be freely changed and controlled. This original exploration of the texture of the images produces new iconic motifs, a kind of dance of lines on the screen which, synchronised with an experimental soundtrack, follows a pattern of "theme and variations," as in a musical composition. We follow a variety of moving forms on the screen, with the bodies of Santos Dumont and Rolls variously engaged in a rhythmical repetition of gestures, depicted in slow motion, seen in a reverse negative image, or rotated on a horizontal or vertical axis. The controlled pace of these special effects produces a sense of deliberate choreography that becomes especially expressive in connection with Santos Dumont's performative explanations concerning his aircraft, and particular emphasis is given to a close-up of his finger performing the spinning movement of the aircraft propeller to illustrate his description (Figures 7.1 and 7.2). This free shaping of the image track follows the design of the film's soundtrack, on which fragments of ironic quotations from old carnival songs interact with the flicking and fluttering supposedly produced by the rotating cards of the Mutoscope mechanism.

On the one hand, *Santoscópio = Dumontagem* was made possible by the Mutoscope and its collection of photographs that Adriano found in the Museu Paulista, but in its formal procedures and visual effects the film's main dialogue is with older devices. This becomes clear as the film proceeds: aside from its last segment that replays the original *Santos Dumont* film it in its entirety, over the course of Adriano's work its compositions move away increasingly from the experience provided by the continuous scene that gave rise to his experiment. The newer digital film offers a great variety of rearrangements of Santos Dumont's and Rolls's gestures and expressions in order to create a totally discontinuous flow of the scene.

In so doing, *Santoscópio = Dumontagem* also explores some of the distinctions between the older proto-cinematic toys and the Mutoscope, as well as laying bare the device itself. In the case of the Mutoscope, which permitted a film to be shown in its continuous form and in a speed controlled

Figures 7.1 and 7.2 *Santoscópio = Dumontagem* (2010), by Carlos Adriano. Two moments of Dumont turning his hand and extended finger to imitate the movement of a propeller.

by its operator, Adriano's film makes explicit its manipulation by means of a quite distinctive visual structure: one of the sequences shows the cards placed inside the Mutoscope and being moved by its gears in order to produce their replacement on the screen and the effect of continuous movement as viewed by its spectators (Figure 7.3).

By showing its internal mechanism and revealing how the Mutoscope worked, Adriano adds a new dimension to his experimental gesture which

Figure 7.3 *Santoscópio = Dumontagem* (2010), by Carlos Adriano. In the animation that evokes the mutoscope system, this shot captures an instant similar to the rotation of consecutive cards.

discloses the very process of production of the continuity effect elicited by the original fifty-five-second film (Figures 7.4–7.6). Perhaps the most singular effect in the film is produced in a passage in which the image composition moves as if in a kaleidoscope, combining the bodies of Santos Dumont and Rolls within multiplied patterns of symmetrical forms placed side by side and occupying the entire screen (Figures 7.7 and 7.8).

The structure of "theme and variations" is developed for several minutes around gestures made by Santos Dumont and Rolls, both still visible as recognisable bodies. However, this kaleidoscopic sequence radicalises the formal experiment with motion as it produces a more radical deformation of their figures through a game of mirrors, a play of symmetries formed by waves, and an extreme stretching of the image. This radical malleability allows for the generation of mathematically rooted visual patterns that multiply themselves in the composition and suggest the historical mixture of optical studies and a fascination with magic that would lead to the creation of the kaleidoscope around 1817.

In both its formal dynamic and its studied historical references to domestic proto-cinematic toys as "content," the film clearly draws its inspiration from the past. And yet its intermedial dimension brings these museum artefacts into meaningful relations with digital technology. The memory of the old

Figures 7.4 and 7.5 *Santoscópio = Dumontagem* (2010), by Carlos Adriano. Two shots of the conversation between Dumont and Rolls, exemplifying the image's circular movement around a vertical axis.

devices embedded in *Santoscópio = Dumontagem* is an example of the technical procedures typical of digital cinema that produce its intermedial dimension; here, the twenty-first century meets the nineteenth century, and the two discover an affinity related to the interconnections of looking, perception, and movement. Taking as his frame of reference "the larger cultural history of the moving image," Lev Manovich (2001: 295) has referred to this dynamic between the digital image and its distant ancestor, observing that

Figure 7.6 *Santoscópio = Dumontagem* (2010), by Carlos Adriano. Dumont and Rolls shown upside down in a negative print as part of the reanimation of a moment of their conversation.

"the manual construction of images in digital cinema represents a return to the proto-cinematic practices of the nineteenth century, when images were hand-painted and hand-animated. At the turn of the twentieth century, cinema was to delegate these manual techniques to animation and define itself as a recording medium. As cinema enters the digital age, these techniques are again becoming a commonplace in the filmmaking process place." It is in this intermedial meeting of past and present that the film also challenges us to remain attentive to its very calculated procedures. *Santoscópio = Dumontagem* privileges certain visual games and technical procedures that lend to the film a quality that resonates with Laura Mulvey's (2006) figure of the pensive spectator. Mulvey writes on the prerogative of the spectator who can use the remote control to redefine her power of control when watching a digital film: she can stop, see a passage again, and command other operations that allow her to develop an analytical curiosity and acquire a better understanding of the procedures that had solicited special attention and created new challenges. This is exactly what we experience when viewing Adriano's film, which is contingent on the possibilities of the digital beyond simple citation or preservation.

What is particularly noticeable in Adriano's film is how it derives from a type of perception that is attuned to a baroque sense of the world's dynamics, one that sees the order of time as modulated by force fields, always in tension.

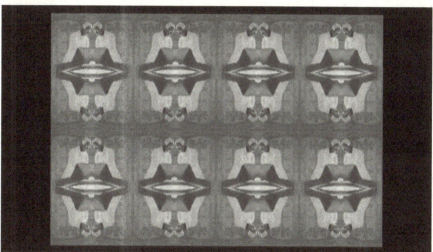

Figures 7.7 and 7.8 *Santoscópio = Dumontagem* (2010), by Carlos Adriano. Two shots taken from different moments of the kaleidoscopic dynamics as performed by the digital animation that create and multiply geometrical patterns in motion.

An incessant game of attraction and repulsion marks the relationship between the moving figures on the screen, orchestrated by a variable movement of lines created by the texture of the image, and the specific content of the original scene involving Santos Dumont and Rolls. This movement radically explores the plasticity of forms that acquire a ludic-poetic dimension, contributing to a mode of attention that fluctuates between fascination/aesthetic pleasure and conceptual reflection. The film's invitation to pleasure rests on the elucidation of the very processes in which the viewer becomes involved and that hark back to the inventory of moving image devices.

The mobilisation of digital effects allows for the creation of metaphors linking moving image devices to the field of aviation and its conquests, which is the very subject being explained by Santos Dumont to Rolls. The Brazilian was in England to receive a prize for experiments related to his pioneering flight conducted in Paris. By then, Santos Dumont was already a well-known personality, thanks to his prodigious flight with the aircraft "No. 6" around the Eiffel Tower in 1901; another well-known flight would come later when he flew over the Parisian Field of Bagatelle in 1906. In a small studio made into a theatre, the cameraman captures the meeting of the two distinguished men in a single take that keeps them framed in a medium shot. Rolls, sitting to the left of Dumont, hears the inventor, who stands up and talks, gesticulates, shows his compass and rulers, displays the drawing of one of his projects, points his finger at certain details, and sometimes looks directly at the camera. He is the protagonist of the scene, but Rolls too plays his part well, conducting his performance with perfect mastery of etiquette; playing the gentle host, he is genuinely interested in what his interlocutor has to say, given its close connection to his own personal interest: the incipient production of automobiles.

The novel modes of mechanical transportation in *Santoscópio = Dumontagem* are more obviously associated with the aeroplane, an historical correlation that has implications for cinema more broadly. The inventions of cinema and aviation present a near-synchronicity that was noted by Edgar Morin (2005) in "The Cinema, the Airplane," the first chapter of his 1958 anthropological approach to film and modernity, *The Cinema, or the Imaginary Man*. Here, Morin notes that, like moving images and automobility, aviation was a dream born in the nineteenth century that gave rise to visionary efforts to conceive a machine heavier than the air that would be capable of flying. Morin observes that this period of invention, especially around the fin de siècle, was a special moment that cemented the connection between art and science, technical skills and imagination, giving emphasis to cinema and aircraft inventions where "the technical and the dream are linked at birth" (9).

Digital Montage and the Structural Film

Santoscópio = Dumontagem revolves around a symbolic dialogue involving two personalities connected to that decisive period of inventions at the very moment of the accomplishment of that nineteenth-century dream. But as a contemporary experimental work, Adriano's film might also be situated with respect to a quite separate cinematic tradition, which informs its structure from another direction. More specifically, the "theme and variations" game in *Santoscópio = Dumontagem* is organised as a radical example of the "structural film," a type of experiment developed in the 1960s and 1970s by North American avant-garde artists such as Hollis Frampton, Ken Jacobs, Ernie Gehr, and Michael Snow. Coined by P. Adams Sitney, the term "structural film" includes a set of works that give radical emphasis to the formal exploration of one of the cinematic technical procedures or "figures of visual language" proper to films, in order to create an experience that rigorously follows a formal rule. The idea is to make the spectator concentrate on a dominant formal strategy in the film and on its effects—the film's "laws of composition" and their motivation. In the sphere of found-footage films, the structural film becomes an experiment about the ways of reading a film, making one notice a certain procedure and consider what is implied in its use in specific formal experiments.

A notable example can be found in Ken Jacobs's film *Tom, Tom, the Piper's Son* (1969), a reworking of the visual structure of the eponymous 1905 Biograph production shot by Billy Bitzer, belonging to the early-film period nowadays known as the "cinema of attractions" (Gunning 1990). Jacobs selected and enlarged a great number of fragments taken from the few continuous and extended medium-long shots that accounted for Bitzer's eight-minute narrative. He then reedited the 1905 film by playing with its fragments and so allowing for a much more detailed depiction of the same line of action. A quick sequence of very short close-ups combined with other shots gave a detailed description and intensified the effect of the frenetic movement performed by a group of adults chasing a mischievous boy. Repeating the process in many variations, Jacobs made an eighty-six-minute structural film as an experiment on the dramatic and informational effects produced by different editing strategies applied to that same 1905 film.

By enlarging details, reconfiguring actions, and reanimating some symbolic passages, Adriano enters into a dialogue with Jacobs, applying his game of repetitions and fragmentations to a very short single-shot film. But Adriano goes further than the American experimental filmmaker in his manipulation of the original images, given that his structural film was made as an experiment in the realm of digital cinema. In his 1969 film, Jacobs dealt with a copy of the 1905 film before the advent of digital media and had to work within a more limited range of visual reconfigurations and editing processes available. His film unfolds at an impressive pace by the accelerated succession and repetition of fragmented shots combined with variations in light and still images, but the variety of reconfigurations contained in Adriano's film were technically unavailable to him.

A product of the digital epoch, *Santoscópio = Dumontagem* departs from its structural film forebears in making an intentional point about the distinctions between analogue and digital media. In so doing, however, the film avoids a chronological teleology of distinct media that would suggest digital media as a kind of advanced stage in the history of technological changes in filmmaking. In this regard, we might read Adriano's film in connection with Thomas Elsaesser's (2016) proposal of a new method of "film history as media archaeology." Elsaesser analyses the impact of digital technologies on our understanding of film history, including the multimedia interactions it enables. He defends a method which would overcome the opposition between "old" and "new" media as they mix and merge in current practices. Rather than a clean break with the past, new media for him function as a catalyst for a paradigm shift in historiography. As he explains elsewhere, "Rather than directly enter the debate about whether digitization is merely an improved or accelerated technology of the visible and the audible, or whether it is indeed a radical, qualitative change in their respective ontologies, I take digital media as the chance to rethink the idea of historical change itself, and what we mean by inclusion and exclusion, horizons and boundaries, but also by emergence, transformation, appropriation, i.e. the opposite of rupture" (Elsaesser 2004: 77). Elsaesser criticises the linear and teleological views of the present configuration of media as accomplishing a kind of vocation prefigured in the past and announced at each step that led from proto-cinematic experiences to our twenty-first-century digital cinema. For him, the complex networks of media production and exhibition, among a slew of other technical and socioeconomic factors, play a crucial role in the history of different media and complicate the process of their development and inscription within any historical narrative. In addition, he critiques received perspectives that see all novel experiences as inscribed within a cyclical pattern of repetition of the past.

Both Jacobs, reimagining the strategies of the "cinema of attractions," and Adriano, reworking visual forms of the nineteenth-century proto-cinematic devices, revisit formal experiences of the past without adhering to either the teleological scheme or the cyclical repetition of patterns. Both have made genuinely innovative formal compositions within the genre of found footage films: the former in 1969, long before the advent of digital technology; the latter in 2010 with the help of digital technology as a unique intermedial experiment inspired by proto-cinema devices, which nonetheless enabled the expression of his radical authorship.

Figure 7.9 *Santoscópio = Dumontagem* (2010), by Carlos Adriano. A shot of the pixels that form digital images.

In Adriano's film, there are many close-ups produced by the separation of fragments of the original medium-shot of Santos Dumont and Rolls, but in addition to this the film calls our attention to the material texture of digital cinema, at times magnifying the pixels to the extent that they occupy the entire screen (Figure 7.9). There is, for instance, an evocation of the rapid intermittence of the image on the screen through the use of a flickering effect. There are also passages in which the technique of animation automates the human gestures in their repetitions, chiming with the new mechanical modes of visual media and transportation that the film evokes. But there is a level of symbolism here, too, and the film's concentration on particular gestures also serves to develop them as unexpected visual metaphors: most notably in this regard, the act of opening a large sheet of paper over the table, repeated in slow motion, evokes nothing less than a wing (Figure 7.10).

The variations of speed and the mechanical repetitions of certain actions obtained through editing create a choreography of the two bodies placed side by side, as if in roboticised rhythms to the sound of either a loom, a locomotive, a printing press, or a telegraph. In the articulation of these procedures, there is playful attention to Santos Dumont as an inventor-bricoleur rather than a scientist of mathematical rigour, but one who knows how to create with the elements at his disposal and think of unexpected connections transversely. This ludic *ballet mécanique* generates an element of irony towards the

Figure 7.10 *Santoscópio = Dumontagem* (2010), by Carlos Adriano. This image, duplicating a shot of Dumont holding a large sheet of paper, is a fragment of an animated scene in which the large white sheet takes the form of moving wings while he emphatically performs the gesture of placing it on the table.

bodies of the two renowned figures, who through digital manipulation are placed on an equal footing with all other objects that compose the image. In the new structure of fragmented scenes, they are two ergometric attractions on an intermedial assembly line.

The original 1901 Mutoscope film scene evoked respect for the performing characters. Through the use of special digital effects, the experimental film creates a humorous theatrics of Santos Dumont's and Rolls's performances that is inflected by their original composition. They are subjected to the parameters of a pantomime typical of the variety spectacle, echoed by sound effects alluding to the circus. The moments of prestidigitation deconstruct the ceremonial aspect associated with the heroes of technological progress, bringing them close to normal people.

Past and Present

I will conclude with a final comment on the intermedial mirroring effect produced by the comparison between the "philosophical toys" from the pre-cinematic era and Carlos Adriano's digital film. I believe that this comparison opens our perception to what Walter Benjamin (1969) called the "dialectical image," that is, an image that makes a direct connection between two separate moments in time, a distant past and the present. This dynamic goes against the grain of both the linear retreat to the past and the teleological drive to the future, nor does it embrace the cyclical pattern of repetition. In tune with Benjamin's "dialectical image," *Santoscópio = Dumontagem* constitutes a playful tête-à-tête between past and present. This experimental film is an invitation to connect the different moments of the history of moving images separated by more than a hundred years. The visual materials acquire an original form when inscribed in digital processes that demonstrate their malleability and sometimes radicalise the "mathematical" origin of the world of visual forms available to perception. Images and sounds in this film may or may not find their referents in the outside world, in the sociohistorical space we inhabit, but they certainly produce a meaningful effect, either from a radical self-referential deconstruction or from intermedial exchanges with archival material. More than simply reviving lost footage from the past for consumption in the present, in its very structure and without any words, *Santoscópio = Dumontagem* makes a strong case for a shift in the way that film scholars and filmmakers approach the moving image in its various interlinked historical moments.

Note

1. For more on Adriano's research and creative process, see Adriano (2015, 2018) and MacDonald (2019), as well as the longer documentary about the Brazilian aviator, *Santos Dumont: Pré-Cineasta?* (Carlos Adriano, 2010).

References

Adriano, Carlos. 2015. "Reapropriação de arquivo e imantação de afeto." *Visualidades* 13 no. 2 (July–December): 60–80. https://doi.org/10.5216/vis.v13i2.40736.
Adriano, Carlos. 2018. "O mutoscópio de Santos Dumont e a poética do found footage." *Anais Do Museu Paulista: História E Cultura Material* 26, e08: 1–42. https://doi.org/10.1590/1982-02672018v26e08.
Benjamin, Walter. 1969. "Theses on the Philosophy of History." In *Illuminations*, edited by Hannah Arendt, 253–264. New York: Schocken Books.
Elsaesser, Thomas. 2004. "The New Film History as Media Archaeology." *Cinémas* 14, nos. 2–3 (Spring): 75–117. https://doi.org/10.7202/026005ar.
Elsaesser, Thomas. 2016. *Film History as Media Archaeology: Tracking Digital Cinema*. Amsterdam: Amsterdam University Press.
Gunning, Tom. 1990. "The Cinema of Attractions: Early Film, Its Spectator and the Avant-Garde." In *Early Cinema: Space, Frame, Narrative*, edited by Thomas Elsaesser and Adam Barker, 56–62. London: BFI.

MacDonald, Scott. 2019. "Carlos Adriano." In *The Sublimity of Document: Cinema as Diorama (Avant Doc 2)*, edited by Scott MacDonald, 337–355. New York: Oxford University Press.
Manovich, Lev. 2001. *The Language of New Media*. Cambridge, MA: MIT Press.
Morin, Edgar. 2005. *The Cinema, or The Imaginary Man*. Translated by Lorraine Mortimer. Minneapolis: University of Minnesota Press.
Mulvey, Laura. 2006. *Death 24x a Second: Stillness and the Moving Image*. London: Reaktion Books.
Oubiña, David. 2009. *Una juguetería filosófica: Cine, cronofotografía y arte digital*. Buenos Aires: Ediciones Manantial.
Sitney, P. Adams. 1974. *Visionary Film: The American Avant-Garde, 1943–2000*. New York: Oxford University Press.

8
Panoramic Views, Planetary Visions
An Intermedial Analysis of *Medium Earth* and *Walden*

Tiago de Luca

In this chapter I look at two artists' films that are bound together through their allegiance to the panoramic shot—in both its 360-degree and 180-degree incarnations—as a mode of Earth-seeing: *Medium Earth* (2013), by the British duo the Otolith Group, and *Walden* (2018), by the Swiss artist Daniel Zimmermann.[1] Given the importance of the circular pan in the history of experimental cinema (especially in the 1970s) and the place of what is now referred to as "artists' cinema" within this genealogy (Connolly 2009), this allegiance may seem unsurprising. While a full survey of this device is beyond the scope of this chapter, suffice it to note, as does Teresa Castro (2011), that films as diverse as *La Région centrale* (Michael Snow, 1972), *La Chambre* (Chantal Akerman, 1972), *Fortini/Cani* (Jean-Marie Straub and Danièle Huillet, 1976), and *Riddles of the Sphinx* (Laura Mulvey and Peter Wollen, 1977) all employed the panoramic shot in order to call attention to the reality of the medium and as a way to erode representational illusionism. For Castro (2011: 80), this understanding of the cinematic panorama as a tool of liberation from conventional "narrative and formal constraints" sits in opposition to its nineteenth-century precursor, often deemed "indissociable from a quest to appropriate and subjugate the world."[2] Like Castro, in this chapter I also consider *Medium Earth* and *Walden* within a panoramic media lineage. More specifically, I contend that the idea of the panorama as a world-embracing view is key to an understanding of these two films, hence the necessity of a historiographic method that transcends the confines of the film medium.

Invented by the Irishman Robert Baker, the panorama opened in 1794 in London's entertainment quarter of Leicester Square. Initially baptised "La Nature à coup d'oeil" (French for "nature at a glance"), it soon became "panorama" (Greek for "see all"). Indebted to landscape painting, the panorama was a large-scale, 360-degree canvas surface placed inside a dimly lit rotunda, with natural light let in through an upper aperture. The cylindrical attraction was contemplated by walking spectators from the vantage point of a centralised and elevated platform, and the content varied from military battles and imperial imagery (particularly from 1815) to "views" (as they were called) of far-flung places, often cities, that offered the surrogate of travel. As Erkki Huhtamo (2013: 5) sums up: "Although it was not wired in the sense of broadcasting or the Internet, [the panorama] was capable of teleporting its audience to another location, and dissolving the boundary between local existence and global vision." Unlike landscape painting, however, the circular panorama abolished the borders of the frame and the single-perspective system. In so doing, it enveloped the observer while implying a world that extended beyond one's visual grasp through a meticulous reproduction of cityscapes beyond which the line of the horizon was clearly demarcated.

The world-encompassing vision of the wraparound panorama thus functioned on two intersecting levels: as a mode of virtual global travel on the one hand and through the suggestion of a planetary expanse that stretched beyond the spectator's perception on the other. As Tanya Agathocleous (2003: 305) notes, panoramas "were global not only because they depicted a range of cities from around the world but because, in their emphasis on the infinite and all-encompassing extension of the horizon, they situated their landscapes in the world as a whole." In turn, this global expanse was depicted in the panoramic "keys" distributed to patrons (Figure 8.1), whose design, as Denise Blake Oleksijczuk (2011: 128) notes in relation to Baker's keys from 1794 to 1816, "shifts from locating the spectator within a flat, immersive landscape that ends at the limit of the horizon to an elevated view at the pinnacle of the globe that extends the space encompassed by pushing the horizon back into the distance." By implying a planetary vastness that stretched into infinity, the panorama thus provided the figurative and phenomenological means through which to confront and make sense of a rapidly expanding world and one's place within it.

Dominant accounts of the wraparound panorama often formulate it as a disciplinary mode of viewing enabled by the elevated platform, from which the spectator, not unlike a military commander, surveyed the surrounding landscape, in tune with Jeremy Bentham's contemporaneous idea of the panopticon as an architecture of surveillance (Griffiths 2013: 77; Comment 1999: 136; Miller 1996: 35–36). According to these accounts, the panorama fostered a sense of ocular mastery that was part and parcel of an "imperial visuality" (Mirzoeff 2011: 17) that aimed to demarcate and appropriate the world. Yet, as contemporaneous descriptions also tell us, the gigantic size and circularity of the panorama overwhelmed spectators and divested them of control, producing disorienting sensory experiences and even unpleasant

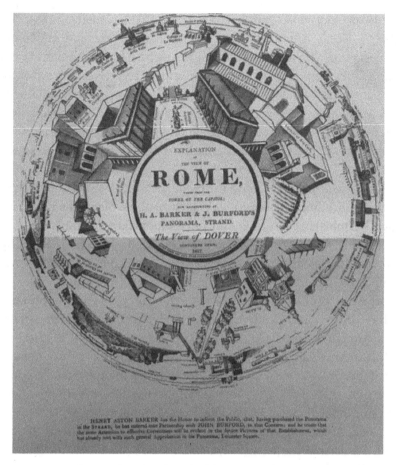

Figure 8.1 A panoramic explanation (1817) of the "view" of Rome crystallises the planetary aspirations of the form. Courtesy of the Bill Douglas Cinema Museum.

physical sensations such as nausea and vertigo (Oettermann 1997: 12). In this sense, as Agathocleous (2003: 301–302) notes, the panorama is more profitably understood as "a deeply ambivalent formation, complex enough to be read as both conservative and progressive; adaptable enough to serve as imperial propaganda-tool or as champion of cosmopolitan democracy." Promising the exacting reproduction of specific sites, the panorama gestured towards the whole world through the horizon, engendering what Agathocleous terms an "urban sublime" (see also Agathocleous 2013) in the context of an acutely felt and confounding globalisation.

The subject of many authoritative histories (Oettermann 1997; Comment 1999; Oleksijczuk 2011; Huhtamo 2013), the panorama has also been examined as a genealogical precursor of cinema (Gunning 2006; Castro 2011;

Miller 1996; Grau 2003; Griffiths 2013; Belisle 2015). Understood as a circular mode of looking, it immediately finds cinematic expression in 360-degree shots described as "panoramic," when the technical possibilities of the new medium were often explored as an end in and of themselves. Nevertheless, the term "panorama" was employed quite liberally in early cinema catalogues to signify a *continuously moving camera* rather than the fully circular shot only, which remained relatively scarce, going on to disappear almost entirely and surviving only in more radical cinematic experiments, such as the ones cited above.[3]

In *Medium Earth* and *Walden*, the recourse to the circular shot is striking, given its application to make visible planetary phenomena: the Earth as a geological landmass in the former film and the global trading routes subtending the economic world system in the latter. As such, these films are uniquely suited case studies to demonstrate the way in which a panoramic gaze has been updated in the context of contemporary globalising processes, including the Earth's environmental breakdown and the so-called Anthropocene. They therefore invite a historically capacious understanding of intermediality as espoused by current media-archaeological approaches, which, as Jussi Parikka (2012: 2) summarises, often "focus on the nineteenth century as a foundation stone of modernity," "excavating the past in order to understand the present and the future." As Parikka (3) notes, via Bolter and Grusin's (1999) influential concept of "remediation," "old media" never disappear but are "continuously remediated, resurfacing, finding new uses, contexts, adaptations." Indeed, as current scholarship has extensively demonstrated (Grau 2003; Griffiths 2013; Belisle 2015), the wraparound panorama did not so much vanish as transmogrify into media as diverse as giant-screen experiences, immersive internet technologies, and VR experiments, many of which, significantly, often have "the world" as their representational and conceptual substratum.

Here I hope to contribute to this important work by showing that, as one of the earliest iterations of the panorama as a mutating medium, the rotating camera shot reappears in *Medium Earth* and *Walden* as an attempt to grasp elusive global and geophysical processes. The intermedial method is thus here necessary for an excavation of the deep media history of Earth-seeing within which both films are implicated. At the same time, both films (especially *Walden*) are indicative of the dissolution of the physical spaces of cinema, as the medium morphs into installations and migrates to art galleries, thus reinstituting the ambulatory character of the panorama into the cinematic experience. If, as Maeve Connolly (2009: 18) suggests, it is possible to "conceptualize artists' cinema through references to broader notions of the interstitial, intermediate or in-between," then *Medium Earth* and *Walden* add to and extend these notions by bringing the panorama into the polymorphous space of the gallery.

The Panorama as Geohistory: *Medium Earth* (2013)

The London-based duo Anjalika Sagar and Kodwo Eshun, or the Otolith Group (formed in 2001), is known for creating research-based works that straddle filmmaking and installation, experimental cinema and audiovisual essay, (science) fiction and documentary. This includes a series of political essay films made between 2003 and 2009, known as the *Otolith Trilogy*, and more recently a number of video and installation works that grapple with ecological questions involving human and nonhuman histories.

Medium Earth (2013), commissioned by the Los Angeles media art centre REDCAT and the Haus der Kulturen der Welt (HKW) in Berlin, is no exception to this rule. The film was part of the Anthropocene Project, a partnership between HKW and other cultural and educational institutions which brought together artists, scientists, and scholars for a series of exhibitions, conferences, workshops, and publications in 2014. Its aim was to reflect on the concept of the Anthropocene from interdisciplinary perspectives, including its implications for an understanding of the planet as related to and dramatically changed by human activity. Originally coined in 2000 by Paul Crutzen and Eugene Stoermer, the now much-debated concept of the Anthropocene describes a new geological epoch the planet has entered due to momentous human-induced changes in its biogeophysical constitution (Crutzen 2002). According to this idea, humanity has remodelled the planet to the point that it is now a geological force in its own right, jeopardising the conditions that make possible the existence and sustenance of human life on Earth. For some, the geological periodicity of the concept acts as a welcome decentring of humanity in the context of wider planetary scales and timeframes (Chakrabarty 2009). For others, the Anthropocene "magnifies the irruption of human action as a telluric force" (Bonneuil and Fressoz 2017: 85), often in the guise of a universalising rhetoric according to which the whole of humanity is responsible for the state of the world, as opposed to specific historical processes and economic systems, such as colonialism and capitalism (Haraway 2016; Demos 2017; Yusoff 2018; Mirzoeff 2018).

Filmed on location in Yucca Valley, the Joshua Tree National Park, and Los Angeles, *Medium Earth* is implicated in these debates and engages with the Anthropocene as an opportunity to demonstrate the interplay between human and geological temporalities. Although there are no humans in

Medium Earth, the film is critical of unchecked progress and depicts anthropogenic meddling with natural landscapes through recurrent shots of subterranean parking lots and highways cutting through mountainsides. As Eshun (2015) explains, "Vast chunks of California were 'reclaimed' from the desert. That's why *Medium Earth* features so many parking garages." Yet no sooner do these human-shaped environments appear than they are shown to be susceptible to the Earth's own tectonic doings. In this sense, the film simultaneously attempts to respond to the dangers of self-aggrandising human narratives in the age of the Anthropocene by suggesting that the Earth is also endowed with agency and volition. Through an exploration of geological fissures and rock formations, *Medium Earth* frames the planet itself as a medium that records and inscribes its own history, while resorting to the medium of panorama, in the form of circular and semicircular shots, as a way to access this geohistory. Intermediality thus appears here as a phenomenon whose imbrications involve and extend to the Earth itself.

Take the film's opening sequence, which strings together several static images filmed in a number of empty underground garages, some of which are many levels below the Earth's surface. Then a shot showing a fissure on the ground snaking its way across the floor compels the camera to slowly tilt down and gradually close in on the crack, as if aiming to penetrate deeper. The following sequence, as if acting upon this quest, is filmed amidst gigantic rocks dominating the screen, with the camera slowly rising from the depths and revealing only a patch of the sky and tree branches blowing in the wind as the camera moves up. Throughout the film, the camera closely inspects a number of cracks winding their way through deserts, concrete floors, and asphalt freeways, often via circular movements. These images disclose the indexical traces of a planetary calligraphy as a process of tectonic mediation. No matter how many vaults humans may carve out in its structure, *Medium Earth* suggests, the Earth may still impose its own design.

As seen in an explosion of photographic projects, documentaries, and IMAX films—including *Home* (Yann Arthus-Bertrand, 2009), *Anthropocene: The Human Epoch* (Jennifer Baichwal, Nicholas de Pencier, and Edward Burtynsky, 2018), *Overview: A New Perspective of Earth* (Benjamin Grant, 2016), and *A Beautiful Planet* (Toni Myers, 2016)—the visual signifier of the Anthropocene is often the "view from above" and/or the "view from space." The rationale for this is often attributed to the idea that only from a distance can one measure and monitor the impact of human activity on the planet. In some ways, the space overview can be seen as the logical culmination of a panoramic mode of looking, which, already at its dawn, visualises an expanding world as seen through an elevated and centralised viewpoint, in tandem with an aesthetic interest in the horizon as contemplated from great altitudes, and the popularity of mountaineering and balloonism (Oettermann 1997: 7). By contrast, the recurrent low-angle shots in *Medium Earth*, taken amid rocks through which tiny glimpses of the sky are only just visible, act as the reverse mirror-image of overviews in their rendering of the planet from an earthly, underside standpoint. This reversal of perspective also finds its counterpart in the many circular and half-circular panoramas utilised in the film, which subvert its perceived constitutive features by precluding the distance often seen as intrinsic to the form.

Shot at both ground and underground level, these pans convey their attachment to the Earth as a historiographic soil rather than an object one coolly examines from a distance. In one of these, a slow-moving camera placed at a high angle and from a short distance films the rugged surface of a desert. In a 180-degree shot, the initially stationary camera frames two busy highways flanked by mountains to the noise of cars flashing past. Then, as the camera begins moving, an eerie soundtrack by Thomas Köner, featuring muffled detonations and atmospheric static music, is superimposed on the audio. The gentle handheld camera continues panning, moving past the highways and onto a ragged mountainside, patiently surveying its crevices and folds as though contouring their outlines, to then return to the other side of the highways. By interspersing its tactile embrace of undulating sedimentary structures with sped-up cars on a busy highway, all the while respecting the physical contiguity of both phenomena via a panoramic shot, *Medium Earth* discloses the material coexistence and interaction of geological and human times.

That the circular pan is here put in the service of an intimate, haptic look at the surface of the Earth challenges the omniscient and all-encompassing vision normally associated with the panorama as a medium. This is especially visible in a 360-degree shot executed by handheld, oscillating camerawork. The camera surveys boulder outlines while mimicking the shape of these geological formations, with the spatial movement of the shot dictated by and enfolded onto the geo-temporalised form of its content. At the same time, when viewed in the context of its original launch at REDCAT, *Medium Earth* offers a phenomenologically different panoramic experience as part of the "in-betweenness" that, for Connolly (2009: 18), characterises artists' cinema. Neither exactly cinema nor gallery work, the single-screen film was housed in a "black box" built within the gallery with a view to faintly simulating a theatrical experience, including dimmer lighting and a single row of eight chairs across its width for visitors to enjoy the film seated. As with most gallery installations, however, viewing protocols ultimately rested with the gallery visitor, meaning that the film's mobile panoramic shots could have been experienced by an equally mobile viewer, thus reconfiguring the traditional panoramic and cinematic experiences into one of conjoined, doubled-up movement, both within and outside the screen.

Movement is further underlined in *Medium Earth* as a characteristic of the Earth itself, with the planet described in the soundtrack as in continuous and convulsive tectonic motion by the softly spoken voice-over (Sagar's): "Under the sedimentary strata, thrust faults move in the dense thickets." Later, as the camera moves with the movement of boulder crops, she asks, "Who does the Earth think it is? We are sinking below its crust, into the plates colliding, forming new mountains." By referencing geological formations, *Medium Earth*, as per its title, taps into the idea of the Earth as a medium, one that shares its genesis with the birth of geology as a discipline. As Parikka (2014) notes, nineteenth-century geology and evolutionary theory "implicitly perceived the earth as media. In these disciplines the earth was a sort of a recording device." Incidentally, a panoramic attraction such as the Great Globe (1851), created by James Wyld, attempted to make visible such recordings at a time geology started to garner popularity. Modelled on the georama, first created in France in 1825, the Great Globe was erected in Leicester Square on the occasion of the Great Exhibition in Hyde Park, London. Like previous georamas (and unlike traditional panoramas), the attraction consisted of a gigantic concave world map spread inside the spherical building, measuring 188 feet in circumference and 60 feet in diameter (Lightman 2012). The concave map was three-dimensional, made up of plaster casts and geographical features differentiated by colours and materials, including, as Rick Altick (1978: 465) has noted, tufts of cotton wool that simulated the eruption of volcanos. The idea that "the earth has been at various periods violently convulsed," as observed in "the throwing out and heaping up of volcanic rocky matter," was further reiterated in a substantial booklet titled *Notes to Accompany Mr Wyld's Model of the Earth* (1851), distributed to patrons during the attraction's first year of existence.[4]

Although miles away from the Great Globe's imperial imaginary, duly nominated in the booklet as a celebration of the "political and moral preponderance of the Germanic race," *Medium Earth* updates a quest to visualise geological (un)doings through a panoramic gaze whose cinematic form is meant to mimic that of rock formations.[5] As such, the film resonates with Parikka's (2015: 12) understanding of a "geology of media" according to which our "relations with the earth are mediated through technologies and techniques of visualization": "it is through and in media that we grasp earth as an object for cognitive, practical, and affective relations." Dominant modes of visualisation in the age of the Anthropocene, however, often reproduce the aforementioned planetary overview, which Hannah Arendt (1998: 11) once cautioned as the epitome of a modern science that "owes its great triumphs to having looked upon and treated earth-bound nature from a truly universal viewpoint, that is, from an Archimedean standpoint taken, wilfully and explicitly, outside the Earth." For Arendt, this universal perspective not only contravenes our phenomenological and cognitive limitations as Earth-bound humans; it fuels dangerous delusions that the world can be mastered as a "world picture" standing "at man's disposal as conquered," as Martin Heidegger (1977: 133) would have it. More recently, Bruno Latour (2018: 67, 70, emphasis in original) has similarly suggested that the "nature-as-universe" dictum that *to know is to know from outside*" has made us "see less and less of what is happening on Earth."

By contrast, *Medium Earth*'s underground and ground-level panoramas respond to Latour's (2018: 81) call for a "terrestrial" mode of seeing that digs "deep down into the Earth with its thousand folds," offering us close-up images of the Earth as a way to open up and access its deep nonhuman history. In so doing, the film recalls Nigel Clark's (2011: xviii) contention, in his book *Inhuman Nature: Sociable Life on a Dynamic Planet*, that we must confront "how the world actually works" beyond human activity if we are to produce correct answers "to the question of what sort of planet and cosmos we inhabit and what kinds of imperatives arise out of this inhabitation." Expounding on Kant's formulation of the sublime, according to which the human mind reaches sublimity through recourse to the faculty of reason when faced with overwhelming and terrifying natural phenomena, Clark shows that this formulation responded to a very specific event: the 1755 Lisbon earthquake, which haunted the philosopher as he recognised that "the temporal and spatial dominion of our species was disturbingly inconsequential when viewed in the context of the earth's eventful history" (xii). *Medium Earth* responds to this imperative by deploying the panorama as an aesthetic tool that can be used to invoke and evoke the geological instabilities traversing space and time. Put differently, it makes visible the eventful history of the Earth as a medium via the mixed—panorama-inflected and now gallery-sited—medium of film.

Mapping Out Globalisation: *Walden* (2018)

If *Medium Earth* utilises the panorama as a way to delve deep into the geological Earth, *Walden* (2018) adopts it as a vehicle to map out the contemporary trajectories and vectors of globalisation. *Walden* is the debut feature film by Daniel Zimmermann, a Swiss artist and wood sculptor, who, over a career spanning nearly thirty years, has worked across many mediums, including theatre, performance, and installation art. Often classed as a documentary, the film was initially exhibited at traditional cinematic institutions such as film festivals, including the Sundance Film Festival (2019), the International Film Festival Rotterdam (2019), Cinéma du Réel (2019), and the Karlovy Vary International Film Festival (2019), where it scooped up the Documentary Special Jury Prize. It must be noted, however, that the film is no spontaneous recording of the objective real, nor is it entirely factual. Instead, it is a confounding tale of stacks of wood mysteriously imported from Europe into the heart of the Amazon rainforest by means of meticulously orchestrated panoramas, which update the form's indelible ties with the trope of global travel. Comprising thirteen 360-degree shots filmed in Austria and Brazil, *Walden* painstakingly tracks the journey of wood planks from the former to the latter location as they travel by train, trucks, boats, and ferries. The film's panoramic intermediality, as we shall see, was then brought to full completion upon its relocation to an art gallery, where it underwent radical mutations in shape and form via the application of multiple screens, thus reinstituting the ambulatory spectator of the wraparound panorama back into the film experience.

Walden starts in Admont forest, Austria, with pines dominating the screen and some tree stumps occasionally visible. Then a tractor comes into view, its engine turned on by a man, followed by the whirring sound of an electric chainsaw and another man felling a tree, which collapses in front of the gyrating camera. The following shots depict the journey of tree logs turned into wood planks: we see them being loaded onto a train wagon (shot 2), an interminable freight train rattling past (shot 3), a pulled-over truck inspected by two policemen on a busy motorway (shot 4) and then parking in an open-air garage (shot 5), and a cargo ship sailing off against the backdrop of wind turbines and factories (shot 6). The seventh shot, positioned exactly halfway through the film and the only one filmed at night, is set at a dock in Manaus, Brazil, with the continuously rotating camera disclosing a proliferation of cargo ships. The remaining six shots are all set in Brazil, as the wood planks continue their journey at a ferry port (shot 8), on a cargo ferry sailing at sea (shot 9), on a small ferry boat sailing off the banks of a river (shot 10), through the waters of an estuary (shot 11), and then inside a mangrove (shot 12), where we see five small boats sailing past the camera one after the other. In the film's final shot, set inside a jungle, we see five men carrying wood planks on their shoulders as they consecutively walk past the camera and disappear into the forest. As the camera continues rotating on its axis, densely tangled vegetation made up of tropical plants and foliage take up the screen while cicada and animal noises dominate the audio.

The spectator of *Walden* is therefore asked to observe and look out for stacks of wood as they travel by land and water. Even when these objects are not visible, we assume that the numerous means of transportation on show in the film carry them along. Often, as in the shot at the Manaus ferry port, the planks are only furtively captured by the continuously revolving camera. Doane (2002: 154) writes that the lure of the panorama in early-cinema actualities was down to its ability to consolidate "the impression of the real" through "the unpredictability of the random movement of figures within the frame." *Walden* capitalises on this association while undermining it from within. Filmed entirely on location, many shots in the film do indeed display a documentary quality, especially those filmed in Brazil, where locals and Indigenous people often look inquisitively into the camera. Nevertheless, while the appearance of elements within the frame is meant to be experienced as something that the rotating camera simply happened to record, the exact timing in which the wood planks and vehicles appear confirms that this film is not simply recording but is meticulously staging the real.

Walden can be loosely situated within the "structural" tradition of experimental filmmaking which P. Adams Sitney (2002: 348), in his field-defining *Visionary Cinema*, describes "as a cinema of structure in which the shape of the whole film is predetermined and simplified, and it is that shape that is the primal impression of the film." All shots, filmed with the identical lens, follow exactly the same format, with the camera mounted on a purpose-built remote head, conceived by cinematographer Gerald Kerkletz, that ensures the same deliberate pace in each take, even if the duration of each shot varies slightly. As the description above shows, there is also a structural mirroring in the film: the bookending shots are each set at the heart of forests, implying that the wood planks that originate from the trees being felled in the first shot somehow find a new home in the Amazon forest.

Two things immediately stand out here. The first, which I will explore shortly, concerns the peculiar trajectory of this trade route, which inverts its usual geographical course. The second relates to the transformation of trees from living into nonliving beings, depicted in the first shot. As the film methodically trails these trees-turned–wood planks traversing vast distances, it builds up the expectation that another transformation is to take place at the end of this supply chain, namely the transformation of wood into objects for human use. But this never happens. On the contrary, we may be forgiven for assuming that these planks are given a second chance of life as they are reabsorbed into another forest, in a completely different location on the globe. The first and last shots are important in this context given that their focus, before and after the brief appearance of some human figures, are almost entirely devoted to plants, trees, and other vegetation: the man-planted temperate forest of Northern Europe, with its supremely vertical pines, and the Amazon rainforest, with its lush tropical foliage, both of which are on full display as the camera rotates on its axis.

Given the director's Swiss German nationality and that the name Walden comes from *Wald* (forest) in German, the film could be deemed the cinematic equivalent of recent anthropological and philosophical treatises on *How Forests Think* (Kohn 2013) or *Plant-Thinking* (Marder 2013). In line with nonhumanist branches of thought such as speculative realism (Shaviro 2014), new materialisms (Bennett 2010), and object-oriented ontology (Harman 2018), these treatises endeavour to describe the world "from the hermeneutical perspective of vegetal ontology (i.e. from the standpoint of the plant itself)" (Marder 2013: 37), and thus as a strategy to displace the human from the centre of representation, thought, and action. The central placement of the camera within both forests as it scans its botanical environs contributes to this idea of the vegetal world seen from an insider's perspective (Figures 8.2 and 8.3).

According to its director, however, the title *Walden* is a reference to Henry David Thoreau's 1854 book, in which the American transcendentalist recounts, with aesthetic precision and delight, his experience of living in the woods in Walden Pond, Massachusetts, for two and a half years. A manifesto for simple living in nature, *Walden* interrogates the materialist excesses that were beginning to take hold in the US industrial modernity, arguing for a minimal and respectful engagement with nature's resources. The film's nod to this book, however, can only be deemed ironic. For, in spite of its bookending shots examined above, *Walden* is predominantly concerned with the large-scale exploration of nature in the age of global capitalism through an observational rendition of the numerous terrestrial and maritime networks connecting interregional and intercontinental routes.

As noted earlier, the panorama was bound up with the idea of travel (and explicitly marketed as such) since its inception: while its popularity more or less coincided with the rise and formalisation of the tourism industry, it was lauded on the basis of its ability to transport spectators to faraway places without the hassle and expense of actual travel. This was also true of the moving panorama, which stitched together scenic views mounted on rollers and then rotated by cranks, thus giving the impression of a continuous journey "around the world," as it was often advertised. Indeed, unlike

Figures 8.2 and 8.3 Forest-seeing in *Walden* (2018), by Daniel Zimmermann: the bookending shots highlight a vegetal ontology.

the circular panorama, its moving counterpart paraded images before an immobile spectator, which for many prefigures the cinema spectator's traditional position. In his study of the moving panorama, Huhtamo (2013) has further stressed its own autonomous cultural history: unlike the wraparound panorama, moving panoramas were itinerant enterprises that travelled through the countryside, often accompanied by a lecturer and other performance and musical acts. They likewise failed to deliver the immersive experience associated with the circular rotundas located in the big cities, and further harboured tighter links with concepts such as narrativity and sequentiality as connected with the trope of global travel.

 It could be argued that *Walden* retains and conjoins traces of both the circular and the moving panorama, the former because of its 360-degree shots, the latter because of its splicing of images that together imply a continuous journey. Yet if travel is a structuring principle of *Walden*, this is certainly not the type of travel bolstered by the tourism industry but the trade routes undertaken by circulating goods and the people and machinery that transport these goods. In the film, there are no touristic sites, monuments, or attractions, but only nondescript and drab spaces of circulation, transit, and liminality, or, to use Marc Augé's (2009) influential concept, the "non-places" of globalisation.

If one of the most enduring lessons Marx has taught us is that, in capitalism, the product is valued according to a logic that fetishises its final appearance and consequently obliterates the material conditions and processes underlying its production, then *Walden*'s revelatory dimension resides in the way it unveils these conditions and processes in the age of intensified global trading and online buying. As Ian Hudson and Mark Hudson (2003: 418) argue, online consumption has emphasised commodity fetishism through "the increasing distance between the production and the consumption of products." While discussions of late-capitalist globalisation often centre around the frictionless flows of finance capital and 24/7 online networks (Castells 2010; Crary 2013), *Walden* provides a counterpoint to these discourses by taking its time to show the very physical infrastructures networking the globe and subtending online worlds. Through its focus on container cargos travelling by outsourced trains, trucks, and ships, the film comments on what Frank Broeze (2018: 9) calls the "containerisation" of the globe, a process which, by streamlining and homogenising the "cargo into a standardised unity of a handy shape and volume," creates "an effective multi-modal sea and land system" that has made globalisation possible in reality. *Walden* makes this reality visible by showing not only globalisation's dependence on extractivist processes but also the dumbfounding physical distances traversed by goods which, today more than ever, appear magically on our doorsteps.

However, *Walden* is no mere record of reality, and nowhere is this more evident in its befuddling narrative about stacks of wood that are mysteriously imported from Europe into the heart of the Amazon rainforest. According to the director (*Walden* Press Kit 2018), this route reversal is a defamiliarising device to highlight the "absurdity of the economic rationale that underlies our globalized world." While wood does account for a considerable share of Austria's overall exports, no one would expect this product to be shipped to the Brazilian Amazon forest, where illegal deforestation for timber exports, incidentally, has exorbitantly increased since President Jair Bolsonaro took office in 2019 (Phillips 2020). Given that the film was released in 2018, one may conclude that this is a coincidence, yet given the director's credentials as a wood sculptor, we can speculate that he is aware of the fact that Brazil owes its very name to a timber tree named *pau-brasil*, or Brazilwood. This was the first product exploited by the Portuguese crown after its "discovery" of Brazil in

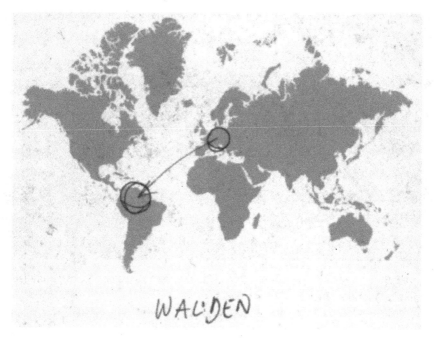

Figure 8.4 The cover of *Walden*'s (Daniel Zimmermann, 2018) "visual screenplay" indicates its world-encompassing ambitions.

the early 1500s, although the timber, valued because of its red dye, was mostly found along the Atlantic coast rather than in the Amazon forest. Whatever the case, there is little doubt that *Walden* attempts to provoke critical thought about our globalised world system by rehearsing the encounter between European and Amerindian worlds. In fact, the film's world-encompassing ambitions were made still more visible upon the publication of its "visual screenplay," which includes pictures of many discarded 360-degree shots. Its cover shows a world map, on which the trade route depicted in the film is indicated by a hand-drawn arrow connecting its original location to its final destination, thus confirming the planetary intentions of this panoramic film (Figure 8.4).

No less important, the illustrated screenplay was launched to accompany the installation version of the film (2020) at the Kunsthaus Pasquart art gallery in Switzerland on the occasion of the first retrospective of Zimmermann's work. Comprising thirteen screens arranged in a circle, each of which plays a different shot from the film, the installation spatialises *Walden*'s internal panoramic structure, with the spectator free to turn around and choose their focus of attention (Figure 8.5). Unlike *Medium Earth*, which still allows for a traditional cinema experience via a row of chairs and dimmed lighting,

Figure 8.5 The installation version of Daniel Zimmermann's *Walden* (2018) spatialises the film's panoramic structuring principle.

Walden the installation dispenses with seating entirely. Once transmogrified into a cinematic technique that does the moving in lieu of the viewer, the panorama here reasserts itself as an enveloping and ambulatory attraction, with movement then compounded by the camera shots in each of the screens. The result of the current migration of moving images to art galleries, or the mutation of film into installation, this transformation heralds one more chapter in the unceasing interaction between the panorama, the cinema, and the world.

Notes

1. This chapter expands on topics explored in de Luca (2019) and de Luca (2022: ch. 1).
2. My translation. "À en croire certains auteurs, le geste panoramique, en particulier quand il implique une rotation complète, est indissociable d'une volonté d'appropriation et de subjugation du monde. . . . Dans le cadre du cinéma, le panoramique peut même servir des intentions diamétralement opposées, dont la nécessité de se libérer de certaines contraintes narratives et formelles ressenties par la praxis cinématographique comme une 'technique disciplinaire'" (Castro 2011: 80).
3. One could further cite *Shoah* (Claude Lanzmann, 1985) and, more recently, many films by Carlos Reygadas, among other examples where the full circular shot is used.
4. *Notes to Accompany Mr Wyld's Model of the Earth* (London: Blackburn & Burt, 1851), pp. 20–21. Item held at The British Library. System number: 003988954.
5. Ibid., p. xvii.

References

Agathocleous, Tanya. 2003. "Wordsworth at the Panoramas: The Sublime Spectacle of the World." *Genre* 36, nos. 3–4: 295–316.
Agathocleous, Tanya. 2013. *Urban Realism and the Cosmopolitan Imagination in the Nineteenth Century: Visible City, Invisible World*. Cambridge: Cambridge University Press.
Altick, Richard D. 1978. *The Shows of London*. Cambridge, MA: Belknap Press.
Arendt, Hannah. 1998. *The Human Condition*. Chicago: University of Chicago Press.
Augé, Marc. 2009. *Non-Places: An Introduction to Supermodernity*. London: Verso.
Belisle, Brooke. 2015. "Nature at a Glance: Immersive Maps from Panoramic to Digital." *Early Popular Visual Culture* 13, no. 1: 313–335.
Belisle, Brooke. 2020. "Whole World within Reach: Google VR." *Journal of Visual Culture* 19, no. 1: 112–136.
Bennett, Jane. 2010. *Vibrant Matter: A Political Ecology of Things*. Durham, NC: Duke University Press.
Besse, Jean-Marc. 2003. *Face au monde: Atlas, jardins, géoramas*. Paris: Desclée de Brouwer.
Bolter, J. David, and Richard Grusin. 1999. *Remediation: Understanding New Media*. Cambridge, MA: MIT Press.
Bonneuil, Christophe, and Jean-Baptiste Fressoz. 2017. *The Shock of the Anthropocene: The Earth, History and Us*. Translated by David Fernbach. London: Verso.
Broeze, Frank. 2018. *The Globalisation of the Oceans: Containerisation from the 1950s to the Present*. Liverpool: Liverpool University Press.
Castells, Manuel. 2010. *The Rise of the Network Society*. Malden, MA: Wiley-Blackwell.
Castro, Teresa. 2011. *La pensée cartographique des images: Cinéma et culture visuelle*. Lyon: Aléas Editeur.
Chakrabarty, Dipesh. 2009. "The Climate of History." *Critical Inquiry* 35 no. 2: 197–222.
Clark, Nigel. 2011. *Inhuman Nature: Sociable Life on a Dynamic Planet*. London: Sage.
Comment, Bernard. 1999. *The Panorama*. London: Reaktion Books.
Connolly, Maeve. 2009. *The Place of Artists" Cinema: Space, Site and Screen*. Bristol: Intellect.
Crary, Jonathan. 2013. *24/7: Late Capitalism and the Ends of Sleep*. London: Verso.
Crutzen, Paul J. 2002. "The 'Anthropocene.'" *Journal de Physique IV* 12, no. 10: 1–6.
de Luca, Tiago. 2019. "Global Visions: Around-the-World Travel and Visual Culture in Early Modernity." In *Journeys on Screen: Theory, Ethics, Aesthetics*, edited by Louis Bayman and Natália Pinazza, 19–35. Edinburgh: Edinburgh University Press.
de Luca, Tiago. 2022. *Planetary Cinema: Film, Media and the Earth*. Amsterdam: Amsterdam University Press.
Demos, T. J. 2017. *Against the Anthropocene: Visual Culture and Environment Today*. Berlin: Stenberg Press.
Doane, Mary Ann. 2002. *The Emergence of Cinematic Time: Modernity, Contingency, the Archive*. Cambridge, MA: University of Harvard Press.
Eshun, Kodwo. 2015. "The Otolith Group: *The Radiant* and *Medium Earth*." *Conversation Pieces*, 2 June. https://agratza.wordpress.com/2015/06/05/the-otolith-group-the-radiant-and-medium-earth-2/.
Grau, Oliver. 2003. *Virtual Art: From Illusion to Immersion*. Translated by Gloria Custance. Cambridge, MA: MIT Press.
Griffiths, Alison. 2013. *Shivers Down Your Spine: Cinema, Museums, and the Immersive View*. New York: Columbia University Press.
Gunning, Tom. 2006. "'The Whole World within Reach': Travel Images without Borders." In *Virtual Voyages: Cinema and Travel*, edited by Jeffrey Ruoff, 25–41. Durham, NC: Duke University Press.

Gunning, Tom. 2008. "Early Cinema as Global Cinema: The Encyclopedic Ambition." In *Early Cinema and the "National,"* edited by Richard Abel, Giorgio Bertellini, and Rob King, 11–16. Bloomington: Indiana University Press.
Haraway, Donna. 2016. *Staying with the Trouble: Making Kin in the Chthulucene*. Durham, NC: Duke University Press.
Harman, Graham. 2018. *Object-Oriented Ontology: A New Theory of Everything*. London: Penguin.
Heidegger, Martin. 1977. *The Question concerning Technology and Other Essays*. Translated by William Lovitt. New York: Garland.
Hudson, Ian, and Mark Hudson. 2003. "Removing the Veil? Commodity Fetishism, Fair Trade, and the Environment." *Organization & Environment* 16, no. 4: 413–430.
Huhtamo, Erkki. 2013. *Illusions in Motion: Media Archaeology of the Moving Panorama and Related Spectacles*. Cambridge, MA: MIT Press.
Kohn, Eduardo. 2013. *How Forests Think: Toward an Anthropology beyond the Human*. Berkeley: University of California Press.
Latour, Bruno. 2018. *Down to Earth: Politics in the New Climactic Regime*. Translated by Catherine Porter. Cambridge, UK: Polity Press.
Lightman, Bernard. 2012. "Spectacle in Leicester Square: James Wyld's Great Globe." In *Popular Exhibitions, Science and Showmanship, 1840–1910*, edited by Joe Kember, John Plunkett, and Jill A. Sullivan, 19–39. London: Pickering & Chatto.
Marder, Michael. 2013. *Plant-Thinking: A Philosophy of Vegetal Life*. New York: Columbia University Press.
Miller, Angela. 1996. "The Panorama, the Cinema, and the Emergence of the Spectacular." *Wide Angle* 18, no. 2: 34–69.
Mirzoeff, Nicholas. 2011. *The Right to Look: A Counterhistory of Visuality*. Durham, NC: Duke University Press.
Mirzoeff, Nicholas. 2018. "It's Not the Anthropocene, It's the White Supremacy Scene; or, The Geological Color Line." In *After Extinction*, edited by Richard Grusin, 123–149. Minneapolis: University of Minnesota Press.
Oettermann, Stephan. 1997. *The Panorama: History of a Mass Medium*. Translated by Deborah Lucas Schneider. New York: Zone Books.
Oleksijczuk, Denise Blake. 2011. *The First Panoramas: Visions of British Imperialism*. Minneapolis: University of Minnesota Press.
Parikka, Jussi. 2012. *What Is Media Archaeology?* Cambridge, UK: Polity Press.
Parikka, Jussi. 2014. *The Anthrobscene*. Minneapolis: University of Minnesota Press. https://manifold.umn.edu/projects/the-anthrobscene.
Parikka, Jussi. 2015. *A Geology of Media*. Minneapolis: University of Minnesota Press.
Phillips, Tom. 2020. "Amazon Deforestation Surges to 12-Year High under Bolsonaro." *The Guardian*, 30 November. https://www.theguardian.com/environment/2020/dec/01/amazon-deforestation-surges-to-12-year-high-under-bolsonaro.
Shaviro, Steven. 2014. *The Universe of Things: On Speculative Realism*. Minneapolis: University of Minnesota Press.
Sitney, P. Adams. 2002. *Visionary Film: The American Avant-Garde, 1943–2000*. 3rd edition. New York: Oxford University Press.
Walden Press Kit. 2018. https://walden-film.com/9-download/.
Yusoff, Kathryn. 2018. *A Billion Black Anthropocenes or None*. Minneapolis: University of Minnesota Press.

9
Elemental Intermedia

Stefan Solomon

In the vast majority of the scholarship focused on the intermedial dimensions of cinema, "media" designates a very specific assortment of anthropogenic technological and artistic means for the storage, processing, and transmission of information. Responding to its composite ontology—including what Christian Metz (1973) called its assorted "substances" or "purports" of expression—and its historical emergence nearly 130 years ago, the intermedial approach brings cinema into conversation with both the six venerable arts that preceded it (dance, theatre, architecture, painting, sculpture, literature) and the cognate analogue and digital mechanical media that were fellow travellers on its journey from the nineteenth century on: photography, sound recording, and computing. In attending to the relations between cinema and these ostensibly "stable" art forms and mediums, so the theory posits, we are able to see past the modernist project that would assert cinema's "purity" or medium specificity, and to find harboured within it a more fluid and expansive version of itself.

While such efforts to analyse film by way of its forebears, rivals, allies, and descendants have certainly borne fruit, more recent trends in media studies scholarship have broadened and interrogated the concept of media significantly (see Mitchell and Hansen 2010; Grusin 2015; Somaini 2016). With a deeper historical and suprahuman sense of media as not only designating communications technologies and art forms but also betokening more abstract processes of "mediation" (see Guillory 2010), such scholarship is also useful in now rethinking cinema's intermedial nature with respect to nature itself: to the environment as a medium.[1] As John Durham Peters (2015: 3) has written, in the book from which this chapter derives its title, "The old idea that media are environments can be flipped: environments are also media." Just as the past century has witnessed the increasing proliferation of technological devices across the face of the Earth, including cameras, computers, and a range of ambient screens, there is an increasing awareness that the Earth

Stefan Solomon, *Elemental Intermedia* In: *The Moving Form of Film*. Edited by: Lúcia Nagib and Stefan Solomon, Oxford University Press. © Oxford University Press 2023. DOI: 10.1093/oso/9780197621707.003.0010 itself possesses many of the functions we usually associate with such media; it is nothing less than a giant light-processing optical medium (Maddalena and Russill 2016; Russill 2017) which, as Tiago de Luca writes in his chapter in this collection, "records and inscribes its own history" with millennia of data, living and dead.

There are of course differences in kind between human "semiotic" and environmental or elemental media, as Peters (2015: 4) points out, but the similarities are clear: "If we mean mental content intentionally designed to say something to someone, of course clouds or fire don't communicate. But if we mean repositories of readable data and processes that sustain and enable existence, then of course clouds and fire have meaning." With such reframing in mind, all manner of phenomena and elements of the more-than-human world have been embraced as media, capable of achieving what is usually assumed to be the province of human-originating cultural technologies: water (Jue 2020; Zylinska 2020), air (Sloterdijk 2009), salt (Young 2020), fog (Furuhata 2019), smog (Parikka 2017), light (Somaini 2020), and weather (Randerson 2018) have all been conceptualised in this way.[2] In this more capacious understanding of the media concept—and perhaps signalling its dissolution as that which can be identified in a wide variety of elemental forms—media are no longer solely the province of the human but function as conduits for all manner of phenomena that unfold in our world irrespective of any human agent. Nicolás Salazar Sutil (2018: 168), to whose work I turn in the next section, summarises the distinction between different ideas of "media" that I am working with here: "If 'media' is a word that refers to how communication or transmission is established by an agent that serves as go-between, then at least two meanings of the word are being pulled apart here: one concerns the technologization and industrialization of mediation, the other concerns a vitalization of mediation through landscape-based transmission." It is in the bringing together of these two meanings, and in observing the entanglements of elemental media with anthropogenic media forms, that the tensions and similarities between the two are most pronounced.[3] Such an encounter is especially relevant to the history of film, primarily on account of analogue and digital film's material existence as the refined byproduct of the Earth, by way of cellulose nitrate (Duncan 2019), silver halides, and an array of "premediatic" rare earth elements and conflict minerals (Parikka 2015; Morton and Škarnulytė 2016). But there are also contingencies at the site of its inscription—where the film shoot is often beholden to the caprices of the weather (see McKim 2013)—and in its much longer afterlife in cold storage, where it must face down the elemental forces of decay and destruction: bacteria, light, damp, fire (see Groo 2019).

While ecomaterialist film scholarship abounds today, it is by no means only a scholarly endeavour that links the medium with environmental matters. Aware of its implication in the world, and spurred on all the more by the illusion of digital technology's seemingly ethereal or immaterial existence, experimental filmmakers have turned their attention to the Earth not only as source of profilmic images to be captured but as the sine qua non of cinema and as a medium that is perhaps even capable of self-representation in a way heretofore little acknowledged. In this regard, there has been a concerted and often self-reflexive effort of late to map the connections between filmmaking and its material substrates: *Gravesend* (Steve McQueen, 2007) cross-cuts between the mining of columbite tantalite (coltan) in the Congo and its processing for use in communications technologies in the developed world; *All That Is Solid* (Louis Henderson, 2014) unearths the recycling of precious metals from computer waste in Ghana; and *Kasiterit* (Riar Rizaldi, 2019) offers a speculative look at the extraction of tin from Bangka Island, Indonesia. Elsewhere the elements themselves have had a direct hand in the making of cinema, as in the case of *Pink Beach Red Desert Dream Sand Film* (Jennifer West, 2017), in which a print of *Red Desert* (Michelangelo Antonioni, 1964) was coloured by dragging it over the pink coral and crushed shells on the Sardinian beach in which parts of the film were shot, and *Sound of a Million Insects, Light of a Thousand Stars* (Tomonari Nishikawa, 2015), in which the negative film stock was buried at Fukushima, exposing it to the nuclear radiation still emanating from the site (see Zinman 2019).[4]

While the elements are no stranger to experimental filmmaking practice, it is cinema's appraisal of the elements *as* media, and even *as* cinema, that represents an even more radical development. In her work on the capacity of nonhuman matter to bear witness, Susan Schuppli (2020: 289) argues that "ecological matter has long been performing a series of technical operations akin to the functions of various media systems." Examining the 2010 Deepwater Horizon oil spill in the Gulf of Mexico, Schuppli points out that this global media event, in which the 4.1 million barrels of crude oil leaking into the ocean were live-streamed around the world, also contained its own "independent mode of filmmaking": "When the smooth viscosity of oil comes into contact with the rough surface tension of the sea—the point at which water molecules are exposed to air—rapid transformations in the thickness of the oil film occur, resulting in extraordinary and rapid shifts of color" (301). On the one hand, the representational images that we saw of the damaged oil rig constituted a film about oil; on the other, the "molecular structure and behaviour" of the slick as it came into contact with the water constituted in its very ontology an "oil film." Here, as the title of Schuppli's 2010 simulation work responding to the event suggests, "nature represents itself": it is not simply a case of the oil's reflective capacity mimicking the cinema screen and "projecting an aesthetic event back at us" but that its capability of appearing this way indexes directly its "very mode of production" (301): the ecological disaster itself.

In Schuppli's (2020: 295) work, the oil spill is rendered as a "horror film" through a detailed technical explanation of the phenomenon. But more specifically for our purposes here, it is the capture of such phenomena on film that is crucial to bringing the intermedial to light; seeing elemental media on screen introduces a level of conscious or unconscious irony or self-reflexivity that would not otherwise obtain were they never represented in cinematic images. When we observe in a film a reflection in a pool of water that serves as something like a natural screen, we are given to understand that makeshift *dispositif* in relation to the digital screen on which we are viewing the image (a screen within a screen), as well as the similarities and differences between the two surfaces. While it may be true, as Douglas Kahn (2013: 205) has written, that "[i]t is possible to see cinema everywhere," the capacity of cinema (as we most commonly know it) to record, archive, and exhibit this othered, "everywhere" cinema is precisely what prompts us to see our environments as offering that which is for the most part identified only with the camera and the screen.

In this chapter, I explore a number of recent works that suggest the intermedial potential of elemental media, to the extent that we are given to see backgrounds, settings, and earthly matter as precursors, imitators, or heirs of cinema itself. What I will here designate as "elemental intermedia" is made visible in cinema principally through experimental filmmaking. Indeed, several of the examples below are drawn from films identifiable under the aegis of "landscape cinema," but the approach taken here also suggests ways in which it might be applied to cinema broadly speaking.[5] In the interest of providing a focused use of the concept, I consider specifically how elemental intermedia might emerge on screen both in ways that predate cinema's very existence—in the legacies of Plato's cave allegory and in naturally occurring camera obscuras—and how such phenomena might also be predicted to outlast cinema, especially insofar as a "remembered" film (Burgin 2004) might effectively embed itself on the landscapes in which it was shot, rendering environments as the ground of cinematic afterimages. In what follows, I consider the historiographical possibilities for cinema when elemental intermedia is brought into the reckoning. By exploring visions of the medium through the (unstable) temporal categories of "pre-cinema," "cinema," and "post-cinema," I seek to understand how cinema sees itself elsewhere in the natural world and how we might see cinema in places not limited to the screen.

Pre-cinema

The paradigmatic image of cinematic spectatorship today remains that vision conjured by Plato's famous allegory of the cave, along with its key ingredients: a darkened space in which a group of chained prisoners view shadows projected on a wall before them, powerless to turn their heads to the fire and objects behind them that together create the shadowy images, and thus unaware that their circumscribed reality is only a simulacrum of a world outside of the cave. Plato's illustration suggests itself to any filmgoer as a broad, albeit anachronistic approximation of the filmgoing experience, especially considering questions of the medium's powers of mystification and oppressive ideological effects. So it is no surprise that the cave allegory has had wide-reaching implications for thinking through the active and passive affordances of viewing cinema in a darkened theatre. It has functioned as a key trope for psychoanalytic and apparatus theories of cinema, and despite its surface-level differences to an actual theatrical *dispositif*, even prompted Alain Badiou (2013: 212), in his reading of the *Republic*, to make the connections to the seventh art quite literal: for him, the cave is an "enormous movie theater" with a screen "which goes right up to the ceiling," while the heads of the prisoners are "held in place by rigid headphones" and there are "enormous projectors flooding the screen with an almost unbearable white light."[6] Such are some of the possible interpretations offered by Plato's text from the contemporary standpoint (see also Baudry 1976).

But if we take seriously the mediality of elements, then might cinema not really have begun its existence in dark underground spaces, in the half-light of real existing caves? Might not the operations of earth, fire, and sunlight have combined long ago to produce the kind of shadow play that could be equated with the mechanical projection of moving images in a theatre? "Everything has always been around," writes Siegfried Zielinski (2006: 3), "only in a less elaborate form; one needs only to look." In this vein, the philosopher's cave presents us with one of many instances in which something like "cinema" might be fashioned from the interaction between humans and the natural environment, prior to the invention of the camera and projector, which provide for the capture, storage, and multiple transmission of images over time.[7] Such a notion is nothing new; recently, certain instances of karst cave painting have been submitted as proto-cinematic media, given the way that the images created work together with the contours of their earthly supports—the cave walls—and the reflections of light from crystals accreted over the images, making them appear as if in motion. In his work on the intermedial dimensions of expanded cinema, Jonathan Walley (2020) has analysed how the Prehistoric Picture

Project, an initiative exploring Copper Age rock carvings across western Europe, renders such media as "ambient cinema" through a particular reading that combines medium specificity with a willingly expansive understanding of what cinema is, or could be. This particular project "relies upon metaphors of 'projection' (the sun), the interplay of flatness and depth (the shadows of the carvings creating '3D' effects), multiple 'screens' (the numerous carved rock faces simultaneously visible to an observer), and of 'stills' and 'animation' (actions represented serially)" (8). A more well-known interpretation of an earthly proto-cinema is Werner Herzog's *Cave of Forgotten Dreams* (2010), which locates a modicum of "specificity" while also extending cinema out of the theatre and into the distant past.[8]

Such retrofittings of parietal art or "paleomedia" (Sutil 2018: 169) as proto-cinema are commonplace in archaeological approaches to film and media studies and throw into relief cinema's supposedly very recent invention. But while they are concerned with gilding the ostensibly primitive forms of the past by association with the modern medium of cinema, such comparisons between ancient and modern media are, as Sutil has argued, rarely sustained and mostly inaccurate. Refusing the distinctions between life and art as suggested by the term "cave art," Sutil prefers to think through such images as forms of subterranean landscape or "landesque" media, in which "no such separation of life and art is possible" (173). In this way, he cautions against a historiographic approach to cave images that would cast them as part of an evolutionary continuum bringing us to the cinema of today; to do so constitutes a form of category mistake, not only because those images were produced through "expression and creativity" that was recognised as "emerging from a geomorphological and other-than-human basis" (173), but also because they are still being produced today. For Sutil, the point is that cave imagery is not situated "in the past" but continues to exist and, more important, to transform: "the cave is a transhistorical imperative" (174) through which "the limestone, the fire, the body, and even the color and materiality of charcoal and ochre could be considered to be living and moving in a continuous present" (169). Does a pursuit of an elemental cinema relegate it to the past or force it into relation with the media of the present?

Cinema

Rather than approaching media like cave images as proto-cinema alone, and thereby extending the origins of the medium by tens of thousands of years, we might be better served by considering how such images alert us to the fact that cinema continues to exist "everywhere" today, in elemental approximations of the camera and screen but also in the capacity of our very environments to archive cinema itself. *Umbra* (2019), a short experimental work by German filmmakers Florian Fischer and Johannes Krell, which takes its name from the section of the moon or the Earth that is cast in shadow during an eclipse, pursues exactly this question. It forms the third part of a trilogy titled *Nature(s) as Spaces of (Self-)Perception*, which also comprises *Still Life* (2014) and *Kaltes Tal* (2016), works that in their own ways interrogate anthropocentric perception and explore how the natural world may return the human gaze. Specifically, *Umbra* seeks to capture age-old "proto-cinematic" phenomena in the world that continue to present themselves to observers today, exploring the capacity of various refractions of light on screen to give us images not of human or technical origin. Fischer and Krell's film proceeds as a kind of survey of different naturally occurring processes, some of which are more or less clear to the viewer, such as sunlight glinting off the ocean, whereas others are revealed only at the end of the film. At this point, text informs us that one part of the film, featuring what look like "images of multiple suns on the ground," were captured in Oregon during the total solar eclipse in 2017 and were "visible in the shadow of a tree, caused by little holes in the leaves which act like apertures—a setting like a natural camera obscura." We are then informed that the film's final sequence features images from a particular peak in the Harz Mountains in Germany, whence the "Brocken spectre" derives its name. This optical phenomenon, which the film tells us "can only be experienced subjectively," involves an observer having their shadow cast upon clouds by the sun, appearing in ghostly form at a larger scale and with a series of diffracted "halos" encircling their head (Figure 9.1).

While the film includes a number of static shots and images of the ocean courtesy of a drone, there is also the pointed use of a pinhole camera, which allows only a small beam of sunlight to enter into the camera's lens, and of a handheld camera, whether the filmmakers are moving underwater through a murky creek bed or traipsing through the forest, their footsteps audible on the soundtrack. Such scenes are suggestive of the work's overarching aim: to "question film as an image-producing procedure" (Berlin Shorts 2019). The searching nature of the moving shots betrays a restless dissatisfaction with the assured visions that cinema, even in its most experimental forms, might offer us of the more-than-human world. But surprisingly, the film ends with a passage of digital manipulation, as the reality of the Brocken spectre gives way to a pixelated disintegration of the image as it fades to black. While both the environment and the camera alike might produce images obtained from the profilmic world, the digital—which here both mimics and supersedes the real

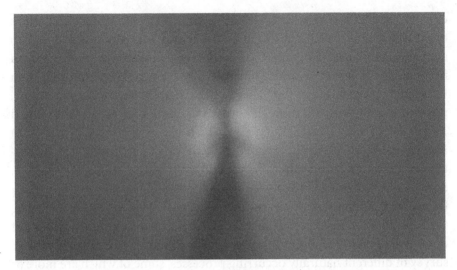

Figure 9.1 The Brocken spectre in *Umbra* (Florian Fischer and Johannes Krell, 2019).

through its immaculately conceived images—presents a point of equivalence that is also a point of tension. But there is commonality, too, as expressed in this evaporating image: just as the Brocken spectre will fade, so too will the ostensibly more stable digital image, which is itself susceptible to the ravages of time.

The "pure light images" that are the "protagonists" of *Umbra* are part of a rapid elemental cycle of light, shade, and air that "fundamentally questions the nature of the image" as associated with cinema (Rosen Pictures 2019).[9] If we look for these cinematic forms today, they still reveal themselves at particular places and times, but absent the storage capability of other technical media are never observable for very long. James Benning's *EASY RIDER* (2012), a loosely "structural" remake of Dennis Hopper's 1969 film of the same name, suggests some of these tensions between the ephemerality and permanence of elemental media. In particular, fire is of great importance here: numbered among the film's thirty-four separate shots, each one corresponding to a scene in the original, are five shots of flames in close-up pitched against a black night sky. As punctuation marks of sorts, these are intended to match the five campfire sequences of Hopper's film, but in the context of Benning's exercise in appropriation they attain vastly different proportions. These images of fire, the flames of which die down progressively over the course of the film, are held for a cumulative total of seventeen minutes, during which time the viewer is provided with some snippets of dialogue—especially from Jack Nicholson's key speech about freedom—but not much more as bearings. Given Benning's refining of his film in these shots to the element of fire alone, they become for Alison Butler (2014) a vision of "primordial pre-cinema," a cinema before its time, when looking at a domestic fire or campfire provided its own form of unpredictable shadow play.

Yet just as these images appear to send the viewer back to a time before cinema's invention, the central conceit of Benning's film is to explore a time after cinema, or, at least, a time four decades since the release of *Easy Rider*, attending to the change and decay that the intervening years have wrought upon the built and natural environments depicted in the film. In his shots of mountains, a flowing river, a spent lava flow, and dilapidated dwellings, Benning offers a meditation on stillness that the original film, in its obsession with travelling and motion, could not. Beyond this refashioning of Hopper's film for the twenty-first century—replete with updated music choices, attention to erstwhile marginalised women, and a decelerating that carves out room for environmental and political contemplation—what the work presents is *Easy Rider* not exactly in absentia but as mediated through the landscapes that formed its milieu. Here Benning stages a figure-ground reversal whereby the environmental backdrop is brought to the fore, functioning as a medium for tracing the narrative contours of the earlier film. Even if the first *Easy Rider* might now be seen as outmoded politically or asking for critical revision in some other respects, for Benning the film can still be sensed through its landscapes, which even in their changed state serve to channel the mood of the original. So, while fire as the source of short-lived images in the film might cast us back into a kind of ancient cinema, the landscape itself takes on the more perdurable storage function of media, whereby specific moments in film history are now archived as environments.[10]

While Benning sought to conjure and modify Hopper's work by showcasing all locations from the earlier film, the iconic shot of Monument Valley, captured from John Wayne's Point, perhaps cements the landscape as media most forcefully, considering how it serves to usher in, and utterly transform, the setting not only of the original but also of a whole host of other films shot in the same location (Figure 9.2). This exemplary site in film history is not simply cinematic by association but is inseparable from its many representations on screen. Similar to but in an important way distinct from the "most photographed barn in America" in Don DeLillo's (1986: 12–13) *White Noise*, the unmistakable buttes of Monument Valley not only are here conceived as the simulacral subject of the films that have been shot in this area but themselves function as media insofar as they have accumulated a storehouse of cinematic memories that are inextricable from the site itself. Referenced here as a very specific citation of Hopper's film, the overdetermined Arizona landmark

Figure 9.2 Monument Valley in *EASY RIDER* (James Benning, 2012).

signifies further back to the American West of John Ford, and even alludes by extension to Benning's earlier visit to the site as captured in his *North on Evers* (1991) (see MacDonald 2018: 21).

In its southern Californian setting, Lukas Marxt's *Victoria* (2018) pursues a strategy in some ways akin to Benning's. In this hour-long film, Marxt also recalls Hopper's *Easy Rider*, albeit with several degrees of difference: the motion proper to the road movie is restored, and the repeated lines of dialogue from the film are rendered only as subtitles (and so never vocalised), placing the earlier film at one further remove from the landscape yet still locating it there. "We don't have much longer. We'll be there soon": lines we read that are spoken in the original by a hippie hitchhiker, and which are here superimposed over a long, slow tracking shot swooping low across the desert. And there is more besides: later subtitles reveal the continued presence of another film made in this area, with a few oft-cited lines from Michelangelo Antonioni's contemporaneous *Zabriskie Point* (1970) spoken over the top of a shot that very much resembles the Death Valley dunes that featured in the original film (Figure 9.3). "I always knew it would be like this," Mark says to Daria cynically in the afterglow of the film's orgy sequence. "Love?" Daria asks. "The desert," Mark replies.

In a more radical departure from the schema of Benning's *EASY RIDER*, Marxt finds in his Californian landscapes the films that were shot there and also traces by association of Joseph Losey's *Figures in a Landscape* (1970) and Werner Herzog's *Fata Morgana* (1971): the former because it was shot in the Sierra Nevada mountain range (albeit of Granada rather than California), the

Figure 9.3 Dialogue from *Zabriskie Point* (Michelangelo Antonioni, 1970) reverberating in the Californian landscapes of *Victoria* (Lukas Marxt, 2018).

latter because of its own desert sites of production in the Sahara and Sahel. *Victoria* thus presents us with southern California as a mediatised desertscape that once played host to films by Hopper and Antonioni and now finds them embedded in its rock and sands, but also as a site of cinematic *lieux de mémoire* that could perhaps conjure "false" memories of events that had never taken place there, as in the case of Losey's and Herzog's works. It is at once a surprising but logical development of the film: given the countless global locations for which this region has been made to stand in since the emergence of the Hollywood studio system, Marxt now asks us to see the very environment (not unlike Monument Valley) as cinema itself, as ineluctably mediated by the camera that has passed over it so many times for different purposes. "People have the impression of the American West's deserts as an uninhabited space," he says, "but it's not true" (Ross 2019: 108). As with his approach to environments as media elsewhere in his body of work, here the land becomes the medium even after it is no longer subjected directly to the camera's gaze.[11] And now, by also following in Benning's wake, Marxt's film equally conjures—intentionally or not—the *EASY RIDER* of 2012, which also lives on in the landscapes in which it, too, has been made.

Post-cinema

After cinema disappears, so it will remain, and when history calls time on the last picture show, the dimly lit cave images and the myriad naturally occurring camera obscuras alike will continue to flicker on, mediating the world for a human audience or for no audience at all. At the same time, if we are to see environments as in some way storing cinema's images, or taking on the function of cinema itself, then it will be only because of the a priori significance of that art form to us as its viewers. The lights of sun and fire will submit themselves for our consideration as "films" when they cast shadows in a way that suggests abstract or figural shapes we associate with the projector's beam. The noise made by a gust of wind passing before us will conjure the three-dimensional sound of Dolby Atmos, wherein voices and music piped from multiple speakers in concert appear to float around the space.

Viktoria Schmid's *A Proposal to Project in Scope* (2020) meditates on such aspects of the cinematic experience, positing a nontheatrical cinema while also holding fast to the memory or awareness of cinema as the framing device that allows environments to signify as media. As part of her longer sculptural series, "Proposals," Schmid installs cinema screens in sylvan surrounds, erecting large white canvases that correspond in size to various aspect ratios used in film projection—4:3, CinemaScope, and even her own fabricated "Viktoriascope" in 4:1—and films them using matching stock; her latest work is, indeed, filmed in 'Scope. While she has previously embedded her outdoor screens in California, *Proposal to Project in Scope* sees Schmid positioning the 2.35:1 screen more deliberately on the shores of the Curonian Spit near Nida, Lithuania, which offers a sympathetically wide landscape of sea, sand dunes, and forests (Figure 9.4).

In capturing the play of light and shadow on her screen as it is embedded in different parts of the coastal environment, Schmid's work depicts a cinema bereft of technologically produced images, and one therefore in which the focal points are simply those elements already present in the landscape: the leaves of the trees that pattern the screen, the wind that blows over it, the shifting

Figure 9.4 The screen outside the theatre in *A Proposal to Project in Scope* (Viktoria Schmid, 2020).

crepuscular light that modulates its colours. And indeed, the screen itself takes centre stage here, manifesting unusually as a kind of *parergon*, a framing device that also invites us to consider it as the very work itself (Derrida 1987). Across a series of static shots of this screen—and also shots between tree branches that seem to chance upon "found" frames in the woods—it appears as if "the sun's rays and the nearby sea work towards the abolition of the cinema or towards its birth" (Holzapfel 2020):[12] the setting equivocates between past and present, apocalyptic in its lack of all human presence, but equally evocative of a time before the mechanised cinema with which we are more familiar and in which such a screen would routinely form the backdrop for shadow puppetry and magic lantern shows.

But of course, for viewers circa 2020, cinema cannot but exist, even if as a fading memory (a fact redoubled during the lockdowns of the pandemic). Schmid's screen cannot help but call to mind the moving images and sounds of the cinema—and perhaps in particular those belonging to the sword-and-sandal epics of the 1950s or the westerns of the same period, also shot as they were in the widescreen formats available at the time. The screen holds *in potentia* the capacity to catch celluloid or digital footage thrown by a projector. But where darkness is usually a prerequisite for screening in a theatre, here nightfall signals the end of this outdoor cinema, since we are no longer able to see the screen or the environmental images that pass across it. While cinema might exist beyond its usual technical and spatial confines, the properties of the medium as we know it can extend only so far into the environs outside of the theatre, and might also be limited by the viewer's willingness to accept the elemental as cinema itself. As Patrick Holzapfel (2020) has said of this work, "There is no clarity to be found on questions between the end and the beginning of cinema, except that which lies in the existence of film itself: Does film need a screen or does the screen need a film? Is cinema beyond the screen or is it always on the screen even when there is nothing there? Is the sun a projector, the shadows the film?"[13] When depicted on screen, elemental intermedia that suggest the cinematic medium invite such comparisons: of cinema with all that precedes and surpasses it. Films approaching this tension between cinema and environment exhort us to consider these questions, even if we cannot answer them conclusively.

Notes

With thanks to Sasha Litvintseva, Susan Schuppli, Nadim Samman, Boris Ondreička, Lukas Marxt, and Leo Goldsmith for generously sharing their work and thoughts with me.

1. Christer Johansson and Sonya Petersson (2018: 9–10) gesture towards some of the implications of this recent media studies scholarship for research into intermediality.
2. For a fuller overview of developments in this area, see Starosielski (2019).
3. Although I pursue a vitalist argument here about the existence of cinema in the natural world, I do so from an intermedial perspective, which preserves the distinctions between the technologised medium and its approximations elsewhere rather than flattening the differences between them. For an important survey of ecological approaches to the "natural aesthetics" of cinema, see Guan and O'Brien (2020) as well as the articles included in their accompanying edited dossier in *Screen*.
4. Similar approaches can be discovered much earlier, for example in the work of British Canadian experimental filmmaker Chris Welsby: his *Weather Vane* (1972), in which gusts of wind determine the oscillations of the panning camera, is a case in point.
5. Given Sasha Litvintseva's (2018: 122, my emphasis) helpful reminder that "the form and content of *any film*, and thus the perceptual and durational experience it engenders, are rooted in geological materiality," there are also clear possibilities for extending the concept of "elemental intermedia" elsewhere. In a similar vein, Ludo de Roo (2019) argues that the "elemental imagination" underwrites the spectator's experience of and immersion in a given filmworld.
6. Or, as Badiou (2013: xxxiii) describes it elsewhere in the book, "The Cave of the famous myth is so like an enormous movie theater that it only takes describing that movie theater and having Plato's prisoners become spectator-prisoners of the contemporary sphere of media for it to be the same thing, only better."
7. In her brilliant survey of responses to the cave allegory, Jean Ma (2020: 61) discusses Robert Smithson's 1971 essay "A Cinematic Atopia," in which the land artist envisions the ideal theatre as a "geologic object" constructed in an actual cave.
8. For an alternative reading of Herzog's film that focuses on the way it "uses the aesthetics of deep time to point to earth movement beyond the scope of all human activity," and which is more sympathetic with Sutil's position, see Evans (2020: 307).
9. In this regard, Thomas Elsaesser (2016: 311) has written of one alternative way of conceiving of the cinematic image: "We can now recognize Lucretius as describing the effects of a *camera obscura* before the light shapes itself into an image as representation. Following his lead, what if we were to see the cinematic image not as solid picture, analogous to paint on canvas, but as precisely such a constantly agitated surface whose elements—specs of dust, which is what the silver grain particles also amount to—are in suspended animation or suspended agitation?"
10. In his revaluation of ecocinema and the landscape film, Leo Goldsmith (2018: 5) points to the possibility in films by Benning and others of reading the "immediate sensory data" of the planet's surface alongside its "embedded" and extractable meanings.
11. *Reign of Silence* (Lukas Marxt, 2014) might serve as an indicative example of the filmmaker's practice: a body of water in a carefully framed and seemingly untrammelled "natural" locale—in this case a frozen Arctic sea shore—is disrupted by a rigid inflatable boat, which on Marxt's command moves in concentric circles before leaving the scene, its ripples still in motion minutes after it exits the locked-off shot.
12. "Die Sonnenstrahlen und das nahe Meer an einer Abschaffung des Kinos arbeiten oder an dessen Geburt" (my translation).
13. "In Fragen zwischen dem Ende und dem Anfang des Kinos gibt es keine Klarheit zu finden, außer jener, die in der Existenz des Films selbst liegt: Braucht der Film eine Leinwand oder

braucht die Leinwand einen Film? Ist das Kino jenseits der Leinwand oder ist es immer auf der Leinwand, selbst wenn da gar nichts ist? Ist die Sonne ein Projektor, die Schatten der Film?" (my translation).

References

Badiou, Alain. 2013. *Plato's Republic: A Dialogue in 16 Chapters*. Translated by Susan Spitzer. New York: Columbia University Press.
Baudry, Jean-Louis. 1976. "The Apparatus." Translated by Jean Andrews and Bertrand Augst. *Camera Obscura* 1, no. 1: 104–126.
Berlin Shorts. 2019. "An Interview with Florian Fischer and Johannes Krell about 'Umbra.'" 19 February. https://shortsblog.berlinale.de/2019/02/19/an-interview-with-florian-fischer-and-johannes-krell-about-umbra/.
Burgin, Victor. 2004. *The Remembered Film*. London: Reaktion Books.
Butler, Alison. 2014. "'You Think You've Been There': A Conversation with James Benning about *Easy Rider* (2012)." *LOLA* 5 (November). http://www.lolajournal.com/5/benning.html.
DeLillo, Don. 1986. *White Noise*. New York: Penguin.
De Roo, Ludo. 2019. "Elemental Imagination and Film Experience: Climate Change and the Cinematic Ethics of Immersive Filmworlds." *Projections* 13, no. 2 (Summer): 58–79.
Derrida, Jacques. 1987. *The Truth in Painting*. Translated by Geoff Bennington and Ian McLeod. Chicago: University of Chicago Press.
Duncan, Pansy. 2019. "Celluloid^{TM}: Cecil M. Hepworth, Trick Film, and the Material Prehistory of the Plastic Image." *Film History: An International Journal* 31, no. 4 (Winter): 92–111.
Elsaesser, Thomas. 2016. *Film History as Media Archaeology: Tracking Digital Cinema*. Amsterdam: Amsterdam University Press.
Evans, Georgina. 2020. "Deep Time in *Cave of Forgotten Dreams*." *Screen* 61, no. 2 (Summer): 306–314.
Furuhata, Yuriko. 2019. "The Fog Medium: Visualizing and Engineering the Atmosphere." In *Screen Genealogies: From Optical Device to Environmental Medium*, edited by Craig Buckley, Rüdiger Campe, and Francesco Casetti, 187–213. Amsterdam: Amsterdam University Press.
Goldsmith, Leo. 2018. "Theories of the Earth: Surface and Extraction in the Landscape Film." *World Records Journal* 2 (Fall). https://vols.worldrecordsjournal.org/02/05.
Groo, Katherine. 2019. "Let It Burn: Film Historiography in Flames." *Discourse* 41, no. 1 (Winter): 3–36.
Grusin, Richard. 2015. "Radical Mediation." *Critical Inquiry* 42, no. 1 (Autumn): 124–148.
Guan, Cassandra, and Adam O'Brien. 2020. "Cinema's Natural Aesthetics: Environments and Perspectives in Contemporary Film Theory: Introduction." *Screen* 61, no. 2 (Summer): 272–279.
Guillory, John. 2010. "Genesis of the Media Concept." *Critical Inquiry* 36, no. 2 (Winter): 321–362.
Holzapfel, Patrick. 2020. "Notiz zu A proposal to project in scope von Viktoria Schmid." *Jugend ohne Film*, 14 July. https://jugendohnefilm.com/notiz-zu-a-proposal-to-project-in-scope-von-viktoria-schmid/.
Johansson, Christer, and Sonya Petersson. 2018. "Introduction." In *The Power of the In-Between: Intermediality as a Tool for Aesthetic Analysis and Critical Reflection*, edited by Sonya Petersson, Christer Johansson, Magdalena Holdar, and Sara Callahan, 1–21. Stockholm: Stockholm University Press.

Jue, Melody. 2020. *Wild Blue Media: Thinking through Seawater*. Durham, NC: Duke University Press.

Kahn, Douglas. 2013. *Earth Sound Earth Signal: Energies and Earth Magnitude in the Arts*. Berkeley: University of California Press.

Litvintseva, Sasha. 2018. "Geological Filmmaking: Seeing Geology through Film and Film through Geology." *Transformations* 32: 107–124.

Ma, Jean. 2020. "Deep in the Cave." In *Deep Mediations: Thinking Space in Cinema and Digital Cultures*, edited by Karen Redrobe and Jeff Scheible, 57–69. Minneapolis: University of Minnesota Press.

MacDonald, Scott. 2018. "Surveying James Benning." In *James Benning's Environments: Politics, Ecology, Duration*, edited by Nikolaj Lübecker and Daniele Rugo, 15–38. Edinburgh: Edinburgh University Press.

Maddalena, Kate, and Chris Russill. 2016. "Is the Earth an Optical Medium? An Interview with Chris Russill." *International Journal of Communication* 10, no. 1: 3186–3202.

McKim, Kristi. 2013. *Cinema as Weather: Stylistic Screens and Atmospheric Change*. New York: Routledge.

Metz, Christian. 1973. "Methodological Propositions for the Analysis of Film." *Screen* 14, nos. 1–2: 89–101.

Mitchell, W. J. T., and Mark B. N. Hansen. 2010. "Introduction." In *Critical Terms for Media Studies*, edited by W. J. T. Mitchell and Mark B. N. Hansen, vii–xxii. Chicago: University of Chicago Press.

Morton, Timothy, and Emilija Škarnulytė. 2016. "Yttrium Hypnosis." In *Rare Earth*, edited by Nadim Samman and Boris Ondreička, 102–110. Vienna: Thyssen-Bornemisza Art Contemporary and Sternberg Press.

Parikka, Jussi. 2015. *A Geology of Media*. Minneapolis: University of Minnesota Press.

Parikka, Jussi. 2017. "The Sensed Smog: Smart Ubiquitous Cities and the Sensorial Body." *Fibreculture Journal* 29: 1–23.

Peters, John Durham. 2015. *The Marvelous Clouds: Toward a Philosophy of Elemental Media*. Chicago: University of Chicago Press.

Randerson, Janine. 2018. *Weather as Medium: Toward a Meteorological Art*. Cambridge, MA: MIT Press.

Rosen Pictures. 2019. *Umbra*. https://www.rosenpictures.com/en/projects/umbra.

Ross, Julian. 2019. "Landscape, Video, and the Anthropocene: An Interview with Lukas Marxt." In *Lukas Marxt: From Light to Cold*, edited by Claudia Slanar, 99–112. Vienna: Verlag Für Moderene Kunst.

Russill, Chris. 2017. "Is the Earth a Medium? Situating the Planetary in Media Theory." *Ctrl-Z: New Media Philosophy* 7. http://www.ctrl-z.net.au/articles/issue-7/russill-is-the-earth-a-medium/.

Schuppli, Susan. 2020. *Material Witness: Media, Forensics, Evidence*. Cambridge, MA: MIT Press.

Sloterdijk, Peter. 2009. *Terror from the Air*. Translated by Amy Patton and Steve Corcoran. Los Angeles, CA: Semiotext(e).

Somaini, Antonio. 2016. "Walter Benjamin's Media Theory: The Medium and the Apparat." *Grey Room* 62 (Winter): 6–41.

Somaini, Antonio. 2020. "'The Surface Becomes a Part of the Atmosphere': Light as Medium in László Moholy-Nagy's Aesthetics of Dematerialization." *Screen* 61, no. 2 (Summer): 288–295.

Starosielski, Nicole. 2019. "The Elements of Media Studies." *Media+Environment* 1, no. 1. https://doi.org/10.1525/001c.10780.

Sutil, Nicolás Salazar. 2018. *Matter Transmission: Mediation in a Paleocyber Age*. New York: Bloomsbury.

Walley, Jonathan. 2020. *Cinema Expanded: Avant-Garde Film in the Age of Intermedia*. New York: Oxford University Press.

Young, Liam Cole. 2020. "Salt: Fragments from the History of a Medium." *Theory, Culture & Society* 37, no. 6 (November): 135–158.

Zielinski, Siegfried. 2006. *Deep Time of the Media: Toward an Archaeology of Hearing and Seeing by Technical Means*. Translated by Gloria Custance. Cambridge, MA: MIT Press.

Zinman, Gregory. 2019. "Echoes of the Earth: Handmade Film Ecologies." In *Process Cinema: Handmade Film in the Digital Age*, edited by Scott Mackenzie and Janine Marchessault, 108–124. Montreal: McGill-Queen's University Press.

Zylinska, Joanna. 2020. "WATERKINO and HYDROMEDIA: How to Dissolve the Past to Build a More Viable Future." In *Deterritorializing the Future: Heritage in, of and after the Anthropocene*, edited by Rodney Harrison and Colin Sterling, 220–243. London: Open Humanities Press.

PART III
NATIONAL AND REGIONAL PHENOMENA

10
Cinema from the Perspective of the Stage

For an Integrated History of Theatrical Entertainment in Brazil

Luciana Corrêa de Araújo

Recent scholarship on the relations between theatre and silent cinema has overhauled traditional approaches and explored previously underresearched topics.[1] It has moved away from placing stage and screen in opposition, typical of the early years of film scholarship, as observed in studies such as Münsterberg's *The Photoplay: A Psychological Study*, published in 1919 (Ingham 2016: 6). Instead, over the past decades, intermedial approaches have given film studies the tools to explore the cross-pollination between these two mediums. Ivo Blom (2017: 19), for example, remarks that "performing intermedial research in film studies has become easier than it was a few decades ago," because film studies are not as reliant on the specificities of the medium as they were in the 1950s and 1960s, when the discipline first took shape.

In order to investigate intermedial encounters between silent cinema and theatre, this chapter will focus on stage plays so as to explore the moving form of film from the perspective of the stage. In so doing it will follow in the footsteps of Michael Ingham (2016: 10), who, in the book *Stage-Play and Screen-Play: The Intermediality of Theatre and Cinema*, examines "stage plays that either incorporate cinema, literally or by overt reference, or are derived from cinema." I will also draw on Charles Musser's proposal for an integrated history of theatrical entertainment, which embraces both live stage performance and the cinema. In a 2004 article, Musser (2004b: 6) argues that writing this integrated history can "reveal exciting convergences and interactions obscured by many years of scholarship that has treated them separately, as rival arts."

Building on this scholarship, this chapter will focus on plays staged in Rio de Janeiro and São Paulo from the late 1910s to the 1920s, a period marked by the rise of the mass entertainment industry. I will investigate the connections between stage plays and cinema from different points of view: a film being at the centre of the plot; commercial ties that linked film and stage business; cinema's influence on stage performance and mise-en-scène; the incorporation of Hollywood stars and characters into stage plots; an adaptation from screen to stage; and references to films and filmgoing, including film reception, audiences, and censorship. Because the manuscripts of most of the plays were submitted to censorship before being staged, they have been preserved and can be accessed at the Arquivo Nacional in Rio and at the Arquivo Miroel Silveira in São Paulo. In addition to the plays, the analysis will rely on accounts by critics and journalists, as well as promotional materials; unfortunately, very few images of the plays being performed on stage have survived.

This chapter is largely inspired by the remarkable research and in-depth analysis conducted by historian Tiago de Melo Gomes (2004) in his book on Brazilian popular theatre in the 1920s, in which he addresses the relationship between cinema and theatre as part of a broader cultural discussion that values the close examination of stage-play manuscripts as a way to access contemporary trends and debates. By adopting stage plays as primary sources to study the relations between theatre and silent cinema, this chapter adopts a similar methodological approach to Danielle Crepaldi Carvalho's (2020) article on the play *O cinematógrafo* (*The Cinematograph*), staged in Brazil in the early twentieth century.

All the plays covered here belong to the so-called light theatre, most of them revues from the *teatro de revista*, a popular genre of the musical theatre. As Lisa Shaw (2015: 89–90) summarises, "the *teatro de revista* first emerged at the end of the 1850s, became a recognized entertainment format in Brazil by the 1880s, and enjoyed its golden age in the 1920s and 1930s. By the 1920s revues were characterized by a range of stock characters, such as the Portuguese immigrant, the *mulata* and the *caipira; quadros* or sketches that poked fun at everyday life in the capital; musical and dance numbers; and a grand finale or *apoteose* that brought together on stage the entire cast." Although contemporaneous critics and traditional theatre historians yearned for a legitimate national theatre, from the end of the nineteenth century up to the first decades of the twentieth century the Brazilian theatrical scene was dominated by comedies of manners and the musical theatre. Décio de Almeida Prado (1999: 113), one of the most renowned theatre critics and a central voice in Brazilian theatre historiography from the 1940s onwards, argues that musical theatre "achieved a considerable increase in audience, with economic benefits for artists and authors, and a decrease in literary aspirations."[2] In his view, "the very nature of musical theatre, judged inferior, did not allow it to bring the reality of the theatre to full fruition" (165).[3] This approach, which favours dramatic theatre as the "true" theatre, has been refuted since the 1980s by the new generations of historians who have reevaluated the language of musical theatre, in particular the *teatro de revista,* and its historical importance (Mencarelli 2003: 7). Mencarelli underlines the vibrant urban culture in Rio at the turn of the century, when cinema and the phonograph ascended as major popular cultural practices in the circuit previously formed by the musical theatre, circus, carnival, and street festivities. He draws attention to the strong interconnections between these practices, which offered a variety of attractions to large audiences, whenever they could afford them (2–3).

Unlike popular theatre, the film business in Brazil expanded and developed by relying mostly on foreign productions. Before the First World War, the local exhibition market was dominated by European films, particularly from France, Italy, and Denmark. However, within a few years, American cinema took over the Brazilian market. Around 1916–1917, American films surpassed for the first time the number of European productions released in the Brazilian market (Freire 2011: 294). In 1925, less than a decade later, 83.6% of the films submitted to censorship were from the United States, followed by French films (a mere 6.67%), with Brazilian productions, most of them newsreels and nonfiction short films, representing 4.08% (Butcher 2019: 108). "The internal market began to function for the benefit of the industrial products from abroad," Stam and Johnson (1979) remark, also noting that "the foreign film became the standard by which all films were to be judged, thus making the exhibition of the more artisan-style Brazilian product problematic." Often considered a "threat" to theatre, foreign films and film culture also provided a variety of themes and strategies that were incorporated on stage. Theatre would thus take advantage of cinema's growing popularity, establishing creative exchanges while also promoting attractions that would appeal to the general theatrical audience.

According to Musser (2004b: 8), "a history of theatrical entertainment must keep in mind the relationship between stage and screen on many levels: that of personnel, subject matter and treatment, production methods, distribution of productions, advertising and promotion, as well as spectatorship." As a means of articulating some of these intersections, I will start by looking at the example of the comedy *A viuvinha do cinema* (*The Little Widow of the Cinema*), in which a film constitutes a stage element, as well as the centre of the plot. The play was staged in Rio de Janeiro in 1919 by the Companhia Leopoldo Froes, named after its director, the most famous Brazilian actor of the time.

In the plot, a husband (Froes), caught by his wife arriving home in the early hours after a night out, takes her to the movies in order to distract her, not knowing that one of the films of the programme has captured him wooing another woman at Guarujá beach during a trip he had made a couple of years before. He bribes the exhibitor to remove the film from the programme, but then it is replaced by a similar one, featuring the same lady having a romantic date, this time with a close friend of the protagonist.

In this play, film and filmgoing provide the very core of the plot. In addition, film is also a scenic element, since the movies watched by the characters are projected on stage at the beginning of the play. This attraction, which saw the screening of a film functioning as a prologue to the play itself, was proclaimed by the Rio newspaper *A Razão* (1919b: 8) as "the *dernier cri* in modern theatre."[4] As another promotional piece suggests ("De sábado para cá" 1919: 14), the innovation was not the film screening prologue itself but its close connection to the plot: "the hilarious play is greatly original for having a filmic prologue which is the *motor* of all the action, interspersed with utterly comical situations."[5]

A viuvinha do cinema is the adaptation by actors Apolonia Pinto and Brandão Sobrinho of a German play. Although not mentioned in reviews or promotional materials, similar versions of the play had been staged earlier in Rio, in 1908 and 1911 (Carvalho 2020).[6] In the handwritten script submitted for censorship, changes were introduced, also by hand, in order to adapt the original plot, set in late nineteenth-century Turin, and in Ostende, on the Belgian seaside, to contemporary Rio and the beachtown of Guarujá in the state of São Paulo. It is important to note, however, that neither the manuscript nor the changes made to it mention the film screening, and there is no evidence that this attraction was integrated in the other versions of the play previously staged in Rio. Everything suggests that it was an idea especially developed for the 1919 staging of the play by the Companhia Leopoldo Fróes at Teatro Trianon. This historic venue was owned by Jácomo Rosário Staffa, one of the most important film exhibitors and distributors in Rio until 1917, when he left the film business. Inaugurated in 1915 in the premises of a former movie theatre, Teatro Trianon was adjacent to Cinema Parisiense, also owned by Staffa. For a short time in 1916, Parisiense and Trianon were turned into one movie theatre (see Pontes 2016). Trianon, therefore, had a strategic connection to cinema, both geographically and commercially.

The actor Leopoldo Froes had already worked in film, starring in the 1916 production *Perdida* (*Fallen*), directed by Luiz de Barros. A key person related to the filmic prologue was Alberto Botelho, who shot the film. He was a well-known cinematographer, with a solid and prolific career in both fiction and nonfiction films. The year before *A viuvinha do cinema*, in 1918, he or his brother Paulino Botelho (the source is unclear on the matter) had captured in film and photographs the occasion at which Froes offered lunch to Gastão Tojeiro, author of another successful play starring Froes (Ferreira 2004: 199).

This constellation of names and facts draws attention to the circulation of professionals between film and stage within the theatrical entertainment sector as a whole. Besides the relations between "personnel" and "subject matter"—to return to Musser's categories—the relations between film and stage conjured by *A viuvinha do cinema* can also be traced in terms of advertising and promotion. The filmic prologue, in its direct connection to the plot for presenting the entire cast on screen, was an important selling point in the play's promotional campaign, which advertised the addition as a unique and modern novelty. In the advertisements, the prologue also received a cosmopolitan touch, through the use of foreign expressions: "dernier cri," "great attraction" (the latter in English) (*A Razão* 1919a: 10; 1919b: 8). An eloquent example of the intermedial content of Brazilian stage dramas in the 1910s, *A viuvinha do cinema* indicates how cinema's modernity could be incorporated by stage productions in different ways, whether by having cinema as the subject of the play, as a stage element, or as a component in its promotional strategies.

Whereas *A viuvinha do cinema* offered its audiences an actual film screening, the prologue of another play, *Cinema-troça* (*Cinema-Mockery*; *troça* also refers to a small carnival street group), which opened in Rio de Janeiro in 1917, provided instead an artistic re-creation of the experience of watching a movie. A review of the play suggests a rather elaborate staging simulating the projection of a film: rather than a screen, there was a diaphanous veil, behind which the actors performed, in silence, a drama of adultery, while actor and director Henrique Alves narrated the plot, in a way similar to the function of early cinema commentators ("*Cinema-troça* no Recreio" 1917: 7). While *Cinema-troça* demonstrates the clear impact of cinema in terms of performance and stage mise-en-scène, it was apparently not to the taste of all audience members; the theatre critic Mário Nunes (n.d.-a: 130) defined *Cinema-troça*'s prologue as "banal and immoral."

Nunes would be more congenial to *O coco de respeito* (*First-Rate Coco*, *coco* being a musical rhythm and dance), a play staged in 1921. Nunes (n.d.-b: 34) wrote that one of the sketches of that play, in which the action takes place on a beach, was remarkably staged and showed the influence of Mack Sennett, who in his films had "replaced the beauty of the statues by well-shaped bodies in swimsuits, with life and movement."[7] In his early review, Nunes conveys enthusiasm for what he calls "Sennettism." As everybody knows, he writes,

"Sennettism" is a "new genre of fine arts in movement, invented by Mack Sennett, the great North American comedy director, who, rather than classical statuary masterpieces, preferred the exquisite living beings of today, veiled only by tight-fitting swimsuits, a constant and ever-renewed glorification of the beauty of the female body" (Nunes 1921a: 6).[8]

These remarks demonstrate how Mack Sennett and his popular bathing beauties crossed cinema's borders and reached Brazilian stages, inflecting the actresses' looks and stage performances. Theatre studies usually emphasise that foreign revue companies, such as the French Ba-ta-clan and the Spanish Velasco, had a decisive influence on Brazilian *teatro de revista* throughout the 1920s (see Veneziano 2013; Shaw 2015). Ba-ta-clan, in particular, whose first tour was in 1922, is considered to have made a decisive contribution to the improvement of the Brazilian *teatro de revista* as concerns mise-en-scène style and the chorus girls' performance, which gained consistency and increased the exposition of the female body on stage (see Veneziano 2013). Nunes's reviews of *O coco de respeito*, however, suggest that even before Ba-ta-clan's first Brazilian tour some of these changes had already started, under the influence of Hollywood and the film culture it spawned, which played crucial roles in valorising the display of the female body, performing sensual movements and choreographies on stage. Grounded in both stage and screen studies, this line of research entails a different historiographical perspective on foreign influences in Brazilian popular theatre, standing as a significant example of the uses of intermediality as a historiographical method.

Gomes (2004: 54) highlights the key role played by Hollywood cinema and the *teatro de revista* in the process of cultural massification. As extremely popular forms of entertainment, the screen and stage forms developed alongside one another to create a common repertoire, shared by a large and heterogeneous audience. It can be argued that the systematic and diverse film references in stage plays implied a spectator familiar with both stage and screen subject matters, stylistic aspects, and practices.

However, the intermedial dynamic was unevenly weighted towards the North American cultural product. Hollywood's hegemonic position in the Brazilian exhibition market and its centrality among social and cultural practices had a direct impact on Brazilian theatre, especially on the *teatro de revista*, whose plays always dealt with current events and trends, as well as "the novelties of modern life, exposing with humour some situations resulting from these novelties" (Gomes 2004: 203).[9] Considering the many interactions between theatre and cinema, Gomes points out how quickly the theatre found ways to take advantage of film elements, even if, he argues, those strategies of interaction also expressed cinema's great power (66).

Faced with the pervasiveness of the Hollywood star system, Brazilian stage plays often incorporated references to foreign film stars, usually portrayed in connection to local culture. Though also resorted to in Brazilian films—as in the comedy *Herói do século XX* (*Twentieth-Century Hero*, Ary Severo, 1926), with a Buster Keaton type as protagonist, or in the project *Tal e qual Harold Lloyd* (*Just Like Harold Lloyd*), announced in 1926 but never completed (Araújo 2018: 101)—this strategy was more fully developed and recurrent in popular theatre. In contrast to the scarce production of local fiction films, the frantic staging of new plays allowed (or rather demanded) fast-paced and constant responses to topics of the day—film culture among them.

The impact of Rudolph Valentino's death in 1926, for instance, resonated in Brazilian plays staged the following year. In *Mosaico* (*Mosaic*), a play staged by Luiz de Barros's theatre company Ra-ta-plan (whose name is a direct allusion to Ba-ta-clan), the singer and actor Luiz Barreira impersonated some of Valentino's most famous characters. He performed in three sketches named after Valentino's films: "Sangre y arena" (*Blood and sand*, Fred Niblo, 1922), "Paixão de bárbaro" (*The Sheik*, George Melford, 1921), and "Monsieur Beaucaire" (*Monsieur Beaucaire*, Sidney Olcott, 1924). Two other plays staged in 1927 referred to Valentino. *As valentinas* (*The Female Valentinos*) included a sketch in which women sing and dance in admiration of the beloved artist, praising his irresistible, languid appearance. Apart from the title and this sketch, though, there is no other reference to Valentino or to cinema in the play.

A quite different approach can be found in *Rodolpho Valentão* (*Rudolph the Bully*), staged in Rio and São Paulo in 1927. The protagonist is described as a ridiculous type in his obsessive imitation of Valentino, with exaggerated sideburns, bell-bottom trousers, and short jacket. As the play unfolds, many situations and dialogues revolve around Valentino and film. One of these involves the arrangements for shooting a promotional film for the protagonist's company, which is a rice powder factory—a joke about Valentino's sleek appearance and makeup. The play's promotional campaign took advantage of Valentino's popularity while also highlighting the well-known leading actor Jayme Costa, drawing an interesting parallel between Hollywood and the local theatre star system (*A Noite* 1927: 5). Some years before, in 1921, the same Jayme Costa had performed in a role related to another Hollywood star, George Walsh, in the play *Brutalidade* (*Brutality*). Interestingly enough, the play not only featured references to cinema but was itself a stage adaption of the 1916 production *The Beast* (Richard Stanton). The film, a blend of comedy, drama, and western, was adapted into an operetta, most of it performed following that modern American musical style, ragtime.

Besides the musical and dance numbers, *Brutalidade* also incorporated some traditional iconography of western movies, such as a saloon with cowboys, bandits, and gamblers and a fight scene in which the hero throws a bandit out of a window and then defeats the rest of the gang. In order to emulate the landscapes of westerns, sets were painted and a number of structures were built to re-create a hill—where the leading couple performed a farewell song—and trenches, placed backstage but visible to the audience, in which Indians and cowboys fought (Nunes 1921b: 6; n.d.-b: 30). These descriptions suggest that, in *Brutalidade*, not only was cinema the source of the plot but—as with the play *O coco de respeito*, performed in the same year—it also provided inspiration for the stage mise-en-scène.

Another important connection between *Brutalidade* and cinema concerned exhibition practices. The play was staged at Teatro São Pedro, run by the Paschoal Segreto Company, which had two other theatres located in the same square, Praça Tiradentes, the hub of popular theatre in Rio. At one of its venues, the Teatro São José, dedicated to *teatro de revista*, the company had implemented since the early 1910s the so-called *teatro por sessões* or *espetáculos por sessões* (theatre in sessions), in which at least three daily shows were scheduled. With this practice, they managed to reduce ticket prices to the level of movie tickets (Martins 2004: 140–141). Similar to film exhibition practices, the programme at the Teatro São José was constantly renewed. Although quite controversial, especially among overworked artists, "theatre in sessions" turned out to be a very efficient practice for the purpose of attracting large audiences, as well as a means to face down competition from cinema. Even at the two other theatres run by the Paschoal Segreto Company at Praça Tiradentes—Teatro São Pedro and Teatro Carlos Gomes—the plays were shown twice each evening.

This connection to film practices is no surprise, considering that the founder of the company, Paschoal Segreto, had a pioneering role in the Brazilian film business. He opened the first permanent venue for film exhibition in 1887 and was the first to produce local actualities. Segreto remained active in the film business until the early 1910s, when theatre started to take up most of his attention. Even then, however, cinema continued to be a strong reference point for his company, as the practice of theatre in sessions demonstrated. After Paschoal Segreto's death in 1920, the company continued to connect with cinema. When *Brutalidade* opened the following year, Nunes (1921b: 6) wrote that a new trend had been discovered: the stage adaptation of successful film productions. While such screen-to-stage adaptations might not have become a trend, film-related plays seem to have been produced on a regular basis, so much so, in fact, that in a review of *Rodolpho Valentão* in 1927, another critic declared that the play belonged to the genre of "cinemania" ("*Rodolpho Valentão* no Trianon" 1927: 14).

In considering this so-called genre, we might also do well to explore a popular subgenre of cinemania, comprising plays featuring characters inspired by Charles Chaplin. This reflected the growth of Hollywood cinema in the Brazilian film market, as well as the artist's emergence on the Brazilian cultural landscape. Only one year after the release of his first films in Rio in 1914, Chaplin and his screen character were nicknamed "Carlito" or "Carlitos." By 1920 the exhibition of Chaplin's comedies had peaked, with at least twenty-eight of his films having being screened in twenty-four Rio movie theatres over a total of 230 days that year (Pontes 2016: 130). In the early 1920s Chaplin was celebrated by the press not only as a comic star and a gifted filmmaker but also as an artist endowed with a superior and universal genius (113). The legion of Chaplin fans spanned different ages and social classes and included groups from the cultural elite, such as the young film critics who in 1928 founded the Chaplin-Club, a pioneering cine-club dedicated to discussing film as an art form. The Chaplin-Club's last activity was the premiere screening of *Limite* (1931), the fabled avant-garde film directed by Mário Peixoto, which itself contains an homage to Chaplin in the form of a clip from *The Adventurer* (Charles Chaplin, 1917).

Chaplin's popularity could also be measured by the wide coverage he received in the press (about his films, personal life, millionaire contracts, and so on), as well as through the stage performances he inspired, from references and characters in the revues to the many Carlitos imitators who took part in stage shows. In his comprehensive study of the exhibition and reception of Chaplin's films in Brazil between 1914 and 1922, Igor Andrade Pontes (2016: 86) mentions that many plays from the *teatro de revista* featured a character based on Chaplin's famous screen persona, a practice that seems to have lasted from the late 1910s until the end of the 1920s. His survey of the newspaper *Correio da Manhã* resulted in a list of eight Chaplin-related titles, including such works as *É o suco!* (1919), *Se a bomba arrebenta* (1920), and *Carlito & Chico Boia* (1920). In the second of these revues, Carlitos's imitators on stage are adopted as the theme of a musical number. One of the characters in *Se a bomba arrebenta* (literally, *If the Pump Bursts*, meaning "if things go wrong") is a newsreel cameraman. When a young lady asks for a film featuring Carlitos, he says he has a very interesting one, showing a Carlitos lookalike contest that took place in New York, in which Chaplin himself, one of the contenders, was not the winner. "Do you want to watch it?" he asks. This is the cue for the entrance of a group of Carlitos imitators, who perform a musical number. The play draws inspiration from the widespread rumour that this contest actually took place, though there is no clear proof of this. Between fact and legend, imitators and the original, Carlitos proves to be an engaging attraction, on both stage and screen.

In the two other plays, Carlitos appears as a stage character. In the revue *É o suco* (literally, *It's the Juice*, meaning "it's the best"), one of the sketches takes place in a movie theatre lobby. When the doorman mentions the comedy that will be screened, Carlitos tears up the poster and makes his entrance. Despite its being a small part, his brief amusing lines stand out for the way they mimic fast-paced silent slapstick comedies, translating into words some of their characteristic situations: "Ah! Ah! Ah! I left home—bumped into a cop—the cop swallowed the baton—Ah! Ah! Ah!—I took a cab—the cab sped up—it skidded in the mud—I fell on the street—Ah! Ah! Ah!—a bike ran over me"[10] and so on. Although there are no particular stage directions for the Carlitos character in this scene, one can easily picture the actor reproducing on stage Chaplin's well-known acrobatic movements.

Finally, in the 1920 play *Carlito & Chico Boia*, Carlitos is the protagonist alongside Chico Boia, a nickname for the very popular slapstick character played by Roscoe "Fatty" Arbuckle. The first act begins at the entrance of a movie theatre, where several characters appear and talk to the doorman. One of them is an infuriated husband looking for his wife and her lover, threatening to kill them both. After a while, shots are heard and patrons run out of the theatre. Among them are Carlitos and Chico Boia, walking robotically—the pair has somehow come to life outside of the silver screen. They evade the doorman, who tries in vain to capture them and put them back into the film can from which they escaped. In the following act, Carlitos and Chico Boia find themselves silent and paralysed in an operating room before they are given the elixir of life.

Later they are involved in dialogues and musical numbers with allegorical characters personifying the National Theatre, Politics, the Public Health Service, the City, and the Vices (Cocaine, Gambling, Alcohol, Cigarettes, among others). Through these scenes, the two foreign visitors are introduced to problems and peculiar situations of the city's everyday life—a typical narrative strategy in *teatro de revista* plays to address Brazilian social and political affairs. To this traditional structure the revue *Carlito & Chico Boia* provides an additional attraction, connecting two of the most famous Hollywood comedians to real life in Brazil. They interact with well-known urban characters and become acquainted with local current events, all of them already familiar to the audience.

The pair of film characters also make room for elements of slapstick comedy, as in *É o suco*. One of the sketches in *Carlito & Chico Boia* takes place outside a tenement house, from which a number of people run down the stairs to escape from an anarchist on the first floor, who threatens to detonate a bomb. Carlitos stands with a hammer at the bottom of the staircase, hitting the heads of all the characters who pass by him. While everyone is still dizzy, tottering around, Carlitos and Chico Boia hammer them even harder, making them drop to the ground. In the last act, the stage setting incorporates a gigantic film projector. Carlitos and Chico Boia, finally captured by the doorman, are put back into the projector, which starts to work.

Although the revue portrays the two characters in a positive way, emphasising their charisma and popularity, this conclusion introduces a twist. Before Carlitos and Chico Boia are captured by the doorman, there is a musical number featuring an allegorical character called Maxixe, the name of the most popular dance in Brazil at the time, known abroad as the "Brazilian tango." The maxixe was condemned by many for its sensuous movements and its lower-class, Afro-Brazilian origins. The revue stages a popular protest against the banning of the maxixe from the list of Brazilian attractions that would be performed before the King of Belgium in his visit to the country later that year (1920). In the song performed by the Maxixe character, he complains that "the so-called nationalism is ashamed of what is ours." After that musical number, another allegorical character, the Popular Spirit, enters the stage, managing to trick Carlitos and Chico Boia as a way "to pull out of them the fictitious life they had." It is in the following scene that the doorman captures them and puts them back in the film projector.

These final sketches cast some ambiguity over the beloved Hollywood characters and their experience amid Brazilian types and controversial affairs. On the one hand, they allow the revue to take advantage of the hegemonic Hollywood cinema and star system, while incorporating not only two of its most famous characters but also some well-known elements from the slapstick comedies in which they starred. On the other hand, the revue also suggests a nationalistic approach to Brazilian popular culture, which was often undervalued when not overtly attacked. The review sheds a positive light on the foreign visitors, whether the real-life King of Belgium or the fictional characters of Carlitos and Chico Boia, but also introduces allegorical characters connected to Brazilian culture, representing the Maxixe and the Popular Spirit. It is the latter who manages to paralyse the two Hollywood characters, taking their fictitious lives away from them so they can be captured and put back where they belong: not in a Brazilian setting but in the film projector. The end of the revue draws on the tensions between local theatre and foreign film. Thus, returning Carlitos and Chico Boia to the projector can be read as both a nationalist gesture and an intermedial manoeuvre that sees theatre dominating film.

This ambivalent approach to foreign elements and Brazilian popular culture derives from the polysemic nature of the *teatro de revista*, as pointed out by Gomes (2004: 35): "[B]eing an essentially comic form of entertainment, the *teatro de revista* counted on the polysemic humour to attract a varied audience to the theatre. The result was a constant debate on current events, in terms that allowed multiple understandings by a diversified audience."[11] Many possible meanings also emerge from the Brazilian stage plays of the era through the countless references to filmgoing. In relation to the Hollywood star system, we can keep track, through the plays, of the main trends and popular stars: in the 1910s, the popularity of westerns and slapstick comedies and their famous artists Walsh, Chaplin, and Arbuckle; in the mid-1920s, the alternately passionate and mocking reactions provoked by Rudolph Valentino; and throughout that decade, the impact of actresses who personified the modern woman, such as Bebe Daniels, mentioned in the revue *Meia-noite e trinta* (*Half Past Midnight*, Luís Peixoto, 1923), where a group of devils discusses the creation of the "perfect woman for modern times" (Gomes 2004: 216).[12] In line with the polysemic nature of *teatro de revista*, cinema and filmgoing could be depicted in a positive light, as a major and welcome sign of modernity, yet also looked upon with suspicion, as a threat to traditional values. When discussing gender conventions in the 1920s, Gomes underlines the importance of the movie theatre regarding social mores (210). As a place where a large number of people, many of them young and single who had never met before, gathered together in a dark room, the movie theatre attracted great attention, not only from journalists and playwrights but also from society as a whole. In the plays of this period, there are countless references to harassment in movie theatres, usually depicted in a light, amusing tone. Still, it is not uncommon to find characters who, despite being portrayed in a satirical way, are able to express widespread concerns about cinema's threat to morality.

Playing such a central role in city life, the movie theatre could not fail to be addressed in the revues. Moreover, as a space in which all manner of people circulated (coming from different social classes, races, backgrounds, and ages), the movie theatre provided rich narrative possibilities. In the revue *É o suco*, in which Carlitos tears up the film poster, the sketch in a movie theatre lobby brings together an interesting variety of characters: the pair of protagonists, one a capitalist, the other a revue playwright referred to as Author, who, having bought a ticket for a second-class seat, tries to sneak into the first-class section; the doorman, whose faulty speech indicates his poor background; an old lady and her young daughter, who is harassed by a man who calls himself a respectable family man; the French female musician who conducts the all-female orchestra playing in the lobby and whom Author insistently woos. From this sketch we can also infer the movie theatre's ticketing policy, whereby a range of ticket prices attracted a varied audience that, although separated into distinct sections, still shared common areas. The theme of harassment is also recurrent, always in a humorous tone, in the inappropriate advances from the supposed respectable man toward the young lady and from Author toward the orchestra conductor. Finally, the doorman's explanation to the protagonists about the first film to be screened in the programme contains revealing and amusing remarks about film genres. It is a serial film with twenty-two episodes. "Very complicated," says the doorman. "I have been watching this thing ever since it started, and I still don't know which of the two is the bad guy."[13] A highly popular genre in Rio since 1915, thrilling audiences with titles such as *Lucille Love, the Girl of Mystery* (Francis Ford, 1914), *The Broken Coin* (Francis Ford, 1915), and *Les Vampires* (Louis Feuillade, 1915), serials could easily puzzle viewers with their action-packed episodes.

Controversial topics regarding local filmgoing are also to be found in a number of revues. In the 1928 revue *Viva a mulher* (*Long Live Women*), written by stage and film director Luiz de Barros, one of the sketches addresses censorship in films and the new rules surrounding the admission of children to movie theatres, through a dialogue between a Police Inspector and a Girl who is barred from watching a film. Although the Girl's age is not mentioned, the implication is that she must be under fourteen: shortly before, in 1926, a federal decree had established that no child under fourteen was allowed to attend movie theatres in the evenings unless accompanied by an adult. Aside from its commentary on the so-called Minors Code, the sketch also takes aim at the state Censorship Board, which used to cut daring scenes from films, especially kissing scenes. In a rather malicious tone, the sketch ridicules the rigours of censorship and regulations, reinforcing the contrast between them and the bold, even impudent young people they were supposed to protect. The Girl complains that when Valentino or Ramon Novarro kiss passionately, the film jumps and no one sees anything. She asks the Police Inspector, "What's the big deal about a kiss? Do you think I've never kissed? What do I have a cousin for?" Then she adds, "I have three cousins, thank God." At one point the Girl mentions a statue on Paulista Avenue of a naked couple kissing. "In the movies," she remarks, "people don't kiss naked." When the Inspector argues that it is a statue and doesn't move, she replies, "So immorality is in the movement? Then we had better tie everyone in a straitjacket."[14] Of course this sketch, itself about censorship, ended up being entirely censored.

Although far from exhaustive, the research contained in this chapter confirms stage plays as a rich yet underexplored source for the study of cinema and film culture in Brazil during the 1910s and 1920s. By understanding these plays—by consulting their manuscripts as well as reviews, advertisements, books, and other documents on them—it is possible to identify "convergences and interactions" (Musser 2004b: 6) as well as conflicts and tensions between cinema and theatre. This intermedial approach also offers ways to reframe the history of both cinema and theatre in Brazil. The study of film references in stage plays brings to the fore the influence of cinema on theatrical themes, characters, and plots and also points to early and innovative contributions of foreign films, especially Hollywood productions, to staging and performance styles. Conversely, approaching cinema from the perspective of stage plays opens up productive avenues for research. One of these would be the circulation of personnel and how it strengthened creative and economic connections between different media and cultural practices. Another would be to explore stage plays as a privileged source through which to study reception and film culture in Brazil. Considering the moving form of film, we might do well to reframe traditional categories such as "Brazilian cinema" and "Brazilian films" by embracing the broader notion of "cinema in Brazil," with all the rich intermedial and transnational relations it implies.

Notes

Research supported by grant #2014/50821-3, São Paulo Research Foundation (FAPESP). "The opinions, hypotheses, conclusions or recommendations contained in this material are the sole responsibility of the author and do not necessarily reflect FAPESP opinion."

1. See, for example, Brewster and Jacobs (1997) on stage pictorialism in cinema; Musser (2004a) on stage-to-screen adaptation; Burrows (2003) on the work of stage actors in films; Waltz (2012, 2015) on film projections integrated with live performance on stage; Askari et al. (2015) on performance in relation to cultural practices. For an extensive list of studies on the relations between theatre and cinema, covering a broader temporal scope, see Ingham (2016: 7).
2. "O teatro musicado, em suas várias encarnações, significou um aumento ponderável de público, com benefícios econômicos para intérpretes e autores, e o decréscimo de aspirações literárias." Unless otherwise indicated, all translations are by the author. For the titles of plays containing colloquial and/or slang terms, both the literal translation and an approximate meaning are given.
3. "Mas a natureza mesma do teatro musicado, julgada inferior, não lhe permitia enxergar a realidade teatral plena."
4. "O 'dernier cri' do teatro moderno."

5. "A hilariante peça apresenta a grande originalidade de ter prólogo cinematográfico que é o *motivo* do qual decorre toda a ação entrecortada de situações as mais cômicas."
6. Carvalho's (2020) research allows us to conclude that *A viuvinha do cinema* reproduces, with few changes, the play *O cinematógrafo* (*The Cinematograph*), which is, in turn, the Portuguese translation by Acácio Antunes of the German play *Hans Huckebein* (1897), written by Oscar Blumenthal and Gustav Kadelburg.
7. "Notável a marcação do quadro do banho de mar, influência de Mack Sennett, que substituiu a beleza das estátuas por corpos bem modelados pelo maiô com vida e movimento.".
8. "O sennettismo, como todo mundo sabe, é esse novo gênero de arte plástica em movimento, inventado por Mack Sennett, o grande diretor de comédias cinematográficas norte-americano, que resolveu antepor às obras-primas de estatuária da antiguidade clássica, os primores vivos de hoje, velados apenas por maiôs modeladores, glorificação constante e sempre renovada à beleza do corpo feminino."
9. "As novidades da vida moderna e expondo com humor algumas situações que as novidades proporcionavam."
10. "Ah! Ah! Ah!—Saí de casa—dei tranco no polícia—o polícia engoliu o pau—Ah! Ah! Ah!—tomei o taxi—o taxi saiu voando—derrapou na lama—caí na rua—Ah! Ah! Ah!—vinha a bicicleta—passou em cima de mim."
11. "Sendo uma forma de entretenimento essencialmente cômica, o teatro de revista apostava no humor polissêmico para atrair ao teatro uma plateia variada. O resultado era um permanente debate sobre os temas do momento, em termos que permitiam múltiplas compreensões por parte de uma plateia diversificada."
12. "A mulher perfeita para os tempos modernos."
13. "É muito complicado. Eu tenho visto todo o troço desde que se principiou-se e ainda não sei quá dos dois é o marvado."
14. "E que é que tem de mais um beijo? Xentes! Você pensa que eu nunca dei um beijo? Pra que que eu tenho um primo! . . . Tenho mesmo três, graças a Deus!"; "No cinema ninguém se beija nu!"; "Ah! É no movimento que está a imoralidade? Então era melhor prender a gente toda na camisola de força."

References

Print Sources

A Noite. 1927, 5. 18 June. http://bndigital.bn.gov.br/hemeroteca-digital/.
Araújo, Luciana Corrêa de. 2018. "O cinema em Pernambuco (1900–1930)." In *Nova história do cinema brasileiro*, edited by Sheila Schvarzman and Fernão Pessoa Ramos, 90–123. São Paulo: Edições Sesc.
A Razão. 1919a, 10. 8 June. http://bndigital.bn.gov.br/hemeroteca-digital/.
A Razão. 1919b, 8. 10 June. http://bndigital.bn.gov.br/hemeroteca-digital/.
Askari, Kaveh, Scott Curtis, Frank Gray, Louis Pelletier, Tami Williams, and Joshua Yumibe, eds. 2015. *Performing New Media, 1890–1915*. Bloomington: Indiana University Press.
Blom, Ivo. 2017. *Reframing Luchino Visconti: Film and Art*. Leiden: Sidestone Press.
Brewster, Ben, and Lea Jacobs. 1997. *Theatre to Cinema: Stage Pictorialism and the Early Feature Film*. Oxford: Oxford University Press.
Burrows, Jon. 2003. *Legitimate Cinema: Theatre Stars in Silent British Film 1908–1918*. Exeter: University of Exeter Press.

Butcher, Pedro. 2019. "Hollywood e o mercado de cinema brasileiro: Princípios de uma hegemonia." PhD dissertation, Universidade Federal Fluminense, Niterói.

Carvalho, Danielle Crepaldi. 2020. "O cinema no palco: *O Cinematógrafo* (1897) na cena teatral carioca dos anos de 1900." *Vivomatografías* 6: 19–51.

"Cinema-troça no Recreio." 1917. *O Imparcial*, 12 April, 7. http://bndigital.bn.gov.br/hemeroteca-digital/.

"De sábado para cá." 1919. *Comédia*, 24 May, 14. http://bndigital.bn.gov.br/hemeroteca-digital/.

Ferreira, Adriano de Assis. 2004. "Teatro Trianon: Forças da ordem x forças da desordem." PhD dissertation, Universidade de São Paulo.

Freire, Rafael de Luna. 2011. "Carnaval, mistério e gangsters: O filme policial no Brasil (1915–1950)." PhD dissertation, Universidade Federal Fluminense, Niterói.

Gomes, Tiago de Melo. 2004. *Um espelho no palco—Identidades sociais e massificação da cultura no teatro de revista dos anos 1920*. Campinas: Editora Unicamp.

Ingham, Michael. 2016. *Stage-Play and Screen-Play: The Intermediality of Theatre and Cinema*. New York: Routledge.

Martins, William de Souza Nunes. 2004. "Paschoal Segreto: 'Ministro das diversões' do Rio de Janeiro (1883–1920)." Master's thesis, Universidade Federal do Rio de Janeiro.

Mencarelli, Fernando Antônio. 2003. "A voz e a partitura: O teatro musical, indústria e diversidade cultural no Rio de Janeiro (1968–1908)." PhD disseration, Universidade Estadual de Campinas.

Musser, Charles. 2004a. "The Hidden and the Unspeakable: On Theatrical Culture, Oscar Wilde and Ernst Lubitsch's *Lady Windermere's Fan*." *Film Studies* 5: 12–47. http://doi.org/10.7227/FS.4.2.

Musser, Charles. 2004b. "Towards a History of Theatrical Culture: Imagining an Integrated History of Stage and Screen." In *Screen Culture: History and Textuality*, edited by John Fullerton, 3–19. Eastleigh: John Libbey.

Nunes, Mário. 1921a. "Burletas e revistas." *Palcos e Telas*, 2 June, 6. http://bndigital.bn.gov.br/hemeroteca-digital/.

Nunes, Mário. 1921b. "Theatros." *Palcos e Telas*, 17 March, 6. http://bndigital.bn.gov.br/hemeroteca-digital/.

Nunes, Mário. n.d.-a. *40 anos de teatro*. Vol. 1. Rio de Janeiro: Serviço Nacional de Teatro.

Nunes, Mário. n.d.-b. *40 anos de teatro*. Vol. 2. Rio de Janeiro: Serviço Nacional de Teatro.

Pontes, Igor Andrade. 2016. "Os caminhos de Carlitos—A exibição dos filmes de Charles Chaplin no Rio de Janeiro, suas histórias e seus personagens (1914–1922)." Master's thesis,: Universidade Federal Fluminense, Niterói.

Prado, Décio de Almeida. 1999. *História concisa do teatro brasileiro: 1570–1908*. São Paulo: Editora da Universidade de São Paulo.

"*Rodolpho Valentão* no Trianon." 1927. *O Imparcial*, 16 January, 14. http://bndigital.bn.gov.br/hemeroteca-digital/.

Shaw, Lisa. 2015. "The *Teatro de Revista* in Rio de Janeiro in the 1920s: Transnational Dialogues and Popular Cosmopolitanism." *Luso-Brazilian Review* 52, no. 2: 73–98.

Stam, Robert, and Randal Johnson. 1979. "Brazil Renaissance, Introduction: Beyond Cinema Novo." *Jump Cut* 21: 13–18. https://www.ejumpcut.org/archive/onlinessays/JC21folder/BrazilStamJohnson.html.

Veneziano, Neide. 2013. *O teatro de revista no Brasil: dramaturgia e convenções*. São Paulo: SESI-SP Editora.

Waltz, Gwendolyn. 2012. "'Half Real-Half Reel': Alternation Format Stage-and-Screen Hybrids." In *A Companion to Early Cinema*, edited by André Gaudreault, Nicolas Dulac, and Santiago Hidalgo, 360–380. Malden, MA: Wiley-Blackwell.

Waltz, Gwendolyn. 2015. "20 Minutes or Less: Short-Form Film-and-Theatre Hybrids–Skits, Sketches, Playlets, & Acts in Vaudeville, Variety, Revues, &c." In *Performing New Media, 1890–1915*, edited by Kaveh Askari, Scott Curtis, Frank Gray, Louis Pelletier, Tami Williams, and Joshua Yumibe, 245–253. Bloomington: Indiana University Press.

Plays

As valentinas. Authors: Marques Junior and A. Campos. Music: Zequinha de Abreu. Genre: revue. Censored in São Paulo on 21 July 1927. Arquivo Miroel Silveira (São Paulo), DDP0604.

A viuvinha do cinema. Adaptation: Apolônia Pinto and Brandão Sobrinho. Genre: comedy. Censored in Rio de Janeiro on 14 May 1919. Arquivo Nacional (Rio de Janeiro), BR_RJANRIO_6E_CPR_PTE_0037.

Brutalidade. Author: J. Ribeiro. Music: Adalberto de Carvalho. Genre: opereta. Censored in Rio de Janeiro on 8 March 1921. Arquivo Nacional (Rio de Janeiro), BR_RJANRIO_6E_CPR_PTE_0205.

Carlito & Chico Boia. Author: Gastão Tojeiro. Music: Griselda Lazzaro Schleder. Genre: revue. Censored in Rio de Janeiro on 3 September 1920. Arquivo Nacional (Rio de Janeiro), BR_RJANRIO_6E_CPR_PTE_0164.

Cinema-troça. Authors: J. Brito e Vieira Cardoso. Music: Felipe Duarte. Genre: revue. Staged at Teatro Recreio, Rio de Janeiro, in 1917.

Coco de respeito. Author: Henrique Junior. Music: Sacramento and Raul Martins. Genre: revue. Staged at Teatro Recreio, Rio de Janeiro, in 1921.

É o suco. Author: J. Praxedes. Musical compilation: Verdi de Carvalho. Genre: revue. Censored in Rio de Janeiro on 4 January 1919. Arquivo Nacional (Rio de Janeiro), BR_RJANRIO_6E_CPR_PTE_0002.

Mosaico. Authors: Celestino Silveira and Annibal Pacheco. Music: Antonio Lago. Genre: revue. Censored in Rio de Janeiro on 14 May 1919. Arquivo Nacional (Rio de Janeiro), BR_RJANRIO_6E_CPR_PTE_0961.

Rodolpho Valentão. Author: Gastão Tojeiro. Genre: farce. Censored in São Paulo on 18 June 1927. Arquivo Miroel Silveira (São Paulo), DDP0594.

Se a bomba arrebenta . . . Authors: Rego Barros, Cardoso de Menezes, and Carlos Bittencourt. Genre: revue. Censored in Rio de Janeiro on 17 December 1920. Arquivo Nacional (Rio de Janeiro), BR_RJANRIO_6E_CPR_PTE_0189.

Viva a mulher. Author: Luiz de Barros. Genre: revue. Censored in São Paulo on 1 February 1928. Arquivo Miroel Silveira (São Paulo), DDP0746.

11
Flamenco on Screen

The Intermedial Legacy of Carmen Amaya in *Bajarí*

Albert Elduque

On the Barcelona seaside, at the end of Carrer de la Marina and just under the looming presence of the Torre Mapfre and the Hotel Arts, stands Somorrostro, a typical swimming beach with restaurants, usually crowded with tourists. Walking along the seafront promenade, four hundred metres to the south, it is possible to drink at a modest public landmark with a limestone relief showing five angels, two of them playing guitars and the other three dancing. Unveiled in 1959, this monument honours Carmen Amaya (1913–1963), the most important dancer in the history of flamenco. Amaya was born in a Roma community in Somorrostro when it was just a shantytown, and thanks to her talent became an international star who lived and toured in Latin America and the United States, performed at Carnegie Hall and in Hollywood movies, and was admired by international politicians and artists while remaining true to her cultural roots. However, despite her worldwide acclaim and popularity among audiences, in Spain her talent was not properly recognised: General Franco's government supported Andalusian folklore for the purpose of tourism, but not flamenco, which was feared for its embodiment of social and racial inequalities (Moix 2013: 29–30).

According to the legend, Carmen Amaya learned flamenco from the motion of the waves on Somorrostro beach, and the effort she exerted walking barefoot on the sand gave her legs an unusual strength which allowed her to perform an intense, violent *zapateado*. This technique, which involves a strong, even violent percussive effect by tapping one's feet, was usually exhibited by male performers but was rare in female dancers. Amaya was able to turn such an ability into her personal trademark, highlighting it by rolling up her skirt or by wearing trousers, thus adding a masculine outfit and dance style to her feminine behaviour (Moix 2013: 26). Throughout her life, a few films recorded those extraordinary skills in different countries and different times. In 2011, Eva Vila directed *Bajarí*, a music documentary which explored the legacy of Amaya in the present, by delving into the connections between flamenco dancing gestures and its visual translation on the screen.

In his brief text "Notes on Gesture," Giorgio Agamben ([1992] 2000) includes both dance and cinema among the artistic expressions which can record the social and political loss of gestures and reclaim them for the present. According to Agamben, since the late nineteenth century pathological tics have prevailed over naturalness and coordination, as if the whole population suffered from Tourette syndrome, and as a result life has become indecipherable. Within this scene of general confusion, isolating and highlighting gestures stands as an action of social empowerment, and both dance and cinema are privileged spaces to make these gestures visible and politically significant. By placing silent movies alongside the dances of Isadora Duncan and Sergei Diaghilev, as well as the novels of Proust and the *Jugendstil* poetry, Agamben highlights the mediality of gestures and explains that reclaiming gestures implies understanding them as means without ends: "If dance is gesture, it is so... because it is nothing more than the endurance and the exhibition of the media character of corporeal movements. *The gesture is the exhibition of a mediality: it is the process of making a means visible as such*" (58).

In this chapter I will explore the ways in which the medial understanding of gesture is articulated in the case of Carmen Amaya and the music documentary *Bajarí*. To this purpose, I will first analyse the intermedial history of Amaya's dancing gestures in her cinematic performances, most notably in *María de la O* (Francisco Elías, 1936) and *Los Tarantos* (Francisco Rovira Beleta, 1963), and then explore the ways in which *Bajarí* not only finds and recovers these gestures for the present but also uses specific techniques to suspend them and exhibit their mediality by introducing a reflexive dimension.

From Somorrostro to Hollywood, and Back: An Intermedial History of Flamenco Gestures

Throughout the twentieth century, flamenco gestures have been either stigmatised for their social origin or commodified as tourist attractions. Their representation in visual culture, including painting, postcards, cinema, television, and advertising, has widely contributed to separating them from their social origins. Even if this history is different from the generalisation of Tourette syndrome described by Agamben, his reflection on gesture is a relevant approach to the interaction between flamenco and film in the case of Carmen Amaya. Gesture, following the Italian philosopher, is a space in which dance and cinema converge, and such a confluence makes it a privileged place for intermedial encounters. Indeed, a crucial work in this area, Erin Brannigan's (2011) *Dancefilm: Choreography and the Moving Image*, places gestures at the centre of the analysis, whether or not they have a defined social function. For this reason, tracing the genealogy of a specific dancing gesture (whether a ballet *fouette*, a tango step, or a twist move) may contribute to an intermedial history of dance and cinema.

Emerging from Somorrostro, Amaya's dancing travelled all over the world and was recorded in film and television, thus opening intermedial dialogues between flamenco and audiovisual mediums. Her dancing always featured intense hand clapping, fast movements, and a deep, penetrating gaze. The oldest recordings of it date back to 1929, in a short sequence in *Wine Cellars* (*La bodega*, Benito Perojo, 1929), and a few years later she was offered a secondary role as a dancer in *Juan Simon's Daughter* (*La hija de Juan Simón*, 1935), directed by José Luis Saénz de Heredia under the supervision of Luis Buñuel, and a role as the main character in *María de la O* (Francisco Elías, 1936). In the latter she played María, the daughter of a Roma woman and a non-Roma painter, whose mother was killed for betraying blood ties when she was a child, and who was then abandoned by her father. After growing up within her Roma community, as an adult woman she meets her father again. In *María de la O* Amaya performed two solo dances, which balanced a fictional story with techniques to highlight her movements within the scene. For example, in the first dance the long shots are intercut with closer shots/reverse-shots of Amaya and the newcomer, who happens to be her father, in order to emphasise their meeting and to signify a turning point in the narrative; in the second dance, her body often appears in a low-angle shot against a gridded floor, which highlights the circularity and sensuality of her gestures and isolates her from the surrounding public, turning the number into something more abstract (Figure 11.1).[1]

According to Eva Woods Peiró (2012: 26–27), Amaya's film career in 1930s Spain failed to develop because she left the country to tour Latin America soon after *María de la O*, but also for racial reasons. At that time, the Romani were absent from the Spanish star system, which was composed of white singers and dancers who performed an assimilated, commodified version of Roma; these artists, popularly known as *folklóricas*, were what Woods Peiró has identified as "white gypsies," borrowing the term from the film *La gitana blanca* (Ricardo de Baños, 1919). In this way, the successful careers of non-Roma artists Raquel Meller and Imperio Argentina overshadowed the skills of real Roma performers such as Amaya. While her film career in Spain was thus thwarted, she started a successful international trajectory which brought her opportunities in the film industry, and over the years she appeared in features

Figure 11.1 Carmen Amaya dancing on a gridded floor in *María de la O* (Francisco Elías, 1936).

in Cuba, the United States, Mexico, France, and Argentina.[2] However, in most of these cases her contribution was limited to secondary musical numbers which merely complemented the main storyline, even if they were considered relevant for the success of the films and were used in promotional posters. Being independent from the plot, they created an intermedial interruption which brought to the fore her dancing gestures, such as the *zapateado*, often highlighted by camera framing and editing.

After this modest career in cinema, which could not compare to her fame as a live performer, Amaya's most important role came at the end of her life, in the Spanish film *Los Tarantos* (Francisco Rovira Beleta, 1963). Based on an original play by Alfredo Mañas, it adapted the story of Romeo and Juliet to the universe of rival Roma families in Barcelona, aiming to describe life in the already vanished Somorrostro and its musical traditions (Benpar 2000: 106). Though indebted to Neorealism, Rovira Beleta's portrait of the city was stylised by the garish quality of Eastmancolor and the conventions of the musical genre (Gubern 1997: 542). An example of the latter is the night scenes in La Rambla in which Antonio Gades dances between water hoses spraying the street from both sides. Dancing is pervasive throughout the film: Roma children and adults dance at special events, such as a wedding and Christmas, and also in their daily activities.

In *Los Tarantos* Amaya starred as Angustias, the mother of the protagonist, a poor boy who is tragically in love with the daughter of the rival family. She performs three solo dances, always together with the Roma community rather than as an exotic artist on the stage, as in most of her film career. The first of these dance numbers, taking place in Somorrostro, is the most significant. Angustias has just met Juana (Sara Lezana), her future daughter-in-law, and reconciles with her "when she sees her dancing beautiful *bulerías*, in which she recognises their shared identity" (Gubern 1997: 541).[3] Encouraged by others, Angustias begins singing and dancing *bulerías* as well, exhibiting her explosive clapping, stomping, rolling around, and even tapping on a table with her fingers (Figures 11.2 and 11.3). Looking at this sequence carefully, it is possible to locate a tension between the supposed improvisation and careful cinematic staging. A table is initially placed in the scene as a functional object to sustain some drinks and glasses, but as soon as Angustias gets close to it, the others remove these objects to give her enough space to perform on the table's wooden surface, which seems to be an action planned beforehand.

In "Tierra y conmoción o el arte de la grieta (Dos fragmentos)" (Earth and Shock, or the Art of the Breach [Two Excerpts]),[4] Georges Didi-Huberman (2017: 196) analyses this musical number by focusing on Amaya's *zapateado* and stresses its mystical and atavistic connotations, arguing that "the ground, fought to death, seems to exhale its last sighs, materialized and visible in the dust which is raised."[5] Highlighting this connection to the earth, he establishes a dichotomy to conceptualise *cante jondo* (a style of flamenco singing from Andalusia); it can be understood either as a landscape (*paisaje*), rooted in its unmovable, pure origins, or as a journey (*viaje*), in constant nomadic movement. He argues for the second option, concluding that, if *cante jondo* is earth, it is because of its dynamism, its impurity, and its resistance to essentialism.

Such a connection between gesture and place is reminiscent of Jean-Louis Comolli's (1994) reflections on the documentary approach to the cityscape. Comolli wonders if filmmakers should invert the classic formula of filming a body in scenery by instead finding scenery in a body. That is because, he says, people embody the contradictions, tensions, and idiosyncrasies of their environment in their gestures. He cites as an example the gesture of a lookout scrutinising the horizon in the port of Marseille, which synthesises the identity of the city: "[S]omething essential about Marseille (the port, the watch, the commerce, the horizon, the effigy of the lookout) is inscribed in this

Figures 11.2 and 11.3 Carmen Amaya singing *bulerías* and tapping on a table with her fingers in *Los Tarantos* (Francisco Rovira Beleta, 1963).

gesture. . . . There is a continuity from the gesture to the city, from the body to the port. There is the symbolisation of a collective history in an individual gesture" (42).[6]

Similarly, Amaya's *zapateado* in *Los Tarantos* condenses the relationship between Roma communities and the city of Barcelona. The dust that is raised evokes the sand of Somorrostro beach, which, according to legend, was traversed by Amaya daily and strengthened the legs of the future dancer. It therefore makes visible a life of marginalisation, misery, and resilience at the origin of her artistic creation. As Comolli (1994) would put it, a scenery (Barcelona) is filmed in a body (Amaya's) that symbolises a collective history. At the same time, she is performing a dancing style which was acclaimed worldwide, and the footage is therefore charged with the intermedial memory of her previous performances. Amaya's *zapateado*, which had toured the world on a nomadic journey (*viaje*), came back to its original landscape (*paisaje*).

In addition, her dancing has a spectral quality, because some days after the commercial release of Rovira Beleta's film in 1963 she died from renal failure and was never able to see it. The film went on to gain critical acclaim and a nomination for the Oscar for Best Foreign Picture. However, Amaya's *viaje* and *paisaje* were passed on to other bodies. Eva Vila's purpose in *Bajarí* was to retrieve these gestures in the present.

Bringing Gestures Back: The *Bajarí* Project

In 2011, Vila decided to explore the legacy of Carmen Amaya in Barcelona, a city in which she had not been given the honours she deserved. Working together with flamenco connoisseur Cándido Álvarez, she soon discovered that Karime Amaya, Carmen's great-niece and a flamenco dancer herself, had just moved to Barcelona from her birthplace in Mexico and was performing in the Palacio del Flamenco *tablao*. Encouraged by this coincidence, Vila and Álvarez organised *Bajarí*, a live event which brought together local artists of flamenco and rumba, the two main genres of Roma music in Barcelona, to perform with Karime and her mother, Mercedes "Winny" Amaya, also a dancer. "Bajarí" means "Barcelona" in *caló*, the language of the Spanish Roma, and the purpose of the show was to pay tribute to Carmen Amaya with bands from her hometown and members of her family. Vila and her crew filmed the rehearsals and the show, which took place on September that year for the city's annual festival La Mercè, and also recorded Mercedes and Karime talking about their relationship with Carmen, an international idol whom neither of them had personally known. At the same time, thanks to Cándido Álvarez, Vila was given access to the Roma communities in Sant Roc, a working-class neighbourhood in the Barcelona metropolitan area, on the left flank of the Besòs River. There she met Juanito, a skilled five-year-old dancer and the nephew of El Coco, a flamenco singer who was rehearsing with Karime for the *Bajarí* show.

The intertwining of Karime's and Juanito's stories became the backbone of Vila's documentary *Bajarí* (2013). The project was developed in partnership across a number of different film production companies and the Universitat Pompeu Fabra's Master's Programme in Creative Documentary, which since

1998 has produced a wide range of works blending fiction and documentary narrative techniques, combining a focus on social inequalities with a reflection on artistic processes. From its inception, *Bajarí* was to be a work devoted to an unknown, marginal Barcelona, but also an intermedial project that delved into the interplay between dance performances and documentary filmmaking. In addition, its screenings were complemented by live performances and other events. Screenings at the International Documentary Film Festival Amsterdam in November 2012 and in DocsBarcelona in May 2013 were accompanied by live flamenco performances by Karime Amaya, and in 2013 the Barcelona City Council commissioned Vila to write a book, *Bajarí: Històries de la Barcelona gitana*, about the long-marginalised Roma families in the city, featuring photographs by Joan Tomás. Moving between dance, cinema, writing, and photography, Eva and her team explored the past and the present of Roma communities in a city where they have historically been, and continue to be, marginalised, despite their major contribution to its cultural development.

In this project Amaya's dancing gestures take centre stage. In the prologue of the *Bajarí* book, Vila (2013: 8) writes, "The city becomes new through the gestures of her dancing, the sounds of her music, the lyrics that describe a world. Gesture through the city, or the city through gesture."[7] These words resonate with Comolli's (1994) linking of gesture and city and with Didi-Huberman's (2017) distinction between "landscape" and "journey": the gesture in *Bajarí* embodies anthropological, rooted meanings, but it is also circulation. For Vila, her documentary is, above all, a piece about transmission: the main goal was to emphasise the ways in which flamenco is passed from one generation to another, rather than to show its formal wonders.[8] Transmission is in *Bajarí* a way of connecting tradition and modernity, past and present, mythology and reality.[9]

In this process, gesture is transmitted, but at the same time it is the medium of transmission. As stated above, according to Agamben ([1992] 2000) both cinema and dance allow for the isolation of gesture, regardless of its end, through which gesture itself becomes a self-reflexive medium. Along the same lines, theorists of intermediality, such as Joachim Paech, have stressed that self-reflexivity is a condition for the perception of intermedial phenomena (cf. Pethő 2011: 39), which bring mediality to the fore and create critical distance. *Bajarí* explores different self-reflexive techniques to isolate gesture, in both dance and cinema, and in doing so it highlights its mediality and ability to move between these mediums. The next sections will address the ways in which these techniques are used in Juanito's and Karime's stories, as well as their relationship with the legacy of Carmen Amaya.

Juanito and the Spirit of Somorrostro

During the shooting of *Bajarí*, Vila heard that an open-air screening of Rovira Beleta's *Los Tarantos* was taking place in Sant Roc and she decided to film it. In the resulting footage, which became the opening sequence of her documentary, Juanito and other members of the local Roma community are shown watching the movie from fifty years before and commenting on the real characters who appear on the screen. Sitting in the audience with his father and grandmother, who explain who the characters are, Juanito watches the film with fascination (Figures 11.4 and 11.5) and becomes irritated by a young girl who stands up and disturbs his experience. When Carmen Amaya starts performing the *zapateado*, Juanito and his father compare it to a submachine gun, and the boy starts clapping and cheering her on, shouting "Olé!" He imitates Carmen's gestures but is unable to keep up with her speed: "I can't make that!" he moans. At the end of the performance, he applauds and looks to the camera, raising his hands as if celebrating a victory.

In this sequence the mirroring effect between Carmen and the young boy via shot/reverse-shot montage brings to the fore the mediality of cinema. Juanito's imitation of Carmen makes him embody the film experience, and his movements establish a physical, sensual relationship with the screen. Flamenco practice, especially clapping, flows from Carmen on the screen to Juanito in the audience, and dance and gesture provide an intermedial passage that connects different people and different times.[10] His irritation with the girl hampering his vision highlights his visceral relation with the footage. Here, the medial and sensual connection is performed through dancing; that is, it is rendered possible intermedially.

The sequence is inspired by a famous scene from *The Spirit of the Beehive* (*El espíritu de la colmena*, Víctor Erice, 1973), in which six-year-old Ana (Ana Torrent) attends a screening of James Whale's *Frankenstein* (1931) in her village in the aftermath of the Spanish Civil War. Discovering the monster in the projected images, Ana becomes interested in the mysteries and contradictions of adult life, which she will explore throughout the film, both within her family and in her encounter with a fugitive Republican soldier. The spirit which is discovered on the screen is conjured up by Ana, then becomes the object of some games between her and her sister, and soon materialises in the figure of the soldier, with whom Ana starts a friendship (Pena 2004: 99).

In *Bajarí*, Juanito undergoes a similar process, in this case discovering flamenco under the guidance of his uncle El Coco, and attending shows in which the latter performs: first, a gig for tourists in the El Cordobés *tablao*, where his attentive gaze contrasts with quick shots of the visitors; and at the end of the

Flamenco on Screen 177

Figures 11.4 and 11.5 Juanito watching *Los Tarantos* and imitating Carmen Amaya's gestures in *Bajarí* (Eva Vila, 2013).

film, when, excited, he claps during Mercedes Amaya's dancing at Barcelona's annual festival La Mercè. While in *The Spirit of the Beehive* the spirit on the screen is embodied in another character (the Republican soldier), in *Bajarí* Juanito decides to imitate Carmen's gestures and incarnates the spirit himself.

Towards the end of the film, this process is made visually explicit and acquires a cosmic dimension. Following Mercedes's visit to the Carmen Amaya Fountain in the Barceloneta, with the five limestone cherubs playing and dancing, the film cuts to Juanito dancing to the song "Caramelos" in the public fountain of the town square of Sant Adrià del Besòs. While bathing there was not an extraordinary event for the boy, bringing the two images together provides an aquatic link: the water from Carmen Amaya's fountain seems to be showering Juanito, transmitting her energy to him, turning him into a new dancing cherub. The image is reminiscent of Antonio Gades's night dancing with hoses in *Los Tarantos*, making this baptism of dance movements also an evocation of former flamenco stars and flamenco films. It is a transformation for the future which also brings back images from the past.

Isolated Feet, Multiplied Gestures, and Compartmentalised Clapping

After the initial open-air screening of *Los Tarantos*, no other archival footage of Carmen Amaya is used in *Bajarí*. She is seen in photographs and evoked in dialogues, as happens when Karime, her great-niece coming from Mexico to perform at the homage event, explains that as a teenager she felt intimidated when practising in a large room filled with Carmen's photos that seemed to be judging her ability. However, footage featuring the deceased idol is absent throughout the film. In fact, some scenes in *Bajarí* have a ghostly quality: the sequence of Karime's first meeting with flamenco musicians in the rehearsal studio is preceded by some shots of this same studio, first showing Karime practising alone and then some empty spaces with a few items of furniture but no human presence.

Throughout the film, the invisible ghost of Carmen Amaya will gradually gain shape, not through moving images or photographs but in the gestures of Juanito, Karime, and Mercedes. The boy will represent an intuitive, noneducated love for flamenco dancing, almost as the unconscious assimilation of a tradition, while the two women will reproduce on stage the dancing of the deceased idol, even dressing like her. Juanito's spiritual embodiment is produced through spectatorship; gestures, even if they are central to him, are not ostensibly highlighted with aesthetic strategies. This is not the case in other sequences, most notably those showing Karime and Mercedes rehearsing, in which techniques are employed to suspend gesture and underscore its intermedial dimension.

In *Dancefilm: Choreography and the Moving Image*, Erin Brannigan (2011) explores the ways in which dance and theory of dance can enrich film studies. In one of her chapters, she analyses Béla Balázs's and Gilles Deleuze's theorisation of the filmic close-up and argues that approaching mise-en-scène through dancing techniques can challenge the hierarchical dominance of the face in traditional film narrative: "[C]horeographic strategies generally work to develop corporeal modes of articulation or expression that involve any and every part of the body and challenge the vertical ordering resulting from the effects of gravity" (51).

In the films from the 1930s, 1940s, and 1950s featuring Amaya's dancing, close-ups of her feet performing a *zapateado* were used to highlight her skill while keeping her gestures within a global, organic performance. In *Bajarí*, the isolation of gesture is pushed further and radicalised, thus suspending it from the context and revealing, as Agamben would put it, its mediality. Right after the opening sequence with the screening of *Los Tarantos*, Karime is introduced with a close-up of her feet wearing flamenco ankle boots and stamping violently on the stage. The shot is ninety seconds long, and no other images are used to show this initial performance. Its placement right after the excerpt from Rovira Beleta's film suggests a continuity between Carmen's *zapateado* and that of Karime, and therefore an embodiment of the former through their feet.

In fact, *Bajarí* is littered with shots of feet and shoes, both Karime's and Juanito's: their feet are alternately bare and clad, dancing and resting (Figures 11.6 and 11.7). At one point Karime's and Juanito's feet are edited together, thus connecting two characters who in reality are in separate places. Shoes also play a crucial role: El Coco asks Juanito to choose the colour of his dancing boots, and different stages of their crafting are shown, as if those objects had a sacred quality. In *Bajarí*, both the feet and their movements are suspended,

Figure 11.6 Karime's feet on stage in *Bajarí* (Eva Vila, 2013).

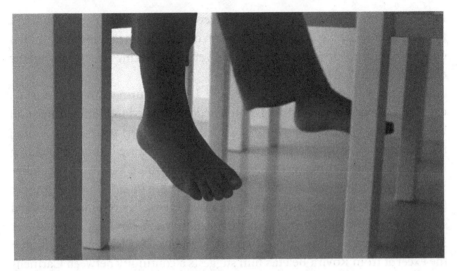

Figure 11.7 Juanito's bare feet in *Bajarí* (Eva Vila, 2013).

isolated, becoming characters with their own story, a story of dancing gestures that circulate across bodies and which, through their own mediality, allow the circulation of a legacy.

The close-up is probably the most intuitive and obvious technique to isolate and suspend gesture, but it is not the only one. In *Bajarí*, gesture is also multiplied and compartmentalised. During the rehearsals, Karime and Mercedes practise in front of two mirrors next to a photo of Carmen dancing, which is reminiscent of the mirroring effect between Carmen and Juanito at the open-air screening, but with a different result. In this case it occurs in long shots of practising, hesitations, and efforts, and equivalent gestures are not only juxtaposed with shot/reverse-shot montage but framed and multiplied within the same shot, as if the film was trying to capture them from different perspectives simultaneously, despite the impossibility of such a total visualisation (Figure 11.8). Sometimes the real body is out of frame, and we see only reflections, which provides a paradoxical effect: while Karime's and Mercedes's bodies become virtualised in the reflective surfaces, the ghost of Carmen seems to incarnate in their movements.

In other cases, percussive techniques of flamenco are reinterpreted through editing. *Zapateado* and clapping are appealing for their intensity and speed; here, they are fused both with other sounds and with cinematic techniques. During the performance at the El Cordobés *tablao*, the film cuts to the hands of the shoemaker crafting Juanito's ankle boots while keeping the *zapateado* in the soundtrack; at this moment, working gestures are put together with

Figure 11.8 Karime practises in front of mirrors and a photo of Carmen Amaya in *Bajarí* (Eva Vila, 2013).

the rhythm of dancing, and the future sound of the boots is heard over their physical conception, bringing together two different stages in the life of these specific objects. Early in the film, Juanito and his brother are playing with the pigeons bred by their father, most of them with their wings colourfully painted. After a dialogue in which the boy expresses his desire to attend dance lessons, we see him holding a pigeon and being followed by a flock of them. When he starts running, the image is slowed down and El Coco's clapping is heard over the wingbeats, introducing the next sequence, in which Juanito is improvising some dance steps in a bar while El Coco claps along. For some seconds, the coincidence between wingbeat and clapping suggests that flamenco rhythms are created by the movement of the birds. In these aural experiments, when flamenco percussion is heard over the crafting of shoes or the flapping of wings, gestures are not visualised in images but evoked in sounds, and editing techniques allow for their compartmentalisation, thus suspending them in a semantic limbo between the original movements and their relocation.

Intermedial and Intergenerational Encounters

Following Jean-François Lyotard's essays "Gesture and Commentary" and "The Unconscious as Mise-en-Scène," Brannigan (2011) establishes a model of gestural exchange in dancefilm. For Brannigan, the body of the performer provides the "originating gesture," which is autonomous but at the same time produces a circuit of exchanges that determines the film's mise-en-scène: "What is specific to the movement of bodies or objects in dancefilm is the way in which they trace trajectories, loitering along gestural routes, *calling attention to themselves*, and resisting any impulse to be digested into existing orders, establishing an *autonomy* to which the entire film must 'bend' or 'accede'" (175). Objects, lighting, camera movements, and editing, as well as the response from the spectator and the analyst, are understood as gestures within Brannigan's encompassing model.

Similarly, gestures in *Bajarí* become the juncture that brings two images together, or a specific image with a specific sound. The dancing gesture that provided an intermedial connection between the screen and Juanito is also the gesture that guides editing techniques, such as the cut from the open-air screening to Karime's feet performing the same *zapateado* as her great-aunt, or the combination of the hand-clapping with the pigeons' wingbeats. The intermedial relationships in *Bajarí* lie between cinema and dance and its transmission through what Brannigan calls "a gestural exchange," and which involves Carmen Amaya, her relatives Mercedes and Karime, and the boy Juanito.

Indeed, techniques used in *Bajarí* such as mirroring, isolation, multiplication, and compartmentalisation could be analysed in relation to Brannigan's (2011) model of gestural exchange. However, while the latter "is based on the autonomy of the gestural articulations in dancefilm—that is, their status beyond the realm of the language of knowledge" (183), in *Bajarí* personal and collective stories are embedded in flamenco gestures, and the intermedial phenomena respond to a logic of intergenerational encounters. Gestures do not have a strict purpose, and, as Agamben would have it, they are means without end; however, their mediality establishes pathways with strong social and historical connotations and makes visible the history of a marginalised community. Intermediality is here fused with intergenerational transmission.

The process of transmission culminates at the end of the film. Karime is seen performing her impersonation of Carmen in the 2011 show. She ends the performance, dressed as a man as Carmen used to do, and showing her back to the public, surrounded by darkness and steam. Then the image fades to a black-and-white photograph of Carmen in *Los Tarantos*, her back with a dark shawl to the camera, before cutting to Juanito dressed in black with his younger brother, teaching him how to dance. In this sequence, we are presented with the consecration of gesture on stage, the freezing of gesture in an image of a deceased person, and the practice of a particular gesture by a child to teach another child. The immobilisation of flamenco gestures on the stage, which sanctifies them, connects with the absence of life suggested by a black-and-white image of a deceased woman, but is then revived in the body of a five-year-old boy. The gesture of dance, then, brings images together, establishes an intermedial connection between them, but shows that to be transmitted it must be destroyed and re-created. The gesture here swings between immobilisation and movement, thus creating a dance between life and death, which is the condition for a successful transmission across images and across generations.

Notes

This chapter is the result of research conducted as part of the AHRC-Fapesp-funded project Towards an Intermedial History of Brazilian Cinema: Exploring Intermediality as a Historiographic Method (short title: IntermIdia). *Bajarí* was discussed in the Sewing Circle study group (University of Reading, 2019), and I am indebted to the comments of the participants in that session. I am also thankful to Eva Vila for sharing with me her memories of *Bajarí* and her passion for Carmen Amaya, and to Alba Daroca (Filmoteca de Catalunya), Marga Carnicé Mur, and Enric Ros, for their help and bibliographic advice.

1. An in-depth analysis of this film can be found in Sanz Díez (2019).
2. According to the filmography compiled by Montse Madridejos and David Pérez Marinero (2013: 282–287), Amaya appeared twenty times in total in films made in Spain and abroad. Not all copies of these films are preserved; some were short films with limited distribution, and others simply reused footage from previous works.
3. "Al verle bailar unas hermosas bulerías, en las que reconoce su identidad común" (my translation).
4. This was originally a keynote speech delivered at the conference La noche española: Flamenco, vanguardia y cultura popular, held at Universidad Internacional de Andalucía (Sevilla), 27 November 2006.
5. "El suelo, atacado a muerte, parece exhalar sus últimos suspiros, materializados y visibles, de hecho, en el polvo que se levanta" (my translation).
6. "Quelque chose d'essentiel à Marseille (le port, la veille, le commerce, l'horizon, l'effigie même de la vigie) s'inscrit dans le geste. . . . Il y a continuité du geste à la ville, du corps au port. Il y a symbolisation d'une histoire collective dans un geste individuel" (my translation).
7. "La ciutat es fa nova a través dels gestos del seu ball, del so de la seva música, de les lletres que descriuen un món. El gest a través de la ciutat, o la ciutat a través del gest." (my translation)
8. Eva Vila, interview with author, Barcelona, 27 November 2020.
9. Transmission is a crucial concept in the teaching philosophy at Universitat Pompeu Fabra's Master's Programme in Creative Documentary, which encourages collaboration between new and experienced filmmakers (cf. Balló 2010).

10. In my 2020 interview with her, Vila pointed out another mirroring effect: in the sequence screened in the open-air cinema, the young dancer (Juana, played by Sara Lezana) has just shown her abilities to the experienced one (Angustias, played by Carmen Amaya). This situation in Rovira Beleta's 1963 film mirrors the fact that in *Bajarí* young Karime is dancing in honour of Carmen.

References

Agamben, Giorgio. (1992) 2000. "Notes on Gesture." In *Means without End: Notes on Politics*. Translated by Vincenzo Binetti and Cesare Casarino, 49–60. London: University of Minnesota Press.
Balló, Jordi. 2010. "Cronología de una transmisión: (El Máster de Documental de la UPF)." In *Realidad y creación en el cine de no-ficción*, edited by Casimiro Torreiro, 105–21. Madrid: Cátedra.
Benpar, Carlos. 2000. *Rovira-Beleta. El cine y el cineasta*. Barcelona: Laertes.
Brannigan, Erin. 2011. *Dancefilm: Choreography and the Moving Image*. New York: Oxford University Press.
Comolli, Jean-Louis. 1994. *La Ville filmée*. Paris: Centre Georges Pompidou.
Didi-Huberman, Georges. 2017. "Tierra y conmoción o el arte de la grieta (Dos fragmentos)." Translated by Pedro G. Romero and Nadine Janssens. *Revista Anthropos* 246 (January): 194–213.
Gubern, Román. 1997. "Los Tarantos." In *Antología crítica del cine español 1906–1995*, edited by Julio Pérez Perucha, 540–41. Madrid: Cátedra and Filmoteca Española.
Madridejos, Montse, and David Pérez Merinero. 2013. *Carmen Amaya*. Barcelona: Edicions Bellaterra.
Moix, Ana María. 2013. "El Marlboro de la Capitana." In *Carmen Amaya 1963: Taranta, agosto, luto, ausencia*, by Ana María Moix, Colita, and Julio Ubiña, 12–32. Barcelona: Libros del Silencio.
Pena, Jaime. 2004. *El espíritu de la colmena*. Barcelona: Ediciones Paidós Ibérica.
Pethő, Ágnes. 2011. *Cinema and Intermediality. The Passion for the In-Between*. Newcastle-Upon-Tyne: Cambridge Scholars.
Sanz Díez, María. 2019. "*María de la O*: Copla y película del 36." *Trama y Fondo: revista de cultura* 47: 93–118.
Vila Purtí, Eva, and Joan Tomás. 2013. *Bajarí: Històries de la Barcelona gitana*. Barcelona: La Fábrica, Ajuntament de Barcelona.
Woods Peiró, Eva. 2012. *White Gypsies: Race and Stardom in Spanish Musical Films*. Minneapolis: University of Minnesota Press.

12
Impurity and Identification
Historicising Chinese Cinema through Opera

Cecília Mello

Throughout its history, the cinema of mainland China has displayed a particular affinity with Chinese opera in its different regional and national varieties. An overview of this intermedial history reveals how Chinese opera intermingled with film in myriad ways. This chapter suggests that an intermedial history of Chinese cinema, framed through the opera lens, blurs the divide between old and new media, socialist and postsocialist arts, theatrical and photographic ontology, foreign and national styles, operatic and realist modes, allowing for a more encompassing appreciation of what are, in effect, necessarily impure and hybrid artistic manifestations. The intermedial approach also encourages a reevaluation of what I deem to be Brecht's misinterpretation of the antinaturalistic performances of Mei Lanfang and the Peking Opera as alienation effects. Instead, I suggest that the intermedial relationship between cinema and opera purposely promotes spectatorial identification at both individual and collective levels.

The proposed approach places an emphasis on the historical and cultural specificities of Chinese cinematic practices, thus deliberately eschewing a Eurocentric perspective in favour of an understanding of Chinese cinema beyond the paradigms of dominant film cultures. I believe that film art is in tune not only with the Western experience of modernity but also with proto- and pre-cinematic forms that contributed to the creation of several local and national cinematic modernities (Nagib and Jerslev 2014), including shadow theatre, literature, painting, architecture, and opera. Ending my approach with an analysis of Chen Kaige's *Farewell My Concubine* (霸王别姬, *Bawang Bie Ji*, 1993), I hope to trace some vectors for a future comprehensive study of Chinese cinema's intermedial history, one that will find in operatic theatre, among other arts, hybrid elements capable of inspiring new, nonteleological, and nonbinary configurations and understandings of history.

Towards an Intermedial Method

Mainland Chinese cinema has been traditionally organised according to different phases or divided into generations of filmmakers, following important historical events that have, time and again, changed the course of the country's trajectory throughout the twentieth century (Tan and Yun 2012). Within these phases or generations, operatic theatre has acquired multiple forms and functions in China's cinematic landscape and has been the subject of political and aesthetic debates. While both the nationalist and the communist regimes called, at different times, for the Sinicisation of film production and favoured cinema's interaction with local and national forms of art, others defended the modernisation of Chinese cinematic language via the enhancement of its medium-specific qualities, which was possible only through cinema's divorce from traditional theatrical forms.

The modernisation anxiety was especially felt during periods normally associated with a realist turn in film production, including the 1930s Shanghai leftist film movement and the output of the fifth and the sixth generations of filmmakers in the 1980s and 1990s. This was in tune with a much wider debate around the modernisation of the Chinese civilization as a whole, spearheaded by the May Fourth Movement of 1919 and with consequences in different spheres of the country's life. In the 1980s, the historical background was Deng Xiaoping's 改革开放 (gaige kaifang, or "reform and opening-up)," and ensuing debates revolving around the specificity of the cinematic language led to a critique of cinema's theatrical roots and to calls for its divorce from theatre as the only possible route towards the modernisation of Chinese cinematic narratives and aesthetics (Zhang and Li 1979; Bai 1979). As Bao Weihong (2012: 379) explains, film language modernisation required a move away from "the confines of theatre" and from "the ideological function of film associated with the tableau-like acting style, static camera framing, overdramatized lighting schemes, and verbose didactic dialogue" in favour of "purity" and "internal principles" of the medium.

Another particularly influential and controversial debate in the 1980s refers to the notion of 影戏 (yingxi, or "shadow play") as proposed by film theorists Zhong Dafeng (1986, 1994a, 1994b) and Chen Xihe (1986). Evoking a 1920s discussion between screenwriters Gu Kenfu and Hou Yao, Zhong and

Chen located an enduring theatrical tradition at the base of Chinese cinema, which they termed "shadow-play ontology" as opposed to the "ontology of the photographic image," as famously proposed by André Bazin (2009). For Zhong and Chen, the ontology of cinema is due to its nature as a form of *xiju* (play-drama) rather than to its photographic base, as theorised by Bazin. For Bazin, as a mechanical reproduction of reality, cinema entertains an ontological relationship with it and is thus endowed with traces of the real, in contrast to other mimetic or representational arts. In its turn, as Victor Fan (2015: 25) explains, the "shadow-play ontology" of Zhong and Chen is symptomatic of a socialist methodology and rejects universality in favour of a historically conditioned notion. These theorists locate the origins of their "shadow-play ontology" in the thought of 1920s critics in Shanghai, the centre of Chinese film production between the 1920s and the 1940s, when China was still under semicolonial rule and cinema was seen exclusively as a form of entertainment. Still, they "aspired to elevate the shadow play theory from a historically conditioned view of cinema ontology to a philosophical system that could potentially compete with Bazinian ontology" (27). However, as Fan argues, this only perpetuates the dichotomy between Western film theory and an East Asian alternative, obscuring the obvious resonances between the two (29). Moreover, as Bao (2012: 378) has shown, in its limited definition and application of what Chinese theatre is, both the modernisation debate and the *yingxi* theory and historiography have contributed more to "mythologizing quintessential 'Chinese' film aesthetics than to addressing the changing dynamics between cinema and theatre in modern China on concrete terms." Therefore, they have little to do with an intermedial understanding of Chinese film history.

A move away from this contradictory historiography came with Berry and Farquhar's (2006) identification of the operatic and realist modes, running diachronically and taking on different forms in Chinese film history. However, this replaces the teleological with a dichotomous approach to film language, which is equally at odds with the border-crossing nature of this intermedial production. While acknowledging the existence of predominant modes in individual films, a focus on intermediality—understood as the interconnections and interferences between different media (Pethő 2020)—allows for a more encompassing, democratic, and suitable approach to the study of cinema, an art form located at the juncture of different media and spectatorial regimes. The intermedial method, tributary to Bazin's defence of cinema as an impure art form (Nagib and Jerslev 2014), prompts the investigation of commingling narrative strategies and aesthetic resources across different art forms, including their cultural determinants.

Chinese Opera and Cinema: Aesthetic and Political Affinities

Broadly speaking, Chinese theatre can be divided into two types, the traditional and long-lived operatic theatre, known as *xiqu* (戏曲), and the imported form with Greek origins, known as *xiju* (西剧). The *xiqu* is a form of dramatic and musical theatre that harks back to Chinese antiquity. Starting as a relatively simple performative art, it gradually incorporated other forms of art such as music playing, singing, dancing, martial arts, acrobatics, and a whole catalogue of stories deriving from Chinese classical literature. It attained maturity during the Song dynasty (960–1279) and developed into a great number of regional variations, with their own specificities regarding dialects, basic melodies, singing style, the use of masks, face paint, musical instruments, and themes. There are more than two hundred regional operatic forms, chief among which is the Peking Opera or *jingju* (京剧), which derived from the Hui Opera (徽剧) from Anhui and developed, from the Qing dynasty onwards (1644–1911), into the most popular and well-known form of Chinese operatic theatre around the world.

In the first decades of the twentieth century, the Peking Opera grew in prestige and continued to assimilate other regional traditions—such as southern Kun opera (昆剧) gestures and singing style—into its repertoire, especially through the work of Mei Lanfang and his collaborator Qi Rushan (Iovene 2010). Mei is considered one of the greatest Chinese opera actors of all time, performing in the female role, *dan* (旦). With the help of Qi he made this art form known in the West through seasons in the United States and the Soviet Union in the 1930s.

At the same time, there were efforts by the Chinese Nationalist Party (the Kuomintang, 国民党), led by Sun Yat-sen, the father of the Chinese Republic, and by Chiang Kai-shek, his successor, to transform, from 1912 to 1949, local traditions such as the Peking Opera into national traditions. As a result, the Chinese opera, which manifested with local peculiarities in different regions of the country, came to be recognised as a national form by adopting the specificities of the Peking Opera, transformed by the cultural and political nationalism of the Kuomintang into an expression of the whole country. Cinema was employed as a tool in this process of dissemination (Berry and Farquhar 2006: 48).

Film first came to China as a foreign technology, but it was soon associated with previous Chinese theatrical traditions, predominantly operatic theatre. It is not by chance that the first film allegedly made in China in 1905, *Conquering the Jun Mountain* (定军山, *Ding Junshan*, Ren Jingfeng), brought to the screen a performance by the most famous Peking Opera star of the time, Tan Xinpei, sponsored by the Empress Dowager Cixi.[1] In the film, which is said to have travelled around China and attracted great popularity, Tan plays the role of General Huang Zhong from the opera based on the cycles 70 and 71 of the *Romance of the Three Kingdoms* (三国演义, *Sanguo Yanyi*). *Conquering the Jun Mountain* is the first example of how cinema, an imported art/technology at the time, tried to become more Chinese by incorporating opera. At the same time, it set the trend for filming opera scenes as a guarantor of success for cinema in China, where a vast array of classical stories that came from the oral tradition, moved to literature and then to opera, could now nourish the new art form and turn it into a more popular and familiar medium (Berry and Farquhar 2006: 48). This amalgam allowed at the same time for the dissemination of operatic pieces beyond their regional origins and their linguistic barriers. Cinema thus emerged as a lingua franca and, from then on, the "opera film" became a well-established genre in the Chinese cinematic landscape, even if it would fall in and out of favour with audiences and the government over the decades.[2]

Following *Conquering the Jun Mountain*, three landmark films made in the first four decades of production in China, before the Communist Revolution of 1949, attest to the centrality of this intermedial relationship. They are *Heavenly Maidens Spread Flowers* (天女散花, *Tian Nü San Hua*, 1920), directed by and starring Mei Lanfang; *Sing-Song Girl Red Peony* (歌女红牡丹, *Ge Nü Hong Mudan*, Zhang Shichuan, 1931), China's first sound film; and *Remorse at Death* (生死恨, *Sheng Si Hen*, 1948), China's first colour film, directed by Fei Mu and also starring Mei Lanfang (Figure 12.1). The first of these is a filmed performance by Mei that attests to the changes the Peking Opera had been going through in the first decades of the twentieth century, including the introduction of dance numbers. The 1919 performance, followed by the 1920 film and the reproduction and distribution of still photographs of Mei, launched his career into national and international stardom (see Yeh 2016: 29).

Beyond the "opera film" genre, the presence of opera is also evident in several films across mainland Chinese cinema history, including realist tales and melodramas. In the 1930s, for instance, Shanghai leftist cinema, epitomised by Sun Yu's oeuvre, developed a remarkable form of realism that, though rejecting what was seen as a "feudal" tradition, also incorporated elements of operatic theatre such as song-and-dance numbers and the representation of popular types, aimed at a form of collective identification (Pang 2002: 221).

Things changed considerably after the 1949 Communist Revolution, which established the People's Republic of China, but opera persisted as an expression of a national aesthetic concept. Genre films such as *Wild Boar Forest* (野猪林, *Ye Zhu Lin*, 1962), an opera adaptation directed by Cui Wei and Chen

Figure 12.1 A poster for China's first colour film, *Remorse at Death* (Fei Mu, 1948), starring Mei Lanfang.

Huai'ai (Chen Kaige's father), continued to be made in the first years of the PRC but were later abandoned in favour of social realist films and historical melodramas, including *Two Stage Sisters* (舞台姐妹, *Wutai Jiemei*), directed by Xie Jin in 1964, a landmark in Chinese film history set in and around the world of opera.

It should be noted that Mao Zedong had always nurtured an interest in China's traditional arts and cultures. Based in Yan'an during the years of the war with Japan, he discussed in pronouncements the importance of creating a "cultural army" in China's battle against foreign and domestic enemies (Marchetti 1997: 66). The Yan'an Literature and Art Forum, which took place in May 1942, determined that all art should reflect the life of the working class and regard it as its target audience, in order to serve the advancement of socialism. Mao's (1971: 259) speech on the occasion emphasised the need to develop a new revolutionary art form that served the masses above all else, but which could start from traditional forms found in literature, theatre, opera, and other Chinese art. These guidelines became the basis for the Maoist "revolutionary romanticism," responsible for the persistence of Chinese opera's influence in the first seventeen years of the PRC (1949–1965). Thus, after 1949 the relationship between opera and cinema took on revolutionary overtones, revealing the desire to make both Marxism and proletarian cinema more Chinese, so they could become the voice of the whole country.

Later, during the Cultural Revolution (1966–1976), the phenomenon of the Peking Model Operas (京剧样板戏, *jingju yangbanxi*) gave rise to a whole new intermedial phenomenon. Following the national turmoil in the early years of the Cultural Revolution, Chinese film production, which had until then been a fundamental part of the communist propaganda effort, was brought to a halt. After 1971, under a rigid censorship imposed by the Gang of Four,[3] some films began to be produced from what was known as the "model for revolutionary operas," originally eight operatic, dance, or symphonic works established as models available for adaptation in different media. This followed Maoist directives that propagated the importance of the "model" since the Great Leap Forward period, in the arts, agriculture, and other spheres. During this period, Peking Opera itself came under attack and was banned for ten years. Jiang Qing, Mao's wife, who had been a film actress in the 1930s, led the creation of the revolutionary model theatrical works and their filmed versions, including the opera *Taking Tiger Mountain by Strategy* (智取威虎山, *Zhi Qu Weihu Shan*, Xie Tieli, 1970) and the ballet *Red Detachment of Women* (红色娘子军, *Hongse Niangzijun*, Pan Wenzhan and Fu Jie, 1971). The filmed versions of the "eight model works," promoted and supervised by Jiang, became effective propaganda pieces and found a very large and popular audience throughout the country. Its formula aimed to modernise the Peking Opera through the inclusion of new topics, gender equality, and military values, as well as incorporating Western elements, such as orchestras and ballet, put at the service of the Revolution and a new and truly proletarian art in form and content. These operas and ballets no longer had emperors, kings, generals, chancellors, princesses, or concubines; instead they presented heroic workers, peasants, and soldiers, as Mao had long demanded and as Jiang finally brought to fruition.

After the Cultural Revolution, the "opera film" genre might have lost its strength, but operatic traditions subsisted in films of the fifth and sixth generations, including the auteurist work of such maverick filmmakers as Chen Kaige and Jia Zhangke, which continued to incorporate operatic modes in their narrative and style. The films of the fifth and sixth generations were responsible for the renewal of Chinese cinema and its international recognition, largely thanks to their realistic aesthetics. However, they also incorporated impurity as a means to establish a dialogue with an idea of Chinese tradition and identity (Mello 2019), which is evident in films from Chen Kaige's historical melodrama *Farewell My Concubine* to Jia Zhangke's masterpiece *A Touch of Sin* (天注定, *Tian Zhuding*, 2013). They are the latest chapter in a long history of intermedial phenomena embedded in Chinese arts, combining oral tradition, literature, painting, theatrical opera, shadow theatre, and cinema over millennia, through repeated adaptations of canonic narratives.

Attractions and Identification

The relationship between Chinese cinema and opera, in both genre and realist films, often attests to the persistence of the principle of "attractions" within narrative films, identified by Tom Gunning (1990) as the predominant mode during the first decade of cinema production. The principle of attractions, contrary to the narrative principle, produces an exhibitionist cinema, based on images that solicit the attention of the spectator and incite their curiosity. Despite its decisive narrative inclination, cinema never completely abandoned its attraction modes, and moments of brief narrative suspension are frequent in certain cinematic genres such as musicals and action films.

The exhibitionist mode, which often includes direct address, or the actor's gaze to the camera, is redolent of vaudeville, the circus, and the music hall, which constituted the cradle of cinema in the late nineteenth century. The origins of Brecht's notion of epic theatre can also be traced back to the music hall and is usually associated with the "breaking" of the presumed fourth wall separating the actors on stage from the audience. As is well known, Brecht's epic theatre was based on the encouragement of active spectatorship, the rejection of voyeurism, and the production of "alienation effects" (*Verfremdungseffekte*). Brecht (2015: 65) proposed some techniques to achieve these goals, such as the use of sketches resulting in narrative interruptions and the separation between the real person of the actor and the fictional character in order to prevent spectatorial empathy and psychological identification with them. Brechtian propositions and practices were very influential on the new politicised cinemas that emerged around the world in the late 1950s, liberating them from the conventions and imperatives of the classical narrative cinema (Stam 2000).

Brecht found in East Asia a source of influence on his 1930s revolutionary propositions. He used the term *Verfremdungseffekt* for the first time circa 1936 in an essay entitled "*Verfremdung* in Chinese Acting" ("Verfremdungseffekte in der chinesischen Schauspielkunst") (Brecht 2015). In this foundational essay, Brecht describes a type of performance that is not based on spectatorial identification and proposes that his epic theatre should embrace a similarly distanced mode. His inspiration came from a Chinese opera performed by Mei Lanfang, which he had the opportunity to attend in Moscow in the spring of 1935, accompanied by Meyerhold, Stanislavsky, Eisenstein,[4] and other artistic personalities of the time.

If Chinese opera informed Brecht's notion of alienation effects, its forms and functions within Chinese cinema history do not translate into reflexivity. The lingering effect of operatic traditions in Chinese cinema suggests that these works have been promoting, instead of an alienation effect, a heightened form of spectatorial identification, thus bringing into question, within the Chinese context, the Brechtian proposition that equates the artifice of this art form with reflexivity. If Brecht saw in Mei's performances a form of distanciation which could be employed by progressive art as a political tool, I argue that in China opera performances produced a privileged form of identification, binding together actor, character, and the audience on a psychological, corporeal, and collective level.

Writing on the relationship between Brecht's concept of the alienation effect and Chinese opera, Min Tian (2008: 40) has shown how his reading of Mei's performance in 1935 was informed by his previous experiments with epic theatre and the breaking down of the fourth wall, a technique he probably borrowed from medieval and Elizabethan theatres (Marlowe and Shakespeare), as well as the music hall. In his fascinating piece, Min also develops a detailed reading of Brecht's concept of the alienation effect and demonstrates how it bears little or no affiliation with the Chinese opera. Rather, the absence of a fourth wall, the actor's performance based on self-observation and self-alienation, and the style of quotation in the Chinese opera all work towards the creation of a poetic atmosphere that involves the spectator in a synthesis of poetry, singing, and dancing (46–56).[5]

As previously mentioned, opera was absorbed by mainland Chinese cinema in order to make it more understandable, more popular, more ideological, and more Chinese, often all at the same time. This is corroborated by the positive response from the audience that, as Berry and Farquhar

(2006: 49) point out, often enjoyed this interaction to the point of knowing by heart the operatic numbers and singing along during the performances and screenings, especially during the Cultural Revolution. Therefore, opera, despite its antinaturalistic nature, entered Chinese cinema not as distancing effect but as an element of identification. It is perhaps the case that the terms "distancing effect" and "identification," anchored as they are within Western critical thinking, should be rethought in the face of the artistic and cultural specificities embedded in the history of Chinese cinema.[6]

The Impurity of *Farewell My Concubine*

I will now offer a brief reading of an eloquent example of the interbreeding of film and opera in China, *Farewell My Concubine*, with a focus on its mixed nature, following Teri Silvio's (2002: 179) understanding of the film as a "border-crossing," "meta-opera film." This stands in opposition to a number of readings that have insisted on Chen's film as promoting an Orientalist aesthetics and an idea of "Chineseness" fit for the outsider's gaze (see, for instance, Chiang 2011). In fact, rather than denying these views, I suspect that the issue of Chinese or Western traditions and their cultural representations is not so relevant to a work that should be defined as inherently impure.

Farewell My Concubine belongs to the second phase of the fifth-generation film production in mainland China and has been the subject of numerous analyses and debates after winning the Palme d'Or at Cannes in 1993.[7] The film spans five decades, focusing on the story of Douzi and Shitou, who later become Peking opera stars and take on the stage names Cheng Dieyi and Duan Xiaolou. Its intricate narrative reveals that Dieyi—who is trained to become a *dan,* the female role in Peking Opera—nurtures a lifelong love for his childhood friend Xiaolou, who himself had been trained to play the Jing, a face-painted male lead. The film thus happens in the interstices of life and art, history and imagination, appearance and truth, in what could be seen as an allegorical reflection on cinema itself.

The film nurtures an intermedial relationship with both the traditional Peking Opera and the Cultural Revolution "model operas." While inevitably antithetical, both the "model operas" and *Farewell* are exemplary of periods of change in the Chinese cinematic landscape, purportedly breaking with old ideas and traditions. "Model operas" reflected the strident and delusional reaction against a perceived capitalist threat that in part precipitated the Cultural Revolution, whereas *Farewell* emerged in opposition to Maoist cinema by the hands of the filmmaker who inaugurated the fifth generation in 1984 with *Yellow Earth* (黄土地, *Huang Tudi*). Yet both share the Peking Opera lineage, which is so adaptable that it can serve the rupture with the past whilst paradoxically maintaining tradition.

The Peking Opera *Farewell My Concubine*, which lends the film its title, constitutes the main characters' stage performance—shown in different occasions along their turbulent trajectories—and inspires to a certain extent the events portrayed. It is significant that the character of the concubine was imortalised by Mei Lanfang, who also choreographed the sword dance. The innovative inclusion of dance numbers in Peking Opera performances in the 1910s and 1920s, led by Mei, was in part a response to the growth of cinema and the nascent "opera film" genre. Dance solos enriched filmed performances and were thought of as cinematic spectacles, demonstrating the intermedial dialogue between the two arts in his time. The sword dance was replicated in contemporaneous opera and film performances and finds a place again in Chen's film (see Silvio 2002: 187–188).

The film's first part focuses on the harsh training to which young children are submitted in a Peking Opera school in order to become actors, and includes two sequences that I believe to be revealing of how identification works within this tradition. In the first, Douzi and his opera schoolmate Laizi run away from the school one day and sneak into an opera theatre to watch a stage performance of *Farewell My Concubine*. The editing of this sequence interweaves the roaring audience and the stage performance, and enhances the organic connection between the two. At first, Laizi begins to cry when he sees his master's favourite pupil mesmerise the audience with his acting. "Think of all the beatings he suffered," he says. But if Laizi cries because of all the toil and abuse that he has gone through in school, a close-up of Douzi further on reveals his awe at the opera's poetic atmosphere, enhanced by the smoke and the golden light that softens his face, soon to be crossed by a single tear, as if shaping his future (Figure 12.2).

The second sequence in question is perhaps the film's most controversial and debated and seals Douzi's traumatic transformation into the opera star Cheng Dieyi. Having been assigned by his master to train in the *dan* role (the female role perfected by Mei), the boy Douzi suffers repeated beatings after he fails time and again to recite a line from the opera *A Nun Dreams of the Outside World* (*Si Fan*): "I am by nature a girl, not a boy." Instead he says, "I am by nature a boy, not a girl," but is forced into a complete identification with his new assigned role after Shitou pushes a hot pipe into his mouth, shouting "I'll teach you how!" He finally recites the correct verse, seen at first in close-up,

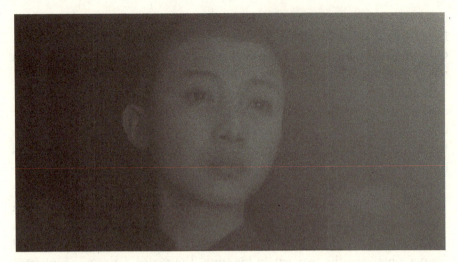

Figure 12.2 Douzi cries during the opera performance in *Farewell My Concubine* (Chen Kaige, 1993).

Figure 12.3 "I am by nature a girl": Douzi's painful transformation into a *dan* in *Farewell My Concubine* (Chen Kaige, 1993).

with tears rolling down his face and blood running from his mouth (Figure 12.3). He is now, according to tradition—and in opposition to what Brecht saw as a distanciation effect—completely converted into the opera character, in tune with the Chinese style of acting (see Min 2008: 51), and is destined to live his life in complete emotional and spiritual identification with it.

One last point I wish to make regarding *Farewell* relates to the inclusion of a final sequence which did not exist in the novel by Lilian Lee, on which it was based, concerning the events of the first years of the Cultural Revolution. This was done at Chen Kaige's request and, while it reveals his desire to come to terms with his own traumas related to this period, it also exists in tandem with the film's interbreeding with opera. In one poignant scene in which revolutionary youngsters discuss the new directions in the arts with the two Peking Opera stars, both rupture and continuity are at stake. For, as an intermedial approach to the history of Chinese cinema reveals, the "model operas," in all their strangeness and peculiarity, derive from the centuries-old popularity of Chinese operatic theatre, in its various forms and styles. The fact that Jiang Qing and the Cultural Revolution leaders chose performing arts for their model works, insisting on calling them Peking model operas, shows how opera could have seemed more suitable to populist reforms than other artistic expressions. Moreover, given their impure character, operas are more prone to "model presentation," easily lending themselves to different adaptations and versions.

Therefore, despite breaking with the past, tradition still persists in "model operas." In *Farewell My Concubine*, the tension between disappearance and persistence, new and old, revolution and tradition is constantly alluded to, especially in the recurring sequences where characters burn items such as clothes, opera props such as swords and flags, and papers (Figure 12.4). From the coat worn by the young Douzi in the beginning of the film, which he burns

Figure 12.4 Burning the opera wardrobe in *Farewell My Concubine*.

at the opera school to erase his past as the son of a prostitute, to the opera wardrobe and other memorabilia destroyed during the Cultural Revolution, the film seems to suggest, rather contradictorily, not the annihilation of the past but its very insistence in remaining.[8] Moreover, *Farewell My Concubine*'s recurring motifs, such as suicide, prostitution, political movements and revolutions, and most of all opera itself, which despite all the political turmoil never completely vanishes, point towards circular rather than linear movements. Thus the film caters to an intermedial history of Chinese cinema, which complicates teleological categories and challenges the specificity of different media, proposing instead a pluralistic historicisation of an impure art form.

Notes

1. The accuracy of this information (regarding the first film made in China) has been disputed in recent scholarship (see, for instance, Huang 2012; Rojas 2013), but, for the purposes of this argument, it still matters that the real or invented film, which survives only in a still photograph of Tan Xinpei, is concerned with an operatic performance.
2. The *wuxia* (武侠) genre can also be deemed a tributary to the opera film genre. Most notably, the highly stylised choreographic style of maverick filmmaker King Hu's action sequences is an inheritor of operatic theatre and, more specifically, the Peking Opera.
3. The Gang of Four (四人帮, *si ren bang*) was a political group composed of Jiang Qing, Zhang Chunqiao, Yao Wenyuan, and Wang Hongwen. All of them had been relatively obscure before 1966 but rose to prominence during the Cultural Revolution and came to occupy high positions in the Chinese government. After Mao's death in 1976, they lost their power and were imprisoned, and later tried and convicted for the events of the period.
4. Eisenstein, whose notion of attraction derives from his work with the Moscow Proletkult, a revolutionary theatre in the early years of the Soviet Revolution, also rejected the naturalist methods of Stanislavsky and embraced the biomechanical approach of Vsevolod Meyerhold. The desire to break with the anti-illusionist project proposed by Brecht in the 1930s, therefore, finds in Eisenstein and Meyerhold important predecessors. In addition to the biomechanics of Meyerhold, Japanese language and artistic traditions, notably the Kabuki theatre, had a great influence on Eisenstein's development of his taxonomy of montage, culminating in his notion of dialectical montage. Later on, he saw the Mei Lanfang performance in Moscow in 1935 and wrote "To the Magician of the Pear Orchard" (Eisenstein 2010: 56–67), an ode to the Chinese method of acting.
5. Gina Marchetti (1997: 72) has offered a reading of Xie Jin's masterpiece *Two Stage Sisters* (1964) from the point of view of its roots in Chinese theatre, Hollywood melodrama, and socialist realism, an aesthetic combination that, revolutionary politics is added, "places it very close to Brecht's notion of epic theatre." She then locates principles of distanciation in the film and evokes Brecht's connection with Mei Lanfang, but fails to question what I believe to be his misapprehension of Mei's art form. This is not to say that Xie Jin's film should be

seen as an expression of Chineseness—quite the contrary, its impurity and hybridity are the product of diverse cinematic experiences, including Soviet cinema, Hollywood cinema, and Chinese opera. Yet to evoke Brecht's epic theatre risks obscuring the importance of identification promoted by the use of opera in film.
6. Lúcia Nagib's (1995, 2011) definitive work on Nagisa Oshima has already demonstrated how the notion of distanciation as proposed by Brecht and his epic theatre, however revolutionary, was still based on established Western philosophical traditions, such as the Christian-inflected mind-body dualism, going back to Kantian metaphysics (2011: 200). Nagib explores what she calls the "eroticized apparatus" in Nagisa Oshima's cinema, demonstrating that the marks of enunciation in his films, seen as responsible for the suspension of "cinematic illusionism" and "spectatorial identification," worked in fact as an antidote to the reason-emotion/mind-body dichotomies, combining alienation with identification/emotion.
7. The film was produced by Taiwanese *wuxia* actress Hsu Feng, then based in Hong Kong and working as a film producer. It was in fact Hsu who initiated the project by approaching Chen Kaige to adapt the eponymous 1985 novel by Hong Kong writer Lilian Lee, and one could speculate on whether it was due to her *wuxia* credentials that she felt attracted to adapting a novel set in the world of the Peking Opera, *wuxia* being a genre with very strong links to Chinese cinema's operatic traditions.
8. In her brilliant reading of the film as "a reevaluation of the disavowed theatricality of the Cultural Revolution," Teri Silvio (2002: 179) shows how *Farewell* draws parallels between the violence of Master Guan's academy and that of the Cultural Revolution, and how, in its ambivalence, it mourns the (unnatural) ways of being a person generated by this violence (183).

References

Bai Jingsheng. 1979. "丢掉戏剧的拐杖" (Diudiao xiju de guaizhang/Throw Away the Crutches of Drama). In 电影艺术参考资料电影艺术研究资料 *Dianying yishu can kao ziliao* 1: n.p.
Bao, Weihong. 2010. "The Politics of Remediation: Mise-en-scène and the Subjunctive Body in Chinese Opera Film." *Opera Quarterly* 26, nos. 2–3: 256–290.
Bao, Weihong. 2012. "Diary of a Homecoming: (Dis-)Inhabiting the Theatrical in Postwar Shanghai Cinema." In *A Companion to Chinese Cinema*, edited by Yingjin Zhang, 377–399. Oxford: Wiley-Blackwell.
Bazin, André. 2009. "Ontology of the Photographic Image." In *What Is Cinema?*, translated by Timothy Barnard, 3–12. Montreal: Caboose.
Berry, Chris, and Mary Farquhar. 2006. *China on Screen: Cinema and Nation*. New York: Columbia University Press.
Brecht, Bertolt. 2015. "*Verfremdung* in Chinese Acting." In *Brecht on Theatre*, edited by Marc Silberman, Steve Giles, and Tom Kuhn, 151–159. London: Bloomsbury.
Chen Xihe. 1986. "中国电影美学的再认识一谈~影戏剧本做法" (Zhongguo dianying meixue de zai renxi: Tan yingxi juben zuofa/Rethinking Chinese Film Aesthetics: On Filmscript Writing). 当代电影 *Dangdai dianying* 1: 82–90.
Chiang, Chih-Yun. 2011. "Representing Chineseness in Globalized Cultural Production: Chen Kaige's *Farewell My Concubine*." *China Media Research* 7, no. 1: 101–111.

Eisenstein, Sergei. 2010. "To the Magician of the Pear Orchard." In *Sergei Eisenstein Selected Works*, vol. 3: *Writings 1934–1947*, edited by Richard Taylor, 56–67. London: I. B. Tauris.

Fan, Victor. 2015. *Cinema Approaching Reality: Locating Chinese Film Theory*. Minneapolis: University of Minnesota Press.

Gunning, Tom. 1990. "The Cinema of Attractions: Early Film, Its Spectator and the Avant-Garde." In *Early Cinema: Space, Frame, Narrative*, edited by Thomas Elsaesser, 56–62. London: British Film Institute.

Huang De Quan. 2012. 中国早期电影史事考证 (*Zhong guo zao qi dian ying shi kao zheng*). Beijing: 中国电影出版社 (China Film Publishing House).

Iovene, Paola. 2010. "Chinese Operas on Stage and Screen: A Short Introduction." *Opera Quarterly* 26, nos. 2–3: 181–199.

Mao, Zedong. 1971. "Talks at the Yenan Forum on Literature and Art" (1942). In *Selected Readings from the Works of Mao Zedong*, 250–286. Beijing: Foreign Languages Press.

Marchetti, Gina. 1997. "*Two Stage Sisters*: The Blossoming of a Revolutionary Aesthetic." In *Transnational Chinese Cinemas*, edited by Sheldon Hsiao-peng Lu, 59–80. Honolulu: University of Hawai'i Press.

McGrath, Jason. 2010. "Cultural Revolution Model Opera Films and the Realist Tradition in Chinese Cinema." *Opera Quarterly* 26, nos. 2–3: 343–376.

Mello, Cecília. 2019. *The Cinema of Jia Zhangke: Realism and Memory in Chinese Film*. London: Bloomsbury.

Nagib, Lúcia. 1995. *Nascido das cinzas: Autor e sujeito nos filmes de Oshima*. São Paulo: Edusp.

Nagib, Lúcia. 2011. *World Cinema and the Ethics of Realism*. London: Continuum.

Nagib, Lúcia and Anne Jerslev. 2014. "Introduction." In *Impure Cinema*, edited by Lúcia Nagib and Anne Jerslev, xviii–xxxi. London: I. B. Tauris.

Nagib, Lúcia. 2014. "The Politics of Impurity." In *Impure Cinema*, edited by Lúcia Nagib and Anne Jerslev, 21–40. London: I. B. Tauris.

Pang, Laikwan. 2002. *Building a New China in Cinema: The Chinese Left-Wing Cinema Movement, 1932–1937*. Lanham, MD: Rowman & Littlefield.

Pethő, Ágnes. 2020. *Cinema and Intermediality: The Passion for the In-Between*. 2nd enlarged edition. Newcastle upon Tyne: Cambridge Scholars.

Rojas, Carlos. 2013. "Introduction: Chinese Cinemas and the Art of Extrapolation." In *The Oxford Handbook of Chinese Cinemas*, edited by Carlos Rojas and Eileen Cheng-Yin Chow, 1–20. Oxford: Oxford University Press.

Silvio, Teri. 2002. "Chinese Opera, Global Cinema and the Ontology of the Person: Chen Kaige's *Farewell My Concubine*." In *Between Opera and Cinema*, edited by Jeongwon Joe and Rose Theresa, 177–197. New York: Routledge.

Stam, Robert. 2000. "The Presence of Brecht." In *Film Theory: An Introduction*, edited by Robert Stam, 145–150. Malden, MA: Blackwell.

Tan, Ye and Zhu Yun. 2012. *Historical Dictionary of Chinese Cinema*. Toronto: Scarecrow Press.

Tian, Min. 2008. *The Poetics of Difference and Displacement: Twentieth-Century Chinese-Western Intercultural Theater*. Hong Kong: Hong Kong University Press.

Yeh, Catherine Vance. 2016. "Experimenting with Dance Drama: Peking Opera Modernity, Kabuki Theater Reform and the Denishawn's Tour of the Far East." *Journal of Global Theatre History* 1, no. 2: 28–37.

Yeh, Yueh-yu. 2002. "Historiography and Sinification: Music in Chinese Cinema of the 1930s." *Cinema Journal* 41, no. 3: 78–97.

Zhang Nuanxin and Tuo Li. 1979. "谈电影语言的现代化" (Tan dianying yuyan de xiandaihua/The Modernization of Film Language). 电影艺术 *Dianying Yishu* 3: 40–52.

Zhong Dafeng. 1986. "影戏理论历史所愿" (Yingxi lilun lishi suoyuan/The History of the Shadow Play). 当代电影 *Dangdai dianying* 3: 75–80.

Zhong Dafeng. 1994a. "中国电影的历史及其根源(上)：再论影戏" (Zhongguo dianying de lishi jiqi genyuan (shang): Zailun "yingxi"/History and Origins of Chinese Cinema (I): Another History of the "Shadow Play"). 电影艺术 *Dianying yishu* 1: 29–35.

Zhong Dafeng. 1994b. "中国电影的历史及其根源(下)：再论影戏" (Zhongguo dianying de lishi jiqi genyuan (shia): Zailun "yingxi"/History and Origins of Chinese Cinema (II): Another History of the "Shadow Play"). 电影艺术 *Dianying yishu* 2: 9–14.

13
Historicising the Story through Film and Music

An Intermedial Reading of *Heimat 2*

Lúcia Nagib

My hypothesis in this chapter is that intermedial relations in film can serve to ground it in historical reality. In order to test it, I will focus on *Heimat 2: Chronicle of a Generation* (*Die zweite Heimat: Chronik einer Jugend*, 1992), the second part of the monumental *Heimat* TV and cinema series, which started with *Heimat: A Chronicle of Germany* (*Heimat: Eine deutsche Chronik*, 1984) and continued with *Heimat 3: A Chronicle of Endings and Beginnings* (*Heimat 3: Chronik einer Zeitenwende*, 2004) and *Home from Home: A Chronicle of Vision* (*Die andere Heimat: Chronik einer Sehnsucht*, 2013), all scripted and directed by German filmmaker Edgar Reitz. Altogether, the project spans over sixty hours, *Heimat 2* being the longest instalment at thirteen episodes totalling more than twenty-five hours of film.

From its first series, the *Heimat* cycle has enjoyed milestone status as a sweeping representation of German political and artistic history, eliciting excellent scholarship as well as heated debates on the accuracy of its historical representations. Indeed, history features high on the agenda of all four parts of the cycle, which are bookmarked by major historical events in Germany: the First and Second World Wars in the first *Heimat*, set between 1919 and 1982; the birth and development of new artistic movements, as well as the students' revolts between 1960 and 1970, in *Heimat 2*; the fall of the Berlin Wall in *Heimat 3*, set between 1989 and 2000; and the great wave of emigration from Germany to Brazil in *Home from Home*, where the story loops back to the 1840s. Binding all of them together runs a national as much as subjective motif, the untranslatable concept of *Heimat,* involving the ideas of "home" and "homeland," whose romantic and nationalistic overtones had been embraced by the sugary and conservative genre of *Heimatfilme* in post–World

War II Germany and radically rejected by the "anti-Heimat" films that made up a strand of the New German Cinema in the late 1960s and early 1970s.

Rather than focusing on the representation of the past, however, my objective here will be to evaluate the ways in which the *Heimat 2* series *presents history in the making* by means of intermediality, that is, through the use of music as theme, diegetic performance, and organisational principle of all episodes. Set in the clearly demarcated decade of the 1960s, *Heimat 2* is devoted to chronicling the development of the Neue Musik (New Music) movement amidst the artistic effervescence in Germany at the time, including the beginnings of what was initially known as Junger deutscher Film (Young German Cinema) and later Neuer deutscher Film (New German Cinema). Beyond its many allusions to real facts and personalities in film and music, all the musical roles in the series feature real instrumentalists, singers, conductors, and composers, who were all, almost miraculously, also brilliant actors, able to enact on camera as fiction their actual musical performances. It is in the reality of this musicianship, and the way it inflects the series' form and content, that lies, I wish to claim, an element of incontestable truth, beyond the inevitable, even necessary betrayals of history taking place on the level of the fable. By being faithful to the contingent event of real-time musical performances, *Heimat 2* injects an element of unpredictable reality into the normative fictional situation that actualises history and constitutes the project's major political contribution, as I hope my analysis will demonstrate.

In *Heimat 2*, the borrowing of techniques typical of another medium, in this case, music, is purposely and constantly highlighted, positing the work as an ideal object for an intermedial approach. Granted, the series is first and foremost cinema in the conventional sense, reliant as it is on the medium's properties of spatiotemporal movement and real-life mimesis for narrative purposes. As in the other *Heimat* instalments, here too storytelling takes the upper hand by means of minutely crafted life-like characters whose unfulfilled desires and ambitions propel the narrative relentlessly forward. Within this context, music could be seen simply as an element of cinematic function, at least as concerns the all-pervading nondiegetic music track, mostly authored by Greek composer Nikos Mamangakis, whose name was made precisely by his work on the first three of the four *Heimat* instalments, but also including a host of other existing classical and popular pieces. As customary in fiction film, this nondiegetic music is there to suture the seams between shots and scenes, provide the desired emotional atmosphere, and fill in ellipses of time and space. Even the fact that music is the very subject of the series, in the form of the life story of instrumentalist, composer, and conductor Hermann Simon, as well as of those musicians, filmmakers, poets, and other artists around him, does not in itself pose a threat to the medium's specificity, aligning it instead with the consecrated cinematic genre of music biopics.

However, a radical intermedial intervention takes place on the diegetic level, in the form of the real-life musical performances which recur throughout the series' extended duration and punctuate the entire narrative. The effect of these passages is consistent with what Werner Wolf (1999: 43) famously defined as "overt intermediality," when a medium other than the dominant one makes an appearance with its "typical and conventional signifiers," remaining "distinct and quotable separately." This mode coexists with its companion piece, "covert intermediality," which Wolf illustrates with "abstract modernist works by Wassily Kandinsky, Paul Klee, Georges Braque and others that constitute a kind of musicalized painting: while the result is still painting, music (its rhythm, certain non- or self-referential patterns) is the avowed structuring principle of the artefact" (43). In *Heimat 2*, covert intermediality is equally at play, not only for being the subject of the fable but also for the stylistic and thematic continuum between diegetic and nondiegetic worlds provided by music, which is mostly in the charge, in both cases, of the same composer, Mamangakis. As in the abstract art quoted by Wolf, music, consisting of a "music-historical panorama of the 1960s" encompassing "dodecaphonic, aleatory, bruitist, phonetic, theatrical, and electronic music" (Schönherr 2010: 130), inflects all aspects of the *Heimat 2* episodes, including spoken language, camerawork, editing, mixing, colour patterns, and the serial structure of storytelling itself.

This musical way of thinking film is inscribed into Reitz's (2004: 184) filmmaking career—partly fictionalised in the series—going back to his early films, when he adopted a method of writing scripts in the form of musical scores, including a self-devised notation system. In *Heimat 2*, music-making often took precedence over the writing of the script, as Reitz retells: "In *Heimat 2*, music is not a matter of post-production, but a constitutive part of the action. While still in the middle of script writing, I was already in contact with Nikos Mamangakis. In many of the film scenes music is played, and these musical pieces had to be ready long before the completion of the script, so that the actors could study them" (177).[1] It is this combination of overt and covert intermediality in Reitz's method of filmmaking that allows for historical realism to freely migrate from a true-to-life mode of production to an entirely fictional mode of address.

I have elsewhere explored the ways in which the utilisation of other media within film can serve as a passage to physical reality, for example, by the filming of the act of painting or theatrical performances as they happen (Nagib 2020: 173ff.). In *Heimat 2*, this passage is opened up by music, which provides film with the proof of the material reality at its base, by means of artists who take upon themselves the difficult task of representing as fiction their actual musical skills. This procedure, uncommon in standard biopics of musicians and other artists, is embraced here as part of director Reitz's own realist pursuits. As one of the founders and intellectual heavyweights of the New German Cinema, Reitz remained faithful in the *Heimat* project to the principles of the Nouvelle Vague, so influential on his generation of filmmakers, of breaking out of the studios and taking to the streets to make their films. For him, on-location shooting brings into the ready product "a piece of life [that] really took place," as well as forcing the filmmaker to think the film according to a place that is alive and evolving (Reitz 2004: 154–155). Thus, the fictional rural village of Schabbach, the home of the Simon family at the centre of the *Heimat* cycle, is the combination of locations from a group of around ten villages in the German region of the Hunsrück, where the dialect, domestic habits, art craft, and housing were painstakingly reconstituted by piecing together lost and surviving traditions. In *Heimat 2*, viewers are presented with the real Munich, with its recognisable districts and landmarks, though duly modified to fit its 1960s appearance; all other secondary locations are equally real, albeit adapted to a period in the past. But even when changes were required for the representation of the past, an effort was made to avoid the studio at all costs and instead identify real apartments, houses, shops, and offices, as well as real used furniture, costumes, and props, to compose the sets.

This insistence on historical realism that embeds presentation within representation is probably the reason the *Heimat* project as a whole, and *Heimat 2* in particular, has often been understood as an attempt at faithfully retelling the history of the 1960s rather than a historically inspired fictional story, most notably by Johannes von Moltke (2003), who laments the flaws in the series' historical account of the New German Cinema. In a book chapter titled "Home Again: Revisiting the New German Cinema in Edgar Reitz's *Die Zweite Heimat* (1993)," von Moltke meticulously locates and weaves together all mentions, allusions, and metaphors regarding this film movement in the series, noting its defeatist, nostalgic, and melancholy tone, with its focus on individual artists and their emotional and professional dramas that ascribe a secondary and rather simplified role to the political struggles so prominent in the 1960s. However, I find little justification in von Moltke's demand that *Heimat 2* "mines the 1960s for the ways in which they speak to the film-historical present in Germany," a function more typical of written essays or documentary films than of an openly fictional work like this. On the other hand, the fact that the *Heimat* project was launched in the 1980s—precisely as the New German Cinema started to disperse and decline—and continued until very recently is the proof of its successful attempt not simply at mourning the past but at giving a new lease on life to this national film movement.[2] It is the permanent actualisation of history through its own existence as a lifelong film that makes *Heimat* so convincing for critics and audiences alike.[3] In short, the fact that the *Heimat* project elicits such a reality effect cannot be dismissed without further reflection.

In what follows I shall attempt to locate history in the making within historical representation in *Heimat 2* by means of an intermedial approach to film and music. I will first examine music as a structuring principle that informs camerawork, colour pattern, editing, and special effects in the series' episodes. I will proceed by focusing on the musician actors who contributed to fiction the reality of their own bodies and skills. The last section will investigate the ways in which the avant-garde and serial experiments portrayed in the film combine with the serial format of *Heimat 2*, giving it a sense of presentness and continuity that enables spectators to be immersed into a kind of parallel life and advances by a few decades the addictive effect of the series produced by today's streaming services.

Film as Music

I would like to start by looking at *Heimat 2*'s title musical piece, because it gives us the clue, in a nutshell, to the intermedial and structuring function of music in the entire series. Composed by Mamangakis, the piece that opens and closes all episodes is a variation of the theme the composer had devised to open the episodes of the first *Heimat* series, in which it appears over the series' title and Reitz's credit as director and screenwriter, prolonging into the first narrative scene. In *Heimat 2,* the theme is restricted to the opening vignette containing the title cards in red lettering, "DIE ZWEITE HEIMAT," that advances towards the viewer in a zoom forward, followed by the line "CHRONIK EINER JUGEND IN 13 FILMEN von Edgar Reitz"; at the end of each episode, the theme reemerges over the rolling credits. The vignette contains one single static, high-angle long shot of a city easily identifiable as Munich thanks to its picture-postcard framing of the town centre, with landmarks such as the church of St. Michael (St. Michael in Berg am Laim) on the centre-left of the picture, enveloped in bright yellow light, and the Cathedral of Our Lady (Frauenkirche), less prominent on the centre-right. Altogether the vignette lasts for thirty seconds, but in that very short period we see the cityscape quickly going from daylight to dusk and night thanks to the use of time-lapse photography, a trick that accelerates exponentially the passage of time. Thus, the lights on the windows of the apartment buildings go on and off in split seconds, whereas in reality this process would have taken hours. The same effect applies to the clouds that race across the top of the image and the several airplanes that traverse the frame in the blink of an eye like little dots of light.

Time-lapse filming technique had become popular in the 1970s and 1980s within Reitz's circle of filmmakers, being resorted to by Reitz himself since his first *Heimat* as well as by his colleague and collaborator Alexander Kluge, in order to, as Lutze (1998: 105) suggests in relation to the latter, "compress time so that a relatively invisible movement is revealed or an entire process becomes visible." In *Heimat 2*, the speed that compresses the day cycle is of a different nature, and in fact is aimed at capturing the "musical" quality of the city's dynamics, even when apparently in standstill. Mamangakis's imposing musical track, involving piano, orchestra, and choir, as well as a number of synthesiser effects, is entirely conventional in its quaternary beat, tonal harmonic field in F-minor, and repetitive chord of fifth (C) and octave, with a final unresolved modulation that makes room for the introduction of the film's storyline. Meanwhile, a loud, aleatory percussive line cuts across the orchestral arrangement in complete disaccord with its regular beat. On closer inspection, however, it becomes clear that this irregular drumming is remarkably in sync with the blinking lights of the apartment buildings, and even seems to be *caused* by them. The fact that the earlier version of this title theme, used in the first *Heimat* series, had no percussion suggests that the drumming line was created for *Heimat 2* to match the city's blinking lights as captured through time-lapse photography.

By this means, the vertiginous compression of time in the vignette unveils the musical shape of Munich with its irregular beating heart that anticipates the film's main subject: music. Indeed, in the first episode, immediately after the vignette, we find protagonist Hermann Simon grieving the end of his romance with his beloved Klärchen, who met with the opposition of his family for being almost twice his age and a mere servant in the parental home. On his knees in his bedroom, Hermann vows (1) to never love again; (2) to leave forever his Schabbach Heimat, the horrible Hunsrück, his mother, and the family home; and (3) to make music his one and only Heimat. Having passed his Abitur (final school exam), Hermann then departs to Munich, where he is admitted into the Musik Hochschule, or Conservatoire, and plunges into a world of music, which identifies the city with his "musical Heimat."

Thus the opening vignette gives us a first example of overt intermediality, in which music and film are in dialogue with each other but can be quoted separately. It is equally a case of covert intermediality, in that music and film inform each other's organisation by combining structured and unstructured elements, so as to highlight the emergence of unpredictable real phenomena within preestablished, conventional modes of music and filmmaking. The short vignette anticipates these counteracting, unstructured events, in the form of the avant-garde, serial, and aleatory music performed in reality by Hermann and his music colleagues throughout the episodes, in both overt and covert modes, as a counterpoint to the conventions of filmic storytelling and nondiegetic music. They constitute irruptions of presentational reality within the fable's illusionist realism, which, clearly detectable as they are, do not go as far as breaking the fourth wall or disrupting the conventional musical and filmic boundaries around them.

This method is a late and compromising development in Reitz's filmmaking career, which started with a radical adherence to music as a filmmaking grammar. Still as a student, in the late 1950s, he regularly attended concerts of New Music in Munich, as well as the series Musica Viva led by symphonic composer Karl-Amadeus Hartmann. He also frequented the circle around the electronic music composer Josef Anton Riedl, a former student of Carl Orff, in whose Munich studio he had the opportunity to meet such avant-garde eminences as Pierre Boulez, György Ligeti, Karlheinz Stockhausen, Luciano Berio, and Mauricio Kagel (Reitz 2004: 181). Mamangakis, a former student at the Conservatoire where Hermann enrols in *Heimat 2*, was also a member of that group. What impressed Reitz most about electronic music production of that time was its similarity to the process of filmmaking: "First a kind of script was sketched, and then the material was produced with sound generators and recorded. The electronic means allowed for the production of rhythmic forms that could not be played manually. The music track would come together as in the shooting of a film" (181). On the basis of that experience, Reitz devised a method of "scoring" for films, which garnered the admiration and support of Norbert Handwerk, the owner of Insel Film, in Munich, who gave him carte blanche to create his short experimental films. Handwerk finds an endearing representation in *Heimat 2* in the figure of Consul Handschuh, head of the production company Isar Film, whose enthusiasm for Hermann's electronic experiments is so extreme that he offers to make Hermann the heir of his company and fortune. As for Reitz's film scoring method, it was entirely based on movement and speed, which he justifies by the fact that "until the mid-1970s progress was synonymous with speed and car driving" (184). Thus, his fascination with cinematic speed, as seen in the use of time-lapse photography in the *Heimat* cycle, harks back to his beginning as a filmmaker in the late 1950s. But he finally had to compromise on this kind of "pure cinema" (123), as it resulted in "a world of forms that are not communicative anymore" (184). He says, "The avant-garde opened up new worlds, but—and this is its tragedy—the contact with the audiences was broken" (184).

To redress this problem, Reitz (2004: 123) had to resort to storytelling, that is, to the language-based film script, which brings into cinema the impurity of literature. *Heimat 2* deploys a veritable catalogue of the ways in which the two methods of "film scoring" and "film scripting" interact, resulting in covert and overt intermediality, respectively. An example is the following scene of episode 2, "Two Strange Eyes." Having recently arrived in Munich, Hermann attends a concert by two prominent students of the Conservatoire, Volker Schimmelpfennig (incarnated by composer and piano virtuoso Armin Fuchs) and Jean-Marie Wéber (Martin Maria Blau), who pay homage to two of Reitz's filmmaker colleagues, Volker Schlöndorff and Jean-Marie Straub. The concert is a multimedia chamber opera, with the instrumentalists and singer dressed as clowns, playing music (in reality composed by Mamangakis) on a poem by Günter Eich titled "Wacht auf, denn eure Träume sind schlecht!" (Wake up—your dreams are bad). Meanwhile, a wide screen on the back of the stage shows Reitz's most emblematic scored film, *Speed* (*Geschwindigkeit*, 1963)—credited in the episode to the characters of Reinhard Dörr (Laszlo I. Kish), a nod to filmmaker Reinhard Hauff, and Stefan Aufhäuser (Frank Röth). In *Speed*, "the protagonist is the camera" (Rauh 1993: 55), for which a new technique was developed that allowed for changes in the filming speed during the shoot. In permanent movement during the piece's thirteen-minute duration, the car-mounted camera captures landscape images in increasing velocity until they blur into abstraction. *Speed*'s original music score was composed by Riedl, but nowadays the film is often screened as part of avant-garde music concerts by other composers (Sobhani 1997: 201). However, this piece of "pure cinema" and its accompanying chamber opera are not allowed to speak for themselves in the scene, as the editing frequently cuts away from the performers to focus on the intrigue going on in the audience: Jean-Marie taking his seat next to Clarissa, who looks back at an anxious Hermann, who is in turn being hassled by an overbearing wannabe actress, Renate. We are also introduced to the publishing heiress, Fräulein Elisabeth Cerphal, accidentally sitting next to Juan Subercaseaux, the actual focus of this episode, who bluntly expresses his dislike for the concert. Thanks to these fictitious goings-on in the audience, the real-life avant-garde performance, itself a self-reflexive satire, is normalised and rendered "communicative," in Reitz's terms.

This use of storytelling as a means to facilitate access to the intricacies of avant-garde art forms resonates remarkably with the idea of "impure cinema" once formulated by André Bazin (2009), in his anticipation of intermedial theory in the early 1950s. For Bazin, the mission of cinema, as a mass entertainment par excellence, was to popularise the other arts: "[T]he success of filmed theatre serves the theatre, as literary adaptation serves literature.... In truth, there is no competition or replacement at work, only the addition of a new dimension, one gradually lost by the other arts since the Renaissance: an audience" (137).

"Impurity" as a "popular" device is even more clearly deployed in a scene in the first episode. Hermann has been given the key to a rehearsal room in the Conservatoire but finds it already occupied by a group of musicians, led by Volker and Jean-Marie, who invoke their priority use of the room. They then resume the performance of an experimental piece for two pianos and two xylophones while the camera closes in on Hermann, who is visibly riveted. Rather than leaving the spectator on their own to grapple with the intricacies of the musical piece, the film brings in Hermann's voice-over to offer an explanation: "How I envied the older students. They were the lords of creation, haughty, against the whole world. They were the proud prophets of the New Music. Whatever shocked the old generation, they did it." By interpolating this explanatory voice-over that verbalises the music's rebellious character, this very rebellion is neutralised while the music remains audible in the background. Real-life performance, offering the actualised evidence of a historical musical movement, is by this means integrated into narrative, while history for the few turns into storytelling for the many.

Musicians/Actors/Characters

Biographism is a key element in obtaining actualisation of history in *Heimat 2*. A great deal has been said about the ways in which Reitz brings to the screen his own experience as filmmaker and music expert in the series, including sections of his own early films, such as *Speed*, but also his Mexican documentary *Yucatan* (1960), the multicamera and multiscreen experiment *Varia Vision* (1965), and the faux-documentary adaptation of E. T. A. Hoffmann, *Cardillac* (1969) (see further details in Sobhani 1997). Equally decisive, however, is the way the cast's own talents and abilities inform both form and content of the episodes. One notable case is that of Juan Subercaseaux, played by Chilean multiartist and polymath Daniel Smith, who introduces the subject of language "as" music. According to autobiographical details he relays to Hermann the first time they meet, in a corridor of the Conservatoire, and which coincide with his self-authored online CV,[4] Juan speaks eleven languages, or "actually ten, music being my eleventh," as he says. This first dialogue between the two is captured with enhanced focus on Juan's lips as he speaks each of the words, bringing to the spectator's awareness the German declinations and the original sound of the names of each of the ten languages. The dialogue culminates with general merriment among the surrounding students when Hermann is called to the exam room and replies out loud, "Eisch!" (I), giving away his provincial origin through his dialectal pronunciation of the High German pronoun *Ich*.

This sets out the pattern prevailing across the film of the use of language as music. Not only do we follow Hermann's uphill struggle in learning High German and its impossible "ch" sound, but we are enlightened on the choice of people's names in the series according to their resonance, as in the case of Hermann's lovers, Klara, Klärchen, Clarissa, that he spells out to Juan. In the Cerphal villa, called Fuchsbau (Foxhole), where musicians and filmmakers gather under the heiress's protection, a lot of the artistic exercise revolves around language, including Clarissa's singing with Juan in Spanish, a male avant-garde duo who turn words into guttural and percussive sounds with their mouths, and a kind of "cadavre exquis" exercise between the poet Helga Aufschrey (a nod to filmmaker Helga Sanders-Brahms) and Hermann around the fortuitous word *Katze* (cat) and its derivations, which results in an atonal song, jointly authored by Helga and Hermann (in reality, a poem by Reitz set to music by Mamangakis) and subsequently sung by Evelyne Cerphal, the heiress's niece. As well as melody, language is percussion, as conveyed by Juan's marimba-and-drums piece "Prelude," which he rehearses in the Conservatoire's majestic concert hall. Displayed as Juan's personal and cultural expression, which is misunderstood and rejected by the Conservatoire as "folklore," the haunting marimba melody, authored by Smith himself, then migrates to the nondiegetic realm for atmospheric effect. The marimba scene resonates with another entertaining example of phonetics turned into bruitism, which is the improvised "spoon concert" performed at the university cantina where students, joined by Juan, break out in concerted tongue noises, slapping their cheeks, groaning, stamping, then resorting to cutlery to hit objects around them—crockery, radiators, kettles, the windows—while a rapidly sliding high camera surveys the tables in the same beat of the drumming, as if under its command. As Sobhani (1997: 203) points out, this concert is "reminiscent of a performance by John Cage in 1942, when he created a savage rhythm with his percussion group by playing . . . anything they could lay their hands on in an attempt to make *all* the field of audible sound available to music."

Thus the communicative vector is music in its widest sense, governing everything, not least the central love story between Hermann and Clarissa, whose arc is drawn by the sounds emanating from their own biographies as pianist and cellist, respectively, both in real life and on screen. They first bump into each other on the Conservatoire's stairs, where they merely exchange inquisitive glances. They are then shown having separate but near-concomitant encounters with their celebrity music masters. Hermann's is none other than Mamangakis himself, in a cameo that allows him to pass the baton of his real-life musicianship to his fictitious alter ego (Figure 13.1).[5] Hermann, overawed by the famous master, very tentatively shows him a short dodecaphonic piece for piano, flute, and voice. To his embarrassment, Mamangakis asks him to sing the melody, which is not at all Hermann's forte, but he obliges anyway, accompanying himself on the piano. The next shot, from Hermann's point of view, shows, through the window, Clarissa down below approaching the building with her cello. The reverse shot goes back to Mamangakis, who comments, "Our great composers wrote their best works for people they loved, a woman perhaps," a veiled reproach on the formulaic dodecaphonic piece Hermann has just presented and a premonition of the love story to come.

The next scene offers a similar setup, with Clarissa receiving a cello lesson from another celebrity, Professor P., an elderly man who courts her explicitly,

Figure 13.1 *Heimat 2* (Edgar Reitz, 1992): Hermann's master is the film's composer Nikos Mamangakis himself, in a cameo that allows him to pass the baton of his real-life musicianship to his fictitious alter ego.

suggesting that she is excessively devoted to her cello and should enjoy herself more as a woman (Figure 13.2). Clarissa immediately rejects this approach, which points to a kind of abusive, even sinister side to this master-student relationship. Clarissa had started by playing a romantic piece, Johannes Brahms's Cello Sonata in E-minor, Opus 38, and now the professor takes up the cello to show her how the Brahms resonates in a piece by Anton Webern, an exponent of atonality and dodecaphony of the Second Viennese School, "Three Little Pieces for Cello and Piano," Opus 11. He first plays a "very male, aggressive" note, which is followed by what he describes as "a very feminine, gentle reply," during which the camera zooms in on Clarissa, who half-smiles and raises her eyes away from the professor, as the image cuts back to Hermann, now walking in a corridor of the Conservatoire. In these two scenes, it is the music, as produced by two actual musicians and their instruments, that dictates the acting, editing, and soundscape, giving meaning and political content to the representation of romance within the fable. More pointedly, these scenes enlighten the viewer on how best to appreciate serial and atonal music, as

Figure 13.2 *Heimat 2* (Edgar Reitz, 1992): Clarissa receives a cello lesson from Professor P.

represented by Webern's and Hermann's pieces, by interweaving them with a romantic melody and a love story.

The stunningly beautiful notes by Brahms and Webern played on the cello by Clarissa and Professor P., moreover, launch the kind of power structure dominating the relationships among the characters. Professor P. is the first example in *Heimat 2* of the recurrent figure of elderly, lustful mentors longing for their young, attractive pupils, such as Hermann's former teacher in Schabbach, Herr Schüller, who suddenly turns up at his Munich accommodation accompanied by one of his young sexy pupils and former colleague of Hermann, Marianne Elz. Clarissa herself is supported by an infatuated, softspoken, and mildly repulsive elderly patron, Dr. Kirchmayer, an ally of her autocratic mother, who has funded her cello learning from the beginning and finally buys her a priceless antique instrument with the undisguised intention of tightening his grip on her. The unfavourable light in which these elderly men are shown, an indictment of the kind of abusive behaviour in the artistic milieu brought to light by the #MeToo movement decades later, might also be understood as a disclaimer for Reitz himself, who became involved with Salome Kammer, the actress who plays Clarissa, during the shoot of *Heimat 2*. He is twenty-seven years older than she. (They remain happily married to this day.)[6]

Whatever the case, the "politics of intermediality" here, to use Jens Schröter's (2010) term, is to question the liberating power of music Hermann and Clarissa abide by to the point of renouncing love. The aggressive male voice against the subdued female response in Webern's piece, played on the cello by Professor P., translates for Clarissa into an oppressive instrument. Later in the plot, Clarissa finds herself pregnant—the father could be either Volker, her future husband, or Jean-Marie—and develops sepsis as a result of a botched abortion. In her illness, she has nightmares of cello F-holes carved on her back, which she desperately tries to get rid of by asking the same charlatan abortionist to sew her fissured skin together. The nightmare is sparked by Hermann's first concert, "Spuren" (Traces), which should have featured Clarissa on the cello but which she has to miss in order to have the abortion. In the actual concert, Hermann marks Clarissa's absence in the orchestra with a live naked model with cello F-holes on her back, exactly as in Man Ray's famous photograph *Le Violon d'Ingres* (Ingres's Violin) (Figure 13.3). As Mattias Bauer (2012: 67) comments, "Clarissa's body thus becomes the scene of the inscription of the experiences she suffers; at the same time, the relation to Man Ray reflects the composition principle that governs *Heimat 2*. On the visual and aural, scenic and diegetic levels of the communication of plot and meaning, assonances and resonances, correspondences and inferences are

Figure 13.3 *Heimat 2* (Edgar Reitz, 1992): Hermann marks Clarissa's absence from the orchestra with a live naked model with cello F-holes on her back, as in Man Ray's photograph *Le Violon d'Ingres*.

introduced, which encourage the viewer and listener to perceive recurrent motifs."

Biographical intermediality here makes room for the political as much as for the haptic perception of the film, according to one of the two main intermedial templates defined by Pethő (2011: 99) as a "sensual" mode, which "invites the viewer to literally get in touch with a world portrayed not at a distance but at the proximity of entangled synaesthetic sensations, and resulting in a cinema that can be perceived in the terms of music, painting, architectural forms or haptic textures." In the series' later episodes, Clarissa will abandon the cello and devote herself entirely to singing. A fact collected from Kammer's own biography, this move represents, in the fable, a break from the male oppressive power and the embrace of feminism. Together with a group of female musicians she had met on a US tour, she forms a troupe which performs the climactic spectacle, "Hexenpassion" (Witches Passion), in the closing episode, with atonal music and *Sprechgesang* composed by Mamangakis on poems by expressionist writer Else Lasker-Schüler, focusing on the trial of the peasant

Katherine Lips, accused of witchcraft in 1672 in Marburg. Again the live performance of a historical fact injects an element of presentational truth into representation. As Schönherr (2010: 123) states, "the textual collage of the historical interrogation records from the witch trials with Else Lasker-Schüler's poems establishes a musical memory for the suffering of women under patriarchy whose artistic reenactment certainly also implies a Utopian element that points to the future."

Historicising Storytelling through Film and Music Serialism

The question remains of where to place the *Heimat* project, and *Heimat 2* specifically, within the development of German film history. As von Moltke (2003) rightly points out, references to the New German Cinema abound in *Heimat 2*, to the point that he perceives it as an attempt at historicising the movement. A closer look, however, discourages such a reading, considering that the film ends in 1970, when the New German Cinema was just starting to conquer the screens. Rather than developing a complete historical picture of the movement, *Heimat 2* concentrates on its nascent phase in the early 1960s. It is the period of the watershed 1962 Oberhausen manifesto, the launchpad for the Young German Cinema—which preceded the New German Cinema—that proclaimed "Papas Kino ist tot!" (Dad's cinema is dead), mimicking the early Nouvelle Vague and its disdain for the *cinéma du papa*. There is no lack of allusions to this memorable event, not least with Reinhardt and Stefan distributing stickers with this slogan all over Munich. There is also an "antifilm" screening by the duo and Rob at the Foxhole, called *Brutalität in Stein* (Brutality in Stone), which is actually the title of the 1961 short film directed by two key figures of the Young German Cinema, Alexander Kluge and Peter Schamoni, though the piece screened at the Foxhole is by Reitz himself. In the early episodes, people are constantly filming in the streets of Munich, to the point that film crews have become a tourist attraction, as a cab driver explains to Evelyne, a newcomer to the city. Hannelore Hoger, in the role of Fräulein Cerphal, is another New German Cinema foundational figure, who came to prominence through her acting in Kluge's films, the same applying to Alfred Edel, a recurrent actor with Kluge and Werner Herzog, who keeps his own name in a short-lasting role as an eccentric intellectual drunkard. More than anyone else, Kluge is the recurrent reference here, a filmmaker and philosopher with whom Reitz collaborated as cinematographer in the landmark *Yesterday Girl* (*Abschied von gestern*, 1966) and other works. In *Heimat 2*,

Kluge is personified by the amusing bookworm Alex (Michael Schönborn), the eternal philosophy student, who claims to be writing three philosophical compendiums at the same time and goes about explaining the love affairs around him in terms of Heidegger, Spinoza, and Adorno, while remaining himself entirely chaste.

All these details demonstrate a focus on the infancy of the New German Cinema movement, and not on its later and more important history, offering little justification to von Moltke's expectations of a full assessment of the period. In contrast, in the early 1960s, the New Music movement had reached an apex marked by a dramatic change in its political direction, and this is the true focus of attention here. As Schönherr (2010: 111) explains, most New Music representatives in the immediate postwar period had had direct experience of the horrors of the front, an example being Stockhausen, a prominent serialist composer in the 1950s, "who was confronted almost daily with the brutality of the battlefield as a paramedic (and who lost his mother in a concentration camp and his father in combat)." For this generation, according to Schönherr, serialism was convenient as a kind of "music that eliminated any historical and personal narrative and suspended the subject from working through its own trauma, guilt, and responsibility" (111). The 1960s, however, "appear to have been a turning point in the postwar history of New Music, which entered a new phase of critical self-reflection and openness that led to a resemanticization reflected in the stylistic and programmatic diversity of the music of that period" (113).

This provides the opportunity, in *Heimat 2,* for history to make a decisive appearance through the revelation of the horrors of the Holocaust at the very centre of creativity and romance: the Foxhole. In the prewar years, famous artists and thinkers, including Bertolt Brecht and Lion Feuchtwanger, had assembled there. But as Elisabeth Cerphal repeats to all her guests, that wonderful villa at the heart of the Munich artistic district of Schwabing was appropriated by her father from his Jewish publishing partner Goldbaum, who perished in the war. Goldbaum's daughter Edith, once Elisabeth's best friend, was sent to the Dachau concentration camp thanks to a tip-off by her own SS-officer husband, Gerold Gattinger, now Elisabeth's "financial adviser" and co-inhabitant of the Foxhole. The revelation of this fact constitutes a rite of passage for the young artists, adding a sense of guilt and responsibility to their hitherto unconcerned artistic exercises. With the old Cerphal's death and before Edith's daughter Esther can claim her right to the property, Elisabeth finally sells it to a construction company that razes it to the ground to make room for lucrative apartment buildings, leading to the artists' disbanding and forced independence.

While the innocence of Fräulein Cerphal, the eternal student and sympathetic patroness of young talents, disintegrates—"Cerphal" being a homonym of *Zerfall*, or "decay," as von Moltke (2003: 130) notes—music acquires historical and political weight. In Reinhard's episode, where he meets Esther in Venice and commits to writing a film about the loss of her mother in the concentration camp, Mamangakis's nondiegetic music is extensively replaced by Olivier Messiaen's "Quartet for the End of Time." Messiaen famously wrote this piece, one of the most important of his prolific career, in 1941, while a war prisoner in Görlitz, then Germany (now Zgorzelec, Poland). This heart-wrenching, poignantly beautiful piece for piano, violin, cello, and clarinet was premiered at the prisoner-of-war camp by Messiaen himself and other musician inmates, with decrepit instruments and under the rain, on 15 January 1941, for about four hundred enraptured prisoners. The presence of Messiaen's music in *Heimat 2* is fitting in many ways, not least for the composer's status as one of the precursors of serialism, which he passed on to Boulez and Stockhausen and other dedicated students. This historical lineage, and the pain and mourning it carries, characterises many other musical choices in *Heimat 2*, the aforementioned Brahms imbedded in Webern being a similar case of historical affiliation with both romantic and sinister undertones.

Historical continuity finds a parallel in the series with the space-time continuum envisaged by avant-garde music, which included the breaking of the boundaries of established categories and art forms (Grant 2001: 110ff.). Atonal, serial, aleatory, and electronic music, as exercised within the New Music movement in Europe, as well as the "indeterminate music" practiced by John Cage in the United States, saw no frontiers between melodic sounds and noises, and even silence. In the Cage-inspired concert "Persona" in *Heimat 2*, for example, the musicians set a stopwatch to one minute, which they mostly fill by quietly mimicking the notes and produce actual sounds for only five seconds. As it moved into the territory of electronics, avant-garde music dissolved its boundaries with engineering, architecture, mathematics, and other sciences. And by surrendering its specificity, it opened up for Reitz the possibility of intermedial cinema, which finds common ground with other arts as well as with real life. The *VariaVision* project, funded by Consul Handschuh and plagued by mishaps which are played out in slapstick style in *Heimat 2*, is based on one of Reitz's actual experiments that had no beginning or end. Combining sixteen screens, a spoken text by Kluge, and electronic music by Riedl, the installation integrated the mediums of film, literature, and music in a continuum which the spectator could appreciate for hours or minutes as they liked (Sobhani 1997: 206).

Likewise, history serves Reitz's storytelling as an open-ended process, which time-based media such as music and film can accurately represent as form and fictionalise as content. By breaking away from the standard two-hour feature format for cinema, Reitz's "lifelong film" responded to a need for change felt by many of his generation. Around the same time the first *Heimat* series was shot, in the 1980s, Kluge gave up on the feature-length format to devote himself entirely to short essayistic documentaries for television. Rainer Werner Fassbinder, in turn, launched his TV series in fourteen episodes, *Berlin Alexanderplatz* (1980), bringing experimentation into a field hitherto dominated by American commercial ventures. *Holocaust* (Marvin J. Chomsky, 1978) is an example of the latter, and actually what made Reitz conceive of his own series, a move that Murray Smith (2017: 172) qualified as "Reitz's refusal of the full-blooded, 'Manichaean' melodrama of *Holocaust*, along with his commitment to an alternative but still emotional form of drama: a kind of synthesis of Brecht's 'epic' and 'dramatic' modes." Combining musical serialism with the television serial format as a mode of telling history through the evolving form of music and film, Reitz ended up anticipating the artistically (and commercially) sophisticated series of our day, which offer to the viewer a kind of parallel reality in which to immerse oneself for months or years of "binge watching." In other words, the actualisation of history by means of music gives material form to the virtual medium of film. Or, in Reitz's (1996: 132) words, "Heimat means for me something that we have lost and maybe can retrieve in cinema as Heimat *Ersatz*."

Notes

This chapter is a revised and shortened version of chapter 9 in Nagib (2020). I would like to thank Stephen Shennan for his helpful comments on this text, as well as Suzana Reck Miranda and John Gibbs for their technical advice.

1. All citations in German were translated into English by the author.
2. The first *Heimat* series enjoyed huge success around the world, but in particular in Germany, where its official TV audience rating stood at 26%, meaning tens of millions of spectators. (See Skrimshire 2009 for a full account of the *Heimat* reception career.) *Heimat 2* garnered stronger enthusiasm internationally—and in Italy in particular—than at home, though there are records of rapturous receptions all over Germany, in marathon cinema screenings lasting several days (Lentz 2005: 63ff.). A veritable *Heimat* cult has emerged since the launch of the first series. Thanks to it, the Hunsrück became a tourist destination, with new hotels, restaurants, and shops. Few films will have elicited such profuse fan pages, such as https://www.heimat123.de/ and https://www.heimat-fanpage.de/, containing hundreds of documents, photographs, films, and links to related websites. This adds to Edgar Reitz's own highly informative homepage, http://www.edgar-reitz.de, and his foundation's online shop,

http://shop.edgar-reitz-filmstiftung.de/, where browsers can find a host of *Heimat*-related materials for sale, not least the full soundtrack recordings of all instalments. Reitz himself has given a great number of long interviews and published widely on the *Heimat* project, including the scripts of the whole cycle, totalling thousands of pages.
3. In a lecture titled "Film und Wirklichkeit" (Film and Reality), Reitz gives amusing accounts of the series' reality effect, including the cases of a lady who identified her own husband in the character of Horst in the first *Heimat* instalment; an English couple who came to one of the villages that make up Schabbach, in the Hunsrück, looking for the tomb of the Simon family; and a doctoral student from Mannheim who wrote a thesis on the development of amateur photography in the twentieth century, using as archival evidence the cameras and photographs shown in the *Heimat* cycle (Reitz 2008: 366–367).
4. See https://heimat123.net/actors/juan.html.
5. It should not be surprising that Mamangakis has only this opportunity of dialogue, alongside a mute appearance conducting a concert for cello and orchestra authored by Hermann, with Clarissa as soloist: he is a clumsy actor and a rare case in which dubbing was used (albeit with his own voice), most likely to camouflage the mishaps in his live utterances.
6. Age difference between couples is an interesting thematic undercurrent in *Heimat 2*. Hermann's first love, Klärchen, who is nearly twice his age, is another example, purportedly lifted from Reitz's own biography.

References

Bauer, Matthias. 2012. "'Responsivität' als Werk- und Wirkungsprinzip: *Die zweite Heimat* (1992)." In *Film-Konzepte 28*, edited by Thomas Koebner und Fabienne Liptay, 64–94. Munich: text+kritik.
Bazin, André. 2009. "For an Impure Cinema: In Defence of Adaptation." In *What Is Cinema?*, translated by Timothy Barnard, 107–137. Montreal: Caboose.
Grant, Morag Josephine. 2001. *Serial Music, Serial Aesthetics: Compositional Theory in Post-war Europe*. Cambridge: Cambridge University Press.
Lentz, Carola. 2005. "'Alles Wesentliche im Leben entzieht sich der Optik einer Kamera—die Liebe, der Tod . . .': Anlässlich der München-Premiere (1992) von Edgar Reitz' *Die zweite Heimat: Chronik einer Jugend.*" In *Heimat: Suchbild und Suchbewegung*, edited by Fabienne Liptay, Susanne Marschall, and Andreas Solbach, 63–74. Remscheid: Gardez!
Lutze, Peter C. 1998. *Alexander Kluge: The Last Modernist*. Detroit: Wayne State University Press.
Nagib, Lúcia. 2020. *Realist Cinema as World Cinema: Non-cinema, Intermedial Passages, Total Cinema*. Amsterdam: Amsterdam University Press.
Pethő, Ágnes. 2011. *Cinema and Intermediality: The Passion for the In-Between*. Newcastle upon Tyne: Cambridge Scholars.
Rauh, Reinhold. 1993. *Edgar Reitz: Film als Heimat*. Munich: Wilhelm Heyne.
Reitz, Edgar. 1996. "Die Zukunft des Kinos im digitalen Zeitalter." In *Der zweite Atem des Kinos*, by Thomas Elsaesser, Jean-François Lyotard, and Edgar Reitz, 115–157. Frankfurt: Verlag der Autoren.
Reitz, Edgar. 2004. *Drehort Heimat*. Edited by Michael Töteberg, Ingo Fliess, and Daniel Bickermann. Frankfurt: Verlag der Autoren.

Reitz, Edgar. 2008. "Film und Wirklichkeit. Lectio doctoralis, Johannes Gutenberg-Universität, Mainz (21. Februar 2006)." In *Edgar Reitz erzählt,* edited by Thomas Koebner and Michelle Koch, 359–369. Munich: text+kritik.

Schönherr, Ulrich. 2010. "Music, Postwar Politics, and Edgar Reitz's 'Die zweite Heimat.'" *New German Critique,* no. 110 (Summer):107–124.

Schröter, Jens. 2010. "The Politics of Intermediality." *Acta Universitatis Sapientiae, Film and Media Studies* 2: 107–124. http://www.acta.sapientia.ro/acta-film/C2/film2-6.pdf.

Skrimshire, Angela. 2009. "'Heimat' of Memory, Imagination and Choice: An Appreciation of Edgar Reitz' Heimat films." http://heimat123.net/Appreciation_of_Heimat_16Jan2009.pdf.

Smith, Murray. 2017. *Film, Art, and the Third Culture: A Naturalized Aesthetics of Film.* Oxford: Oxford University Press.

Sobhani, Mehrnoosh. 1997. "Avant-Garde Music and the Aesthetics of Film: On Edgar Reitz's *Die Zweite Heimat.*" In *Text und Ton im Film,* edited by Paul Goetsch and Dietrich Scheunemann, 199–208. Tübingen: Gunter Narr.

von Moltke, Johannes. 2003. "Revisiting the New German Cinema in Edgar Reitz's 'Die Zweite Heimat' (1993)." *Cinema Journal* 42, no. 3 (Spring): 114–143.

Wolf, Werner. 1999. *The Musicalization of Fiction: A Study in the Theory and History of Intermediality.* Amsterdam: Rodopi.

PART IV
INTERMEDIAL ARTISTS

14
Stephen Dwoskin, an Intermedial Artist

Rachel Garfield, Jenny Chamarette, and Darragh O'Donoghue

The work of Stephen Dwoskin (born 1939 in Brooklyn; died in 2012 in London) is varied in form, subject matter, and genre. Best known for his early underground films, his role in setting up the London Film-Makers' Co-op (LFMC) in 1966, and his groundbreaking book on experimental film, *Film Is...* (1975), Dwoskin was a truly intermedial artist. Having come to artistic maturity in the 1960s New York underground, his practice was informed by, and often incorporated, other art forms, such as dance, painting, performance art, avant-garde theatre, literature, and music. The films discussed in this chapter include, among others, *Chinese Checkers* (1965), *Trixi* (1969), *Dyn Amo* (1972), *Central Bazaar* (1976), *Trying to Kiss the Moon* (1994), and *Grandpère's Pear* (2003), demonstrating the breadth of his oeuvre. All of these films experiment with the limits of the material as a form of portraiture and self-portraiture, ruminating on the nature of relationships—Dwoskin's with others and theirs with him—while also exploring the nature of time, history, memory, generational transmission, haunting, and the representation of the past.

To explore the intermedial connections and contexts of Dwoskin's artwork, this chapter focuses initially on his book *Film Is...* and his relationship to key historical and cultural moments in Anglo-American avant-gardes and experimental film; the postwar American avant-gardes that were such a significant influence and source of inspiration for his filmmaking; and the influential work of French Surrealists and proto-Surrealists, such as Antonin Artaud and Georges Bataille, on Dwoskin and his contemporaries. In the second part of the chapter, we undertake a close and detailed analysis of intermediality within a single work, Dwoskin's autobiographical essay film, *Trying to Kiss the Moon*. We argue that technological and material intermediality overlap in his relationships both to newer technological-aesthetic forms such as video, as a distinct medium and material differentiation from film, and to older modes such as painting, as well as to the modalities of self-portraiture that span both. We also situate Dwoskin's intermediality in relation to the Greenbergian expectation of purity of media as an absolute requirement for art, important at that time and in itself an intermedial aspiration. It is also a possible explanation for the elision of Dwoskin's work in the United Kingdom. Overall, we make the case that Dwoskin, underrepresented and underrecognised in his lifetime, is an outstanding case study to explore intermediality, where intermediality is not only a creative praxis but also a way of acknowledging the integration of artistic self-expression within a wider sphere of cultural influence and a way of writing the intermedial histories of film.

Dwoskin, New York, and Avant-Garde Intermediality

This section proposes that the sources of Dwoskin's intermedial aesthetic are found in his American background: his education, his work as an applied artist, and his association with the New York Film-Makers' Cooperative. His unique position in the United Kingdom as intermedial artist can be exemplified by his book *Film Is . . .*, an inclusive history of experimental film. The interrogatory ellipsis in the title is characteristically exploratory. For Dwoskin film was underground film, Hollywood, dance, theatre, music, happening, painting, photography, sculpture, philosophy, anthropology, literature, television, light show, comic books, and anything else it could draw on to maximise its expressiveness. Part of Dwoskin's strategy in his book was to situate the Structural/Materialist film of his co-workers in the LFMC, of which he was a co-founder, as merely one option among the many other manifestations of experimental film.

For Dwoskin, the postwar American experimental film makes sense only in the context of Beat literature, Abstract Expressionism, Pop Art, the reevaluation of Dada and Surrealism, the visual data of "everyday life" (advertisements, comic books, pin-ups, flags, clothing), and experimental theatre and dance. The key figure was not a filmmaker, such as Maya Deren, Kenneth Anger, Stan Brakhage, Jonas Mekas, or Robert Frank—all very important to Dwoskin— but a composer. Dwoskin (1975: 46) states that John Cage's "philosophical and physical impact was undeniably one of the greatest influences on the post-war generation." Cage was a one-man intermedial phenomenon who combined not only multiple disciplines but whole cultures with his studies in Indian philosophy and Zen religion. Dwoskin praises Cage's attempts to replace formal artistic processes and Western ideology with a commitment to the everyday and chance (via the *I ching*, regularly consulted by Dwoskin, as recorded in his diaries).

Dwoskin (1975: 47) alludes to a famous multimedia event that Cage mounted at Black Mountain College in 1952 with artist Robert Rauschenberg and dancer Merce Cunningham. *Theatre Piece No. 1* has gone down in art history as the first "happening" and the progenitor of modern performance art—art forms that by their very natures are intermedial, "impure" (Kirby and Schechner 1965; Shattuck 1976; Benfey 2016; Palmer and Trombetta 2017: 19). Cage shines throughout *Film Is . . .* as the very emblem of an intermedial aesthetic. There is a direct line between Cage and Dwoskin: Cage, Josef Albers, Willem de Kooning, and other Black Mountain College alumni taught at Parsons School of Design, Pratt Institute, or the New School for Social Research, all in New York, where Dwoskin studied in 1958 (at Parsons) and 1959 (at Pratt and the New School). Parsons School of Design (1958) in particular offered an intermedial curriculum, with courses in applied arts embedded in other fine art disciplines, as well as a broadly humanist curriculum that included the study of philosophy, art history, English, social studies, science, sociology, psychology, and "general cultural [studies]."

More broadly, the Black Mountain College event, the wider "happening" movement that it inspired, and the rediscovery of Dada and Surrealism by artists such as Cage and Rauschenberg (Robert Motherwell had published the influential anthology *The Dada Painters and Poets* in 1951) fed into the artistic milieu within which the New York Film-Makers' Cooperative was established in 1962, where Dwoskin (1975: 55–61) showed his first films and befriended its members. Several of the Cooperative's members engaged in intermedial activities, especially those New York filmmakers to whom Dwoskin was closest or felt most affinity: Jack Smith, who is being increasingly recognised as an important figure in the history of performance art,[1] and Andy Warhol, who would combine film, performance, music, and light shows in his Exploding Plastic Inevitable multimedia events (in 1966) (Mekas 2016: 249–251).

Jonas Mekas from the New York Film-Makers' Cooperative was probably the greatest single influence and mentor. Mekas's widely read "Movie Journal" column in the *Village Voice* expanded the definition of "movie" to include reports on pornography, poetry readings, experimental theatre and dance, performance art, light shows, shadow play, "tactile interactions," Rauschenberg's Experiments in Art & Technology (EAT) organization, pop music, television, home movies, painting, and the circus, as well as the emergence of expanded cinema, which Mekas (2016: 251–254) also calls "intermedia." Mekas (1972) collected several of these columns in *Movie Journal: The Rise of the New American Cinema, 1959–1971*. The fact that Mekas felt it necessary to discuss extracinematic media to account for the "changing frontiers" of American experimental film would influence Dwoskin (1975: 55, 245) in *Film Is . . .*, which frequently cites "Movie Journal" and includes Mekas's (2016: 73–74) byline as a visual insert and the collection *Movie Journal* in the bibliography. The *Film Is*... bibliography also lists texts on contemporary art, Minimalism, happenings, philosophy, sociology, and conceptual art, while the text directly cites practitioners or examples of Buddhist texts, contemporary classical music, Dada/Surrealism and fellow travelers, experimental theatre, literature, philosophy ancient and modern, psychology, and sociology.

Whereas most English avant-garde filmmakers of Dwoskin's era were trained as fine artists,[2] many of the great American experimentalists were first dancers, writers, commercial artists, photographers, mathematicians, art historians, teachers, television editors, anthropologists, and even a banker! By crossing from one discipline or form of expression to another, they were able to inform their work in a new medium with the aesthetic insights or experience gained with the old.

Dwoskin himself demonstrates his interdisciplinarity in his collaborations, as well as his influences. Friendships with literary figures, in particular the Beat writers Allen Ginsburg and Jack Kerouac, manifest in his illustration and graphic design work, as well as his films. For instance, three of his four artist's books and at least eight of his films are adaptations of literary works, while many more cite favourite authors.

A key influence that Dwoskin shared with Cage and his countercultural descendants was the French actor, playwright, and theorist Antonin Artaud. In several of his works, Dwoskin attempted to transpose Artaud's concept of the theatre as a live, visceral rite into the recorded medium of film. In an interview with *The Guardian* in 1968, Dwoskin stated that he wanted his films to have a visceral effect on their viewers, to bypass their minds and affect them somatically (Gilbert 1968). Four decades later, Ricardo Matos Cabo (2006) claimed that Dwoskin's cinema was close to magic, exorcism, and hypnosis, terms invoked by Artaud (1993: 68–78) in his first manifesto for the "Theatre of Cruelty."

In any case, such violence is precisely the relationship between artwork and viewer that Artaud (1993) advocated in his "Theatre of Cruelty" texts. Artaud railed against the psychological drama that dominated bourgeois or "élite" theatre, a theatre that "restrict[ed] itself to probing the intimacy of a few puppets, thereby transforming the audience into Peeping Toms" (64). He called for a direct, violent spectacle analogous to popular forms, such as the cinema, music hall, and circus, that "upsets all our preconceptions, inspiring us with fiery, magnetic imagery and finally reacting on us after the manner of unforgettable soul therapy" (64–65). Only a handful of Dwoskin films have this level of cruelty as their subject matter. Most of his films, however, enact these strategies formally, finding cinematic correlatives for Artaud's theatrical ideas, using techniques to defibrillate the jaded viewer (and the complacent performer), such as long takes, excruciating close-ups, disruptive editing, and unsettling drone soundtracks. *Girl* (1972) achieves most of the effects Artaud called for without any of the shock tactics, by simply by placing a fixed camera at a distance from a vulnerable woman and leaving it there. This bodily directness contrasted with what Dwoskin termed the "analytical" approach to filmmaking practiced by the Structural/Materialists at LFMC after he left (Washington 1972: 36).

Artaud's influence on the "happening" was also crucial for Dwoskin. His experiences of physical impairment and the limitations of accessibility for expanded cinema events prevented him from fully participating in them, even though he performed *Mr Sunshine* with Gavin Bryars and John Tilbury at the 1969 Edinburgh Film Festival. However, he used the happening as a starting point to generate films. Dwoskin would place performers in a particular environment—a bedroom (*Dirty*), a bathroom (*Me, Myself & I*), a living room (*C-film*), or a house (*Central Bazaar*)—for a length of time, from an afternoon to several weeks, and ask them to interact and perform while he recorded the proceedings on camera. The resultant films, however, are not simply documents of private happenings. Just as Kurt Kren, to whom Dwoskin devoted the most pages of any single artist in *Film Is . . .*, reimagined or even undermined or subverted the Viennese actions he was commissioned to film in works like *6/64: Mama und Papa* (1964), so Dwoskin transformed his raw "documentary" material through editing, sound, and manipulation of the image, at once "sculpting" and fragmenting the original "live," time-bound experience, whilst maintaining and intensifying its communal energies.

Central to Artaud's Theatre of Cruelty was dance; one chapter of his influential *The Theatre and Its Double* (1938) focuses on Balinese dance drama. The Black British dance company Les Ballets Nègres was the subject of Dwoskin's documentary *Ballet Black* (1986), but dance has always been fundamental to his own work. In *Take Me* (1968), Clodagh Brown's flirtatious dance before the camera disintegrates into a paint-splattered rite in the manner of the Viennese Actionists Dwoskin (1975: 195–101) admired through the films of Kren and witnessed at the Destruction in Art Symposium in September 1966. *Trixi* documents the mercurial interaction between dancer Beatrice Cordua and Dwoskin's camera, and *Dyn Amo* comprises four progressively brutal sequences of "erotic" dancing, culminating in the protracted torture of the final dancer. The autobiographical comedy *Outside In* (1981) includes slapstick sequences in which Dwoskin fails to dance; he redeems himself by dancing with his fingers in an homage to *Never Fear* (1950), directed by childhood polio survivor Ida Lupino, about a dancer whose burgeoning career is stopped by polio.

The most sustained example of intermedial activity in Dwoskin's work relates to Georges Bataille's (1966) posthumous novella, *Ma mère*. In 1977, Dwoskin worked on screen tests for *My Mother* with artist, musician, pornographer, sex worker, model, and dancer Cosey Fanni Tutti. It is not clear what became of these rushes; perhaps they were shown at the multimedia Georges Bataille celebration Violent Silence Festival: Acts of Transgression at Bloomsbury Theatre, London (25–29 September 1984), co-organised by a former Better Books employee, where an unidentified Dwoskin film was screened (there was also a performance by Cosey) (Buck 1984; Brennan 2013; Tutti 2017). Soon after this, Dwoskin began working on a full-feature adaptation of *Ma mère*, released as *Further and Particular* (1988). As can be gleaned from the several surviving drafts of the script, held in the Dwoskin Archive at the University of Reading, this film fuses *Ma mère* with the speculative (and also posthumously published) novel *Exploits and Opinions of Dr. Faustroll, Pataphysician* (*Gestes et opinions du docteur Faustroll pataphysicien: Roman néo-scientifique suivi de Spéculations*, 1911) by proto-Surrealist Alfred Jarry (1996). The script was reworked as the text for Dwoskin's artist book of photomontages *Ha, ha! La Solution imaginaire* (1993; the title derives from Jarry's *Faustroll*).

Such sustained engagement with a single project over nearly two decades, and in multiple media—film, performance, dance, photography, collage, the artist's book, the framed print—may be attributable to Dwoskin's training and early work as an applied artist in the United States. As a designer of corporate branding, Dwoskin had to imagine the same core image in different shapes, sizes, and contexts. As an art director for Whitney Publications and CBS, and as a creator of artist's books, he laid out and fused material in different media: text, drawings, photographs, etchings, typography. This training and experience gave Dwoskin a facility with and habit of thinking in the combination and recombination of different media. This facility and habit would inform his dense, allusive, and intermedial films.

Trying to Kiss the Moon (1994): Intermedial Praxis, Self-Portraiture, Self-Exile

This chapter has so far focussed on the intermedial contextual environments of Dwoskin's filmmaking practices. This second part turns to a close reading of the later *Trying to Kiss the Moon* (*TTKM*, 1994) as exemplary of Dwoskin's intermedial praxis. We argue that *TTKM* follows several definitions of cinematic intermediality proposed by Ágnes Pethö (2011: 41–48), namely a heterotopic "place" to interrogate self-exile via disability and family memory; an exploration of the configurations of video, film, and performance as figural forms that disfigure a notion of self; and a performative act (and artistic praxis). *TTKM* is a crucial bridge between Dwoskin's earlier work, for which he is best known, and his "late style," which, following Edward Said (2004: 14), can as likely constitute "a form of exile from [one's] milieu" as it can be, "at the end, fully conscious, full of memory, and also very (even preternaturally) aware of the present."

Jointly commissioned by Arts Council England and Channel 4, *TTKM* is subtitled *An Autobiographical Film*. However, this underplays the film's craft as an experimental essay film, which deftly combines sophisticated staging of autoethnography using home movie footage filmed by Dwoskin's father, Henry, with selected segments from Dwoskin's earlier films, while developing distinctive tensions between classical modes of composition and the plastic and material qualities of video images. Drawing on filmed photographs, paintings, televised interviews and outtakes, re-recordings, and commentaries, *TTKM* is a collage film, recombining materials typically described as Dwoskin's "works"—his films—with the filmed material manifestations and fragments of a life. Film as art is combined with film as biographical documentation.

Dwoskin's life could be understood as a series of estrangements, from his position as an American expat living in London to his condition as a diasporic Jew, and his lived experience of disability. Disabled artists and writers also encounter exile, discussed for instance in queer-trans disabled writer Eli Clare's (2015) memoir-manifesto, *Exile and Pride*. But in *TTKM*'s complex interrogation of Dwoskin's self-image alongside his image-making of others, exile takes on a different flavour. Exile and self-exile underpin the forms and aesthetics of autobiographical self-representation exacted in the film. *TTKM* was made at an interstitial moment, between the fully analogue filmmaking of Dwoskin's work from 1969 to 1989 and his prompt adoption of digital filmmaking technologies in the early to mid-1990s, and is therefore not fully a "late" work since several other significant films come after it.[3] Nonetheless, the sense of apartness and paradoxical self-exile and self-integration, as described in Said's vision of lateness and late style, come to the fore in *TTKM*. These thematic dimensions are not simply a result of creative production late in a career; they also demonstrate fine-tuned intermedial approaches to image-making, via portraiture, self-portraiture, and autoethnography, modelled in complex ways throughout the film. And the most significant tool of this intermedial modelling is video, both digital and magnetic.

From the perspective of media history, *TTKM* falls within the high period of video haptics described by Laura U. Marks (1998, 2000). The *haptic* is itself intermedial in conceptual origin, developed from the writing of nineteenth-century art historian Aloïs Riegl which explored the relationships between figure and ground in ancient Egyptian and Roman art, including mosaic, metalwork, and textile (Marks 1998: 335). The haptic remains a powerful alternative theoretical framework for the moving image, because moving images are of course more than flat visual planes; they are also spatiotemporal, auditory environments, with situated and embodied technological relationships to their spectators, as intermedial figural forms, and heterotopias of space-time. Video haptics offer an alternative model of artistic creativity to the models of image-based remediation put forward by Bolter and Grusin (1999), which tend to elide both the material, archival, and plastic qualities of analogue/magnetic video under a broader remit of hypermediated images, and the hotly contested historical debates about artist's film and video which emerged in the 1980s and 1990s. By focussing on video as intermedial technique and figuration rather than technological hypermediation, Marks's work preempts some of the critiques of media archaeology by archival scholars—namely that there is an insufficient focus on the material artefacts, archiving, and content-based analysis of moving image technologies (see Griffin 2015).

Marks (1998: 340) cites low contrast ratios, electronic and digital imaging, and video decay as potential sources of haptic visuality in video, explaining that "the tactile quality of the video image is most apparent in the work of videomakers who experiment with the disappearance and transformation of the image due to digital and other effects." Disappearance and transformation are important techniques in *TTKM*, both as aesthetic practices of self-portraiture and autobiography and as political devices to undermine self-representation. Furthermore, disappearance and transformation (of Dwoskin's body, of other bodies) are a key feature of the film, which both deploys the surface textures of video and expands the frame of the moving image to incorporate re-projection and refilming of preexisting footage and filmed audiences. Each layer, often overlapping as a form of moving collage, competes for the viewer's attention, recombining intermedial techniques of action, place, and figuration.

In *TTKM* Dwoskin's digital videocamera frequently refilms projections of analogue films—including those made earlier in his career—as well as filmed photographs, in segments where the performers discuss the films and photographs "live" with Dwoskin. In one segment, an older Beatrice Cordua observes a projection of *Trixi*, the film that Dwoskin and she made in 1969. Part of the film is superimposed over her head and upper torso, caught part-framed in the left-hand third of the frame (Figure 14.1).

In a striking meeting of the plane of the screen projection with the plane of the observer, Trixi verbally addresses Dwoskin, looking to her left (the viewer's right) off-screen, mentioning that they hardly ever made any other films together. Dwoskin, whom we initially surmise from the close-miked off-screen voice is behind the videocamera filming her, corrects her, saying that they did indeed make only one film together. (Neither is true—she features in three other Dwoskin films.) Seconds later, as the projected film *Trixi* continues to move over the filmed portrait of Beatrice, an arm clad in a light blue denim shirt appears to the right of the frame, moving as if operating the screening of the image. The eyeline match of Beatrice to the owner of the arm surreptitiously reveals Dwoskin, not behind the camera but in front of it.

Figure 14.1 *Trying to Kiss the Moon* (Stephen Dwoskin, 1994). A real-life Beatrice Cordua (left) and Stephen Dwoskin (just visible, far right) look out at a projected image, while the image of Beatrice's younger self in Dwoskin's film *Trixi* from 1969 is superimposed on the frame.

Filmed staging, reenactment, and reflections confuse viewing planes between the artist, the camera, and his former collaborator, lover, and friend (Beatrice) and the gaze of the viewer. This complex technique does not conflate figure and ground, following Riegl, but rather fuses configurations between observer and observed, lived history and art. The historicised and heterotopic-heterochronic environments in which that contact between visual planes takes place—between 1969 and the early 1990s—draw together specific qualities of Dwoskin's life and works through time, through overlapping configurations of projection, liveness, and performance.

This sequence enacts a visual autoethnography of Dwoskin's films, complicating its intermedial modalities of autobiographical filmmaking. Processes of restaging and reperformance are found elsewhere in Dwoskin's work; however, in *TTKM* there is an involution of video and film, performance and documentation, so that transformations of the image are related not simply to surface and depth but also frame and context, the place of observation, and the reconsideration of the artwork. This pushes the formal boundaries of video haptics: video becomes a ground from which staging and reperformance emerge, and an attentiveness to conflations of past and present, which makes the subject in question—Dwoskin himself—more rather than less elusive.

In *TTKM*, Dwoskin's self-image, auditory self-fashioning and self-portraiture deploy tactics of doubling, refracting, and regenerating multiple image-making forms, including filmed family photograph albums and old Super 8 home movies. There is a profound awareness of absence in the retooled, reworked images of Dwoskin in his infancy, childhood, and adolescence. And yet it is not always the absence of another that is being marked; sometimes it is an absence of self. The film invites an estranged and estranging way of looking upon the young Dwoskin's body. In refilmed portions of home movie footage before he contracted polio, when his legs enable him to walk, tumble, and play, there is often a moment of bleed or indistinction that comes about from the imperfections of the image from both analogue film and the video refilming process. In one instance, the young Dwoskin is swinging in a hammock (Figure 14.2). As he falls and returns to the hammock, the camera lens catches the sun, transforming the child's body into a burning glow of a painterly abstracted pattern in the left-hand third of the frame (Figure 14.3).

This is not the only instance when filmed imperfections and loss of granularity in the transfer from analogue film to videotape manifest in Dwoskin's self-representation. In fact, in many instances throughout the film, editing choices favour blur, indistinction, and shifts into abstraction, presenting

Figure 14.2 *Trying to Kiss the Moon* (Stephen Dwoskin, 1994). Dwoskin as a young boy falling from a hammock (home movie footage).

the dissolution of Dwoskin's face and body into abstracted lines and masses of colour, facilitated by the use of freeze frames and slowed-down footage (Figures 14.4 to 14.7).

From a technical and aesthetic perspective, the self-images collated by Dwoskin both embrace the artefactual evidence of "waste"—the bleed, the lens flare, the softness and indistinction of an over-enlarged image and oversaturated colour that obscure facial features—and adopt these side effects as productive tools to explore and undermine the notion of self-portraiture. This is reminiscent of earlier experimental filmmaking by Kurt Kren or Ken Jacobs, but significantly more focussed on self-representation and self-expression, structured in tightly focussed vignettes that develop an orchestrated rhythm and polyphony. The slowing down of the image, facilitated by working with video, foregrounds these techniques, so that they occupy far longer screen durations than they would if run at conventional speed, switching rapidly between photographic documentation and impressionistic form, while regularly returning to the abstracted forms of Dwoskin's own face and body as site and subject matter. Dwoskin's extradiegetic voice only rarely accompanies these younger-Dwoskin sequences, foregrounding the buried

Figure 14.3 *Trying to Kiss the Moon* (Stephen Dwoskin, 1994). Dwoskin as a boy (to left) becomes golden-coloured lens flare and abstracted pattern.

histories of these moving and still images that are refilmed or filmed-while-being-projected (so that the sound of the projector and the fragility of the projection on a wall are visible and audible). There is either nothing to say, or too much: the emotional valence of these sequences powerfully disrupts attempts to narrativise them in the form of spoken commentary.

The performative acts of Dwoskin's work adopt intermedial models of video haptics, complex intermedial replay, and reframing (which is also materially more substantive than mere remediation). Intermedial method produces an incoherent, fragmented subjectivity. As mentioned earlier regarding the reenacted sequence between Dwoskin and Beatrice/Trixi, representations of Dwoskin's artworks in the film invite embodied processes of enquiry and an erotics of looking within a historical and environmental plane. In sequences where Dwoskin refilms projections of home movies of himself, invisible interlocutors—often his mother—are heard off-screen on the film's soundtrack, absent from the images. But Dwoskin's refusal to narrate his self in the film seems also to be a refusal to isolate person from work, and equally a refusal to visually master past images of himself as a linear, coherent autobiographical narrative.

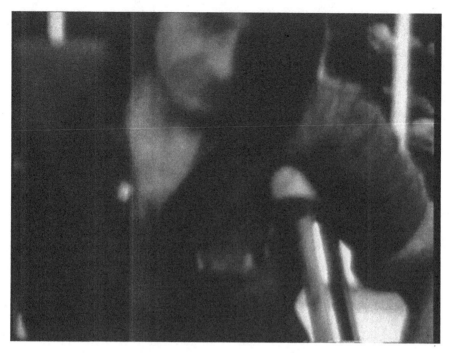

Figure 14.4 *Trying to Kiss the Moon* (Stephen Dwoskin, 1994). Close-up image of young Dwoskin, features shrouded by hair and the bright blue of his shirt.

To this effect, the disruptions of autobiography might also be better critically understood as an effect of autoethnography: a desire to understand Dwoskin's self-image as mediated through language, history, art, and kinship rather than as an individuated account of personhood.[4] In this sense, the resistance to "autobiography" in any normative frame is also indicative of a resistance to other norms prescribed by able-bodied and ableist definitions. Dwoskin's intermedial methodology is thus intrinsically bound up with his sense of self as an outsider—as a working-class, disabled, Jewish man and an artist seeking to blur formal configurations of medium. We can therefore best understand Dwoskin's work as an exemplar of intermedial praxis: not to be claimed *for* Dwoskin's work but an aesthetic underpinning of a life.

Understanding *TTKM* as an activist mode of autoethnography, resisting an individuated body in favour of a plural landscape and community of vision, gives additional depth to the concepts of self-exile explored by Said and by Clare. *TTKM* is not only an example of a late Dwoskin film adopting plural intermedial strategies through video but also an example of disability filmmaking that resists normative calls to produce "late autobiography" in the work and lifetime of an artist. One could even say that self-exile is in *TTKM*

Figure 14.5 *Trying to Kiss the Moon* (Stephen Dwoskin, 1994). Abstracted image of Dwoskin's torso through a balcony door.

a concerted strategy, deployed through intermedial techniques centred on video, to disrupt body-normative models of writing a life.

Trying to Kiss the Moon: Painting with Film

In *TTKM* Dwoskin sets out to exemplify his relationship to the world. Often described as foundational to his oeuvre is the desire to connect to women and to revel in the pleasure of looking. While it is to some extent true, this position misses much in Dwoskin's approach. Visual virtuosity and layered references are as integral a part of his methodology as is the narrative load of his cinema.

Earlier in this chapter, we discussed the relationship of figure and ground and described the way that normative expectations of art, life, and time are disrupted. This is exemplified by a passage in *TTKM* where Beatrice is speaking and being filmed while discussing the earlier film *Trixi* with Dwoskin, also being filmed while concurrently projected onto a wall. The discombobulation of figure/ground demonstrates Dwoskin's ongoing engagement with painterly concerns through the moving image, moving beyond the figure/ground plastic relations in painting towards something more profound. In moving

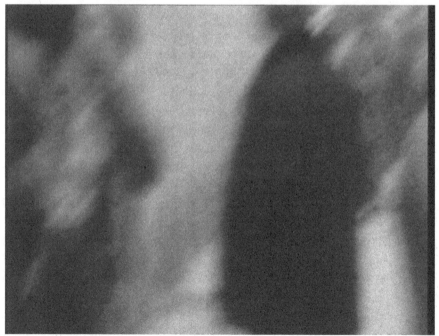

Figures 14.6 and 14.7 *Trying to Kiss the Moon* (Stephen Dwoskin, 1994). Refilmed, slowed-down footage of young adult Dwoskin on a street in Italy, shifting from clearer image to abstract blur.

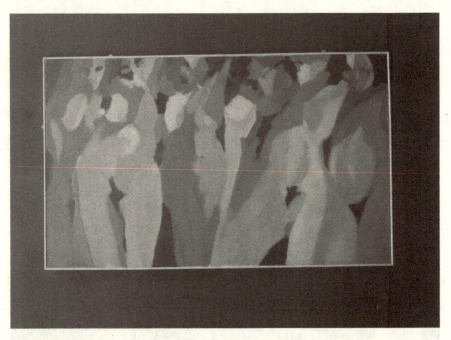

Figure 14.8 Stephen Dwoskin, *Six Figures*. Oil on canvas, mid-1960s.

beyond (as much as through the more-than-haptic), Dwoskin demonstrates his ongoing relationship with the painting concerns of his training. His teachers, amongst whom were Willem De Kooning and Josef Albers (according to Dwoskin's diaries), inculcated the key painterly paradigm of the time as propagated by figures such as Clement Greenberg (1985: 43):[5] "Where the painter still tries to indicate real objects, their shapes flatten and spread in the dense two-dimensional atmosphere. A vibrating tension is set up as the objects struggle to maintain their volume against the tendency of the real picture plane to re-assert its material flatness and crush them to silhouette."

Dwoskin's reflections throughout *TTKM* demonstrate how foundational his training was in the development and conceptualisation of his visuality, particularly in the later works which are not bound by the requirements of TV funding nor the expectations of the feature film. Medium specificity, as outlined by Greenberg (1985: 35–46) in "Towards a Newer Laocoön," was a key component of the paradigm of flattening the picture plain, of using primary colours, of simplifying form—all of which are used in the Dwoskin's paintings. These strategies were also dealt with in his filmmaking, by slowing down the footage, by juxtaposing the different materialities of film and video, by reworking film and stretching the image, by filming visual imperfections. In these ways the focus on the materiality of the film *as image* comes to the fore, as Dwoskin states in the film: "I never thought that people had made films like that before. I just considered it kind of an extension of my painting."

Dwoskin's paintings, made mostly in the mid-1960s, explore portraiture, colour, and space. He eschews any reference to local colour, using colour instead to destabilise the sense of space and the viewer's relationship to it. The figures, mainly women, are constituted through bold blocks of colour where negative and positive space battle: colour and space oscillating in importance. They are iconic and full frontal, but dynamically composed as if in movement. The push/pull[6] of colour in the paintings creates the shallow space of high modernist painting that emphasises its materiality and serves to question the figure-ground relationship by replacing spatial perspective with flatness. This is again reminiscent of the Trixi/Beatrice sequence in *TTKM* where Dwoskin considers the specificity that time affords to the mediums of film and video to reflect on how, in their own way, they destabilise the subject/object differentiation that is central to naturalism in art. Elsewhere in *TTKM* Dwoskin films a collection of his paintings leaning against the wall in his home. The camera pans the paintings, rendering the figuration abstract while at the same time invoking the tableaux of paintings as a wall of objects. A naked woman is filmed passing through the paintings, reminding us of the difference between the plasticity of painting and a body moving in space. Yet the paintings filmed in this way—with the shifts in light across the pan of the paintings back and forth—merely comments on the affinities he finds through his handling of both paint and film, whilst at the same time reflecting on film's distance from painting in its indexical link to the real. Key to this are the ways the film can create a complex and at times puzzling visual world through time and camera work.

However, the influence of his former teacher Albers was not merely in relation to the exploration of colour and the flatness of the image; Albers's emphasis on the experience of looking was a lesson that remained central to Dwoskin's approach throughout his life: "For Albers, colour was in constant flux. In his instruction, he emphasised its relativity as material and its role in creating visual relationships, especially those causing optical estrangement. But in doing so Albers taught his students more than the interaction of colour; he instilled in them a general *approach* to all material and *means* of engaging it in design. In his teaching, Albers put practice before theory and prioritised experience; 'what counts,' he claimed, 'is not so-called knowledge of so-called facts, but vision—seeing'" (Saletnik 2007: 1–2).

Greenberg's emphasis on form as materiality, amplified through Albers's experiential visuality, can be seen in Dwoskin's approach to film in the way that he takes the propositions in abstract painting against the grain and creates a visuality that traverses the push/pull of colour in paint into the inability to situate the subject in film. *TTKM* extrapolates specific characteristics that then become about exploring an embodied lived experience confounded with art.[7] So Dwoskin's focus on colour and space develops through his exploration of the world through film into an idea of visual relationships creating a vision that is not so much about knowledge as about conveying the experience of seeing. Moving from painting to film, he tested the boundaries of material and the boundaries of the image. In film, he could do this not only through composition and colour but also through the bleed and waste of the filmic image, extreme slow motion, digital manipulation of old footage, and dramatic juxtaposition of sound and shots.

Not only does the film feature his own paintings, in several different shots, but he also puts the filmed footage to work as painterly imagery through manipulation and reuse of footage. Almost every shot is classically composed, but the material components of that composition are equally often filled with casual excess, with the messiness of domestic life. This intermediality is not for the sake of formalism, although Dwoskin clearly enjoys the dynamic opportunities the rectangle of the frame/canvas affords. Early in the film he narrates, of his life and his relationship to film, "Trying to find a way of managing a dialogue with other people, something I saw in other people particularly women that triggered some kind of thing I wanted to deal with. I felt I had to deal with on screen to convey abstraction, thinking feeling. Allow people to enter the space of the subject, almost improvise in their minds about what's happening because that's the great thing about imagery in film, to think in time, which you can't do in painting." So painting here, by negation, is presented as the touchstone that propels him into film. Dwoskin reflects on his life through original black-and-white films shot by his father when he was a child. This footage acts as a backbone for the film, fragmented, poignant, intermittent, but present throughout. It is like the underpainting of the film. The footage, put into the digital realm, is reframed, often slowed down, cut up in fragmentary jump cuts or paused on the last frame to create a fuzzy edge, like a smeared charcoal mark on a sheet of paper. This has the effect of making the footage dreamlike, often depicting Dwoskin himself skipping, dancing, hugging his sister, or as a toddler struggling to walk or falling over: a metaphor for his life, perhaps. There is a strong sense of wonder and poignancy about the footage, as if he is looking at himself wondering who that was, or if he was ever actually walking.

Thinking in time allows Dwoskin to look at the specificity of gesture and movement of people around him or what their facial expression and what that might tell you about them, what they reveal and conceal. However, the expression and language he uses in the voice-over conveys an indeterminacy that is central to his visual language. His work is a dialectic of precision and generality that belies his painterly roots and the lifelong engagement with the rectangle as explored through colour, composition, and form. His decisions as a filmmaker always relied on the visual as the main driver (as opposed to narrative, character, or other possible drivers). He works with fuzziness of line set against the sharpness of the digital camera, with saturated colour contrasted with grisaille, with cartoon as drawn imagery alongside shot. But he also pushes the camera to the edge of its capability, where it struggles to focus: the struggle of the camera is a metaphor but also an investigation or experiment at the interface of technology and visuality. He takes a distant shot and expands it on the timeline into a close-up so as to restage a filmed event, but in such as a way that emphasises its painterliness. All these strategies create not only the richness of the palimpsest often found in essay films but also the visual language of collage that gives depth and breadth to the film, fusing the internal language of the subject with the external language of looking.

Conclusion

Dwoskin's intermedial multiplicity is, we argue, an artistic embodiment of the layered complexities of any person's life: the relationship between the individual, the family, and ethnic and national tradition; the interplay between the artist, histories of art, and the historiographies that govern those histories; the conflation of varied temporal, spatial, and even metaphysical coordinates (time and space, the United Kingdom and the United States, continental European and Anglo-Saxon cultures); and the paradox of the organic individual using impersonal reproductive technology to record and provide access to a life. We also want to make the case for the importance of acknowledging intermediality as the combined emergence of aesthetic, political, and cultural influences, collaborations, and practices across a body of work. What the proponents of Structuralist/Materialist film failed to see, and why the exhibition *Film as Film* has failed to excite the canon of experimental film, were the dialectics of figure and ground, form and vision, colour and depth, action and inquiry, that were always in tension in Dwoskin's work. Greenberg effectively set a challenge to future artists and art historians, a challenge which Dwoskin readily took on. By challenging the grounds of purism espoused by artists such as Gidal and Le Grice, Dwoskin instead refused the endgame of experimental film form, opening it out towards a permanent mode of intermediality. The perfect imperfection of his later video works, such as *TTKM*, emphasising the restaging and reenactments that were a constant of his earlier work, the draw of high and low art, continually test the boundaries of film. As opposed to Marcel Duchamp's testing of art by departing from painting, Dwoskin tests film by returning to painting, and to the full intermedial range of the visual, plastic, and performance arts.

Notes

The research in this essay was made possible by funding from the Arts and Humanities Research Council for the Legacies of Stephen Dwoskin's Personal Cinema project (grant reference AH/R007012/1), which ran from 2018 to 2022. Figures 14.1 to 14.7 are reproduced courtesy of the LUX/Dwoskin Estate. Figure 14.8 is reproduced courtesy of the Special Collections at the University of Reading, where the Stephen Dwoskin Archive is housed and where underlying archival research can be accessed. No new data were created in this study, however, the underlying archival material can be accessed via the Dwoskin Archive, with a digital catalogue available here: https://www.reading.ac.uk/adlib/Details/archive Special/110438699 Our heartfelt thanks to the Dwoskin project team—in particular, Guy Baxter, Associate Director (Archives Services) of the University Museums and the Special Collections at the University of Reading, Yunhyong Kim, Frank Hopfgartner, Zoe Bartliff, and Henry K. Miller.

1. See, for example, Monk (1998) and Johnson (2012).
2. We use the term "English" here specifically: very few non-English filmmakers are discussed in this context, such as Margaret Tait and James Coleman. But "English" was also the terminology that filmmakers and institutions used to describe the artist's film movement—for example, the international touring exhibition *A Perspective on English Avant-Garde Film*, organised by David Curtis and Deke Dusinberre for the Arts Council England (1978–1979) and the title of Dusinberre's (1977) seminal thesis "English Avant-Garde Cinema, 1966–1974"; Malcolm le Grice (1969) referred to the new "English" experimental filmmakers in *Cinim* no. 3; Dwoskin's mentor Jonas Mekas (1967) describes LFMC filmmakers as "English" in "Movie Journal"; and Amos Vogel (1974: 234) calls Dwoskin "England's most iconoclastic independent" in *Film as a Subversive Art*. In European publications, when not described as American, Dwoskin is often listed as "English" but rarely "British." For much of his career, the main funding body was Arts Council England.
3. *Pain Is . . .* (1997), *Intoxicated by My Illness* (2002), *The Sun and the Moon* (2008), and *Age Is . . .* (2012).
4. This definition of autoethnography is drawn from Lionnet (1989: 99), in turn cited in Couser (2000: 308).
5. Although Albers was a generation earlier than de Kooning, both were émigrés from Europe, and Albers had both studied and taught at the Bauhaus.
6. "Push/pull" is a phrase coined by the painter and teacher Hans Hofmann in the 1930s. It became ubiquitous with reference to abstract painting, playing on the way that colour recedes or emerges in space on a flat surface.
7. He does this in a different way in *Behindert* (1975), where a relationship is reenacted between the protagonists for whom the events happened but through a film that had prefigured the

events depicted in the film. Dwoskin had the idea for a film about a relationship between a disabled man and an able-bodied woman that failed because of the protagonist's disability; the actual relationship with Carola Regnier provided the specific detail through which Dwoskin made the film in which both Dwoskin and Regnier then acted.

References

Albers, Josef. 2006. *Interaction of Color*. New Haven, CT: Yale University Press.
Artaud, Antonin. 1993. "The Theatre of Cruelty: First Manifesto." In *The Theatre and Its Double*, 68–78. Montreuil: Calder.
Bataille, Georges. 1966. *Ma mère*. Paris: Jean-Jacques Pauvert.
Benfey, Christopher. 2016. "A Wonderfully Ephemeral College." *New York Review of Books*, 26 May.
Bolter, Jay David, and Richard Grusin. 1999. *Remediation: Understanding New Media*. Cambridge, MA: MIT Press.
Brennan, Eugene. 2013. "Aversion to Repetition: Cosey Fanni Tutti Interviewed." *The Quietus*, 2 December. https://thequietus.com/articles/13445-cosey-fanni-tutti-interview.
Buck, Paul, ed. 1984. *Violent Silence: Celebrating Georges Bataille*. London: Georges Bataille Event.
Clare, Eli. 2015. *Exile and Pride: Disability, Queerness, and Liberation*. Durham, NC: Duke University Press.
Couser, G. Thomas. 2000. "The Empire of the 'Normal': A Forum on Disability and Self-Representation: Introduction." *American Quarterly* 52, no. 2: 305–310. https://doi.org/10.1353/aq.2000.0017.
Dusinberre, Peter de Kay. 1977. "English Avant-Garde Cinema, 1966–1974." Master's thesis, University of London.
Dwoskin, Stephen. 1975. *Film Is . . .: The International Free Cinema*. London: Peter Owen.
Dwoskin, Stephen. 1993. *Ha, Ha!: La Solution Imaginaire*. New York: The Smith.
Gilbert, Dick. 1968. "Steve Dwoskin Film Maker." *The Guardian*, 24 April.
Greenberg, Clement. 1985. "Towards a Newer Laocoön." In *Pollock and After: The Critical Debate*, edited by Francis Frascina, 35–46. London: Paul Chapman Publishing Ltd.
Griffin, Ken. 2015. "The Lessons of Counterpoint: Wolfgang Ernst's Media Archaeology and Practical Archival Research." *VIEW Journal of European Television History and Culture* 4, no. 7: 11–20. https://doi.org/10.25969/mediarep/14116.
Jarry, Alfred. 1996. *Exploits and Opinions of Dr Faustroll, Pataphysician*. Translated by Simon Watson Taylor. Boston: Exact Change.
Johnson, Dominic. 2012. *Glorious Catastrophe: Jack Smith, Performance and Visual Culture*. Manchester: Manchester University Press.
Kirby, Michael, and Richard Schechner. 1965. "An Interview with John Cage." *Tulane Drama Review* 10, no. 2: 50–72.
Le Grice, Malcolm. 1969. "The London Filmmakers Co-op Report." *Cinim* 3: 31.
Lionnet, Françoise. 1989. *Autobiographical Voices: Race, Gender, Self-Portraiture*. Ithaca, NY: Cornell University Press.
Marks, Laura U. 1998. "Video Haptics and Erotics." *Screen* 39, no. 4: 331–348.
Marks, Laura U. 2000. *The Skin of the Film*. Durham, NC: Duke University Press.

Matos Cabo, Ricardo. 2006. "A transmissão silenciosa." *Doc's Kingdom: International Seminar on Documentary Film*. Accessed 16 December 2018. https://docskingdom.org/wp-content/uploads/downloads/textosdeapoio_2006-min.pdf#page=91.

Mekas, Jonas. 1967. "Movie Journal (December 23, 1967)." *Village Voice* [unpaginated clipping in Stephen Dwoskin Archive, University of Reading].

Mekas, Jonas. 1972. *Movie Journal: The Rise of the New American Cinema, 1959–1971.* New York: Macmillan.

Mekas, Jonas. 2016. "Movie Journal (May 26, 1966)." In *Movie Journal: The Rise of the New American Cinema, 1959–1971*, edited by Gregory Smulewicz-Zucker, 249–251. 2nd edition. New York: Columbia University Press.

Monk, Philip. 1998. *American Playhouse: The Theatre of Self-Presentation.* Toronto: Power Plant.

Palmer, Jonathan, and Maria Trombetta. 2017. "Black Mountain College: A Creative Art Space Where It Was Safe to Fail." *World Futures* 73, no. 1: 19.

Parsons School of Design. 1958. *[Curriculum] 1958–59*. New York: Parsons School of Design.

Pethö, Ágnes. 2011. *Cinema and Intermediality: The Passion for the In-Between.* Newcastle: Cambridge Scholars.

Said, Edward. 2004. "Thoughts on Late Style." *London Review of Books* 26, no. 15: 3–7.

Saletnik, Jeffrey. 2007. "Josef Albers, Eva Hesse, and the Imperative of Teaching." *Tate Papers* 7. https://www.tate.org.uk/research/tate-papers/07/josef-albers-eva-hesse-and-the-imperative-of-teaching.

Shattuck, Roger. 1976. "Artaud Possessed." *New York Review of Books*, 11 November. https://www.nybooks.com/articles/1976/11/11/artaud-possessed/.

Tutti, Cosey Fanni. 2017. *Art Sex Music*. London: Faber & Faber.

Vogel, Amos. 1974. *Film as Subversive Art*. London: CT Editions.

Washington, Irving. 1972. "The London Film-makers' Co-op." *Time Out*, 21–27 January, 36.

15
Intermedial Voices
Intersections in Feminist Sound and Moving Image

Claire M. Holdsworth

The human voice begins within and travels outside the body and, as such, is a fundamentally intermedial act. The voice is by nature disconnected from the person who spoke it, and the recorded voice in turn forges new connections across and over time. As both a unique spoken event and a recorded artefact it has different meanings and effects that depend on where and how it is heard. The voice as a concept recurs in activist and feminist politics in the form of a reassessment of language, being, and being heard, which are central to struggles for recognition and the reassessment of the intersecting structural biases (of race, class, and gender) perpetuated within culture.

The Feminist Improvising Group, also known as FIG (Figure 15.1) used striking free-vocal refrains in their music, combining live instruments with other sounds. Bizarre and innovative, humorous and intelligent, their multifaceted, unconventional performances were closely connected with feminist and socialist activism in the late 1970s. Its members connect with a wider network of art forms, including feminist experimental filmmaking via (among other overlaps) their inclusion in the soundtracks of feminist films. This is a subtle convergence within and extending beyond the context of the Women's Liberation movement, indicating nuanced exchanges that are easily overlooked when histories are separated according to art form or subcategorised into feminist micro-subjects, processes that simplify this complex ecology, which encompassed concentric circles of overlapping activity (Lippard 1995). These overlaps are further complicated when we consider how, as Laura Mulvey (1979) wrote at the time, these cross-fertilisations were newly emergent and concerned with inventing new methodologies or uncovering hidden histories—to use Sheila Rowbotham's (1973) phrasing. Amy Tobin (2015: 113) emphasises that artists working in this intersectional context "shook the established tenets of old and new media alike, imbuing women's work with a mobility that constantly contravened the borders of museum, art school, gallery and cinema." Building upon these contexts, sound and music represent a significant and often overlooked sphere within this concentric ecology.

Despite the dual audio-visual nature of cinema, the topic of sound, though not neglected, is nevertheless not visible (and difficult to describe), like the complex cultural intersections of historical feminism. The replay of the recorded voice, much like feminist methodologies that critically reexamine the past, blurs boundaries between timeframes, re-forming them in the present. The voice is a phenomenon with compound cultural associations within feminist discourses (Kristeva 1984; Silverman 1988; Cavarero 2005; Whittaker and Wright 2017), some of which informed the use of voices in Laura Mulvey and Peter Wollen's 1980 film *AMY!* (16mm, 32 minutes).[1] This feminist historical reexamination of the aviator Amy Johnson (1903–1941) merges sound and voices from the late 1970s with images from the 1930s and includes music by FIG. Through examination of both FIG and *AMY!*, this chapter explores the intermedial historical dynamics of the voice and how it can be reassociated with other objects, subjects, and contexts over time.

Figure 15.1 The Feminist Improvising Group performing, ca. 1980. Left to right: Maggie Nicols, Annemarie Roelofs, Irene Schweizer, Georgina Born, Lindsay Cooper, and Sally Potter. Lindsay Cooper Digital Archive, #8578 (ID LC01565), Division of Rare and Manuscript Collections, Cornell University Library. Available at: https://digital.library.cornell.edu/catalog/ss:21812300

Expanding Discourse and Intermedia

The "medium" was significant in art from the 1960s onwards. The development and use of new recording technologies in art at this time initiated new discourses that redefined such terms—including video, cassettes, and Super 8 film, all of which were more affordable and available beginning in the late 1960s. Following on from this, until recently, discourses on media/mediums have tended to dissect and separate technologies (e.g., film is often separated from video). By revisiting notions of "intermedia," a number of recent studies (including this collection) have sought to break down these distinctions, acknowledging intersections between other elements (Knowles and Schmid 2020) and how countercultural underground practices from the late 1960s involved a convergence of media, mediums, materials, art forms, and writings. The concept of intermedia originally developed from writings by Fluxus artist Dick Higgins in 1965, who adapted the term from the Romantic poet Samuel Taylor Coleridge. Higgins ([1965] 2021: 50) observed at the time that the "best work being produced today seems to fall between media. This is no accident."

At this time many cooperative groups were established, creating collaborative artistic workshops and spaces that emphasised access to technology along with showing and sharing works. As the 1970s progressed, many such groups actively blurred the lines between performance, music, writing, film, video, and art, creating artworks between "cinema, drama, music, and poetry," the phrase written on the door of the Better Books bookshop on Charing Cross Road, where the London Film-Makers' Co-operative (LFMC) was founded in 1966. Underground organisations and groups in this context emphasised boundary-pushing, collaboration, and nonconformity, boosting technological, social, and artistic innovations that were closely connected to activism (Holdsworth and Blanchard 2017).

This activism extended to free improvisation in the United Kingdom, which emerged as a musical technique and a genre during the 1950s, influenced by UK jazz groups connected with Music for Socialism (Holdsworth 2017). Artists developed alternative approaches to live performances, in which musicians played varied, unexpected instruments or objects, sometimes using nonconventional "scores," diagrams, or sets of instructions (techniques also developed in Fluxus artworks).[2] Instruments were often attached to contact microphones and favoured unconventional sounds and ways of playing. Practitioners tended to be critically alert to the established structures of the art form (e.g., notation, tone, scales, harmony, and other musical conventions), but also the politicised structures of culture and society (Born 2017). In free improvisation, the medium/instrument, its use and forms of conventionalised play were completely reassessed, including vocals and use of the voice.

As more feminist discourses developed over the 1970s, female artists and artists of colour—working in a country with an overwhelming sense of the world established and projected by its colonial and imperial history—questioned preestablished canons and histories (Rhodes 1979) and organised into support systems, collectives, and cooperatives. This criticality did extend to language and mediums, but the term "intermedia" was not commonly used in the United Kingdom until more recently. Instead, concepts such as "expanded field" were used, which, as Rosalind Krauss wrote in 1979, provided "for an organisation of work that is not dictated by the conditions of a particular medium" (42–43). In experimental film and video, this engagement with the audience and physical space moved "beyond materiality to mobilize an 'active spectatorship' through performance, extending the experience of watching [and listening] into other spaces" (White 2011: 110).

Despite this transcendence, recent writings reexamining intermediality tend to focus on expanded performance (Barber 2020; Walley 2020). This emphasis means that the techniques of narrativisation that emerged in the mid-1970s, such as those of filmmakers like Mulvey and Wollen in the six films they made between 1974 and 1983, are perceived as a move away from this "live" expansion (Walley 2020: 91). Yet live-ness was often fundamental to "new narrative" practices, such as works by performance artist Yvonne Rainer (Walley 2020: 94–99), who also participated in Mulvey and Wollen's *AMY!* The use of sound in this film (Figure 15.2), whether recorded voices or music

Figure 15.2 Still from Laura Mulvey and Peter Wollen, *AMY!* (1980). © Mulvey and Wollen. Image courtesy of Laura Mulvey.

by FIG, enacts a peculiar reversal of this expansion, which drags live acts and other politicised spaces back into the filmic frame. Many discourses focus on how mediums record and store the human voice, yet the voice is a kind of medium in and of itself, an intermedial element that traverses both time and technology that, as discussed later, contributes to the overlapping timeframes cycled in *AMY!*

Defamiliar Voices: The FIG

The women-only FIG was founded by composer Lindsay Cooper and vocalist Maggie Nicols with the musicians Georgina Born, Koryne (formerly Corinne) Liensol, and Cathy Williams towards the end of 1977. They were soon joined by Irène Schweizer and Sally Potter, who become core members.[3] Their first performance was at the Music for Socialism Festival at the Almost Free Theatre in 1977 in response to the lack of women on this platform (Gray 2021: 41). The event involved a workshop which explored ways of subverting female stereotypes in life and on stage (41; Nicols 2021: 8). FIG developed an "extraordinary and eccentric style; along with musical and sonic improvisations, performances often entailed the anarchic and uneven use of visual, theatrical and elements that dramatized and parodied aspects of 'women's experience' . . . with a focus on the subversive or hilarious enactment of mundane activities such as domestic labour" (Born 2017: 53). Nicols has described FIG performances as "completely irreverent," a way of playing and performing that was "synchronistic with a women's liberation movement giving birth to itself; we were part of it. You cannot separate the political movement from what FIG was . . . and the absolute joy of discovering that women were important" (quoted in Gray 2021: 42).

FIG's performances used costumes and props and engaged with politics through farce, questioning both the status quo of society and the egalitarian ethos of improv communities, an approach rooted in a socialist politics that, nevertheless, excluded many. Georgina Born (2017: 36, 41) explains that their music reflected the distinct "micro-social" spaces of musical performance. This connects with Tobin's (2015: 112) description of intersecting feminist artistic practices in the 1970s (via Hannah Arendt's concept of the "space of appearance"), which describes "a mobile manifestation of power, supported by the speech acts of the participants. Group members are connected by first rendering themselves incomplete through their openness to others and are bound together by mutual 'inter-est' " via co-habitation and speech in spaces.[4] Like expanded cinema, FIG saw performance as a two-way "co-productive process" between audience and musician (Born 2017: 33) that directly channelled awareness of wider contexts and politics.

The personal became political through the coproductive interactions between FIG musicians and the audience and the centrality of the voice in this interaction. The free vocal sounds of Nicols and Potter were part-sung and spoken, using poetic lines and subversive statements alongside sounds resembling speech, paralinguistic half-heard words, communicating through tone and pitch and rhythm. Multiple singing and spoken voices merged, tuned, and changed with each other and the instruments—with strings, cello, piano, and breath-like exclamations from bassoon and oboe. Humour-laden improvisations were often combined with laughter among the audience and performers alike, a coproductive approach to "music [that] necessitate[d] an expansion of the conceptual framework of social mediation" (Born 2017: 43) beyond notions of the individual and collective as binaries, and which echoes the wider feminist social re-formations to which FIG was connected.

FIG came together just as other organised spaces and groupings dedicated to improvised music were being established in London, such as the London Musicians' Collective (LMC). In 1976, the LMC moved into the same building as the LFMC. Although both organisations were separate physically and institutionally, there were overlaps, and they were neighbours in this building for over a decade (Holdsworth 2017). FIG vocalist Sally Potter was a member of the LFMC and went on to make influential works of feminist performance and cinema (including 1983's *The Gold Diggers*, scored by Cooper), indicating that the concentric connections between experimental feminist practices extended beyond art forms as well as mediums into other spaces.

As a challenge to the seemingly egalitarian yet highly professionalised improvisation community, FIG opened their process to women at all levels of musicianship. The ensemble usually performed with as many as eight improvisers, including white, Black, lesbian, straight, working- and middle-class women, channelling the anarchic ethos of punk music (also emerging in London in 1976) with left-wing meeting formats, overt comedic mime, and audience participation. At times, they received hostile responses from audiences, and their performances tended to take place in spaces very different from the LMC or improvised music venues (including cinemas, see Figure 15.3), including female-only concerts and on one occasion a "gents" toilet (Nicols, cited in Gray 2021: 42).[5] FIG's coproductive performances engaged in "antiphonal" exchanges: back-and-forth, call-and-response passages with the audience. In these settings, antiphonal, live-improvised voices interrupt the tropes of song-singing and musical performance and the boundaries between performers and audience.

Intermedial Voices 253

Figure 15.3 Poster for FIG gig at the Ritzy in Brixton. Illustrations by Sally Potter. Lindsay Cooper Digital Archive, #8578 (ID: LC01353), Division of Rare and Manuscript Collections, Cornell University Library. Available at: https://digital.library.cornell.edu/catalog/ss:21812079

As they were performed largely in live coproductive contexts, recordings of FIG are rare, making their inclusion in film soundtracks significant.[6] By inverting the embodied, sonic materiality of live interaction, recordings of FIG manifest a paradoxical performative gap that is also central to the voice itself. The voice implies and emphasises the subjectivities, inflections, and indexical characteristics unique to the body that produced/projected it out into the air. This self-inscription is rooted in our inclination to connect sounds to sources, a tendency given the name "causal listening" by Michel Chion

(1994: 25). This causal inclination to identify a sound source means that the voice can be reattached to other bodies and objects, a situation of association that is fundamental to the effectiveness of voiceovers in film and video, speech sounds from beyond the camera frame (Chion 1999). Dissociated by the act of throwing, the voice betrays both utterer and receiver by connecting to something other. Yet it channels a veracity, an authority that does not correspond to straightforward notions of appearance (the visible), authorship, or authority. As Mladen Dolar (2006: 106) writes, the voice exists in a paradoxical state, an interstitial space of "inclusion [and] exclusion which retains the excluded at its core." This external existence and parallel ability to connect with other sources is closely bound to the words we use to describe it. In English, the voice attaches "to" as opposed to "away from" other objects (including our ears). The "ventriloquial voice," then, as Steven Connor (2000: 42) describes it, exists in the space between pure vocalisation and the communication or expression of ideas—cleaved to one body, yet associating with another object.

The fact that the voice always exists external to our selves informs its depiction as a recorded phenomenon. In cinema, voices are often disembodied (as voice-overs), with uncanny associations, shifting origins, implying psychic fracture or ghostly apparitions. Voices can trick us and assume the role of unreliable narrators. These participatory states of inclusion/exclusion and potential misappropriation are why the voice as a concept is closely associated with the politics of representation and feminism. It is a signifier of authority or authenticity, yet it is questionable, shifting, and easily reattached or reassociated with an other. The voice is closely associated with both the inclusions and the exclusions to which we as humans are subject structurally.

Intermedial Voices: *AMY!*

AMY! includes multiple voices, which speak from outside the frame, beyond the event horizon of the images seen (Toufic 1996: 48). One of Mulvey and Wollen's last theory films, *AMY!* completes a trilogy along with *Penthesilea* (1974) and *Riddles of the Sphinx* (1977) examining the myths, mythopoesis, and representation of women. Building upon these earlier works, *AMY!* explores ideas of heroine-ism via the story of pioneering British aviator Amy Johnson, the first woman to fly solo from Britain to Australia, in 1930. Conflating this earlier period with the later one (the end of the 1970s) in which it was shot, Mulvey and Wollen intersperse contemporary footage with archive footage, blurring the lines between past and present.

In *AMY!* voices and sounds are layered as carefully as the assembled elements of the image-track, with complex concatenations of image, archive, superimposed text, spoken word, sounds, and music. These are used to establish compound(ed) readings of the ways reality (and a person) can be signified and inscribed via the audio-visual. Although these methods and the many elements that come together in *AMY!* provide rich material for aural analysis, as do the writings of Mulvey and Wollen along with their other five films, discussion here will focus on scenes in *AMY!* that include music by FIG.[7]

Throughout *AMY!* the movement and juxtaposition of elements create a compounded time-space in which 1930 and 1980 converge. In Europe and the United Kingdom, the 1920s were a time of avant-garde advancement, collaboration, and exploration in society, music, art, and culture. Then, in the wake of the worldwide effects of the Wall Street Crash in 1929 and after the onset of the Great Depression in the US in 1930, there was a rise in Fascist politics, culminating in the outbreak of the Second World War in 1939. For Mulvey and Wollen, the 1920s were a mirror for the political shifts of the 1970s, during which time arts, filmmaking, and music flourished, before a dark neoliberal turn to Conservatism in the UK heralded by the election of Margaret Thatcher to Prime Minister in 1979 (an antiheroine of sorts), just before they started making *AMY!*

In *AMY!* music and voices act as conduits connecting 1939 and 1979, both of which are tethered to the present of listening. The sound, like all Mulvey and Wollen's films, was designed by Larry Sider under the name Evanston Percussive Unit.[8] In terms of music, the film can be divided into two halves, dissected by an extended map sequence in the middle (and described briefly later). The first half features the recurring sounds of FIG, whose otherworldly music and half-heard voices contrast with the powerful, clear lyrics and vocals of Poly Styrene, lead singer of the punk band X-Ray Spex used in the second half of the film. The start and end include bright, fast-paced xylophone music by La Troupe des Guinéens (from the record *Xylophones et chœur de femmes*) released in 1977 (and part of Mulvey and Wollen's record collection). We hear these percussive xylophones before seeing black-and-white archive footage from the perspective of a camera eye. The camera travels through a cheering crowd of people who wave into the lens, welcoming Johnson back to Croydon airport after her solo flight from England to Australia in May 1930. As discussed by Esther Leslie and Nicolas Helm-Grovas, these opening elements channel silent and Soviet cinema of the 1930s, when Johnson undertook her flights, recalling the montage techniques of director Sergei Eisenstein— "exhorting, interrogating and inducing excitement in the viewer" (Helm-Grovas 2018: 275).[9] The exclamatory tone and sped-up footage are made playful by the quick-paced percussive tones of the xylophones, which interweave several distinct lines of notes, adding to the pace of this opening section, echoing yet tonally different from the lively piano music that typically accompanied newsreels in the silent era during which the footage was originally shot. These silent-film origins are made more apparent by the contemporaneity of the sound, a reminder that recorded sounds, and Johnson's own voice were not necessarily captured in the same way as her journey or exploits were via the media. Other newsreel footage from the time (not included in *AMY!*) reveals that when her voice was captured, it was heavily scripted and staged (stemming from the complex setups required to record sync-sound in the 1930s). In *AMY!* we see footage of her speaking, but we never hear her voice. Throughout the film, her personal experiences are set against more generalised depictions of Amy the heroine.

The percussive sounds and intertitle cuts of the opening section abruptly change, and Mulvey's voice is then heard, the sound echoing in a very different unseen room-space, asking about heroines. Played over the black and yellow intercut title text at the start, the sound arrives slightly ahead of the images to which it connects, comprising interviews with a class of students from Paddington College (on the Community Care Course), originally shot on video (with the faint sound of a carpentry workshop discernible in the background). A video monitor with curved edges can be seen in the frame (Figure 15.4), indicating that the 16mm film-stock camera used in *AMY!* was used to refilm the video screen. By contrast, the sound is immediate, coming to us through a different (closer), more direct channel. Each element, whether sounded or seen, is separated from its source.

Figure 15.4 Still from Laura Mulvey and Peter Wollen, *AMY!* (1980). Interviews with students at Paddington College (Community Care Course) in the late 1970s. © Mulvey and Wollen. Image courtesy of Laura Mulvey.

The interviewees discuss women working in engineering in the 1970s. One female speaker says they used to fix the family's television set. Her description of the image being "not quite right" reflects Johnson's sense of dissonance, voiced later in the film, between media projections of her as "Amy," which fail to acknowledge her abilities as a skilled mechanic and aviator. Although the interview voices are diegetically connected to the people who speak, the remediation between film and video screens creates a temporal distance between the moment of the shot and the replay of the conversations, reiterated by our hearing these voices slightly before seeing them. This sense of being out-of-sync reflects the use of voiceovers as well as contemporary music from the late 1970s by FIG and X-Ray Spex: a displacement that is also part of the process of recording, compounded by the voice itself. As Connor (2000: 7) explains, perhaps "the commonest experiential proof of the voice's split condition (as at once cleaving to and taking leave from myself), is provided by the experience of hearing one's own recorded voice." This split between speaking and being recorded, between acting and perceiving the voice-act later, is significant to Johnson's struggles with depictions of "Amy, Wonderful Amy"—to use the words of a popular 1930 song about her by Jack Hylton and his Orchestra, which is heard in full towards the end of the film.

Throughout *AMY!* music adds distinct layers to the coexisting realities perceived by the viewer. The choice of music reemphasises the compounded slippage between 1939 and 1979. Mulvey and Wollen were familiar with the work of FIG and moved in similar feminist/social circles at the LFMC and via left-wing activism/writing, women's groups, and music performances in London.[10] We first hear FIG just after the interview scene, which cuts to contemporary footage of a wet London street next to the department store Peter Jones (on Sloane Square), where Johnson worked briefly (the sequence also includes yellow on-screen writing stating how much Johnson earned). The traffic moves as the sound of a bassoon plays, shifting between intricate scale movements and unstructured free playing, as improvised singing voices are heard, starting quiet and gradually getting louder. These sounds stop when the short street scene switches to an indoor setting at first focussed on a small chest of drawers. The shot is accompanied by the voice of the actor Mary Maddox, who plays Johnson. Maddox's voiceover—familiar from earlier films in Mulvey and Wollen's trilogy—reads words from a letter written by Johnson to a lover, whilst hands remove flowers and a pile of envelopes from the small drawers. Adopting a technique of movement that reflects rostrum shots across a map later in *AMY!* (a technique used in other films by Mulvey and Wollen), the voice stops speaking and the camera slowly tracks sideways across the room. The voices and sounds of FIG are heard once again as the camera glides through space, first quiet and increasing in volume as the frame travels across the room and comes to rest on a fireplace. The sounds of FIG's vocal improvisations tune in and out. Sounds hum and harmonise with a piano and other sounds, becoming louder. The musical space of the scene is taken up either by Johnson's voiceover or the sounds of FIG; they are never heard simultaneously. The powerful musical noises made by FIG contrast with the silence of Maddox/Johnson, who then sits down on the floor beside the fire. The other-worldly, barely discerned vocalisations of FIG form abstracted words that are hard to understand, denying semantic identification. They indicate an expansive, unknowable inner world, which no one, not the viewer, Johnson, nor media/historical depictions of her can translate.

Both singing and spoken vocal sounds in this scene echo the paradox of the voice as described by Dolar (2006: 106), who observes that it is constantly haunted by "the impossibility of symbolising" itself. This reflects the situation faced by Johnson, who outlines a conflict between her status as a heroine and her parallel status as an engineer and aviator (as described in the letters voiced by Maddox). The sustained hum of thoughtful activity implied by the music and voices of FIG gradually build to an unstructured cacophony of improvised sounds. These sounds channel tumultuous and extreme emotions, becoming high pitched, singing undiscernible words. There is a dissonance between seeing and hearing, between outward appearance and internal emotion, amplified by these juxtaposing image- and sound-tracks. Finally, Johnson places the letters in the fireplace and burns them.

Figure 15.5 Still from Laura Mulvey and Peter Wollen, *AMY!* (1980). Mary Maddox as Amy Johnson. © Mulvey and Wollen. Image courtesy of Laura Mulvey.

There is then a quick cut to a very similarly composed image of Johnson sitting in the same place, wearing different clothes, the sounds of FIG now gone. She sits on the floor silently making cocoa beside a fireplace, the pan heating directly on the coals. We then hear her voiceover once more, methodically listing the "daily drill" activities involved with testing, greasing, and checking an airplane engine. The shot rests here as the voice speaks, before anticipating Johnson's move back to the desk, and slowly tracking this movement across the room. The voiceover finishes and as the shot moves the sounds of FIG return. Johnson sits at the desk once more, reading and planning, as music by FIG continues to play. The photo of a man on the desk in the earlier sequence has been replaced by a photo of a plane in flight (anticipating the footage of planes and birds in flight later in the film) and reflecting the shift in the phases of Johnson's life described in the voiceover letter extracts (Figure 15.5). The fluctuating sounds of FIG build to form a cacophony of crashing instruments and voices as the camera focuses once more on the chest. This time, Johnson's hand opens the drawers, now filled with screw-bolts and a miniature globe of the Earth, replacing the letters we saw and heard earlier. The sounds of FIG then carry over into the next scene, showing an old-fashioned blue propeller aeroplane parked in a hangar. Yellow text appears on screen—"Flying Dreams" (see Figure 15.2), "Financial Backers," and "Wakefield's Oil"—and the music fades as a black intertitle is seen, after which the film's central scene starts, tracing Johnson's journey across a map, pulling us away from this intimate, internalised depiction of Johnson.

The peculiar timelessness of the dissociated FIG recordings contrasts with the clipped voice heard during the map sequence. In this section, a rostrum shot scans a map, charting the legs of Amy's journey, showing brightly coloured place names and the contours of an atlas, accompanied by the sound of a distant plane in flight. We hear the English-accented male voice of Jonathan Eden reading headlines from *The Times*, describing events all over the world in May 1930, when Johnson undertook her journey, political events that in some ways indicate the slow dissolution of the British Empire, the externalised conflicts we now know to be the start of decolonial history. Like the ventriloquised voice, in this film, image, voice, and source (text) elements are recombined, and voiceovers such as Maddox/Johnson's and Eden's create coexisting narratives that supplement the image-track. The different elements of the film ventriloquially connect, as voices are reattached to new (time) frames.

Voiceovers are, to use composer Pierre Schaffer's (1952) term, "acousmatic"; they are sounds disconnected from their source, which activate a form of "reduced listening," according to Chion (1994: 29). In this situation, auditors "quickly realize that in speaking about sounds they shuttle between a sound's actual content, its source, and its meaning" (29). Simultaneously, voiceovers have a paradoxical presence, existing in defamiliarised disconnection from the subject (the person who spoke them) whilst being remediated, reassociated with something else. The constant shifts between source, content, and meaning are emphasised by the fact that many of the voices in *AMY!* read texts written by others, calling attention to the intermedial process through which stories are inscribed (and to which Johnson is subject). Voiceovers point to other sources, enacting an iterative re-enunciation of contrasting narratives on the experience of flying and the factual reporting of Johnson's journeys in the media. Among these voices, Yvonne Rainer reads a text written by Peter Wollen in which different extracts are merged into each other and sources become indistinguishable, including words by "Bryher, Amelia Earhart, Lola Montez, S. and Gertrude Stein" (*AMY!* film credits). During this section we see dreamily filmed skies, planes, and birds, which cut and repeat. In other sections we hear Katherine Wright, sister and supporter of the Wright Brothers, and Rainer reads a text by the poet H.D. which describes the experience of flying and seeing the land from above. Earlier, Wollen's voice describes a "philobat" (a term from psychoanalyst Michael Balint), a person who enjoys risk-taking and vertigo, which is heard over footage of the now deserted Airport House in Croydon (where Johnson started and ended her solo journey). Mulvey later discusses the symbolism of the heroine over a shot of 1970s Northcliffe House, where the newspaper the *Daily Mail* used to be based. These subjects are pitched forward in time. They speak words that are not their own. Complex and temporally uncertain, they involve a splitting that characterises all voices but to which we as receivers are easily able to reattune, adapt to, and associate with what we see.

The intermedial connection between written and spoken words and the ways in which voices are ventriloquised through mediums is central to the layered realities that converge in *AMY!* Singing and spoken voices perform different functions in the film. The voiceovers are connected to written texts and writings, whereas the singing voices and music are captured in the later moment, 1979. A later mirror camera sequence plays refrains of the X-Ray Spex song "Identity" (1979), and in another scene we hear the song "Obsessed with You" (1978). Contrasting with the otherworldly, unknowable sounds of the FIG voices heard in the first half of the film, in the "Obsessed with You" scene the lyrics are direct and discernible. The lead singer of the band, Poly Styrene, sings, "you are just a concept," a "dream," a "reflection," a "theme," a "symbol" of the "new regime," as Maddox/Johnson walks towards the camera, angrily turning away from its gaze, then turning back and staring defiantly into the lens. Poly Styrene articulates the sentiments echoed by Johnson in her letters, connecting to her sense of individuality, and the grander narratives she resists. The music of FIG and X-Ray Spex resist narrativization by form and content, respectively, and contrast with the old-world nostalgia and oversimplified refraction of "Amy" as sung by the male voice of Hylton. This much older song is played in full over a static shot of Amy's equally still aeroplane, suspended in the Science Museum. The sentimentality of Hylton's singing voice seems absurd after hearing Johnson's letters, discussing how "publicity and public life" were "forced" upon her.

The final shots of the film use newsreel footage of Johnson speaking in public, but we do not hear her voice. Instead, we hear a voice from one of the college interviewees from the start of the film, discussing how heroines do not need to be famous. This image of Johnson ventriloquises the later women's sounded discussion. The recorded video-voice travels back as well as forwards through time. The politicised compounded context of 1930/1979 is emphasised and facilitated via the reassociation of this ventriloquised voice, fostering an exchange of feminist solidarity over and beyond linear timeframes. Through the voice, Mulvey and Wollen expand time and space, emphasising difference and manipulating conventional approaches to linear continuums of history, disrupting the flow of information, and creating a temporal dissonance through voices that denies historicism in the present.

Conclusion

As Rebecca Schneider (2001:101) discusses, performance practices that emphasise live-ness are often associated with terms such as "ephemerality," also used to describe gaps in feminist histories; these dialogues channel an ocular prioritisation via words such as "disappearance." However, performance, actions, and live acts do remain, as Schneider outlines, "the scandal of performance relative to the archive is not that it disappears (this is what the archive expects) but that it *both* 'becomes itself through disappearance' . . . *and* that it remains" (105, italics in original).[11] In terms of music and performance, FIG enacted and subverted narratives of appearance and visibility in complex ways. Even though the intersecting feminist artistic practices of the 1970s and 1980s have been revisited in recent years (Jacquin 2017; Tobin 2015;

Reynolds 2015, 2019), the representation of complex ecologies and overlaps among art forms, artists, and groups who are hard to place such as FIG, remain unmapped.

Notions of visible and invisible histories connect directly with FIG, a group whose works were performed live and who were rarely recorded. Recordings of FIG, by inverting the embodied, sonic materiality of their live performances, manifest the paradoxical performative gap central to the voice. This disembodiment is not purely physical, arising from the apparatus of the body; hearing the voice as well as recording it involves reembodiment through call-and-response, a hyperaware perceptive reinscription and signification at the moment of watching/listening. The levels of self-inscription subverted in FIG's work call attention to the remediative process through which such histories, and particularly stories about individual people, are inscribed.

When considering the concentric ecologies of feminist artistic practices that emerged at this time, Mulvey (1979: 4) wrote of how a "tension arises . . . between celebration of the past and taking it as a guide-line for the future." In *AMY!* the paradoxical immateriality of the voice amplifies the exposure of hidden feminist histories, yet the invisibility of the voice means that it can nevertheless be subsumed into grander "visualised" narratives such as those relating to "Amy" the heroine, whose voice is displaced. In this and other feminist films from the late 1970s[12]—including those of Rainer and Potter—voices and sounds act as conduits, another medium through which narratives can manifest. The sounded historical subject, whether it is Amy Johnson the aviator, *AMY!* the film, or FIG the group, activates a complex and "radical historiography" (Russell 1999: vx) that reflects the paradoxes of the voice itself, dis-associated yet connecting to new subjects and contexts. The voice itself parallels the peculiar ability of these pasts to manifest in the present anew.

The voice as a material, adaptively reembodied substance was and continues to be an important means of breaking and remoulding visually and epistemologically objectified loops in discourse, which overemphasise patrilinear conceptions of immateriality (and the surviving archive) as opposed to reframing our relationship to the past, to artworks and voices that have the potential to reembody.

Notes

Thanks to Laura Mulvey for reading this chapter and answering detailed questions about the music and sound in *AMY!* Thanks also to Oliver Fuke for sharing research and to Nick Helm-Grovas and Stefan Solomon for insightful comments.

1. Among these feminist references, Julia Kristeva's (1984) concept of the "chora" was particularly important in Mulvey and Wollen's theoretical approach to the trilogy of which *AMY!* is part, starting with *Penthesilea* (1974), then *Riddles of the Sphinx* (1977). The trilogy explores representation and mythmaking, which were also significant to the subsequent film *Crystal Gazing* (1981). For a more detailed account of the relationship between Mulvey and Wollen's filmmaking and theories, see Helm-Grovas (2018).
2. For example, the influential *Notations* score book co-compiled by John Cage and Alison Knowles (1969).
3. Artists involved with FIG included Frankie Armstrong, voice; Georgina (Georgie) Born, bass, guitar, cello; Lindsay Cooper, bassoon, oboe, saxophone; Françoise Dupety, voice; Koryne (formerly Corinne) Liensol, trumpet; Maggie Nicols, voice; Sally Potter, voice, tenor saxophone; Annemarie Roelofs, voice; Irene Schweizer, piano, drums; Angèle Veltmeijer, saxophone; Cathy Williams, voice, piano. It has been reported that musician Dagmar Krauss was involved in the foundation of the group. FIG evolved into the European Women's Improvising Group (EWIG) in the early 1980s. See Louise Gray's account in *The Wire* magazine (March 2021). A reply from Nicols (2021) is included in the subsequent (April) edition of the magazine.
4. Tobin (2015: 112, citing Rugoff 2005: 123) connects Hannah Arendt's (1958) "spaces of appearance" to Irit Rugoff's reworking of this idea as a "concept of power constructed in the 'space of appearance' through speech."
5. Ephemera and paper documents relating to FIG are housed in the archives of the University of the Arts London and Cornell University in collections on Lindsay Cooper and the London Musicians' Collective.
6. FIG released a self-published cassette of live performances in Copenhagen, Stockholm, and Reykjavík (1979; see Punk Music Data 2016). The recording "The Seventh Kiss" (1980) is available on *Resonate-Reverberate-Roar*. A recording from live sessions at the Logos Foundation in Ghent, Belgium, in 1979 is also included on *Another Evening at Logos 1974/79/81* (Sub Rosa 2015).
7. The techniques seen in *AMY!* include dual timeframes, split voices, and multiple contexts, building upon the earlier theory films in the trilogy (see previous note).
8. Larry Sider used the title Evanston Percussion Unit when recording video (and recorded the interviews with students at Paddington College in *AMY!*).
9. Esther Leslie discussed this at the retrospective *Laura Mulvey and Peter Wollen: Beyond the Scorched Earth of Counter-Cinema*, curated by Oliver Fuke, Whitechapel Gallery, London, 12–22 May 2016. See also Helm-Grovas (2018).
10. Mulvey and Wollen were introduced to Lindsey Cooper through a mutual friend, the feminist journalist and critic Mandy Merck. Whilst making *AMY!* they visited Cooper's studio to discuss the film and listen to recordings. They were drawn to the ethereal sound of both Nicols' and Potter's voices. Cooper sent a short tape (approximately twenty minutes) of miscellaneous recordings for them to use in *AMY!*
11. Schneider here refers to Peggy Phelan's (1993: 146, cited in Schneider) discussion of "performance as disappearance."
12. *The Song of the Shirt* (Jonathan Curling and Sue Clayton, 1979) was scored by Lindsey Cooper and includes sounds by FIG created in collaboration with two oral history projects, Women's Aid and the Feminist History Project, with multiple voices reading historical accounts of the oppression of women.

References

Barber, Stephen. 2020. "Film and Performance: Intermedial Intersections." In *Cinematic Intermediality: Theory and Practice*, edited by Kim Knowles and Marion Schmid, 11–22. Edinburgh: Edinburgh University Press.

Born, Georgina. 2017. "After Relational Aesthetics: Improvised Music, the Social and (Re)Theorizing the Aesthetic." In *Improvisation and Social Aesthetics*, edited by Georgina Born, Eric Lewis, and Will Straw, 33–58. Durham, NC: Duke University Press.

Cage, John, and Alison Knowles, eds. 1969. *Notations*. New York: Something Else Press.

Cavarero, Adriana. 2005. *For More Than One Voice: Toward a Philosophy of Vocal Expression*. Stanford, CA: Stanford University Press.

Chion, Michel. 1994. *Audio-Vision: Sound on Screen*. Translated by Claudia Gorbman. New York: Columbia University Press.

Chion, Michel. 1999. *The Voice in Cinema*. Translated by Claudia Gorbman. New York: Columbia University Press.

Connor, Steven. 2000. *Dumbstruck: A Cultural History of Ventriloquism*. Oxford: Oxford University Press.

Dolar, Mladen. 2006. *A Voice and Nothing More*. London: MIT Press.

Feminist Improvising Group. 1980. "Feminist Improvising Group, The Seventh Kiss (1980)." *Resonate-Reverberate-Roar*. https://re-re-roar.org/the-seventh-kiss-by-the-feminist-improvising-group/.

Gray, Louise. 2021. "Maggie Nicols: Singing for Change." *The Wire* 445 (March): 36–43. https://www.thewire.co.uk/issues/445.

Hayles, N. Katherine. 2002. *Writing Machines*. London: MIT Press.

Helm-Grovas, Nicolas. 2018. "Laura Mulvey and Peter Wollen: Theory and Practice, Aesthetics and Politics, 1963–1983." PhD dissertation, Royal Holloway, University of London. https://pure.royalholloway.ac.uk/portal/en/publications/laura-mulvey-and-peter-wollen-theory-and-practice-aesthetics-and-politics-19631983(b42d4c87-2f38-4d05-906c-76b57fd18fb7).html.

Higgins, Dick. (1965) 2021. "Intermedia." *Leonardo* 34, no. 1: 49–54.

Holdsworth, Claire M. 2017. "Readings at the Intersection: Social Ecologies in Critical Texts." *Intermédialités: Histoire et Théorie Des Arts, Des Lettres et Des Techniques/Intermediality: History and Theory of the Arts, Literature and Technologies*, nos. 30–31: n.p. https://doi.org/10.7202/1049946ar

Holdsworth, Claire M. 2020. "The Artist Interview—An Interdisciplinary Approach to Its History, Process and Dissemination." *Journal of Art Historiography*, no. 23: 1–22. https://arthistoriography.files.wordpress.com/2020/11/holdsworth.pdf.

Holdsworth, Claire M., and Simon Blanchard. 2017. "Organising for Innovation in Film and Television: The Independent Film-Makers' Association in the Long 1970s." In *Other Cinemas: Politics, Culture and Experimental Film in the 1970s*, edited by Laura Mulvey and Sue Clayton, 279–298. London: I. B. Tauris.

Jacquin, Maud. 2017. "From Reel to Real—An Epilogue: Feminist Politics and Materiality at the London Filmmakers' Co-operative." *Moving Image Review and Art Journal* 6, nos. 1–2: 80–88.

Knowles, Kim, and Marion Schmid, eds. 2020. *Cinematic Intermediality: Theory and Practice*. Edinburgh: Edinburgh University Press.

Kozloff, Sarah. 1989. *Invisible Storytellers: Voice-over Narration in American Fiction Film*. Berkeley: University of California Press.

Krauss, Rosalind. 1979. "Sculpture in the Expanded Field." *October* 8: 31–44.
Kristeva, Julia. 1984. *Revolution in Poetic Language*. Translated by Margaret Waller. New York: Columbia University Press.
Licht, Alan. 2019. "Jonas Mekas (1922–2019)." Obituary. *The Wire*, 23 January. https://www.thewire.co.uk/in-writing/essays/jonas-mekas-alan-licht.
Lippard, Lucy. 1995. "Moving Targets/Concentric Circles: Notes from the Radical Whirlwind." In *The Pink Glass Swan: Selected Feminist Essays on Art*, edited by Lucy Lippard, 3–19. New York: New Press.
McKay, George. 2003. "Maggie Nicols: Telephone Interview, 23 November 2002, Written Revisions 5 February 2003." https://georgemckay.org/interviews/maggie-nicols/.
Mulvey, Laura. 1979. "Feminism, Film and the Avant-Garde." *Framework* 10 (Spring): 3–10.
Nichols, Bill. 1983. "The Voice of Documentary." *Film Quarterly* 36, no. 3: 17–30.
Nicols, Maggie. 2021. "Fig Leaves." *The Wire*, no. 446 (April): 8. https://www.thewire.co.uk/issues/446.
Phelan, Peggy. 1993. *Unmarked: Politics of Performance*. London: Routledge.
Punk Music Data. 2016. "Feminist Improvising Group Official Releases." *Punk Music Catalogue*, 2 January. https://punkmusiccatalogue.wordpress.com/feminist-improvising-group/.
Reynolds, Lucy. 2015. "A Collective Response: Feminism, Film, Performance and Greenham Common." *Moving Image Review and Art Journal* 4, nos. 1–2: 90–101.
Reynolds, Lucy, ed. 2019. *Women Artists, Feminism and the Moving Image Contexts and Practices*. London: Bloomsbury Academic.
Rhodes, Lis. 1979. "Whose History." In *Film as Film: Formal Experiment in Film, 1910–1975*. Catalogue of an Exhibition Held at the Hayward Gallery, London, 3 May–17 June, 1979, 119–120. London: Arts Council of Great Britain.
Rowbotham, Sheila. 1973. *Hidden from History: 300 Years of Women's Oppression and the Fight Against It*. London: Pluto Press.
Russell, Catherine. 1999. *Experimental Ethnography: The Work of Film in the Age of Video*. Durham, NC: Duke University Press.
Schneider, Rebecca. 2001. "Performance Remains." *Performance Research* 6, no. 2: 100–108. https://doi.org/10.1080/13528165.2001.10871792.
Silverman, Kaja. 1984. "Dis-Embodying the Female Voice." In *Re-Vision: Essays in Feminist Film Criticism*, edited by Mary Ann Doane, Patricia Mellencamp, and Linda Williams, 132–133. Los Angeles: American Film Institute.
Silverman, Kaja. 1988. *The Acoustic Mirror: The Female Voice in Psychoanalysis and Cinema: Theories of Representation and Difference*. Bloomington: Indiana University Press.
Stern, Lesley. 1979. "Feminism and Cinema: Feminism and Cinema-Exchanges." *Screen* 20, nos. 3–4: 89–106.
Stover, Chris. 2016. "Musical Bodies: Corporeality, Emergent Subjectivity, and Improvisational Spaces." *M/C Journal* 19 no. 1. http://journal.media-culture.org.au/index.php/mcjournal/article/view/1066.
Tobin, Amy. 2015. "Moving Pictures: Intersections between Art, Film and Feminism in the 1970s." *Moving Image Review and Art Journal* 4, nos. 1–2: 118–134.
Toufic, Jalal. 1996. *Over-Sensitivity*. Los Angeles: Sun and Moon Press.
Walley, Jonathan. 2003. "The Material of Film and the Idea of Cinema: Contrasting Practices in Sixties and Seventies Avant-Garde Film." *October* 103 (Winter): 15–30.
Walley, Jonathan. 2020. *Cinema Expanded: Avant-Garde Film in the Age of Intermedia*. Oxford: Oxford University Press.

White, Duncan. 2011. "Degree Zero: Narrative and Contextual Image." In *Expanded Cinema: Art, Performance, Film*, edited by Al Rees, David Curtis, Duncan White, and Steven Ball, 110–124. London: Tate.

Whittaker, Tom, and Sarah Wright, eds. 2017. *Locating the Voice in Film: Critical Approaches and Global Practices*. Oxford: Oxford University Press.

Wollen, Peter. 1998. *Signs and Meaning in the Cinema*. 4th edition. London: British Film Institute.

Women's Liberation Music Archive. 2010. "F." https://womensliberationmusicarchive.co.uk/f/.

16
Entanglements of Intermediality

Polanski, Pinter, *Steptoe and Son*

Jonathan Bignell

This chapter traces intermedial connections between examples drawn from film culture, the stage, and broadcasting: work by the émigré film director Roman Polanski; the theatre playwright, actor, and screenwriter Harold Pinter; and the TV, radio, and film characters Albert and Harold Steptoe, who were created for BBC television comedy in the mid-1960s. The chapter emerged from and reflects back on the research process for an intermedial research project, "Pinter Histories and Legacies," that documented and analysed Pinter's work for the stage, on radio, on television, and in cinema. The emphasis of the project was on documenting and evaluating a large and diverse body of data relating to people, texts, institutions, and media across a long span of time, and how these entities and agents affected and were affected by wider historical contexts and cultural networks. Methodologically, this meant tracing historiographic connections between media, across chronologies, between Pinter's life and his work, and identifying intertextual relationships between works either by Pinter or by numerous other creative figures. It was a challenging project of comparative intermedial historiography of a kind that this chapter suggests is best approached from an *histoire croisée* perspective (Werner and Zimmermann 2006), involving the identification and analysis of interchange, simultaneity and convergence, invention and reinvention, thus problematising the activity of constructing relationships and flows. The methodological advantage of *histoire croisée* is the capacity to link different types of knowledge and sources to produce a complex understanding. One of the usual English translations of the term is "entangled history," which draws attention to the attractions and also the problems of intermedial research that are discussed and tested in this chapter. Working from a historical and comparative perspective entails reflecting on interconnectedness and the directions of flow between objects of study. Intermediality is too often seen as a one-way process, in which an inherited discourse or form is passed on or a contemporary medium or media text is understood as a remediation of an antecedent (Bolter and Grusin 1999). In contrast, this chapter argues for co-dependency and cross-fertilisation in which the linked elements reconfigure each other.

Tracing this intermedial story, however, prompted debate about the limits and purchase of intermedial methodologies. Although the centrality of the author to the research also potentially constrained the mapping of connections, it positioned "Pinter" productively as a textual entity shaped relationally by the other parts of a textual field. In this chapter, other elements of the textual field include a film by the Hollywood director William Wyler, Samuel Beckett's (1956) play *Waiting for Godot*, and the screening programme at the 1965 Berlin Film Festival. There are many, perhaps too many, illuminating and relevant connections. It is tempting to see Pinter as a node in an infinite intertextual field in which everything becomes connected to everything else. But if everything is connected, repetition becomes stasis, and unlimited semiosis (Barthes 1975) becomes an entrapping entanglement. Theoretically and methodologically, intermediality raises the question of what influence and impact mean, and it is that issue of connection and affect that I explore here.

This chapter thematises dramas about entanglement at a textual level, focusing on stories about entrapment. Moreover, at an interwoven metacritical level the chapter debates the limits of intermedial methodologies and the extent to which they may entrap the unwary (Werner and Zimmermann 2006). I want to reflect on what the activity of connecting means, to avoid the twin traps of reference-hunting and unlimited semiosis. My own work on Pinter's histories and legacies has mainly been in the field of television historiography, using written and audiovisual archival sources to analyse British screen drama of the 1960–1980 period. But doing analyses of Pinter's TV plays and films seems to me less interesting than the opportunity that the Pinter project offered to trace connections across and between media, and how ideas, people, and aesthetic forms are incorporated, shared, transformed, or repudiated. This chapter is a brief account of some of those entangled histories, and it concludes by arguing for a deconstructive understanding of medium specificity that opens up analysis via attention to intermediality. It also argues for respect to be paid to the contingent specificity of the historical event and the specificity of the moment of making research connections, for these two factors limit the potentially unbounded and entangling connectedness that intermediality implies.

Two Mysterious Men

Pinter was already a relatively well-known public figure at the beginning of the 1960s. He was originally a stage actor, became famous as a playwright, and added work as a director, poet, and political activist to his repertoire until his death in 2008. In 1960 the *Oxford English Dictionary* first included the word "Pinteresque," meaning "pertaining to the work of Harold Pinter." His first full-length play, *The Birthday Party* (1963) was premiered in 1958 and is set in a seaside boardinghouse where two unexpected visitors, Goldberg and McCann, arrive and terrorise a long-term resident, Stanley (Figure 16.1). An impromptu birthday party is held for Stanley; a young woman, Lulu, is assaulted when the lights go out; and, at the end of the play, for reasons that remain obscure, Goldberg and McCann take the cowed Stanley away. As the *Sunday Times* reviewer Harold Hobson (1958) summarised in a review of the play's London premiere, it "consists, with all kinds of verbal arabesques and echoing explorations of memory and fancy, of the springing of a trap." The play's dialogue appears demotic and desultory but hints at the powerful emotions and psychological and physical violence that break through its

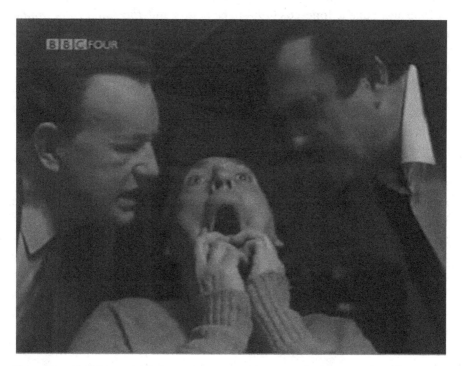

Figure 16.1 Goldberg and McCann terrorise Stanley in Harold Pinter's *The Birthday Party*, 1958.

banal surface. It is that combination of banality and menace that constitutes the Pinteresque.

At least since the late 1950s, Pinter's plays were recognised as socially engaged drama. The New Left writers of the theatre magazine *Encore*, such as Irving Wardle (1958), drew attention to the entrapment of his characters spatially and existentially, seeing this as a recognition of contemporary material circumstances and the passive frustration that they produced. Pinter's language was seen as degraded and constraining, thus equally reflective of modernity, yet his idiomatic turns of phrase were capable of revealing flashes of comic resistance. His work was thought to be relevant, challenging, and intellectually complex. So the implicit model of influence here is that Pinter absorbed existential features of contemporary culture and replayed them back to his audiences via his drama. This familiar trope was also used by other playwrights of the time (Rebellato 1999), especially Samuel Beckett, with whom Pinter was often compared (Esslin 1961). A strand of British theatre culture was strongly influenced by continental European writing, alternative to the apparently more staid British tradition embodied by Terence Rattigan's or John Whiting's plays, and the major London productions just preceding *The Birthday Party* included Beckett's (1956) *Waiting for Godot* in 1955 and Eugene Ionesco's (1958) *The Lesson* and *The Bald Prima Donna* in 1956, each written by authors based in Paris. The other key comparator is John Osborne's (1957) *Look Back in Anger*, first performed in 1956, which became the paradigm for gritty, "kitchen-sink" drama that featured young, frustrated, and entrapped characters in down-at-heel domestic settings. Pinter and the other Angry Young Men of the New Wave benefitted from a transnational context enlivened by an expectation of experiment and challenge.

The Pinteresque has intermedial connections based on textual form and personal networks. The film director Roman Polanski, born in Paris, grew up in Poland, where he made his first full-length film, and then migrated to the United Kingdom. He was a glamorous, international figure associated with art cinema and based himself in Swinging London in 1963, throwing uproarious parties, promenading along the King's Road, and dating fashion models (Sandford 2007: 110–120). He gained financial backing from Compton Films, a British production company that owned a small chain of cinemas in London's Soho and distributed foreign films, to make *Repulsion*, released in 1965. *Repulsion* was the first major success for Compton and its entrepreneurial owner, Michael Klinger, whose career as an executive producer had begun with the nudist exploitation film *Naked as Nature Intended* (George Marks, 1961). He saw Polanski as a creative genius who would enable the small and rather disreputable Compton Films to enter the big time. Polanski was an admirer of Pinter's work, and the 1965 Berlin Film Festival, where *Repulsion* won the Silver Bear award, happened also to include a screening of *The Caretaker* (a.k.a. *The Guest*, Clive Donner, 1963) that Pinter (1960) had adapted from his eponymous stage play. Klinger and his colleague Tony Tenser allocated a budget of £120,000 to Polanski's next project, the script *If Katelbach Comes* that Polanski had co-written with his friend Gerard Brach, about a man and his wife in an isolated mansion who are threatened by mysterious visitors. *The Caretaker* featured Donald Pleasence, and Polanski chose Pleasence to play the main male character in the new film project, partly because he admired Pleasence's performance as Davies in *The Caretaker* (Wine 2001). Tracing this history starts to reveal connections and networks.

If Katelbach Comes had been retitled *Cul de Sac* by the time shooting began in July 1965. Together with the designer Voytek, another London-based Polish émigré, Polanski had toured Brittany looking for a desolate location but chose Lindisfarne in northern England instead. Its isolated castle by the sea separates the film from the contemporary moment and from verisimilitude, and it functions as a home but also as an abstract nonplace, similar to the bare stagings in both Pinter's and Beckett's plays. A causeway flooded twice daily by the sea cuts off the castle from the mainland (hence the film's title), leaving George (Donald Pleasence) with the much younger woman (Françoise Dorléac) he has left his wife for. Her emasculation of him, through her affair with their neighbour and her dressing George in her flimsy nightdress, for example, escalates when two escaping criminals arrive (Figure 16.2). One of them, Dickie (Lionel Stander), physically assaults George, asserting control and exploiting George's submissiveness. Jack MacGowran, cast as the second robber, Albie, was one of Beckett's favourite actors, and Beckett had tried unsuccessfully to cast him (Knowlson 1996: 522) in his only film project, *Film* (Beckett 1965) which was made the year before and was touring the festival circuit in 1965 at the same time as Polanski's *Repulsion*. In Polanski's film the characters wait for the mysterious Mr. Katelbach to arrive, but he never comes, and the motif of fruitless waiting suggests the two tramps of Beckett's *Waiting for Godot* and the terrorisation of a household by the two guests, Goldberg and McCann, in *The Birthday Party*. Investigating these conjunctions and parallels uncovers further intermedial relationships.

Cul de Sac won awards at the 1966 Berlin and Edinburgh film festivals. But the film was hard to market and was never a popular success, largely because of its subject matter of sexualized domination, which Brendan Gill (1966), for example, reviewing the film for *The New Yorker*, called an "odious freak show." These comments closely resemble press reactions to Pinter's *Birthday*

Figure 16.2 A gangster invades the couple's domestic space in Roman Polanski's *Cul de Sac* (1966).

Party, which Derek Granger (1958) reviewed for the *Financial Times*: "Pinter's first play comes in the school of random dottiness deriving from Beckett and Ionesco and before the flourishing continuance of which one quails in slack-jawed dismay." The influences and impacts of these dramas on each other derive from shared dramatic forms and structures, namely the enclosed domestic space, the menacing visitors, and the eruption of suppressed violence and sexual desire. In cinema, the history of the home invasion motif goes back to *The Desperate Hours* (William Wyler, 1955) with Humphrey Bogart, now regarded as a film noir because of its claustrophobic, existential bleakness, the motif of entrapment, and the violence enacted in a familiar suburban home. Bogart played a gangster and drew on the star image he had established in earlier thrillers with home invasion motifs, *The Petrified Forest* (Archie Mayo, 1936) and *Key Largo* (John Huston, 1948) (Weedman 2005). However, the home invasion trope alone is too common to be very useful for comparative intermedial studies because there are so many texts, in cinema alone, that adopt it; Wikipedia ("List of Films Featuring Home Invasions" 2022) lists about 190 films beginning with D. W. Griffith's short *The Lonely Villa* (1909). Intermedial conjunctions between texts, people, and events need to be channelled and disciplined if they are not to become unruly. One way of doing that is to address them historiographically, as I have done here through the networks of a specific mid-1960s milieu mixing British with American and continental European arts and popular culture.

A Laugh in the Trap: Situation Comedy

Thus far this exploration has mainly concerned high culture, but of course entangled histories can also question the hierarchies and separations between "serious" and "popular" culture, such as between dramatic forms in theatre, television drama, and situation comedy. The restricted spatiality that characterises sitcom is a development of theatre Naturalism, and Pinter's spatial pressurisation of Naturalism fed back into sitcom. Dramas set in enclosed domestic rooms (Williams 1974: 56) were adapted from the dominant form of 1950s British theatre to become the main formal convention of television drama's mise-en-scène, across genres from sitcom and the soap opera to the prestigious single TV play. Tom Sloan, head of Light Entertainment at BBC in 1961, reacted to news that the comedian Tony Hancock wanted to concentrate on cinema projects and decline another television series of *Hancock's Half Hour* (1956–1961) by offering Hancock's writers Ray Galton and Alan Simpson the chance to write an anthology of ten half-hour comedy dramas (Kilborn 2016). These one-off plays, collectively titled *Comedy Playhouse* (1961–1975), would fill the empty Hancock slots in the BBC's evening schedule. In 1962 Galton and Simpson's drama *The Offer* for *Comedy Playhouse* introduced rag-and-bone men Albert Steptoe (Wilfred Brambell) and his son, Harold (Harry H. Corbett), in which the ageing Albert's dependency on his son frustrates Harold's vain dreams of escaping to make his own way in the world. The biography of Corbett recounts that Ray Galton said, "I think we have written a little piece of Pinter here" (Corbett 2012: 332). The sitcom attracted huge audiences and eventually extended over nine seasons, in 1962–1965 and then 1970–1974. The Pinteresque had become enormously popular in another medium and genre.

The connection between television situation comedy and Pinter's dramatic work is made possible by an intermedial comparison, but its significance is much greater than simply the noticing of similarities of form, mood, and language. The metropolitan, high-cultural position of Pinter's theatre in the early 1960s overlapped with its visibility in the ascendant popular medium of the time, as television replaced radio in Britain after the launch of the Independent commercial channel (ITV) in 1955. In 1964, *Steptoe and Son* was the most popular programme of the year, with a regular audience of up to 9.7 million viewers. Its success ran alongside Pinter's television heyday. Pinter's single TV plays appeared regularly in the 1960s, but it was ITV, rather than BBC, which screened his work and built his national profile. The ITV output was provided by separate, regionally based franchise owners, and one of them, Associated-Rediffusion, commissioned a television version of Pinter's 1958 theatre play

The Birthday Party in 1960 for the ITV network's anthology series *Play of the Week* (1956–1966), where it was watched by an audience of 11 million (Billington 2007: 110). Another ITV company, Granada, produced Pinter's play *The Room* for ITV's *Television Playhouse* (1955–1967) series in 1961; Pinter's *The Collection* was made by Associated-Rediffusion in 1961, and *The Dumb Waiter* by Granada in the same year. Associated-Rediffusion's production of Pinter's *The Lover* in 1963 won the Prix Italia international prize for television drama, and his *A Night Out* was made by yet another ITV contractor, ABC, for the *Armchair Theatre* (1956–1974) series in 1964. Audiences for each of these dramas probably saw some of the other, thematically similar dramas being broadcast at the same time (Smart 2019). Popular audiences for theatre, although always smaller than for broadcast drama, were also becoming familiar with Pinter's work in regional, amateur, and student productions of his plays and as published texts. Several of his plays had been published in accessible paperback editions, and his media profile was enhanced by newspaper reviews, appearances in television interviews, and talk shows like *Late Night Line Up* (BBC, 1964–1972). Pinter's dramas and Galton and Simpson's sitcom formed part of a shared intermedial supertext.

The interchange between theatre and television broke the boundaries between high and popular culture as well as between media of production. The Pinteresque may not have been "popular" in the sense that it was universally approved, since Pinter himself was regarded as a controversial figure and his plays were considered "difficult." However, there was widespread recognition of Pinter and his distinctive "brand," and his representation of ordinary people and everyday speech was, despite the artifice with which Pinter turned these domestic stories into "menace," an aspect of a cultural current that sought to connect with mass audiences and engage with contemporary experience. Many of the playwrights coming to prominence in the late 1950s and early 1960s in London explored versions of social realism (Lacey 1995) associated with productions at the Royal Court Theatre and the experiments by Joan Littlewood's Theatre Workshop at the Theatre Royal Stratford East. The gritty "kitchen-sink" realism of working-class domestic settings, colloquial speech, exploration of contemporary issues of social class, sexual repression, and gender inequality in this theatre work shared some its foci, creative personnel, and sometimes dramatic texts with radio, television, and cinema. The BBC's *Wednesday Play* (1964–1970) series of original dramas and ITV's *Armchair Theatre*, for example, became associated with the realist project. The British cinema industry adapted dramas from the stage (including Pinter's *The Caretaker* in 1963 and *The Birthday Party* in 1968), and from recent novels by northern working-class writers (such as *Saturday Night and Sunday*

Morning [Karel Reisz, 1960] from Alan Sillitoe's 1958 novel). Social entrapment within manual labour, marriage, regional provincialism, or domination by bourgeois authority was an intermedial framework for dramas about rebellious male (and occasionally female) protagonists on the page, stage, and screen (Hill 1986).

The ensemble working methods and openness to actors from working-class backgrounds that were associated with the Royal Court's and Theatre Workshop's realism contributed to the interchange of actors between London theatre and television comedy, and one of Galton and Simpson's *Steptoe* episodes in particular, "The Desperate Hours" (BBC1, 1972), takes us back to *Cul de Sac*. Leonard Rossiter and J. G. Devlin play a pair of escaped convicts from nearby Wormwood Scrubs prison in West London who come to the Steptoes' ramshackle house in the hope of hiding out. They take Harold and Albert hostage to demand food and a fast car, and parallels between the two pairs' relationships are explored. Each character is trapped with his companion and with the other pair. There is no food, the Steptoes cannot afford to own a car, and, like the Steptoes, the convicts cannot escape their situation, nor the enclosing space of the room in which the episode takes place (Figure 16.3). The episode ends as the convicts decide to go voluntarily back to prison, another enclosure or trap and a more comfortable one than the

Figure 16.3 The convicts with Harold Steptoe (left) and his father (third left) in "The Desperate Hours" episode of *Steptoe and Son* (BBC1, 1972).

Steptoes' shabby home. That same year, Rossiter played the tramp Davies in a revival of Pinter's *The Caretaker*, a role he had first played in 1961. The play's setting is a derelict household into which Davies brings his pretensions to a better life. But Davies never leaves the room in the play, remaining trapped with his dreams of leaving, just as the Steptoes and the two convicts do in "The Desperate Hours." The dramatic trope persists across an intermedial web of texts and people.

Domestic, interior, studio-shot television drama and sitcom each developed from theatre and fed back into it. In 1970, in a review of *Steptoe and Son*, television critic and theorist Raymond Williams (1989: 125) placed the sitcom in "a very old pattern in the drama of the last 100 years. This is the pattern of men trapped in rooms, working out the general experience of being cheated and frustrated, on the most immediately available target: the others inside the cage." Beginning as tragedy with the work of Henrik Ibsen and August Strindberg, then becoming ambivalent in plays by Anton Chekhov, this form becomes comedy in dramas by Ionesco, Osborne, and Pinter that are "at once absurd and sinister" (125). Williams's complaint about this form is that the enclosed world, peopled by a frustrated dreamer paired with a conservative yet vicious figure, allows no possibility of genuine engagement with the lived social world outside the room, and therefore no prospect of material change for the characters. The repetition inherent in the sitcom format and the anachronistic (even in 1962) setting of *Steptoe and Son* in the rundown London docklands meant that while he might represent (comparative) youth and aspiration, Harold's dreams could be ridiculed. The audience's laughter, Williams concludes, is evidence of submission to circumstance, a "rueful laugh in the trap" (127). Entrapment has a politics, and Williams wanted to critique cultural forms that implicitly justified stasis and existential resignation.

Methodological Conclusions

Intertextual and intermedial webs, allusions, and references might also be traps, despite their pleasures (Rolinson 2016), unless their patterns of adaptation and reworking can escape being the endless return of the same. An *histoire croisée* approach such as is used in this chapter makes a feature of intermediality by using different kinds of evidence from primary archival documents; analysis of plays', programmes', and films' mise-en-scène; and interviews with creative figures such as writers and performers. Tracing impacts and influences is a huge task, because they cross media, create chronologies, and link geographies. In the "Pinter Histories and Legacies" project to which this chapter contributes, intermedial research was facilitated by an electronic database, in which hypertext links created and enabled multiple connections. But the aspects of the Pinteresque that I have noted show the tensions at stake, which I argue are as interesting as the links that such work discovers. As Roland Barthes (1972: 112) concluded, "a little Formalism turns one away from History, but a lot . . . brings one back to it." Tracing influences raises the spectre of a boundless territory and the trap of infinite repetition, which need to be countered by looking for difference and historical specificity as much as for correlation and formal resemblance.

Some of the historiographic methodologies that are helpful were devised largely to critique national histories by stressing transnational exchanges (Hilmes 2011: 11–12), and in the examples discussed in this chapter there are intermedial links between Berlin and London and between Parisian theatres and BBC's London studios, for example. The related concept of *transferts culturels* (cultural transfers) focuses on how cultural goods have been appropriated from their place of origin and repurposed to signify in new ways through the networks of globalisation (Barker 1999), a process involving inequalities of power and access. Similarly, work on "entangled histories" has been interested in relationships between colonisers and the colonised, and how identities (in Europe) are established through relationships with otherness (Hall 1995). Each of these approaches to comparative work assumes the necessary instability of such categories as nation, language, institution, and ideology, and looks to the transcultural, transnational, and intermedial nature of modernity. In this chapter, some of the methodological issues identified by Werner and Zimmermann (2006) as key to an *histoire croisée* approach have arisen, and prompt intermedial analysis has noted the fluid, relational nature of the links between texts, people, networks, institutions, media, and technologies that the analysis uncovers. The intermedial way of working needs to continually question the "scales, categories of analysis, the relationship between diachrony and synchrony, and regimes of historicity and reflexivity" that are adopted (32). Pinter was established at the outset as a primary node who would sit at the centre of a web of connected individuals, networks, organisations, texts, and historical events because of my role in leading a research team with a specific remit. This framed the scale and scope of the intermedial entanglements to be accounted for, and the dramatic tropes, moods, and formal choices associated with the Pinteresque. Temporally, there is a tension between a synchronic analysis, here focused around the "long 1960s," and the diachronic lineage identified by Williams's analysis of Naturalism and its movement across theatre and literature and into mass-media forms such as television sitcom. The different axes of intermedial analysis each imply different questions and different results and propose intermedial relationships that would otherwise not come to light.

The reflexivity proposed by Werner and Zimmermann (2006) draws attention to the contingent quality of the divisions and categories that customarily separate media from one another and separate media textualities from the agents that create them. Moreover, the objects of study are themselves constructions whose apparent self-identity can occlude the ways that they are formed, and are best understood not only in relation to one another but *through* one another. This intertextual and intermedial process, moving and changing over time, is also a process of adaptation, inasmuch as adaptation can be thought of as an action of return to and recapitulation of an antecedent (Bignell 2019). The medial identities of film or television, at a particular historical moment, work by taking up a position relative to their comparators rather than by the expression of a self-sufficient essence. Thus, medial identity can be understood as performative, following conceptual approaches deriving from performativity in linguistic theory (Austin 1971), philosophy (Lyotard 1988), or gender studies (Butler 1990), as well as the field of performance studies itself (Parker and Sedgwick 1995). Performance, in somewhat different but related ways in these fields of study, is the social action of articulating identity in a process of continual becoming and remaking. Intermedial analysis offers ways of studying complex processes of interaction, circulation, and appropriation. Media forms, dramatic tropes, and modes of discourse are dynamic and active, as this chapter's brief adventure through work by Pinter and Polanski and the entrapments of television situation comedy has shown. While the focus of this chapter has been on a short chronological period around the 1960s, and in Western Europe and the USA, the focus on processes of interconnection between networks of people, texts, institutions, and technologies has obvious longitudinal and spatial extension (Bignell and Fickers 2008: 11). The *histoire croisée* approach to intermediality suits the study of broadcast media and the circulation of entertainment commodities by the cultural industries particularly well because it is routine for them to operate through processes of adaptation, resistance, inertia, and modification as they work to generate new texts, products, and experiences.

Note

This chapter is one of the outcomes of the research project "Pinter Histories and Legacies: The Impact of Harold Pinter's Work on the Development of British Stage and Screen Practices (1957–2017)," funded by the Arts and Humanities Research Council of England from 2017 to 2020, ref. AH/P005039/1.

References

Austin, John L. 1971. *How to Do Things with Words*. Oxford: Oxford University Press.
Barker, Chris. 1999. *Television, Globalization and Cultural Identities*. Buckingham: Open University Press.
Barthes, Roland. 1972. *Mythologies*. Translated by A. Lavers. New York: Hill and Wang.
Barthes, Roland. 1975. *The Pleasure of the Text*. Translated by Richard Miller. New York: Hill and Wang.
Beckett, Samuel. 1956. *Waiting for Godot*. London: Faber.
Beckett, Samuel. 1965. *Film*. New York: Grove.
Bignell, Jonathan. 2019. "Performing the Identity of the Medium: Adaptation and Television Historiography." *Adaptation* 12, no. 2: 149–164. http://dx.doi.org/10.1093/adaptation/apz017.
Bignell, Jonathan, and Andreas Fickers, eds. 2008. *A European Television History*. New York: Blackwell.
Billington, Michael. 2007. *Harold Pinter*. London: Faber.
Bolter, Jay, and Richard Grusin. 1999. *Remediation: Understanding New Media*. Cambridge, MA: MIT Press.
Butler, Judith. 1990. *Gender Trouble: Feminism and the Subversion of Identity*. London: Routledge.
Corbett, Susannah. 2012. *Harry H. Corbett: The Front Legs of the Cow*. Stroud: History.
Esslin, Martin. 1961. *The Theatre of the Absurd*. Harmondsworth: Penguin.
Gill, Brendan. 1966. "Dead End." *New Yorker*, 12 November, 115.
Granger, Derek. 1958. "Puzzling Surrealism of *The Birthday Party*." *Financial Times*, 20 May, 3.
Hall, Stuart. 1995. "New Cultures for Old." In *A Place in the World? Places, Cultures and Globalization*, edited by Doreen Massey and Pat Jess, 175–213. Oxford: Oxford University Press.
Hill, John. 1986. *Sex, Class and Realism: British Cinema 1956–1963*. London: British Film Institute.
Hilmes, Michele. 2011. *Network Nations: A Transnational History of British and American Broadcasting*. London: Routledge.
Hobson, Harold. 1958. "The Screw Turns Again." *Sunday Times*, 25 May, 11.
Ionesco, Eugene. 1958. *The Lesson, The Bald Prima Donna, Jacques, or Obedience*. London: Calder.
Kilborn, Richard. 2016. "A Golden Age of British Sitcom? *Hancock's Half Hour* and *Steptoe and Son*." In *British TV Comedies*, edited by Jürgen Kamm and Birgit Neumann, 23–35. London: Palgrave Macmillan.
Knowlson, James. 1996. *Damned to Fame: The Life of Samuel Beckett*. London: Bloomsbury.
Lacey, Stephen. 1995. *British Realist Theatre: The New Wave in its Context 1956–65*. London: Routledge.
"List of Films Featuring Home Invasions." 2022. Wikipedia. https://en.wikipedia.org/wiki/List_of_films_featuring_home_invasions.
Lyotard, Jean-François. 1988. *The Differend: Phrases in Dispute*. Translated by Georges Van Den Abbeele. Manchester: Manchester University Press.
Marwick, Arthur. 2000. *Windows on the Sixties*. London: I. B. Tauris.
Osborne, John. 1957. *Look Back in Anger*. London: Faber.
Parker, Andrew, and Eve Kosofsky Sedgwick. 1995. *Performativity and Performance*. London: Routledge.
Pinter, Harold. 1960. *The Caretaker*. London: Methuen.
Pinter, Harold. 1963. *The Birthday Party*. London: Methuen.

Rebellato, Dan. 1999. *1956 and All That: The Making of Modern British Drama*. London: Routledge.

Rolinson, David. 2016. "'You Dirty Old Man!'" Masculinity and Class in *Steptoe and Son* (1962–74)." British Television Drama. http://www.britishtelevisiondrama.org.uk/?p=2346.

Sandford, Christopher. 2007. *Polanski*. London: Century.

Sillitoe, Alan. 1958. *Saturday Night and Sunday Morning*. London: W. H. Allen.

Smart, Billy. 2019. "Harold Pinter at ITV." Pinter Legacies. https://pinterlegacies.com/2019/03/20/harold-pinter-at-itv/.

Wardle, Irving. 1958. "Pinter, Comedy of Menace." *Encore* 5 (September–October): 28–33.

Weedman, Christopher. 2005. "*Cul-de-Sac*." *Senses of Cinema* 34 (February). http://sensesofcinema.com/2005/cteq/cul_de_sac/.

Werner, Michael, and Bénédicte Zimmermann. 2006. "Beyond Comparison: *Histoire Croisée* and the Challenge of Reflexivity." *History and Theory* 45, no. 1: 30–50.

Williams, Raymond. 1974. *Television, Technology and Cultural Form*. London: Fontana.

Williams, Raymond. 1989. "Galton and Simpson's 'Steptoe and Son.'" In *Raymond Williams on Television: Selected Writings*, edited by Alan O'Connor, 124–127. London: Routledge. First published in *The Listener*, 17 December 1970.

Wine, Bill. 2001. "Pleasence, Donald." In *International Dictionary of Films and Filmmakers: Actors and Actresses*, edited by Sara Pendergast and Tom Pendergast, 973–975. New York: Gale.

17
The Intermedial Reworking of History in Peter Greenaway's *The Tulse Luper Suitcases* Trilogy

Fátima Chinita

From a Transmedia Project to an Intermedial Trilogy

Peter Greenaway's *The Tulse Luper Suitcases* project is a high-art transmedia storytelling network of media convergence *avant la lettre,* which ran at full throttle from 2003 to 2005. It encompassed five feature films (including the trilogy this chapter is about), a computer game with ninety-two levels, and several web pages which are no longer maintained. Over the years, other materials have been added to this enterprise, always authored and supervised by Greenaway himself: books, installations, exhibitions, theatrical work, and VJ performances (for more on this, see Chinita 2020: 31–51). As originally conceived, the project is a megalomaniac enterprise, though not all of the instalments announced by Greenaway were actually produced.[1]

The Tulse Luper Suitcases trilogy itself (from now on, *TLST*) is composed of the films *Part 1—The Moab Story* (2003), *Part 2—Vaux to the Sea* (2004), and *Part 3—From Sark to the Finish* (2004). It is a historical saga starting in the aftermath of World War I, encompassing the years of World War II, and extending into the period of the Cold War. The events depicted in the film take place, according to Greenaway, from 1928—which coincides with both the discovery of uranium and the stabilisation of sound (introduced in 1927) in American mainstream cinema—to 1989—the year the Berlin Wall fell, changing Europe forever and anticipating Greenaway's feature *Prospero's Books* (1991), one of the first films ever shot on HDTV and digitally edited.

Fátima Chinita, *The Intermedial Reworking of History in Peter Greenaway's* The Tulse Luper Suitcases *Trilogy* In: *The Moving Form of Film.* Edited by: Lúcia Nagib and Stefan Solomon, Oxford University Press. © Oxford University Press 2023.
DOI: 10.1093/oso/9780197621707.003.0018

This coincidence is relevant since it ties the medium of film—in the form of Greenaway's trilogy—to the making of history, the spatiotemporal stratum on which all art forms develop and evolve and with which Greenaway's trilogy dialogues in an intermedial relationship.

In the "Mission Statement" section of the project's official website, *TLST* was described as a reconstruction of the life of Tulse Henry Purcell Luper, "a professional writer and project-maker." It is a character whom Greenaway has always nurtured as his alter ago and who appears in several of his early films.[2] The opening credits of each film state that the trilogy is "A Life Story in 16 Episodes," that is, sixteen film sequences with different historical and geographical settings. These are spread out across the three films. The protagonist, Luper, is followed from the age of ten onwards, until his tracks disappear in the mists of time and he becomes a myth. In *TLST* he is depicted both as a storyteller (concocting fictions) and a reporter (laying down the annals of history), as well as the subject of many historical events which he experiences firsthand as a prisoner of different parties, including his own father (as a childhood punishment) and the Soviet officers at a "checkpoint on a bridge along the Werra river, near Creuzburg, on the East-West German border," as explained by the character Colonel Kotcheff in *Part 3*. For example, he is held in a desert jail in Utah and in a bathroom of the Antwerp train station, is stranded on a desert island, and is forced to work as an employee at a cinema in Strasbourg, as an elevator boy in the Molle Antoniella in Turin, and as an attendant in the Bucharest morgue, to name but a few of his prisons—enough to make him call himself "a professional prisoner." He is both a picaresque character feeding the episodic narrative, entirely based on his geographical movements, and an Everyman caught up in the circumstances of war and life's fortuitous events. Significantly, he is a fictional character but portrayed in the guise of a real one. Many of the ninety-two characters in *TLST* are presented, in intertitles, as "Luper specialists" and talk straight to the camera (in frontal or profile close shots) about his life, adventures, and work. Taking place from the outset in the film, this procedure begs the question of where truth actually resides, if it exists at all. Indeed, although 1928 is the first date mentioned in the trilogy, Luper's date of birth, according to several Greenaway sources, is 1911, which means that the saga really starts in 1921. This discrepancy in dating, originated by Greenaway himself, proves just how much the events and the essence of the protagonist are portrayed in an impressionistic manner, in broad strokes, so to speak, without real definition.

None of this is relevant, though, because *TLST* is not a real historical saga but one which has History in it, conveyed metaphorically and with a fair share of abstraction. Suffice it to say that many of the actors in the cast play

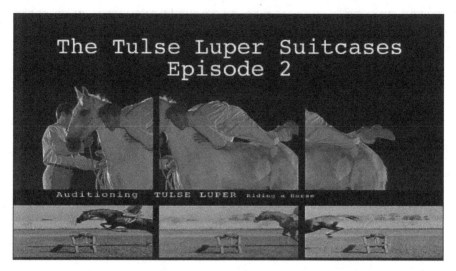

Figure 17.1 J. J. Feild auditioning for the role of Luper in Peter Greenaway's *Part 1: The Moab Story*.

several characters and that one single character may be played by several actors, such as Luper himself (who is played by a child actor and then by three adults), as I will explain later. The opening sequence of each of the three films is made up of images of the project's casting sessions, either real or counterfeit, in order to reinforce the artefactual nature of the films and the dubiousness of the characters' identities (Figure 17.1). Nothing is exactly what it seems to be, although the trilogy plays heavily on the viewer's perception and is highly seductive through its engaging audiovisual strategies (see Chinita 2016: 86–107).

In this chapter—which focuses on the correlation between cinema/other art forms and History—I argue that *TLST* opens itself to media archaeological scrutiny. In it Greenaway himself behaves as a media archaeologist. He makes world history the object of his own cinematic reflection on the history of the cinematic properties where narrative is truly en-*formed* instead of simply being literature set to images. Not only that, but he presents us with an impure cinematic medium, already hybridised by the insertion of many other art forms which share with cinema the same constructed nature, thus contributing to his discourse on audiovisual perception and the question of truth throughout the decades. This mixture of history and fabricated art forms—with cinema and/or cinematic processes taking the foreground—is made quite perceptible in the timeline that appears in the trilogy at particular intervals (Figure 17.2).

Figure 17.2 Timeline containing historical, artistic, and fictional events in Peter Greenaway's *Part 2: Vaux to the Sea*.

Media Archaeology as Historical (Un)Covering

In the *TLST*, Greenaway is a metaphorical media archaeologist equating film with History and, concomitantly, with several other art forms (i.e., older media) with which film both combines and is able to represent intradiegetically. In episode 1 (*Part 1*) of the *TLST*, a Luper specialist lists the protagonist's many activities throughout his adult life, charging him with being an archaeologist as well, quite fitting for Greenaway's alter ego. The Welsh director's position on media archaeology is akin to Erkki Huhtamo's (1996), which is based on the recurrence of media practices (Strauven 2013: 59). Huhtamo's media-archaeological approach "emphasizes cyclical rather than chronological development, recurrence rather than unique innovation" (Strauven 2013: 72). The presentation of the ninety-two Objects That Represent the World, which work as archaeological findings in their own multidisciplinarity and diversity, is not conveyed in any specific numerical order, but randomly. The ninety-two suitcases of the trilogy's title, on the contrary, are seen in ascending numerical order. Although they are reportedly Luper's, they are filled with things he collects and which belong to the world that he comes in contact with in his voyages, rather than with objects/living beings that belong constitutively to him.

Along the same lines, the three instalments of the trilogy are subtly different from one another in terms of their portrayed mediality. The selected focus of each instalment does not correspond to a chronological media order but rather to an interaction between the technical, artistic, and narrative properties of media in general, the triad at the core of Greenaway's aesthetics for the new millennium, which he introduced in his "Cinema Militans Lecture" (2003),[3] his first approach to *The Tulse Luper Suitcases* project.

Part 1 is subdivided into only three life episodes, each time introduced by an intertitle: (1) Newport, in South Wales, where Luper, aged ten, plays war games with his friends in the neighbourhood's backyards; (2) the Moab desert in Utah, where Luper, looking for the Mormon lost cities, finds an old-fashioned community of German origin and Fascist inclinations; (3) Antwerp in 1938, where Luper, then a writer, becomes a prisoner of the Nazis for the first time. *Part 1—The Moab Story* focuses on the technical properties of media. Photographs—shown recurrently throughout the trilogy—appear as the contents of suitcase number 3 in *Part 1*, and Luper is made the subject of a photography session by a professional photographer in the desert jailhouse, starting with Luper's mugshots and ending with erotic photographs of him and the young and beautiful Passion Hockmeister (played by Caroline Dhavernas), a member of the hostile Mormon clan (Figure 17.3). Film is the content of suitcase number sixteen, filled with the celluloid reels of Luper's lost films; it also emerges in *Part 1* in the form of a diagram of a 16mm camera, used by Luper soon after with the soundtrack reinforcing the mechanically noisy piece of equipment. Binoculars, newsreels of the war period, a radio set,

Figure 17.3 Photo shoot in the Moab desert jailhouse in Peter Greenaway's *Part 1: The Moab Story*.

newspapers, and manuscripts (most of them being typed by a row of female typists) complete the *old* media of this film. Although a voice-over mentions that Luper was commissioned to write a hundred stories about time travel and transportation, none of them is heard in *Part 1*.

Part 2—Vaux to the Sea focuses on art forms, perceived as qualified media, that is, "clusters of media products that tend to present a certain type of sensory configuration" (Elleström 2014: 2). The film is divided into three episodes, all set in France: (4) the Palace of Vaux-le-Vicomte, outside of Paris; (5) the movie theatre Arc-en-Ciel in Strasburg; (6) a wealthy estate in Dinard, house of the Moitessiers, where Luper works as a cross-dressing housemaid in order to avoid further detention by the Germans. In such architectural structures—themselves permeated with art objects such as sculptures and bas-reliefs, films, paintings, and ceramic figurines—and in the company of artists or artistically prone people (musicians, painters, draughtspersons, art lovers, and so on), Luper comes into contact with artworks of various forms. Photographs, manuscripts, and stories continue to be present, but now they are perceived by their content rather than their form. For example, the movie theatre Arc-en-Ciel becomes a vehicle for arthouse films. Not only do Luper and his fellow ushers watch Carl Theodor Dreyer's silent film *La Passion de Jeanne D'Arc* (1928), but Joan of Arc (as played by Maria Falconetti in Dreyer's film) is made to be the trilogy's fiftieth character (Figure 17.4).

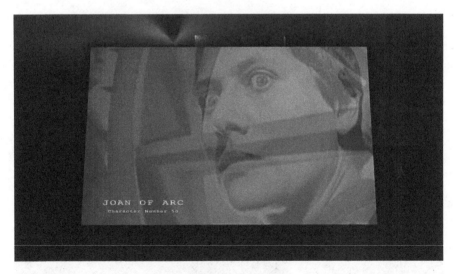

Figure 17.4 Maria Falconetti as Joan of Arc in Carl Theodor Dreyer's film in Peter Greenaway's *Part 2: Vaux to the Sea*.

Part 3—From Sark to the Finish is divided into nine episodes, and the fourteenth contains further CGI subdivisions alluding to several games. Not only does this film rely more heavily on digital technology than the preceding ones—with the practice of layering gaining momentum and attaining its maximum exuberance (five superimposed layers of images and three layers of sounds are used in some shots)—but stories multiply exponentially. One of the recurrent words in this film—but nonexistent in the other two—is "stimulated," which highlights its inherent sensoriality. *Part 3* focuses on storytelling as a creative activity, authored by Luper himself, who, in order to survive at a border checkpoint between East and West Germany, offers to tell bedtime stories to the Soviet commander's wife, becoming a de facto "Gulag Scheherazade," as he says. Yet architecture is still important as Luper travels around occupied Europe. For example, episode 9, set in Barcelona, features the Sagrada Família cathedral, and episode 10, set in Turin, displays at length the Mole Antonelliana, which nowadays, incidentally, lodges a film museum. Photographs, films, and typewriters continue to be present throughout this third instalment.

No matter how distinct Greenaway's "new cinema" might be as per the "Cinema Militans Lecture," it is still based on previous monomedial forms. Greenaway's statement "Cinema is dead, long live cinema" should be understood not in terms of medial replacement but as a way of continuing a tradition by other means, a way of metaphorically devising a new aesthetic vocabulary from the same cinematic alphabet. In fact, Greenaway posits that he aims to direct "a cinema-maker's cinema" in which words and images would be as one and the screen(s) would be filled with text used as image inserted upon it, just as the overall structure is composed of mini-narratives and multiplying narration (storytelling). Thus, the possibility of a visually performative storytelling appears, one in which form and en-*forming* resound with story and story*telling*, both the visual look and the narrative operation(s) coming together in an elaborate film aesthetics. The cinematic style championed by Greenaway is based on "space, ideas, inanimacy, architecture, light and color and texture itself," including the human figure as part of this plastic ensemble, rather than an intradiegetic vehicle for psychology and emotions. Like Picasso, who did not paint what he saw but what he imagined, and Walt Disney, who produced his animated pictures from scratch—because they were conceived, drawn, coloured, and set in motion without a profilmic reality—Greenaway thinks of his films as blank canvases on which he can manipulate the contents via the form, thus en-*forming* the result into "a cinema of virtual unreality." If this is true of many of his films, which contain a historical background, it certainly is the main aspect of the *TLST*, premised on the creative artistry enabled by history as well as on its own fallibility.

Greenaway's dictum in the trilogy, and everywhere he speaks, that "There is no History, only historians" is not a *blasé* comment aimed to shock but the very crux of his art in *TLST*. He firmly believes that history is "always filtered through the perceptions, interpretations, and values of subjects as experiencers" (Peeters 2005: 5). Examples are characters repeating the same sentences on different occasions, as if they were mottos or refrains, and actions replayed two or three times consecutively at a fast-cutting pace (see Peeters 2005 in this respect). The possibility afforded by digital technology of layering several images and sounds on top of one another, combined with juxtaposed shots, allows for a complex reworking of History into narratives that function as variations on a theme.

Yet there is more to this technical combination than the possibility of enhancing artistic expression. Although Greenaway does not explicitly mention this, the way his professedly militant lecture is organised, from the funereal opening statement ("Cinema died on the 31st September 1983") to the proposal of a phoenix-like rebirth ("Let us now reinvent that cinema") by way of taking into consideration several steps in the evolution of media, makes this lecture as much about the technical resources of media as a manifesto on an art form. He says, "Every medium needs to constantly re-invent itself." This, I believe, suggests that the recurrent use of archival film footage of historical events in the trilogy is irrevocably tied to the history of the cinematic medium, an idea that echoes the above-mentioned cinematic dictum and the way it resonates with Greenaways's metacinematic inclination in general. In the *TLST*, the frequently seen timeline, formerly accessible online in the section "Archives" of the project's website, documents the evolution of History in intermedial form (as text on image), proving that media exist in a flux. Indeed, as claimed by Simone Natale (2016: 586), "media constantly change throughout time, resisting clear-cut definitions related to age." Yet cinema, despite its technological base, is also historically, culturally, and socially contextualised, evolving and possibly receding according to specific contexts and their corresponding mentalities (Elleström 2010: 24–25), which is the case with all qualified media (27). In *TLST* the alliances with other arts and the conventions ruling their characteristics are constantly enacted and (re)formulated.

For example, in episode 6, set in Dinard, Madame de Moitessier (played by Isabella Rossellini) copies the garments and allure of her namesake predecessor painted twice by the artist Ingres. Greenaway represents Ingres's

Greenaway's *The Tulse Luper Suitcases* Trilogy   289

Figure 17.5 Ingres's deconstructed painting in Peter Greenaway's *Part 2: Vaux to the Sea*.

paintings only to shamelessly deconstruct them, like a Cubist artwork, by using inner framing combined with layering (Figure 17.5).

Thus, the representation is not a simple act of transference from one medium to another but an altogether new artistic practice based on the utter fragmentation of matter. In Greenaway's opinion in the "Lecture," it is this repurposing of old media in the context of a new aesthetics that will guarantee cinema's survival, albeit under a new form. However, the flat surface of both the screen and the canvas is very much the starting point of this exercise of style, which nevertheless results in proving, as Jacques Aumont (2007: 154) contends, that on the flat surface objects and people can be portrayed in a manner which presents elements of depth, but also length and width.

The same could be said for the medium of writing, which in the analogue age was an inscription on another surface (usually paper or another more or less flat substitute). In episode 2, set in the Moab desert, love letters are referred to and several different calligraphies are seen, but superimposed on one another through layering. This conveys the idea that more than those four perceivable layers exist. This use of depth and volume gives the impression that all love letters are contained in this representation, providing writing with a universalising power. This strategy is used throughout the trilogy. In *Part 3*, episode 8, Luper is on an (initially) deserted island imagining stories which become visible on a rock wall in yellow, the same colour of the paint that one day is washed ashore by the sea current. This visual rendering of typesets in digital form applied as if painted is here made explicit. The practice is reminiscent of the film *Le Mystère Picasso* (*The Mystery of Picasso*, Henri-Georges Clouzot, 1956) in which the eponymous artist is seen painting directly on see-through paper, positioned midway between himself and the camera, until a picture is created and then disappears as he paints over it, in a form of live palimpsest. In Clouzot's work, the old medium does not merely appear in a newer one, because its function and operation have changed drastically. Rather than sketching images, Picasso is illustrating a discourse on painting. A new artwork is made *through* the old one because, ultimately, it is not only the technical properties of the media that are at stake but especially their specific sensory configurations. Also in *Part 3*, episode 14, set on the border between East and West Germany, Luper verbalises his stories, often to the camera, which then appear in written form on the screen in an upwards-scrolling movement. In this case, the typesets are not really inscribed on any intradiegetic surface; rather they are perceived as hanging in the air as subtitles on a 3D film: what they are hanging on is the surface of the extradiegetic screen itself (Figure 17.6).

Thus, although Greenaway presents the audience with an aesthetics for the new millennium, he uses past centuries, past media, and their past materiality to convey his creativity. Like more recent media artists, Greenaway appreciates the "obsolete, old and analogue" but repurposes it (Parikka 2015: 133).[4] His constant use of calligraphy in letters, manuscripts, postcards, and reports,

Figure 17.6 Roger Rees as Tulse Luper, the Gulag Sheherazade, in Peter Greenaway's *Part 3: From Sark to the Finish*.

as well as his use of typewriters and their traditional font, to create art, demonstrates how the product of certain old media can be utilised creatively in their more recent counterparts. In laying out the plan for his historical saga, Greenaway, in the "Lecture" (2003: 8) admits that "[I]t soon becomes evident that [each] film is happening, so to speak, as it is written, and is, in essence, the deliberate product of a writer." Therefore, the scripted text appearing on the screen is none other than the *TLST* script. This occurs on several occasions. For example, in *Part 1,* episode 2, in the Moab desert, Luper and three other characters are seen standing in front of a digital background significantly consisting of a 3D map and recite their lines, which simultaneously scroll up on the screen superimposed on their likeness. This constant repurposing is archaeological, I argue. As Jussi Parikka (2015: 135) observes: "Media archaeology is itself this sort of excavation of the lost ideas, alternative histories and the conditions of the existence of media."

"Once Upon a Time, Cinema": New Cinema, New Methods

In his book *The Lumière Galaxy,* Francesco Casetti (2015: 4, 5)—to whom cinema is above all an *experience*, a mixture of perception (a sentient observation), reflexivity (a cognitive act), and social practices—concurs that cinema will always face deep transformations but will "persist" because it is "no longer necessarily tied to a single 'machine.'" Of the seven keywords for the cinema to come that Casetti advocates, three are highly relevant to my purposes here: expansion (furthering an appeal to the senses), display (free-floating images made available in a wide variety of screens and less dependent on a monolithic narration), and performance (a different modality of watching a film, in which viewers navigate the surface of the story and employ a multifocussed attention).

For Casetti (2015: 111), the word "expansion" has several possible cinematic meanings, some of which are quite pertinent to my approach because they imply "a myriad of products," "an amalgam of discourses that derive from films," "an expressive form at the crossroads of various traditions," and, no less significantly, "a series of stories that take up other stories and give life to new ones." Greenaway practices this in *TLST*, although he does not separate the sensorial impact on the viewers from a self-reflexive metacinematic discourse, as Casetti does.[5] The rich, multilayered overflow of images (and sounds) is intended to bring forth the kinetic stimulation of the viewers' senses throughout the saga, but the metacinematic discourse is made blatantly obvious via self-reflexive devices that expose the constructedness of cinema in general and Greenaway's variety in particular. In fact, episode 5, set in the Arc-en-Ciel cinema (*Part 2* of *TLST*), contains a Greenaway lookalike meant to represent the Welsh director delivering one of his talks. This self-reflexive gesture is simultaneously a nod towards authorship, as the character is listed in the end credits as "Peter Greenaway" himself (albeit played by an actor). Thus, the auteur's "discourse" is enacted for all to see, also working as a diegetic signature in the saga's episode which deals more directly with cinema on a thematic level. In fact, one of the shots in which the Greenaway character appears corresponds to one of the ninety-two Objects to Change the World (number 25 = Cinema) (Figure 17.7).

Figure 17.7 A Greenaway lookalike delivers a metaleptic lecture in the film theatre in Peter Greenaway's *Part 2: Vaux to the Sea*.

In this episode, Luper lives and works in the film theatre, gathering objects left behind by audience members. Such items are seen first as three-dimensional artefacts and then as flat images presented on an inner digital screen, sometimes animated (e.g., a wagging rabbit's tail). By constantly fragmenting the screen image into myriad inner frames, Greenaway proves that almost anything can be made into a screen, thus transforming virtually every space into a potential cinematic environment, that is, a display. When Casetti contends that the new multiplication of screens enables cinema to be found everywhere, he is thinking of the use of disparate and/or unsuspected surfaces for the inscription of images, as in the projection of multimedia images over façades of famous buildings. However, when transposed to the *TLST*, the manifold screens are a metaphorical representation of this phenomenon more than anything else, because Greenaway's own VJ performances (*The Tulse Luper VJ Tour*, 2005–2009, or *The Lupercyclopedia Live Cinema VJ*, 2010–2011) use real screens and not architectural surfaces. In the *TLST*, inversely, screens—and particularly inner screens—do what a display does: they make images present (Casetti 2015: 168) and thus highlight their current existence everywhere in the world. They are on "a continuous flow," a journey, much like Luper himself, available for somebody somewhere one moment and then gone. This may very well be one of the reasons why so many means of transportation are seen throughout *TLST*, in both historical and fictional contexts. In episode 2 (*Part 1*), for example, a montage sequence featuring a train station mixes historical characters walking on the platform with excerpts from a fictional film depicting a couple who is allegedly told to strip and then murdered in front of seventeen presumed witnesses; the two disparate contexts are bound by the timecode imprinted on both classes of images, rendering them historically believable. This pseudo-documental penchant, where "real" images of the war context are used as simulacra for other purposes, can be said to correspond to the old cinematic media exposure, notably through film newsreels shown in movie theatres, although here they are adulterated by inner screens and constitute, therefore, inner diegetic discourses by "specialists." Despite imitating old media, these postcinematic images "are often unstable and the scenes are increasingly composed of collages and mosaics" (Casetti 2015: 175).

This audiovisual flux is intrinsically performative, in that the images appear, disappear, and merge into one another in a fast rhythm, reminiscent of the twists and turns of History, especially during armed conflicts, such as world wars. Yet this flux has consequences in what pertains to the spectatorial attitudes involved in such witnessing. Casetti distinguishes between immersion, in which viewers penetrate the story, identifying with the characters and their predicaments, and ultimately experiencing catharsis as a result; and a kind of surfing of the audiovisual materials, in which attention is distributed among several factors, some extraneous to the film itself, as when one looks at a smartphone while the film is being projected. The latter posture is typical of a dispersed audience, yet it may entail "an aesthetic realization," inasmuch as the beauty of the images themselves, or rather something in the images, outpaces the story (Casetti 2015: 182). Within the scope of his cognitive approach to film, Carl Plantinga (2009) corroborates this assessment by recognising that viewers may be drawn voluntarily or quite unintentionally to the technical aspects of filmmaking that render it a "discourse" (a constructed artefact). He terms these affects "artifact emotions" (90), which may be self-reflexive, possibly furthering a disclosure of their own procedures and the cinematic philosophy behind them. For Daniel Yacavone (2015: 117), such self-reflexivity is appropriate to the status of "films as works of art," conjoining form and narrative. That could be caused by the highlighting of the film's narrative structure, as in a film in episodes or tableaux, which is certainly the case for *TLST*.

Besides the sixteen episodes on which the whole trilogy is structured, each film is based on a stylised formal opposition between wide shots that convey a volumetric dimension of the space—richly ornamented, crossed by patterned shadows and/or Rembrandt lighting—and close shots which are usually inserted in the composition as real or metaphorical cut-ins of the same overall frame, reinforcing its innate two-dimensionality instead. The former strategy is reminiscent of theatre, because the space is large and the characters are more often than not shot frontally and occupy the centre of the composition; the general atmosphere thus conveyed is somewhat velvety and haptic. Moreover, only half the space is shown, as if the camera (and, by extension, the viewers) were positioned on the theatrical fourth wall facing the action. This also corresponds to the term "tableau-like shots" that Ben Brewster and Lea Jacobs (1998: 48) invoke with regard to early cinema, and must not be confused with a cinematic establishing shot, because the whole space is never provided within one single scene. Additionally, in some scenes, the characters are shot against a black background, as if sets had been temporarily removed.

Conversely, the images which are permeated by inner screens, thus splitting the whole, are more allusive to painting; the contrast of the superimposed layers symbolises the viewers' attention to either the full frame or to the scrutiny of certain details which are part of the picture. These images, like the tableaux, can be quite textural and draw attention to the (audio)visual materials presented by the filmmaker, working as a sort of cinematic brushstroke, which can be as appealing as the figurative content.

In fact, as Aumont (2007: 154) points out, there is no clear division between the art forms of painting, cinema, and theatre. Painting is also partly three-dimensional because it illustrates an imaginary event, a story; whether sacred or profane, painting is always an incarnation ("drama") (207). That this is very much what Greenaway believes is proved by the use of scenes which either occur in theatres or depict acts of painting. In addition to the film theatre Arc-en-Ciel in Strasbourg where episode 5 takes place, in episode 3, set in Antwerp, four actors (Nigel Terry, Steven Mackintosh, Raymond J. Barry, and Albert Kitzel) present their professional and personal arguments for the opportunity to play the writers Samuel Beckett and Franz Kafka, but do so in front of what appear to be diegetic theatre director(s)/producer(s), and do it in a real theatre house (Figure 17.8). Not only are they Luper's future jailors,

Figure 17.8 Theatrical auditioning for the roles of Beckett and Kafka in Peter Greenaway's *Part 1: The Moab Story*.

but Luper is attending this session as well. There seems to be no relation to the preceding scene, although both feature the same actors. Also, Beckett and Kafka are marginal to the trilogy, except for the fact that they are important historical storytellers. The only settings which are not filmed as one-sided tableaux are, precisely, the cinema and this theatre house.

What seems to be at stake here is the subject of representation, which is at the core of yet another scene, in episode 6, set at the Moitessiers' estate. Luper is made to pose in the nude at a garden banquet. The guests are presented with a quandary, as one of the Luper specialists points out: as Luper is physically a male, his sex cannot be hidden when he is naked, and yet he has been employed as a female servant, the only kind allowed by the Nazis. Since these guests are political collaborators of one sort or another, they hesitate between painting what they see and being true to nature, or imagining an alternative version that would protect the Moitessiers and themselves from problematic consequences. For some, this experiment becomes an act of imagination instead of observation.

Narrative Complexity and Intermediality

As regards *TLST*, I would not go as far as saying that the viewers enact a performance, multitasking all throughout the length of the film, as Casetti's theory allows, but I do claim that they are more likely to appreciate the versatility and audiovisual multiplication inherent in the film itself. Clearly, *TLST* requires a postcinematic viewer who is able to enjoy an old medium, such as film (depicting even older media), but *dressed up* in a new cinematic language. The constant introduction of inner screens is as much a narrative embedding as it is a visual one and introduces fragmentation and a fast pace which I consider to be highly performative. The postcinematic viewer of *TLST* should be able to relish this saga as both material and metaphor (images and sounds that contain a threefold discourse on cinema, intermediality, and fabrication).

The fact that Greenaway's *TLST* is a trilogy spanning several decades of History allows for interest and attention to set in and be maintained at a very high level. The existence of the film *A Life in Suitcases* (2005, also directed and written by Greenaway), a two-hour abridged version of the five hours and fifty-five minutes of the trilogy, shows that length is a necessary ingredient for this effect to take place. Although *A Life in Suitcases* is made up of materials contained in the trilogy, it lacks its epic scale and picaresque novelty.

The trilogy is inhabited by ninety-two characters overall: some of them are central to the historical developments of the trilogy, appearing in all or two of the films; others are invested with minor actions and are present in only one episode or marginally (and symbolically) in several; the "Luper specialists," who provide false or dubious information about the protagonist in the television documentary-style of the "talking head" (perceived in small inner screens usually in square shape) or occasionally intrude upon the diegetic frame, although in a metaleptic way, as part of another audiovisual layer; and, finally, some are fictional characters featured in other art forms or objects (e.g., Tiger Lily and Rupert the Bear are featured in comics; Dreyer's Joan of Arc and Jean Renoir's Boudou are characters in films). There is also a character called Charlotte des Arbres, known as the Storyteller (played by Ana Torrent), who is endowed with an additional symbolic nature in that her mission in the trilogy is simply to voice two stories—one starting with "Once upon a time there was a beautiful woman who loved unwisely" and another one about three women who crossed Europe pushing prams filled with potatoes hiding gold.

Ultimately, all the accounts are part of the same narrative impetus, forming different points of view or interpretations of the same facts. The most important item under assessment is Luper himself. That nothing of what is reported about him—including "evidence" conveyed by the "specialists"—is conclusive only reinforces the volatile nature of this specific character. The films could be seen as the decoding of one man's life in all its intricacies: Tulse Luper, a man who seems omnipresent in some of the most important (and conspiratorial) events in Europe over an extended period. Tulse Luper, the protagonist of the

Suitcases trilogy around whom the entire project revolves, is a chameleon of sorts. Not only is his identity never firmly established, but he is played by different actors throughout: J. J. Feild in *Part 1* and *Part 2,* Roger Rees in *Part 2* and *Part 3*, and Stephen Billington in *Part 3*; he also has a Belgian lookalike, played by Feild. The same dispersal, typical of the Freudian condensation process, befalls other characters in the trilogy, such as the Contumely sisters, a trio who end up on the same initially deserted island where the protagonist is stranded in episode 8 (*Part 3*). The first time they are seen they appear as three portly women, but when they speak in inner screens, they are played by other actresses with completely different physiques. They reappear in yet another semblance in episode 13, set in the Budapest morgue, as a trio of naked Jewish women who have been tied together and thrown off a bridge by the Nazis.

The same condensation is applied to the couple of Soviet commanders at the border checkpoint between East and West Germany, who are actually played by two different pairs of Russian actors. This practice is highlighted in one scene, in which Greenaway presents them simultaneously to the film viewers via a split screen. Ironically, Colonel Kotcheff, who has saved Luper's life only to have him tell stories to his wife, Lieutenant Alazarin, is a non-believer in narrative. "Storytelling is cheating," he claims in the sex scene in which he tries to impregnate his wife, when she ventures that Luper might be a viable candidate for paternity. Since Kotcheff does not speak English, he communicates with Luper via a translator.

The *TLST* is the ultimate application of the "man-narrative" structure, a pretext to begin a narrative and keep it going by way of an internal dispersal of narratives, as Tzvetan Todorov (2006: 126) claims of structures which are not psychologically motivated. In those cases, which include the *Arabian Nights*, actions are not evidentiary of specific character traits, since all traits generate actions, regardless of their nature. It is the process of engendering stories—the enunciation—that matters, and not their motivation. In this type of structure "any character is a virtual story which is the story of his [or her] life" (122, my translation), since none of them serves any other purpose. The protagonist Luper is the ultimate "man-narrative" character because he performs this role throughout the entire trilogy. He is the male equivalent of Scheherazade in the *Arabian Nights*. Like Scheherazade, he possesses no emphatic or specific character traits other than being a vehicle for storytelling and a storyteller himself. Indeed, many versions of his person and exploits circulate in the film, and in *Part 3* his life literally depends upon the stories he tells to his jailors. Excerpts of these stories are seen scrolling upwards on the screen and resemble mere anecdotes with no real causality or significant progression. They are micro-narratives like those compiled in Greenaway's (2002) book

Gold.[6] In these short passages, as in the entire *TLST*, there is no psychological causality; it is the act of storytelling that advances the story rather than the characters' actions. Todorov (2006: 125, 131) considers that all narratives are self-reflexive and should evince their own process of enunciation. The "narrative-man" is required only as long as the narrative lives on; the end of the narrative equates to the death of the man (128). In the *TLST* this death takes place through a surprising twist: Tulse Luper, in fact, is revealed to have died at the age of ten, and consequently the Tulse Luper myth, built around his supposed manifold imprisonments, denies all the narratives at the same time that it confirms the narration.

With this supreme revelation cinema is further linked to History in *TLST* historical saga in that both are highly unreliable. Even in the official annals, there is no record that is not tainted by the act of (immediate) subjective registry and/or (later) recollection. According to William A. Dunning (1914: 217), truth in History is always relative: "The phenomena of the past are no less complex than those of the present and the truth about them is no less elusive." Historical research is inevitably tainted by many factors: derivative accounts, preconceptions and contextual biases, deliberate falsification for political reasons or personal benefit, and a desire for reconstruction as when researchers start writing their own version of events. Monika Fludernik (1994: 89) argues that the writing of historical accounts resembles the writing of fiction: "History, like fiction, operates by means of emplotment and is based not on empirical cause-and-effect causality but on motivated sequentiality."

If there is no such thing as history, only historians, and "all historians are liars," as *TLST*'s Soviet translator claims upon his death, then perhaps from a media archaeologic perspective, Marshall McLuhan's dictum that "the medium is the message" is still as true today as it was in 1964, when the author wrote his seminal book *Understanding Media*. The importance of Greenaway's *TLST* in this matter resides in highlighting the metamediality involved, in McLuhan's (2001: 7) words, by means of a special aesthetics that mixes the art forms in an intermedial dialogue with one another within the boundaries of History, that is, in a never-ending relationship of artistic products.

Notes

This research was financed by FCT—Portuguese Foundation for Science and Technology, under the project SFRD/BDP/113196/2015.

1. Of the four media Greenaway contemplated using in 1997, when he first had the idea for this project, he dropped television and CD-ROM. The different "episodes" contained in the films can nowadays been seen as separate installments on certain websites.

2. These are *Vertical Features Remake* (1978), *Walk through H—The Reincarnation of an Ornithologist* (1979), *The Falls* (1980). The character is also mentioned in *Drowning by Numbers* (1988) (see Chinita 2020).
3. Unless otherwise stated, all quotations by Greenaway in this chapter come from his "Cinema Militans Lecture" (2003).
4. My use of the term here differs from Bolter and Grusin's (2000: 49) "repurposing," which refers to the representation of a medium embedded in the same medium. I am using the word literally.
5. Casetti (2015: 122) refers to these two stances with the words "adhesion" and "consciousness," two of his three modes of expansion.
6. Published by Dis Voir in 2002, a year before *Part 1* of the trilogy was released, the book contains 101 short accounts related to the disappearance of ninety-two gold bars during the Third Reich.

References

Aumont, Jacques. 2007. *L'Oeil interminable*. Paris: Éditions de la Différence.
Bolter, Jay David, and Richard Grusin. 2000. *Remediation: Understanding New Media*. Cambridge, MA: MIT Press.
Brewster, Ben, and Lea Jacobs. 1998. *Theater to Cinema: Stage Pictorialism and the Early Feature Film*. Oxford: Oxford University Press.
Casetti, Francesco. 2015. *The Lumière Galaxy: 7 Keywords for the Cinema to Come*. New York: Columbia University Press.
Chinita, Fátima. 2016. "I Sing the Body Synaesthetic: Cinematic Embodiment in Peter Greenaway's *Goltzius and the Pelican Company*." In *Image Embodiment: New Perspectives of the Sensory Turn*, edited by Lars C. Grabbe, Patrick Rupert-Kruse, and Norbert M. Shmitz, 86–107. Darmstadt: Büchner Verlag.
Chinita, Fátima. 2020. "Peter Greenaway's The *Tulse Luper Suitcases* Project (2003–2005): Transmedia Storytelling as Self-Reference Multimediality." In *Transmediations: Communication across Media Borders*, edited by Niklas Salmose and Lars Elleström, 31–51. New York: Routledge.
Dunning, William A. 1914. "Truth in History." *American Historical Review* 19, no. 2: 217–229.
Elleström, Lars. 2010. "The Modalities of Media: A Model for Understanding Intermedial Relations." In *Media Borders: Multimodality and Intermediality*, edited by Lars Elleström, 11–48. Basingstoke: Palgrave Macmillan.
Elleström, Lars. 2014. *Media Transformation: The Transfer of Media Characteristics among Media*. Basingstoke: Palgrave Macmillan.
Fludernik, Monika. 1994. "History and Metafiction: Experientiality, Causality, and Myth." In *Historiographic Metafiction in Modern American and Canadian Literature*, edited by Bernd Engler, 81–101. Paderborn: Schöningh.
Greenaway, Peter. 2002. *Gold*. Paris: Éditions Dis Voir.
Greenaway, Peter. 2003. "Cinema Militans Lecture: Towards Re-Invention of Cinema." SCRIBD, 28 September. https://pt.scribd.com/document/58238054/Cinema-Militans-Lecture-Peter-Greenaway#download.
Greenaway, Peter, dir. 2003. *The Tulse Luper Suitcases, Part 1—The Moab Story*. Odivelas: Films4You. DVD.
Greenaway, Peter, dir. 2004. *The Tulse Luper Suitcases, Part 2—Vaux to the Sea*. Odivelas: Films4You. DVD.

Greenaway, Peter, dir. 2004. *The Tulse Luper Suitcases, Part 3—From Sark to the Finish*. Odivelas: Films4You. DVD.
Huhtamo, Erkki. 1996. "From Kaleidoscomaniac to Cybernerd: Towards an Archaeology of Media." In *Electronic Culture. Technology and Visual Representations*, edited by Timothy Druckery, 296–303, 425–427. New York: Aperture.
Kiss, Miklós, and Steven Willemsen. 2017. *Impossible Puzzle Films: A Cognitive Approach to Contemporary Complex Cinema*. Edinburgh: Edinburgh University Press.
McLuhan, Marshall. 2001. *Understanding Media: The Extensions of Man*. New York: Routledge.
Natale, Simone. 2016. "There Are No Old Media." *Journal of Communication* 66, no. 4: 585–603.
Parikka, Jussi. 2015. "Media Archaeology: Questioning the New in Media Arts." In *Histories of the Post-Digital*, edited by Ekmel Ertan, 133–147. Istanbul: Amber Platform/Akbank Sanat.
Peeters, Heidi. 2005. "The Tulse Luper Suitcases: Peter Greenaway's Mediatic Journey through History." *Image [&] Narrative Suitcases* 6, no. 2. http://www.imageandnarrative.be/inarchive/tulseluper/peeters_art.htm.
Plantinga, Carl. 2009. *Moving Viewers: American Film and the Spectator's Experience*. Berkeley: University of California Press.
Strauven, Wanda. 2013. "Media Archaeology: Where Film History, Media Art, and New Media (Can) Meet." In *Preserving and Exhibiting Media Art*, edited by Julia Noordegraaf, Cosetta G. Saba, Barbara Le Maître, and Vinzenz Hediger, 59–80. Amsterdam: Amsterdam University Press.
Todorov, Tzvetan. 2006. *As Estruturas Narrativas*. Translated by Leila Perrone-Moisés. São Paulo: Editora Perspectiva.
Yacavone, Daniel. 2015. *Film Worlds: A Philosophical Aesthetics of Cinema*. New York: Columbia University Press.

Index

For the benefit of digital users, indexed terms that span two pages (e.g., 52–53) may, on occasion, appear on only one of those pages.

Figures are indicated by *f* following the page number; 'n.' after a page number indicates the endnote number.

activism, 35–36, 249
   feminist activism, 247
   See also politics
adaptations
   film adaptations, 42–43
   remixed adaptations, 39–40
   silent cinema and theatre, 154, 158–59
   transmedial adaptations, 33–34
   See also *Up the Junction*: Loach's adaptation; *Up the Junction*: Collinson's adaptation
Adorno, Theodor, 4
   aesthetics, 25, 26
   anti-cinema, 24–25
   art/arts, 23–26, 27n.5, 27–28n.7
   "Art and the Arts," 23
   avant-garde, 23–24, 25
   cinema and arts, 6–7, 24, 25, 26
   hybridity of arts, 23–24
   intermediality, 26, 27n.2
   negative dialectics, 26
   music, 25
   subjectivism, 25–26
   "Transparencies on Film," 23, 78n.3
Adriano, Carlos. See *Santoscopio = Dumontagem*
aesthetics
   Adorno, Theodor, 25, 26
   aesthetic commons, 43–44
   documentary-style aesthetic, 87–88
   film aesthetics and culture, 43–44
   Hegel, G. W. F., 4, 6–7, 15, 25, 26–27n.1
   rasa aesthetic, 30
   realist aesthetic, 85–86
   sampling and cut-and-mix aesthetic, 40
   Tulse Luper Suitcases Trilogy, 284–85, 287–88, 289, 290–91, 298
   See also arts; arts and cinema

Agamben, Giorgio, 169–70, 175, 179, 182
Agathocleous, Tanya, 114–15
Akerman, Chantal: *La Chambre* (1972), 113
Akomfrah, John: *The Stuart Hall Project* (2013), 33–34
Albers, Josef, 238–40, 241
Altick, Rick, 120
Álvarez, Cándido, 174
Alves, Henrique, 155
Amaya, Carmen, 9, 168
   clapping, 170, 172, 176
   death, 174
   fast movements, 170, 176
   as flamenco international star, 168, 174
   gaze, 170
   gestures, 170–71, 173–74, 173*f*, 175, 177*f*
   masculine outfit and dance style, 168–69
   Somorrostro, 168–69, 170, 172, 173–74
   zapateado, 168–69, 170–71, 172, 173–74, 176, 179
   See also Amaya, Carmen: films and TV; *Bajarí*; flamenco
Amaya, Carmen: films and TV, 168–69, 170, 179
   Amaya's film career, 170–71, 183n.2
   Bajarí, 9, 168–69, 175, 176, 178, 180, 181*f*, 182–83
   improvisation and cinematic staging, 172
   Juan Simon's Daughter (*La hija de Juan Simón*, José Luis Saénz de Heredia, 1935), 170
   María de la O (Francisco Elías, 1936), 169, 170, 171*f*
   Tarantos, Los (Francisco Rovira Beleta, 1963), 169, 171–72, 173–74, 173*f*, 176, 177–78, 177*f*, 179, 184n.10
   Wine Cellars (*La bodega*, Benito Perojo, 1929), 170
   See also *Bajarí*

Amaya, Karime, 174–75, 178, 179–80, 179*f*, 181*f*, 182–83, 184n.10
  See also *Bajarí*
Amaya, Mercedes "Winny," 176–77, 178, 180, 182
  See also *Bajarí*
American Mutoscope and Biograph Company, 97, 98–99
AMY! (Laura Mulvey and Peter Wollen, 1980), 10, 256*f*, 263n.1
  "Amy, Wonderful Amy," 257
  archive/contemporary footage, 254, 255–56
  Eden, Jonathan, 259
  "Flying Dreams," 250*f*, 259
  intermediality, 250, 254–61
  interviews with students, 256–57, 258*f*, 261
  Johnson, Amy, 10, 248, 254, 255–56, 258, 259–60, 261
  Maddox, Mary (Amy), 257–59
  Mulvey, Laura, 256, 259–60
  music, 255–56, 257–58
  music by FIG, 248, 254, 255–56, 257–59, 260–61, 263n.10
  music by X-Ray Spex, 255–56, 257, 260–61
  opening section, 255–56
  politics, 255, 261
  remediation, 257
  theory film, 254
  voice, 248, 254–61, 262
  voice-over, 257, 259–61
  Wollen, Peter, 259–60
  See also FIG; Mulvey, Laura and Peter Wollen
Anger, Kenneth, 226
Anthropocene, 116, 117
  Medium Earth (Otolith Group, 2013), 117–18
  planetary overview, 120–21
  visual signifier of, 118–19
Antonioni, Michelangelo: *Zabriskie Point* (1970), 140–41, 141*f*
  See also elemental intermedia
appropriation, 7
  cultural appropriation, 42–43
  cultural transfers (*transferts culturels*), 277–78
  Santoscopio = Dumontagem, 97
Arabian Nights, 297–98
Araújo, Luciana Corrêa de, 4–5, 9

Arendt, Hannah, 120–21, 251–52
Argentina, Imperio, 170–71
Aristotle, 7, 29, 38–39
  categories of analysis, 29–30
  intermediality theory, 29–30
  Poetics, 29–30, 34–35
art/arts, 15
  Adorno, Theodor, 23–26, 27n.5, 27–28n.7
  dialectical nature of, 26
  Hegel, G. W. F. on total, final art, 16, 18, 19
  no clear division between painting, cinema, and theatre, 294–95
  "relational art," 39
  "softwareisation" of the arts, 40
  Wagner, Richard: *Gesamtkunstwerk*/ totalisation of the arts, 9, 16, 23, 34–35
  See also aesthetics; arts and cinema
Artaud, Antonin, 225–26, 228–29
  "Theatre of Cruelty," 228–30
Arthus-Bertrand, Yann: *Home* (2009), 118–19
artists' cinema, 8–9, 113, 116–17, 119–20
arts and cinema, 1, 2, 3–4, 5–6
  Adorno, Theodor, 6–7, 24, 25, 26
  architecture and cinema, 16–17
  Badiou, Alain, 1, 6–7
  Brazilian cinema, 1–2
  cinema and end of art history, 6–7
  cinema as seventh art, 5–7, 15, 16, 19, 21–23, 25, 32
  Dwoskin, Stephen, 225, 226, 228
  Hegel, G. W. F., 6–7, 15, 16, 19, 27–28n.7
  music and cinema, 17–18, 33–34
  painting and cinema, 17
  poetry and cinema, 18
  sculpture and cinema, 17, 33–34
  totalisation of the arts and cinema, 19, 21–23
  Tulse Luper Suitcases Trilogy, 281–82, 283, 284, 286, 287, 288–89, 289*f*, 294–95, 298
  See also Badiou, Alain; Dwoskin, Stephen
audience/spectatorship, 66, 102–4, 135, 153–54
  active/interactive spectatorship, 1, 7, 192–93, 250
  Bajarí, 178
  Chinese cinema, 193
  dispersed audience, 293–94
  FIG, 251–52
  fourth wall between actors and audience, 192–93, 293–94

Natyashastra, 30
"subjective motion," 1
audiovisual media. *See* media (audiovisual media)
Augé, Marc, 125–26
Aumont, Jacques, 289, 294–95
Auslander, Philip, 69
Austen, Jane: intermedia and transmedia, 36–38
authorship, 7, 10, 94–95, 108, 253–54, 291–92
avant-garde, 31–32, 255
　Adorno, Theodor, 23–24, 25
　avant-garde cinema, 24, 25, 37, 38–39
　Dwoskin, Stephen, 225–30
　English avant-garde filmmakers, 228, 244n.2
　Heimat 2 series, 206, 207–8, 209–10, 218
　historical avant-gardes, 24–25, 27n.4, 30–31

Badiou, Alain, 4, 6–7
　arts and cinema, 1, 6–7, 21–23, 27–28n.7, 32–33
　dialectics, 21–23
　on Plato's cave allegory, 135, 144n.6
　subjectivism, 21–22
Baichwal, Jennifer, Nicholas de Pencier, and Edward Burtynsky: *Anthropocene: The Human Epoch* (2018), 118–19
Bajarí (Eva Vila, 2011) 9, 174
　Amaya, Carmen, 9, 168–69, 175, 176, 178, 180, 181*f*, 182–83
　Amaya, Karime, 174–75, 178, 179–80, 179*f*, 181*f*, 182–83, 184n.10
　Amaya, Mercedes "Winny," 176–77, 178, 180, 182
　Bajarí project, 174–75
　Bajarí show, 174
　Barcelona/"Bajarí," 174–75
　clapping, 176–77, 177*f*, 180–81, 182
　close-ups, 179–80
　Coco, El, 174, 176–77, 179–81
　gestures, 169, 175, 176–77, 177*f*, 178–83
　gestures, mediality of, 169, 182–83
　gestures, reflexive dimension of, 169, 175
　ghostly quality of, 178, 180
　intergenerational encounters, 181–83
　intermediality, 176, 181–83
　Juanito, 174–75, 176–78, 177*f*, 179–81, 180*f*, 182–83
　live flamenco performances, 174–75
　music documentary, 9, 168–69, 174–75
　Roma communities, 174–75, 176
　Somorrostro, 176–78
　Tarantos, Los, 176, 177–78, 177*f*, 179, 184n.10
　transmission, 175, 182–83
　zapateado, feet and shoes, 179–81, 179*f*, 180*f*, 182
　See also Amaya, Carmen; flamenco
Baker, Robert, 113–14
Bakhtin, Mikhail, 32, 34, 36–37, 42
　"dialogism," 30–31
　"embeddedness," 30–31, 43–44
Balázs, Béla, 178–79
Baldwin, James, 33–34
Baños, Ricardo de: *La gitana blanca* (1919), 170–71
Bao, Weihong, 186–87
Baradaran, Amir, 31–32, 38–39
Bard, Perry: *Man with a Movie Camera: Global Remake*, 38–39
Barreira, Luiz, 157
Barthes, Roland, 276–77
Ba-ta-clan, 156, 157
Bataille, Georges, 225–26, 230
Bauer, Mattias, 214–15
Bazin, André, 4–6, 34, 66–67, 186–87
　"impure" cinema, 5–6, 187, 209–10
BBC (British Broadcasting Corporation)
　Comedy Playhouse, 273
　Late Night Line Up, 273–74
　Wednesday Play, 81–82, 85–86, 274–75
　See also Steptoe and Son; TV
Beckett, Samuel, 270
　Film (film, 1965), 271
　Pinter, Harold and, 271–72
　Polanski, Roman and, 271
　Waiting for Godot (play, 1956), 268, 270, 271
Bee, Samantha: *Full Frontal*, 38
Bellour, Raymond, 3
Benegal, Shyam, 30
Benjamin, Walter, 110–11
Benning, James, 144n.10
　EASY RIDER (2012), 138–41
　EASY RIDER: Monument Valley shot, 139–40, 140*f*
　North on Evers (1991), 139–40
　See also elemental intermedia
Benson, Susan, 83–84, 84*f*, 89, 91–92, 94–95
　See also Up the Junction (Nell Dunn, 1963)

Bentham, Jeremy, 114–15
Berry, Chris, and Mary Farquhar, 187, 193–94
Bharata, 30
Bignell, Jonathan, 1–2, 10
black-and-white cinema, 17
Blom, Ivo, 151
Bogart, Humphrey, 271–72
Bolter, Jay David, and Richard Grusin, 30–31, 87–88, 116, 232
Bordwell, David, 2, 4–5
Botelho, Alberto, 154–55
Botelho, Paulino, 154–55
Bourriaud, Nicolas, 39
Brakhage, Stan, 226
Brannigan, Erin, 169–70, 178–79, 181–82
Brazilian cinema, 153
  "cinema in Brazil," 164
Brazil's light theatre/*teatro de revista*, 9, 152–53
  Brazilian cinema and theatre as co-constitutive forms, 9, 152–53, 164
  Brutalidade (*Brutality*), 157–59
  Carlito & Chico Boia, 160–62
  Chaplin, Charles/Carlitos, 159–63
  characters, 152–53
  cinemania, 158–59
  Cinema-troça (*Cinema-Mockery*), 155
  coco de respeito, O (*First-Rate Coco*), 155–56
  cultural massification, 156
  É o suco (*It's the Juice*), 160–61, 162–63
  espetáculos por sessões (theatre in sessions), 158–59
  film theatre, 162–63
  foreign influence on, 156, 162
  Hollywood and, 156–58, 159
  Hollywood star system, 157, 161–62
  Mosaico (*Mosaic*), 157
  Rodolpho Valentão (*Rudolph the Bully*), 157, 158–59
  Se a bomba arrebenta (*If the Pump Bursts*), 159–60
  valentinas, As (*The Female Valentinos*), 157
  viuvinha do cinema, A (*The Little Widow of the Cinema*), 153–54, 155, 165n.6
  Viva a mulher (*Long Live Women*), 163
  See also silent cinema and theatre
Brecht, Bertolt, 30–33, 34–35, 37, 219
  Chinese opera and, 185, 193
  Mei Lanfang and, 185, 193, 195–96, 198–99n.5

Verfremdungseffekt/epic theatre, 192–93, 198n.4, 198–99n.5, 199n.6
Bresson, Robert, 5–6
Brewster, Ben, and Lea Jacobs, 294
Bridgerton (Netflix series, 2020), 36–37
British cinema, 10
  colour films, 87–88
  music and, 10
  theatre and, 1–2, 274–75
  TV and, 1–2, 7–8, 87–89
British theatre, 270, 273–74
  Angry Young Men of the New Wave, 270
  home invasion/enclosed world trope, 271–72, 275–76
  Royal Court Theatre, 274–76
  social realism, 274–76
  Theatre Workshop, 274–76
  TV and, 273–74, 275–76
  See also Beckett, Samuel; Pinter, Harold; theatre
broadcasting. See TV
Broeze, Frank, 126
Brooke, Stephen, 83, 89–90
Burroughs, William, 31–32
Butler, Alison, 138–39

Cage, John, 211, 218
  Black Mountain College event, 227
  Dwoskin, Stephen and, 226–27, 228
camera obscura, 8–9, 134, 136–37, 141–42, 144n.9
Canudo, Ricciotto, 3
carousel slide projector/slides, 7–8
  carousel slide projector: characteristics, 65–67, 70–71, 72–73, 75–76, 77
  contemporary art and audio visual media, 65–66, 67, 68–69
  display of "black" in slide projection, 66–67
  economy of reproducibles, 66–67
  educational function, 76
  ephemerality, 65–66
  film projection and, 79n.13
  industrial demise of, 67, 68–69, 77, 79n.14
  installations, 65, 68–69, 73
  intermediality, 65–66, 67, 68–69
  media archaeology, 78n.6
  performance and, 68–69, 70–71, 72–73, 79n.10
  presence and engagement with the present, 65–67, 77

slides: characteristics, 66–67
storytelling, 70–71, 72–73
temporality of the carousel slide
  projector, 69
See also *Casa de Michèle*; *Non-chronological History*
carousel slide projector/slides: exhibitions
  2005 *Slideshow* (Baltimore Museum of Art, United States), 68–69
  2014 Turner Prize exhibition, 65–66, 78n.2
  2017 *Slides: A History of Projected Photography* (Musée de l'Elysée, Lausanne, Switzerland), 65, 68–69, 78n.1
Carters, The (Beyoncé and Jay-Z), 35
Carvalho, Danielle Crepaldi, 152, 165n.6
Casa de Michèle (Pablo Pijnappel, slideshow/performance, 2014), 7–8, 68–73, 75–76, 77
  Reeford, Adaire, 71–73
  synchronisation of audio and image, 79n.12
  See also carousel slide projector/slides; Pijnappel, Pablo
Casetti, Francesco, 291–93, 295–96, 299n.5
Casler, Herman, 98–99
Castro, Teresa, 113
censorship, 152, 154, 163, 191
Chamarette, Jenny, 4, 10
Chaplin, Charles, 159–62
Chekhov, Anton, 276
Chen Kaige, 189–90, 192
  Yellow Earth (*Huang Tudi*, 1984), 194–95
  See also *Farewell My Concubine*
Chen Xihe, 186–87
China
  1919 May Fourth Movement, 186
  1942 Yan'an Literature and Art Forum, 190–91
  1949 Communist Revolution, 189–90
  1966–1976 Cultural Revolution, 191–92, 193–95, 197–98, 199n.8
  Chinese Nationalist Party (Kuomintang), 188
  Deng Xiaoping: "reform and opening-up," 186
  Gang of Four, 191, 198n.3
  Great Leap Forward period, 191
  People's Republic of China, 189–91
Chinese cinema (mainland), 1–2, 185–86
  1930s Shanghai leftist film movement, 186
  censorship, 191

Chinese cinema/opera, 9, 185, 186, 187, 193–94
Chinese cinema/opera: attractions and identification, 192–94
Chinese cinema/opera: intermediality, 185, 188–92, 197–98
exhibitionist cinema, 192–93
identification, 193, 195–96
impurity, 194–98, 198–99n.5
intermedial method, 185, 186–87
Marxism and proletarian cinema, 190–91
modernisation debates, 186
"opera film" genre, 188–89, 192, 195, 198n.2
realism/social realism, 189–90, 192, 198–99n.5
"shadow play" and, 186–87
Shanghai, 186–87, 189
Sinicisation of film production, 186
spectatorship, 193
wuxia genre, 198n.2, 199n.7
See also Chen Kaige; Chinese cinema: specific films
Chinese cinema: specific films
  Cui Wei and Chen Huai'ai: *Wild Boar Forest* (*Ye Zhu Lin*, 1962), 189–90
  Fei Mu: *Remorse at Death* (*Sheng Si Hen*, 1948), 189, 190f
  Mei Lanfang: *Heavenly Maidens Spread Flowers* (*Tian Nü San Hua*, 1920), 189
  Pan Wenzhan and Fu Jie: *Red Detachment of Women* (*Hongse Niangzijun*, 1971), 191
  Ren Jingfeng, *Conquering the Jun Mountain* (*Ding Junshan*, 1905), 188–89
  Xie Jin: *Two Stage Sisters* (*Wutai Jiemei*, 1964), 189–90, 198–99n.5
  Xie Tieli: *Taking Tiger Mountain by Strategy* (*Zhi Qu Weihu Shan*, 1970), 191
  Zhang Shichuan: *Sing-Song Girl Red Peony* (*Ge Nü Hong Mudan*, 1931), 189
  See also *Farewell My Concubine*
Chinese opera, 9, 185
  960–1279 Song dynasty, 188
  1644–1911 Qing dynasty, 188
  Chinese opera/cinema, 9, 185, 186, 187, 193–94
  Chinese opera/cinema: attractions and identification, 192–94
  Chinese opera/cinema: intermediality, 185, 188–92, 197–98

Chinese opera (*cont.*)
   Cultural Revolution "Peking Model
      Operas," 191, 194–95, 197–98
   Hui Opera, 188
   impurity, 197
   Maoist "revolutionary
      romanticism," 190–91
   as national form, 188, 189–90
   "opera film" genre, 188–89, 192, 195, 198n.2
   propaganda, 191
   Qi Rushan, 188
   Tan Xinpei, 188–89, 198n.1
   xiqu, 188
   See also Mei Lanfang; Peking Opera
Chinese theatre
   "shadow play" and Chinese
      cinema, 186–87
   xiju, 188
   xiqu, 188
   See also Chinese opera
Chinita, Fátima, 4–5, 10
Chion, Michel, 253–54, 259–60
Cho, Julia, 37–38
Chomsky, Marvin J.: *Holocaust* (1978), 219
Chuck D, 40
cinema
   dialectical function of, 19–20
   digital environment and, 38–39
   film as universal language, 1–2
   "five tracks" of, 32, 43–44
   hybridity, 2, 4–5, 39, 43–44
   intermediality, 1–4, 6, 10–11, 43–44
   media and, 1, 2, 3, 5–6, 32–33
   movement and film, 1
   moving form of film, 1, 2–3, 4, 6, 10–11
   "objective motion"/"subjective motion," 1
   transartistic nature of, 32
   See also arts and cinema; film festivals; film history; film industry; film philosophy; film studies; film theory
"cinema of attractions," 107, 108
cityscape, 172–73, 206–7
Clark, Nigel, 121
Clouzot, Henri-Georges: *Le Mystère Picasso*
   (*The Mystery of Picasso*, 1956), 289–90
Coleridge, Samuel Taylor, 249
Collinson, Peter. See *Up the Junction*:
   Collinson's adaptation
colour film, 87–88
   Eastmancolor, 87–89, 171–72
   Technicolor, 7–8, 87–88

Techniscope, 87–88, 94–95
Up the Junction: Collinson's adaptation,
   87–88, 89–90, 90*f*, 93–95
Comolli, Jean-Louis, 78n.8, 172–74, 175
Compton Films, 270–71
Connolly, Maeve, 116–17, 119–20
Connor, Steven, 253–54, 257
Conrad, Joseph: *Heart of Darkness*, 39–40
Conrad, Tony: *The Flicker* (1966), 78n.4
Cooke, Lez, 81–82, 89
Cooper, Lindsay, 248*f*, 251, 252, 263n.3,
   263n.10, 263n.12
   See also FIG
Coppola, Francis Ford: *Apocalypse Now*
   (1979), 39–40
copyright, 7, 40, 42–43
   piracy culture and abuse of copyright, 43
Cordua, Beatrice, 232–34, 233*f*, 236, 238–
   40, 241
Costa, Jayme, 157
Covid pandemic, 143
Creative Commons, 31–32, 41–42
Croce, Benedetto, 27–28n.7
culture
   cultural appropriation, 42–43
   cultural massification, 156
   cultural transfers (*transferts
      culturels*), 277–78
   film aesthetics and, 43–44
   high culture, 273–75
   mass culture, 35, 42
   "participatory culture," 39–40
   popular culture, 35, 273, 274–75
Curling, Jonathan, and Sue Clayton: *The Song
   of the Shirt* (1979), 263n.12

Dada, 24–25, 226, 227–28
Daney, Serge, 3–4
De Barros, Luiz, 154–55, 157, 163
De Certeau, Michel, 31–32, 42
De Kooning, Willem, 238–40
Deleuze, Giles, 4–5, 32, 178–79
DeLillo, Don, 139–40
De Luca, Tiago, 4, 8–9, 131–32
Deren, Maya, 226
De Roo, Ludo, 144n.5
Derrida, Jacques, 30–31
Deutsch, Gustav: *Shirley*, 17
Devlin, J. G., 275–76
dialectics
   Adorno, Theodor, 26

art: dialectical nature of, 26
Badiou, Alain, 21–23
dialectical function of cinema, 19–20
Hegel, G. W. F., 15, 17, 19–20, 25, 27–28n.7
Dickens, Charles, 2–3
Didi-Huberman, Georges, 172, 175
digital era/media, 7
　audio-visual-digital arts, 33–34
　digital environments, 38–39, 43–44
　hybridisation and, 39, 43–44
　proto-cinematic practices of the nineteenth century and, 102–4
　"remediation," 30–31
　"softwareisation" of the arts, 40
　transmediality, 34, 39–40
　Tulse Luper Suitcases Trilogy, 287, 288
　See also media (audiovisual media); *Santoscopio = Dumontagem*
Doane, Mary Ann, 123
documentary
　critical documentary, 19–20, 21–22
　"docufiction," 19–20, 21–22, 26
　documentary-style aesthetic, 87–88
　Heart, Beating in the Dark—New Version (2005), 48, 52–57, 56*f*
　Up the Junction: Loach's adaptation (documentary elements), 83–84, 89
　See also *Bajarí*; *Medium Earth*; *Walden*
Dolar, Mladen, 253–54, 258
Donner, Clive: *The Caretaker* (*The Guest*, 1963), 270–71
Dreyer, Carl Theodor: *La Passion de Jeanne D'Arc* (1928), 286, 286*f*
Dunn, Nell
　"Bad Girl" (lyrics), 86
　engagement with different media, 82
　Poor Cow (novel, 1967), 82
　Steaming (play, 1981), 82
　See also *Up the Junction* (Nell Dunn, 1963)
Dunning, William A., 298
Dwoskin, Henry, 26
Dwoskin, Stephen, 4, 10, 225, 243–44
　arts and cinema, 225, 226, 228
　Arts Council England, 231, 244n.2
　avant-garde, 225–26
　Cage, John and, 226–27, 228
　dance and film, 229–30
　diaries, 226, 238–40
　Dwoskin Archive, University of Reading (UK), 230
　expanded cinema, 227–28, 229
　experimental film, 225–26, 243–44
　Film Is…(book), 225–26, 227–28, 229
　Ha, ha! La Solution imaginaire (book), 230
　as intermedial artist, 10, 225, 228, 230
　intermediality, 225–26, 238–44
　"late style," 230–32, 237–38
　LFMC (London Film-Makers' Co-op), 225, 226, 228–29, 244n.2
　locations, 229
　New York and avant-garde intermediality, 226–30
　New York Film-Makers' Cooperative, 226, 227
　paintings by, 240*f*, 241
　painting with film, 238–44
　performance/happening, 226, 227, 229, 233–34, 236
　Structural/Materialist film, 226, 243–44
　Surrealism/proto-Surrealim, 225–26, 227–28, 230
　theatre and film, 228–29
　UK, 225–26
　underground film, 225, 226
　as underrepresented and underrecognised in his lifetime, 225–26
　See also Dwoskin, Stephen: films by; *Trying to Kiss the Moon*
Dwoskin, Stephen: films by
　Age Is…(2012), 244n.3
　Ballet Black (1986), 229–30
　Behindert (1975), 244–45n.7
　Central Bazaar (1976), 225
　C-film (1970), 229
　Chinese Checkers (1965), 225
　Dirty (1971), 229
　Dyn Amo (1972), 225, 229–30
　Further and Particular (1988), 230
　Girl (1972), 228–29
　Grandpère's Pear (2003), 225
　Intoxicated by My Illness (2002), 244n.3
　Me, Myself & I (1967/8), 229
　Outside In (1981), 229–30
　Pain Is…(1997), 244n.3
　Sun and the Moon, The (2008), 244n.3
　Take Me (1968), 229–30
　Trixi (1969), 225, 229–30, 232–34, 233*f*, 236, 238–40, 241
　See also Dwoskin, Stephen; *Trying to Kiss the Moon*
Dyer, Richard, 86

Earth
  media and, 131–32
  Medium Earth, 116–18, 119–20, 121
  Walden, 116–17
  See also elemental media; natural world
Eastwood, Clint, 19–20
Eisenstein, Sergei, 2–3, 193, 198n.4, 255–56
  Battleship Potemkin (1925), 16–17
Elderfield, John, 83–84
Elduque, Albert, 4, 9
elemental intermedia, 8–9, 134, 144n.5
  cinema, 134, 136–41
  cinema: elements *as* media, 133–34
  cinema/environment tension, 143
  experimental cinema, 134
  historiographical possibilities for cinema, 134
  Plato's cave allegory, 134, 135–36, 144n.7
  post-cinema, 134, 141–43
  pre-cinema, 134, 135–36
  See also elemental media; intermediality
elemental media (environment as media), 131–32, 140–41
  Earth and media, 131–32
  ecomaterialist film scholarship, 133
  film (medium) and, 132
  filmmaking and, 133–34, 144n.5
  landscape as media, 139–40
  "semiotic"/elemental media comparison, 132
  See also elemental intermedia; media
Elías, Francisco: *María de la O* (1936), 169, 170, 171*f*
Eliot, T. S., 32–33, 43–44
Elsaesser, Thomas, 108, 144n.9
entanglement, 268
  "entangled history," 267–68, 273, 277–78
  entrapment/entrapping entanglement, 268
  intermedial entanglements, 277–78
entrapment
  entrapment/entrapping entanglement, 268
  home invasion/enclosed world trope, 271–72, 276
  intermedial methodologies, 276–77
  Pinter, Harold, 270, 271–72
  politics of, 276
  Steptoe and Son, 276
Erice, Víctor: *The Spirit of the Beehive* (*El espíritu de la colmena*, 1973), 176–77
European cinema, 4–5

expanded cinema, 72–73, 251–52
  Dwoskin, Stephen, 227–28, 229
  Japanese expanded cinema, 79n.13
experimental cinema, 69
  Dwoskin, Stephen, 225–26, 243–44
  elemental intermedia, 134
  feminist experimental cinema, 247–48
  panoramic shot, 8–9, 113, 115–16
  See also *Medium Earth*; *Santoscopio = Dumontagem*; *Walden*

Facebook, 37
Fair(y) Use Tale, A (2007, collective work led by Eric Faden, Stanford University Fair Use project), 43
Fan, Victor, 186–87
Farewell My Concubine (*Bawang Bie Ji*, Chen Kaige, 1993), 9, 185–86, 197*f*
  1993 Palme d'Or, Cannes, 194
  as "border-crossing," "meta-opera film," 194
  Chinese tradition and identity, 192
  Cultural Revolution, 197–98, 199n.8
  Douzi, 194, 195–96, 196*f*, 197–98
  Hsu Feng, 199n.7
  identification, 195–96
  impurity, 194–98
  intermediality, 194–95, 197
  Laizi, 195
  Peking Opera, 194–98
  Shitou, 194, 195–96
  See also Chen Kaige; Chinese cinema
Fassbinder, Rainer Werner: *Berlin Alexanderplatz* (television series, 1980), 219
feature films, 19–20, 35, 36–37, 42, 240–41, 281
feminism
  activism, 247
  cyberfeminism, 49
  feminist films, 247–48, 262, 263n.12
  Heimat 2 series, 215–16
  historical feminism, 248
  intermediality of experimental feminist practices, 252
  Lizzie Bennet Diaries, The (YouTube vlog series, 2012–2013), 37
  Paley, Nina: *Sita Sings the Blues* (2008), 41–42
  recorded voice, 248
  voice as concept, 247, 248
  See also *AMY!*; FIG

Feminist History Project, 263n.12
Feminist Improvising Group. *See* FIG
Ferguson, Kirby: *Everything Is a Remix* (2010), 43
Feuillade, Louis: *Les Vampires* (1915), 162–63
Fielding, Henry, 42
FIG (Feminist Improvising Group), 10, 247–48, 251–54, 253f, 261–62
  AMY!: music by FIG, 248, 254, 255–56, 257–59, 260–61, 263n.10
  audience, 251–52
  Born, Georgina, 248f, 251–52, 263n.3
  Cooper, Lindsay, 248f, 251, 263n.3, 263n.10
  coproduction, 252–54
  eccentric style, 251
  EWIG (European Women's Improvising Group), 263n.3
  feminist experimental cinema, 247–48
  film soundtracks, 253–54, 263n.12
  improvisation, 252, 257–58
  Liensol, Koryne (Corinne), 251, 263n.3
  members, 248f, 251–52, 263n.3
  Mulvey, Laura and Peter Wollen, 257–58, 263n.10
  music by, 250
  Nicols, Maggie, 248f, 251, 252, 263n.3, 263n.10
  politics, 251–52
  Potter, Sally, 248f, 251, 252, 263n.3, 263n.10
  recordings of, 253–54, 262, 263n.6
  Roelofs, Annemarie, 248f, 263n.3
  Schweizer, Irène, 248f, 251, 263n.3
  voice/vocal sounds, 252, 253–54, 262
  Williams, Cathy, 251, 263n.3
film (medium)
  colour film, 87–88
  elemental media and, 132
  instant film, 78n.5
film festivals
  1965 Berlin Film Festival, 268, 270–71
  1966 Berlin Film Festival, 271–72
  1966 Edinburgh Film Festival, 271–72
  1969 Edinburgh Film Festival, 229
  1984 London Film Festival, 47–48, 59
  2019 Cinéma du Réel, 121–22
  2019 International Film Festival Rotterdam, 121–22
  2019 Karlovy Vary International Film Festival, 121–22
  2019 Sundance Film Festival, 121–22
  Pia Film Festival, 47–48
film history, 1, 2, 3, 4–6, 78n.8, 139–40
  Brazilian cinema, 1–2
  Chinese cinema, 186–87, 193–94
  cinema as heir of millennial traditions, 43–44
  elemental intermedia, 134
  evolution of cinema, 4–6
  "film history as media archaeology," 108
  integrated history, 151
  intermediality and, 4–5, 6–7, 164
  new film history, 6
  nonlinear narratives of film-historical phenomena, 4–5, 49–50
  Santoscopio = Dumontagem, 98, 110–11
  See also parallax historiography
film industry, 19–20, 21–22, 87–88
  Japan's post-studio film industry, 47–48
film philosophy, 4
  See also Adorno, Theodor; arts and cinema; Hegel, G. W. F.
film studies, 2, 3–4, 30–31, 151
  dance/theory of dance and, 178–79
film theatre, 4–5, 162–63, 292–93
  Plato's cave allegory and, 135–36, 144n.7
film theory, 135
  See also Adorno, Theodor; arts and cinema; Badiou, Alain
Fischer, Florian, and Johannes Krell
  Kaltes Tal (2016), 136–37
  Nature(s) as Spaces of (Self-)Perception (trilogy) 136–37
  Still Life (2014), 136–37
  Umbra (2019), 136–39, 138f
  See also elemental intermedia
flamenco, 9
  Barcelona, 9, 168, 171–72, 173–74
  bulerías, 172, 173f
  cante jondo, 172
  gestures, 9, 168–69
  intermedial history of flamenco gestures, 169–74
  intermediality, 170, 175
  male performers, 168–69
  Roma communities, 9, 168, 170–72, 173–74
  transmission, 175
  zapateado, 168–69
  See also Amaya, Carmen; *Bajarí*

flicker films, 78n.4
Fludernik, Monika, 298
Fluxus, 249
Foräs, Johan, 50
Ford, Francis
  Broken Coin, Francis Ford (1915), 162–63
  Lucille Love, the Girl of Mystery (1914), 162–63
Frampton, Hollis, 106–7
  nostalgia (1971), 79n.12
Frank, Robert, 226
Froes, Leopoldo, 153–55

Galton, Ray, 273–74, 275–76
Garfield, Rachel, 4, 10
Garnett, Tony, 81–82, 83
Gates, Henry Louis, Jr, 30–31
Gaudreault, André, 35–36
Gehr, Ernie, 106–7
Germany
  Heimatfilme, 202–3
  New German Cinema, 202–3, 204–6, 216–17
  New Music movement, 217
  Young German Cinema, 203, 216–17
  See also *Heimat 2* series; *Heimat* project; Reitz, Edgar
gestures
  Amaya, Carmen, 170–71, 173–74, 173*f*, 175, 177*f*
  contemporary pathological tics prevailing over naturalness and coordination, 169
  dance and cinema, 169–70, 175
  flamenco, 9, 168–69
  "gestural exchange" model, 181–82
  intermediality (flamenco), 169–74, 175, 182–83
  mediality of, 169
  place/gesture connection, 172–74, 175
  Santoscopio = Dumontagem: Santos Dumont's and Rolls's gestures, 100, 101*f*, 102, 109, 110*f*
  transmission of, 175
  See also *Bajarí*
Gil, Gilberto, 31–32
Gill, Brendan, 271–72
Ginsburg, Allen, 228
globalisation
  panoramic shot and, 116–17
  Walden, 121–28
Godard, Jean-Luc, 29–30, 33–34, 37–38
  Band of Outsiders (*Bande à part*, 1964), 35

Goodbye to Language (*Adieu au langage*, 2014), 17
Goldin, Nan, 70–71, 79n.10
Goldsmith, Leo, 144n.10
Gomes, Tiago de Melo, 152, 156, 162
Graham, Dan, 70–71
Graham, Todd: *Apocalypse Pooh* (2012), 39–40
Granger, Derek, 271–72
Grant, Benjamin: *Overview: A New Perspective of Earth* (2016), 118–19
Greenaway, Peter
  "Cinema is dead, long live cinema," 287–88
  "Cinema Militans Lecture" (2003), 284–85, 287–88, 289
  cinematic style of, 287–88, 289
  en-*forming*, 283, 287–88
  Gold (book) 297–98, 299n.6
  Luper, Tulse Henry Purcell, 282, 299n.2
  as media archaeologist, 10, 283, 284
  New Cinema, 287–88, 291–95
  Prospero's Books (1991), 281–82
  VJ performances, 281, 292–93
  See also Greenaway, Peter: films by; *Tulse Luper Suitcases* Trilogy
Greenaway, Peter: films by
  Drowning by Numbers (1988), 299n.2
  Falls, The (1980), 299n.2
  Life in Suitcases, A (2005), 296
  Vertical Features Remake (1978), 299n.2
  Walk through H—The Reincarnation of an Ornithologist (1979), 299n.2
  See also Greenaway, Peter; *Tulse Luper Suitcases* Trilogy
Greenberg, Clement, 39, 225–26, 238–42, 243–44
Griffith, D. W., 2–3, 98–99
  Lonely Villa, The (1909), 271–72
Gunning, Tom, 192

Hallam, Julia, and Margaret Marshment, 85–86
Hancock, Tony, 273
Handwerk, Norbert, 208–9
Hansen, Miriam, 27n.2
Hartmann, Karl-Amadeus, 208–9
Heart, Beating in the Dark (Nagasaki Shunichi, 1982), 7, 52, 57–58, 58*f*
  1984 London Film Festival, 47–48, 59
  as "blueprint" for *New Version*, 59–60

jishu eiga (self-made film), 51–52, 53–54, 55–57
  lack of closure, 51–52, 59–60
  reflexive techniques, 51–52
  Super 8, 7, 47–48, 53–54, 55
  synopsis, 51–52
  as zero-budget chamber piece, 51–52
  See also *Heart, Beating in the Dark—New Version*; Nagasaki Shunichi
Heart, Beating in the Dark—New Version (Nagasaki Shunichi, 2005), 7, 47–48, 58*f*
  documentary, 48, 52–57, 56*f*
  intramediality, 7, 48, 60
  intramedial passages, 54, 55–60
  "intramedial reference," 59–60
  metareference, 7, 48, 52–53, 59, 60
  opening narration, 57–58
  parallax historiography, 48, 60
  parallel narratives and metafictional stacking, 51–57
  remake, 7, 48, 51, 52–53, 54, 55–58, 56*f*, 59
  remediation, 48, 51, 53–54, 56*f*
  self-reflexive narrative, 47–48, 59
  sequel, 7, 48, 55–57, 56*f*
  See also *Heart, Beating in the Dark*; Nagasaki Shunichi
Hegel, G. W. F.
  Aesthetics, 15, 21–23, 26–27n.1
  aesthetic system/classification of the arts, 4, 6–7, 15, 25, 26–27n.1
  cinema and arts, 6–7, 15, 16, 19, 27–28n.7
  dialectics, 15, 17, 19–20, 25, 27–28n.7
  modern comedy as culmination of its preceding forms, 6–7, 15, 18
  modern comedy leads. . .to dissolution of art, 15–16, 26–27n.1
  total/final art, 16, 18, 19
Heidegger, Martin, 120–21
Heimat 2 series (*Heimat 2: Chronicle of a Generation–Die zweite Heimat: Chronik einer Jugend*, Edgar Reitz, 1992), 9, 202–3
  avant-garde and serial experiments, 206, 207–8, 209–10, 218
  Clarissa (Salome Kammer), 209, 211–16, 213*f*, 215*f*
  closing episode, 215–16
  Elisabeth Cerphal, Fräulein (Hannelore Hoger), 209, 216–18
  feminism, 215–16
  film and music, 203–4, 206–10, 212–14
  Foxhole, 211, 217
  Hermann Simon, 203–4, 207–9, 210–15, 212*f*
  historicising storytelling through film and music serialism, 216–19
  history of Germany, retelling of, 9, 205–6
  Holocaust, 217, 218
  impurity, 209–10
  intermediality: film and history, 202, 203, 206
  intermediality: film and music 203–5, 206, 207–8, 209
  Juan Subercaseaux (Daniel Smith), 210–11
  Klärchen, 207, 211, 220n.6
  Kluge, Alexander (Alex/Michael Schönborn), 216–17
  language as music, 211
  live musical performances, 204, 210, 215–16
  locations, 204–5
  Mamangakis, Nikos, 211–12, 212*f*, 220n.5
  Mamangakis, Nikos (music track), 203–4, 206–7, 209, 215–16, 218
  Munich, 206–7, 209, 216–17
  music as theme, diegetic performance, and organisational principle of episodes, 9, 203
  musicians/actors/characters, 206, 209, 210–16
  New Music movement, 203, 210, 218
  overt/covert intermediality, 204, 207–8, 209
  Professor P., 212–15, 213*f*
  storytelling, 203–4, 209–10, 216–19
  success, 219–20n.2
  time-lapse photography, 206–7
  title musical piece, 206–7
  "Two Strange Eyes" episode, 209
  See also Germany; *Heimat* project; Reitz, Edgar
Heimat project (Edgar Reitz), 4–5, 205–6, 219
  Heimat: A Chronicle of Germany (*Heimat: Eine deutsche Chronik*, 1984), 202–3, 206–7, 219–20n.2
  Heimat 2: Chronicle of a Generation (*Die zweite Heimat: Chronik einer Jugend*, 1992), 202–3
  Heimat 3: A Chronicle of Endings and Beginnings (*Heimat 3: Chronik einer Zeitenwende*, 2004), 202–3
  historical realism, 205–6

Heimat project (Edgar Reitz) (*cont.*)
  history of Germany, 202–3
  Home from Home: A Chronicle of Vision
    (*Die andere Heimat: Chronik einer*
    Shensucht, 2013), 202–3
  Schabbach, 204–5, 207, 214, 220n.3
  success, 205–6, 219–20n.2
  time-lapse photography, 208–9
  See also Germany; *Heimat 2* series;
    Reitz, Edgar
Hellings, James, 4, 6–7
Helm-Groves, Nicolas, 255–56
Henderson, Louis: *All That Is Solid* (2014), 133
Henri, Adrian, 81–82, 87
Herzog, Werner
  Cave of Forgotten Dreams (2010), 135–36
  Fata Morgana (1971), 140–41
  See also elemental intermedia
Higgins, Dick, 2–3, 249
Hill, John, 83, 86
histoire croisée approach, 10, 267–68
  "entangled history," 267–68
  intermedial method and, 276–78
Holdsworth, Claire M., 4, 10
Hollywood cinema, 4–5, 19–20, 21
  cultural massification, 156
  influence on Brazil's light theatre/*teatro de*
    revista, 156–58, 159
  influence on stage plots, 156, 157, 164
  star system, 157, 161–62
Holzapfel, Patrick, 142–43
Hopper, Dennis, 138–39, 140–41
  Easy Rider (1969), 138–40
Hopper, Edward, 17
Hudson, Ian, and Mark Hudson, 126
Huhtamo, Erkki, 113–14, 124–25, 284
hybridisation/hybridity
  cinema, 2, 4–5, 39, 43–44
  digitization and, 39, 43–44

Ibsen, Henrik, 276
India, 30
Ingham, Michael, 151
installations, 3, 73
  Medium Earth, 119–20, 121
  panoramic shot and, 116–17, 119–20
  slide projector/slides and, 65, 68–69, 73
  Walden, 116–17, 121–22, 127–28, 128f
  See also *Non-chronological History*
intermediality
  Adorno, Theodor, 26, 27n.2

Aristotle, 29–30
  from Aristotle to Hollywood, 29–31
aural intermediality, 86
Austen, Jane, 36–38
carousel slide projector/slides, 65–66,
  67, 68–69
Chinese opera/cinema, 185, 188–
  92, 197–98
cinema, 1–4, 6, 10–11, 43–44, 131, 151
  co-dependency and cross-
    fertilisation, 267–68
  concept of, 3–4, 39, 41–42, 70, 82–83,
    230–31, 249
Dwoskin, Stephen, 10, 225–30, 238–44
experimental feminist practices, 252
flamenco, 170, 175
gestures and, 169
gestures (flamenco) and, 169–74,
  175, 182–83
haptic (concept), 232
as highly performative, 82–83
intermedia (concept), 2–3, 29, 249
intermedial artists, 10
"intermedial passages" within cinema, 50
intramediality/intermediality
  distinction, 48
national and regional phenomena, 9
as one-way process, 267–68
overt/covert intermediality, 204, 207–8, 209
parallax historiography and, 49–50
Pinter, Harold, 10, 268, 270–71, 273–
  74, 277–78
"politics of intermediality," 214–15
provenance of terms, 31–35
Reitz, Edgar, 218
scholarship on, 3–4
self-reflexivity, 175
silent cinema and theatre, 151, 164
technologies and environments, 7–9
UK, "intermedia" term, 250
voice as intermedial act, 247
See also hybridisation/hybridity;
  intermediality: specific films/works;
  intermedial method; transartistry,
  transmediality
intermediality: specific films/works
  AMY!, 250, 254–61
  Bajarí, 176, 181–83
  Farewell My Concubine, 194–95, 197
  Heimat 2 series: film and history, 202,
    203, 206

Heimat 2 series: film and music 203–5, 206, 207–8, 209
Heimat 2 series: overt/covert intermediality, 204, 207–8, 209
Medium Earth, 116–17
Santoscopio = Dumontagem, 97, 102–4, 108, 110–11
Trying to Kiss the Moon, 225–26, 230–38
Tulse Luper Suitcases Trilogy, 281–83, 295–98
Up the Junction (Nell Dunn, 1963), 83–84, 94–95
Up the Junction: Collinson's adaptation, 87–89
Up the Junction: comparison between Collinson and Loach's adaptations, 81–82, 87, 90–95
Up the Junction: Loach's adaptation, 82, 86
intermedial method, 1–2, 10
　Chinese cinema, 185, 186–87
　comparative intermedial historiography, 267–68
　"entangled history," 267–68
　histoire croisée approach and, 276–78
　intermedial entanglements, 277–78
　intermediality as historiographic method, 4–5, 6–7, 164
　limits of, 267–68, 271–72, 276–78
　theoretical possibilities of intermediality, 6–7
　See also intermediality
internet, 29, 30–31
　free distribution model, 41–42
　Situationism, 42–43
intramediality
　concept of, 48
　intramediality/intermediality distinction, 48
　"*intra*medial meta-film," 50–51
　"intramedial reference," 59
　metareference and, 50–51
　self-reflexive/metafictional films, 48
　See also *Heart, Beating in the Dark—New Version*
Ionesco, Eugene, 271–72, 276
　Bald Prima Donna, The (play, 1956), 270
　Lesson, The (play, 1958), 270
Israeli cinema, 19–20
ITV (Independent Television)
　Armchair Theatre series, 273–75
　Pinter, Harold and, 273–74

Play of the Week series, 273–74
Television Playhouse series, 273–74
See also TV

Jackson, Lauren Michele, 42–43
Jacobs, Ken, 106–7, 235–36
　Tom, Tom, the Piper's Son (1969), 107–8
Jandl, Silke, 37–38
Japan
　Japanese expanded cinema, 79n.13
　jishu eiga (self-made film), 47–48, 51–52
　Kabuki theatre, 198n.4
　post-studio film industry, 47–48
　See also Nagasaki Shunichi
Jarry, Alfred, 230
Jenkins, Henry, 31–32, 35–36, 39–40, 42
Jiang Qing, 191, 197, 198n.3
Jia Zhangke, 192
　Touch of Sin, A (*Tian Zhuding*, 2013), 192
Jiwarangsan, Prapat
　Aesthetics 101 (slide-based installation, 2019), 76, 79n.19
　Destination Nowhere (digital film, 2018), 74–75, 80n.20
　Dok-rak (*The Asylum*, digital film, 2015), 74–75, 80n.20
　Ploy (digital film, 2020), 74–75, 80n.20
　Wandering Ghost, The (digital film, 2017), 74–75, 80n.20
　See also *Non-chronological History*
Johansson, Christer, 144n.1
Johnson, Amy, 10, 248, 254, 255–56, 258, 259–60, 261
　See also *AMY!*

Kahn, Douglas, 134
Kant, Immanuel, 121, 199n.6
Kerkletz, Gerald, 123
Kerouac, Jack, 228
Kim, Jihoon, 39
King, Jamie: *Steal This Film* (2006), 43
King Hu, 198n.2
Klinger, Michael, 270–71
Kluge, Alexander, 24, 207, 218, 219
　Brutality in Stone (*Brutalität in Stein*, with Peter Schamoni, 1961), 216–17
　Yesterday Girl (*Abschied von gestern*, 1966), 216–17
Kohn, Eduardo, 124
Köner, Thomas, 119
Kracauer, Siegfried, 1

Krauss, Rosalind, 68–69
Kren, Kurt, 229–30, 235–36
Kristeva, Julia, 263n.1
Kubelka, Peter: *Arnulf Rainer* (1960), 78n.4
Kurosawa, Akira: *The Seven Samurai* (*Shichinin no samurai*, 1954), 18

Lagomarsino, Runo: *Sea Grammar* (slides, 2015), 78n.1
landscape film, 134, 144n.10
Lang, Fritz: *Metropolis* (1927), 33–34
Lanzmann, Claude: *Shoah* (1985), 128n.3
Latour, Bruno, 120–21
Lee, Lilian: *Farewell My Concubine* (novel), 197, 199n.7
Leslie, Esther, 255–56
Lévi-Strauss, Claude, 31–32
LFMC (London Film-Makers' Co-op), 225, 226, 228–29, 244n.2, 249, 252
Lindsay, Vachel, 1–2
Litvintseva, Sasha, 144n.5
Lizzie Bennet Diaries, The (YouTube vlog series, 2012–2013), 37–38
LMC (London Musicians' Collective), 252
Loach, Ken
    Cathy Come Home (BBC *Wednesday Play*, 1966), 85–86
    film adaptation of Dunn's *Poor Cow*, 82
    See also *Up the Junction*: Loach's adaptation
London Film-Makers' Co-op. See LFMC
London Musicians' Collective. See LMC
Lookbook, 38
Losey, Joseph, 82
    Figures in a Landscape (1970), 140–41
Losey, Patricia, 82
Lucretius, 144n.9
Lumière brothers: *Train Pulling into a Station* (*L'Arrivée d'un train en gare de La Ciotat*, 1896), 49
Lupino, Ida: *Never Fear* (1950), 229–30
Lutze, Peter C., 207
Lyotard, Jean-François, 181–82

Ma, Jean, 144n.7
MacGowran, Jack, 271
McLuhan, Marshall, 34, 298
McQueen, Steve: *Gravesend* (2007), 133
Mack, Jonathan, 82–83, 88–89
Malraux, André, 19
Mamangakis, Nikos, 208–9
    Heimat 2 series, 211–12, 212f, 220n.5

Heimat 2 series: music track, 203–4, 206–7, 209, 215–16, 218
    See also *Heimat 2* series
Mankiewicz, Joseph L.: *Julius Caesar* (1953), 18
Manovich, Lev, 102–4
Mao Zedong, 190–91
Marchetti, Gina, 198–99n.5
Marder, Michael, 124
Marker, Chris and Alain Resnais: *Statues Also Die* (*Les Statues meurent aussi*, 1953), 35
Marks, George: *Naked as Nature Intended* (1961), 270–71
Marks, Laura U., 232
Martel, Lucrecia, 33–34
Marx, Karl, 126
Marxt, Lukas
    Reign of Silence (2014), 144n.11
    Victoria (2018), 140–41, 141f
    See also elemental intermedia
Matos Cabo, Ricardo, 228
MC Lars: *Moby Dick* (rap version), 39–40
media (audiovisual media), 4, 249
    anthropogenic media, 8–9, 132
    cinema and, 1, 2, 3, 5–6, 32–33
    concept of, 131, 132
    "embedded" in the aesthetic commons, 43–44
    media history, 69, 232
    media studies, 34, 131–32, 136, 144n.1
    See also digital era/media; elemental media; intermediality; media archaeology
media archaeology, 4, 6, 8–9, 67, 116, 136
    carousel slide projector/slides, 78n.6
    concept of, 78n.6
    "film history as media archaeology," 108
    Greenaway, Peter as media archaeologist, 10, 283, 284
    Tulse Luper Suitcases Trilogy, 283, 284–91, 298
Medium Earth (Otolith Group, 2013)
    Anthropocene, 117–18
    Earth, 116–18, 119–20, 121
    experimental documentary work, 8–9
    gallery installation, 119–20, 121
    HKW (Haus der Kulturen der Welt), 117
    intermediality, 116–17
    locations, 117–18
    low-angle shots, 118–19, 121
    movement, 119–20
    panorama as geohistory, 117–21

panoramic shot (circular/half circular), 8–9, 113, 116–17, 118–20, 121
REDCAT, 117, 119–20
soundtrack, 119, 120
See also Otolith Group
Mei Lanfang, 188, 190*f*, 195, 198n.4
　Brecht, Bertolt and, 185, 193, 195–96, 198–99n.5
　Heavenly Maidens Spread Flowers (*Tian Nü San Hua*, 1920), 189
　national/international stardom, 189
　See also Chinese opera
Mekas, Jonas, 226, 227–28, 244n.2
Méliès, Marie-Georges-Jean, 49
　Voyage to the Moon (*Le Voyage dans la Lune*, 1902), 33–34
Meller, Raquel, 170–71
Mello, Cecília, 2, 9
Mencarelli, Fernando Antônio, 152–53
Messiaen, Olivier, 218
metareference, 50–51
　Heart, Beating in the Dark—New Version (2005), 7, 48, 52–53, 59, 60
　intramediality and, 50–51
　"*intra*medial meta-film," 50–51
　"intramedial reference," 50–51
　metaisation, 50–51, 53–54
　remakes, 51
Metz, Christian, 1–2, 6, 32, 34, 39, 131
Milne, A. A.: *Winnie the Pooh*, 39–40
Min Tian, 193
Mittmann, Jörg-Peter, 50–51, 59
Mizoguchi, Kenji: *The Crucified Lovers* (*Chikamatsu monogatari*, 1954), 18
Monáe, Janelle, 7, 33–34, 35
　Many Moons (short film, 2009), 35
Morin, Edgar, 106
Müller, Jürgen E., 4–5
Mulvey, Laura, 102–4, 247–48, 262
　See also AMY!; Mulvey, Laura and Peter Wollen
Mulvey, Laura and Peter Wollen, 250–51
　AMY! (1980), 254, 263n.1
　Crystal Gazing (1981), 263n.1
　FIG and, 257–58, 263n.10
　Penthesilea (1974), 254, 263n.1
　Riddles of the Sphinx (1977), 113, 254, 263n.1
　sound, 255–56
　trilogy, 254, 257–58, 263n.1, 263n.7
　See also AMY!

Münsterberg, Hugo, 151
Murnau, Friedrich Wilhelm: *Last Laugh, The/ The Last Man* (*Der letzte Mann*, 1924), 17
music, 40
　Adorno, Theodor, 25
　Bridgerton (Netflix series, 2020), 36–37
　free improvisation, 249, 252
　hip hop, 40
　musical "remix," 41
　musical theatre, 152–53, 188
　popular music, 41, 86, 92–93
　punk music, 252, 255–56
　sampling and cut-and-mix, 40, 41
　Up the Junction: Loach's adaptation, 86
　See also AMY!; *Heimat 2* series; opera
Music for Socialism, 249, 251
music videos, 7, 33–34, 35
　Rap music videos, 40
Musser, Charles, 151, 153–54, 155, 164
Mutoscope, 98–99
　home entertainment, 99
　Santoscopio = Dumontagem, 100–2, 102*f*
Myers, Stanley, 86
Myers, Toni: *A Beautiful Planet* (2016), 118–19

Nagasaki Shunichi
　After That (*Sonogo*, 1982), 60–61n.3
　jishu eiga (self-made film), 47–48, 51–52, 53–54, 55–57
　Lonely Hearts Club Band in September, The (*Kugatsu no jōdan kurabu bando*, 1982), 52–53, 60–61n.3
　See also Heart, Beating in the Dark; *Heart, Beating in the Dark—New Version*
Nagib, Lúcia, 34, 50, 59–60, 199n.6
Nagisa Oshima, 199n.6
Natale, Simone, 288
natural world, 8–9, 134, 136–37
　See also Earth; elemental media
Neorealism, 171–72
Noah, Trevor: *The Daily Show*, 38
Non-chronological History (Prapat Jiwarangsan, slide-based installation, 2013), 7–8, 68–69, 73–76, 75*f*, 77
　Dust under Feet (photography, 2011), 75–76, 79n.18
　stipulated duration of, 74
　Thai political history, 73–76
　versions, 74, 79n.14
　See also carousel slide projector/slides; Jiwarangsan, Prapat

Nunes, Mário, 155–56, 158–59

O'Donoghue, Darragh, 4, 10
Oliver, John: *Last Week Tonight*, 38
opera, 9
   Brecht: popular opera, 34–35
   "street opera," Brazil, 34–35
   Wagner, Richard, 9, 16
   See also Chinese opera; Peking Opera
Osborne, John, 276
   Look Back in Anger (play, 1957), 270
Otolith Group
   Eshun, Kodwo, 117–18
   installations, 117
   Otolith Trilogy, 117
   Sagar, Anjalika, 117, 120
   See also *Medium Earth*

Paech, Joachim, 175
Paley, Nina: *Sita Sings the Blues* (2008), 41–42
panorama, 113–16
   eighteenth-century panorama, 113–14, 115f
   nineteenth-century panorama, 8–9, 113–14
   1851 Great Globe (James Wyld), 120
   georama, 120
   moving panorama, 124–26
   panorama as world-embracing view, 113–14
   panoramic "keys," 114
   as precursor of cinema, 115–16
   travel and, 113–14, 121–22, 123, 124–25
panoramic shot, 8–9, 113, 115–16, 128n.3
   continuously moving camera, 115–16
   experimental cinema, 8–9, 113, 115–16
   globalisation and, 116–17
   installations and, 116–17, 119–20
   panorama as world-embracing view, 113
   realism, 123
   See also *Medium Earth*; *Walden*
parallax historiography, 49–50
   Heart, Beating in the Dark—New Version (2005), 48, 60
   intermediality and, 49–50
   remakes, 51
Parikka, Jussi, 116, 120–21, 290–91
Peixoto, Luís: *Meia-noite e trinta* (*Half Past Midnight*, 1923), 162
Peixoto, Mário: *Limite* (1931), 159
Peking Opera (*jingju*), 185, 188–89, 191, 197
   ban on, 191
   dance, 195

Farewell My Concubine (film) and, 194–98
Farewell My Concubine (opera), 195
   modernisation of, 191
   twentieth century, 189, 195
   wuxia, 198n.2, 199n.7
   See also Chinese opera
performance/happening, 2–3, 69
   Cage, John: Black Mountain College event, 227
   carousel slide projector/slides and, 68–69, 70–71, 72–73, 79n.10
   "disappearance," 261–62
   Dwoskin, Stephen, 226, 227, 229, 233–34, 236
   lecture performance, 70–71
Perojo, Benito: *Wine Cellars* (*La bodega*, 1929), 170
Peters, John Durham, 131–32
Petersson, Sonya, 144n.1
Pethő, Ágnes, 49–50, 59, 82–83, 215–16, 230–31
Picasso, Pablo, 32–34, 287–88, 289–90
Pijnappel, Pablo, 70
   Lucas (film, 2013), 70, 79n.11
   Pareciam ser de um cinza translúcido (solo show), 79n.11
   See also *Casa de Michèle*
Pinter, Harold, 10, 267–68, 269–70
   Beckett, Samuel and, 271–72
   Birthday Party, The (film version), 274–75
   Birthday Party, The (play, 1963), 269–70, 269f, 271–72, 275–76
   Birthday Party, The (TV version), 273–74
   Caretaker, The (film version), 274–75
   Caretaker, The (play, 1963), 270–71
   Collection, The (TV version), 273–74
   Dumb Waiter, The (TV version), 273–74
   entrapment, 270, 271–72
   home invasion/enclosed world trope, 271–72, 276
   intermediality, 10, 268, 270–71, 273–74, 277–78
   Ionesco, Eugene and, 271–72
   ITV and, 273–74
   Lover, The (TV version), 273–74
   Naturalism, 273
   Night Out, A (TV version), 273–74
   Pinteresque, the, 269–71, 273, 274–75, 276–78
   Polanski, Roman and, 270–71

Room, The (TV version), 273–74
socially engaged drama, 270
Steptoe and Son and, 273, 275–76
textual field, 268
TV sitcom and Pinter's dramatic work, 273–74
"Pinter Histories and Legacies," 267–68, 276–77
Pinto, Apolonia, 154
Plantinga, Carl, 293–94
Plato: cave allegory, 134, 135–36, 144n.7
Player, Mark, 7
Pleasence, Donald, 270–71
Polanski, Roman, 267–68, 270–71
  Beckett, Samuel and, 271
  Cul de Sac (1965), 271–72, 272f, 275–76
  If Katelbach Comes (1965), 270–71
  Pinter, Harold and, 270–71
  Repulsion (1965), 270–71
politics
  AMY!, 255, 261
  cinema and, 19–20, 21–22
  entrapment, 276
  FIG, 251–52
  political talk shows, 38
  See also activism
Pontes, Igor Andrade, 159–60
Potter, Sally, 248f, 251, 252, 262, 263n.3, 263n.10
  See also FIG
Prado, Décio de Almeida, 152–53
pre-cinema, 4, 6, 185–86
  digital cinema and proto-cinematic practices of the nineteenth century, 102–4
pre-cinema "toys," 8–9, 98, 99
  kaleidoscope, 102, 105f
  phenakistiscope, 98
  praxinoscope, 98
  Santoscopio = Dumontagem and, 8–9, 97, 98, 102–4
  zoetrope, 98
  See also Mutoscope

Qi Rushan, 188
Quinn, Julia, 36–37

Rainer, Yvonne, 250, 259–60, 262
Rancière, Jacques, 4–5
Rattigan, Terence, 270
Rauschenberg, Robert, 227–28

realism
  aural realism, 85–86
  British theatre: social realism, 274–76
  Chinese cinema, 189–90, 192, 198–99n.5
  "expositional realism," 85–86
  Heimat project: historical realism, 205–6
  panoramic shot, 123
  realist aesthetic, 85–86
  Reitz, Edgar, 204–5
  Up the Junction: Loach's adaptation, 85–86, 88–89, 92, 94–95
Rebentisch, Juliane, 73
Regnier, Carola, 244–45n.7
Reitz, Edgar, 24
  Brutality in Stone (*Brutalität in Stein*), 216–17
  Cardillac (1969), 210–11
  film and music, 204
  "Film und Wirklichkeit" (Film and Reality, lecture), 220n.3
  intermedial cinema, 218
  "lifelong film," 219
  locations, 204–5
  method of "scoring" for films, 208–9
  music as filmmaking grammar, 208–9
  "pure cinema," 208–9
  realism, 204–5
  Speed (*Geschwindigkeit*, 1963), 209, 210–11
  storytelling/language-based film script, 209
  VariaVision (1965), 210–11, 218
  Yucatan (1960), 210–11
  See also Germany; *Heimat 2* series; *Heimat* project
remakes
  Heart, Beating in the Dark—New Version (2005), 7, 48, 51, 52–53, 54, 55–58, 56f, 59
  metareference, 51
  parallax historiography, 51
remediation, 4, 41, 42, 116, 232
  AMY!, 257
  digital media, 30–31
  Heart, Beating in the Dark—New Version (2005), 48, 51, 53–54, 56f
  Santoscopio = Dumontagem, 97
Reygadas, Carlos, 128n.3
Richards, James: *The Screens* (slides, 2013), 78n.2
Riedl, Josef Anton, 208–9, 218

Riegl, Aloïs, 232, 233–34
Rizaldi, Riar: *Kasiterit* (2019), 133
Rodowick, David N., 6, 82–83
Rolls-Royce Limited, 97
Ross, Julian, 4–5, 7–8
Rossellini, Isabella, 288–89
Rossellini, Roberto: *Voyage to Italy* (*Viaggio in Italia*, 1954), 17–18
Rossiter, Leonard, 275–76
Rovira Beleta, Francisco: *Los Tarantos* (1963), 169, 171–72, 173–74, 173*f*
  opening sequence in *Bajarí*, 176, 177–78, 177*f*, 179, 184n.10
Rowbotham, Sheila, 247–48
Royce, Henry, 106
  See also *Santoscopio = Dumontagem*; *Santos Dumont* film
Russell, Catherine, 49–50
Russian Formalism, 39

Sadoul, Georges, 6
Saénz de Heredia, José Luis: *Juan Simon's Daughter* (*La hija de Juan Simón*, 1935), 170
Said, Edward, 230–32, 237–38
Santoscopio = Dumontagem (Carlos Adriano, 2010), 8–9, 97, 103*f*
  appropriation, 97
  baroque sense of the world's dynamics, 104–6
  choreography, 100, 109–10
  close-ups, 100, 109
  digital animation, 97, 105*f*, 109, 110*f*
  digital cinema: pixels and material texture, 109, 109*f*
  digital cinema/proto-cinematic devices link, 97, 98, 100, 102–4, 108
  digital editing, 8–9, 97, 99–100, 106–10
  experimental cinema, 8–9, 97, 100, 101–2, 106–7, 110
  film history, 98, 110–11
  intermediality, 97, 102–4, 108, 110–11
  kaleidoscopic dynamics, 102, 105*f*
  Mutoscope, 100–2, 102*f*
  past and present, 110–11
  reanimation, 104*f*
  remediation, 97
  Santos Dumont and Rolls's gestures, 100, 101*f*, 102, 109, 110*f*
  Santos Dumont film and, 97, 98–100, 110
  shot on 35mm, 8–9
  soundtrack, 100, 110
  structural film, 106–10
  "theme and variations," 100, 102, 106–7
  "toys" of pre-cinema, 8–9, 97, 98, 102–4
  visual structure, 100–1
  See also *Santos Dumont* film
Santos Dumont, Alberto, 106
  See also *Santoscopio = Dumontagem*; *Santos Dumont* film
Santos Dumont film (short film, 1901), 97, 98–99
  1901 meeting: Albert Santos Dumont and Charles Rolls, 8–9, 97, 106
  American Mutoscope and Biograph Company, 97
  Mutoscope, 98–99, 100
  Santoscopio = Dumontagem and, 97, 98–100, 110
Sasaki, Shirō, 52–53, 60–61n.3
Sauper, Hubert: *We Come as Friends* (2014), 19–20
Schaffer, Pierre, 259–60
Schamoni, Peter, 216–17
Schlöndorff, Volker 24, 209
Schmid, Viktoria: *A Proposal to Project in Scope* (2020), 142–43, 142*f*
  See also elemental intermedia
Schneemann, Carolee, 72–73
Schneider, Rebecca, 261–62
Schönherr, Ulrich, 215–16, 217
Schopenhauer, Arthur, 25
Schröter, Jens, 214–15
Schuppli, Susan, 133–34
screenwriters, 29–30
Segreto, Paschoal, 158–59
semiosis: unlimited semiosis, 268
semiotics, 30–31, 34, 132
Sennett, Mack, 155–56
Severo, Ary: *Herói do século XX* (*Twentieth-Century Hero*, 1926), 157
Shakespeare, William, 18, 43–44, 193
Shaw, Lisa, 152–53
Sider, Larry (Evanston Percussive Unit), 255–56
silent cinema, 16–17, 59, 87–88, 169
silent cinema and theatre, 9, 151, 152
  adaptations, 154, 158–59
  censorship, 152, 154, 163
  cinema's influence on stage performance and mise-en-scène, 155, 158
  exhibition practices, 158

film as centre of the plot, 153–54
film/stage business links, 154, 155, 158–59
Hollywood influence on stage plots, 156, 157, 164
intermediality, 151, 164
references to films and filmgoing, 153–54, 157, 162–63, 164
stage plays, 151, 152–53, 164
See also Brazil's light theatre/*teatro de revista*
Silvio, Teri, 194, 199n.8
Simon, David
  Treme (series, 2010–2013), 19–20
  Wire, The (series, 2002–2008), 19–20
Simon, Hermann: *Heimat 2* series, 203–4, 207–9, 210–15, 212f
Simpson, Alan, 273–74, 275–76
Sinnreich, Aram, 40
Sitney, P. Adams, 106–7, 123
Situationism, 30–31, 42–43
slide projector. *See* carousel slide projector/slides
Sloan, Tom, 273
Smashing Pumpkins: "Tonight, Tonight" (video), 33–34
Smith, Jack, 70–71, 227
Smith, Murray, 219
Snow, Michael, 106–7
  Région centrale, La (1972), 113
Sobhani, Mehrnoosh, 211
Sobrinho, Brandão, 154
social media, 7, 37, 38
Solomon, Stefan, 4
sound/soundtrack
  aural intermediality, 86
  "causal listening," 253–54
  FIG, 253–54, 263n.12
  Medium Earth, 119, 120
  Santoscopio = Dumontagem, 100, 110
  Up the Junction: Loach's adaptation, 85–86, 92, 94–95
  See also voice/human voice
South Sudan, 19–20
spectatorship. *See* audience/spectatorship
stage. *See* theatre
Staiger, Janet, 2
Stam, Robert, 7
Stam, Robert, and Randal Johnson, 153
Steptoe and Son (BBC TV sitcom), 273, 276
  Albert Steptoe (Wilfred Brambell), 267–68, 273

"Desperate Hours, The," 275–76, 275f
entrapment, 276
Harold Steptoe (Harry H. Corbett), 267–68, 273, 276
Pinter, Harold and, 273, 275–76
success, 273–74
See also BBC
Stockhausen, Karlheinz, 27n.6, 208–9, 217, 218
storytelling
  Aristotle, 29–30
  carousel slide projector/slides, 70–71, 72–73
  Heimat 2 series, 203–4, 209–10, 216–19
  Reitz, Edgar, 209
  transmedia storytelling, 38, 281
  Tulse Luper Suitcases Trilogy, 281, 287–88
Straub, Jean-Marie, and Danièle Huillet: *Fortini/Cani* (1976), 113
Street, Sarah, 1–2, 7–8
Strindberg, August, 276
structural film, 106–10, 123
structuralism, 30–31
Styrene, Poly, 255–56
Sun Yu, 189
Surrealism, 24–25
  Dwoskin, Stephen, 225–26, 227–28, 230
Sutil, Nicolás Salazar, 132, 136

Tangnamo, Somkiat, 76
Tenser, Tony, 270–71
theatre
  British cinema and, 1–2, 274–75
  cinema and, 3, 4–5, 6, 18, 153–54, 228–29
  classical Greek tragedy, 29
  Hegel, G. W. F. on modern comedy, 6–7, 15–16, 18, 26–27n.1
  Kabuki theatre, 198n.4
  musical theatre, 152–53, 188
  See also Brazil's light theatre/*teatro de revista*; British theatre; Chinese theatre; silent cinema and theatre
Thompson, Robert Farris, 41
Thoreau, Henry David: *Walden*, 39–40, 124
TikTok, 38
TLST. *See Tulse Luper Suitcases* Trilogy
Tobin, Amy, 247–48, 251–52, 263n.4
Todorov, Tzvetan, 297–98
Tomonari Nishikawa: *Sound of a Million Insects, Light of a Thousand Stars* (2015), 133

transartistry, transmediality, 7, 34, 39, 44n.1, 49–50
   audio-visual-digital arts, 33–34, 35–36
   Austen, Jane, 36–38
   cinema: transartistic nature of, 32
   digital media, 34, 39–40
   "inter/transmedial turn," 30–31
   musical "remix," 41
   overlapping specificities, 38–44
   political talk shows, 38
   "transartistic" methodology, 32–33
   transartistry, 32–34
   transmedia storytelling, 38, 281
   transmediatic, 35–36
   transmediatic actualisations, 35–38
   See also hybridisation/hybridity; intermediality
Troupe des Guinéens, La, 255–56
Truffaut, François: *400 Blows* (*Les Quatre cents coups*, 1959), 37
Trying to Kiss the Moon (*TTKM*, Stephen Dwoskin, 1994), 225, 243–44
   analogue film, 231–33, 234–35
   autobiographical essay film, 225–26, 231–32, 236–37
   autoethnography, 231–32, 234, 237–38, 244n.4
   Cordua, Beatrice/*Trixi*, 232–34, 233*f*, 236, 238–40, 241
   disability, 230–32, 234
   disappearance and transformation, 232
   Dwoskin's earlier films, 231, 232–34, 233*f*, 236
   intermediality, 225–26, 230–38
   paintings, 241
   self-exile, 230–38
   self-integration, 231–32
   self-portraiture, 230–38
   self-representation/self-images, 234–37, 235*f*, 236*f*, 237*f*, 238*f*
   slowed-down footage, 235–36, 239*f*
   video/digital video, 231–33, 234–36
   video haptics, 232, 234, 236
   See also Dwoskin, Stephen
Tulse Luper Suitcases Trilogy (*TLST*, Peter Greenaway, 2003–2005), 4–5, 10
   aesthetics, 284–85, 287–88, 289, 290–91, 298
   archival film footage, 288
   arts and cinema, 281–82, 283, 284, 286, 287, 288–89, 289*f*, 294–95, 298
   audio-visual strategies, 283, 294

   digital technology, 287, 288
   "expansion," "display," "performance," 291–94, 295–96
   from transmedia project to intermedial trilogy, 281–83
   as high-art transmedia storytelling network, 281, 298n.1
   History, 282–83, 284, 288, 293–94, 296, 298
   history/history-telling, 4–5, 281–82, 283, 284–91, 292–93, 298
   intermediality, 281–83, 295–98
   as "Life Story in 16 Episodes," 282
   media archaeology, 283, 284–91, 298
   metamediality, 298
   "Mission Statement" section, 282
   narrative complexity, 295–98
   narrative structure, 293–94, 297–98
   opening sequences, 282–83, 283*f*
   Part 1—The Moab Story (2003), 281–82, 283*f*, 284, 285–86, 285*f*, 290–91, 292–93, 294–95, 295*f*, 296–97
   Part 2—Vaux to the Sea (2004), 281–82, 284*f*, 286, 286*f*, 291–93, 292*f*, 296–97
   Part 3—From Sark to the Finish (2004), 281–82, 287, 289–90, 290*f*, 296–98
   storytelling as creative activity, 287–88
   suitcases, 284, 285–86
   timeline, 284*f*, 288
   writing, 289–91, 290*f*
   See also Greenaway, Peter; *Tulse Luper Suitcases* Trilogy: actors and characters
Tulse Luper Suitcases Trilogy: actors and characters, 282–83, 288, 296–97
   Billington, Stephen, 296–97
   Charlotte des Arbres, the Storyteller (Ana Torrent), 296
   Colonel Kotcheff, 282, 297
   Contumely sisters, 296–97
   Feild, J.J., 283*f*, 296–97
   Greenaway character, 292–93, 292*f*
   Gulag Sheherazade, 287, 290*f*
   Joan of Arc (Maria Falconetti), 286, 286*f*, 296
   Lieutenant Alazarin, 297
   Luper, Tulse Henry Purcell, 282–83, 284, 285–86, 285*f*, 289–91, 292–93, 294–95, 296–98
   "Luper specialists," 282, 284, 295, 296–97
   Madame de Moitessier (Isabella Rossellini), 288–89
   Passion Hockmeister (Caroline Dhavernas), 285–86, 285*f*

Rees, Roger, 290*f*, 296–97
theatrical auditioning for Beckett and Kafka roles, 294–95, 295*f*
See also *Tulse Luper Suitcases* Trilogy
Tumblr, 38
Tutti, Cosey Fanni, 25
TV (television)
  British cinema and, 1–2, 7–8, 87–89
  British theatre and, 273–74, 275–76
  cinema and, 3, 81–82, 87–88
  "cinematic TV," 3
  documentary-style aesthetic, 87–88
  film/TV comparison, 34, 87–88
  TV series, 19–20, 37, 219
  See also BBC; ITV; *Up the Junction*: Loach's adaptation
Twitter, 38

underground/underground film, 225, 226, 249
Universitat Pompeu Fabra's Master's Programme in Creative Documentary (Barcelona, Spain), 174–75, 183n.9
University of Reading (UK): The Moving Form of Film (conference, 2017), 1–2
Up the Junction (Nell Dunn, 1963), 7–8, 81–83, 94–95, 95n.1
  drawings by Susan Benson (1st edition), 83–84, 84*f*, 89, 91–92, 94–95
  English social history, 81–82, 87, 89, 94–95
  female sexuality, 81–82, 83, 92–93
  "Gold Blouse, The," 90–92, 94–95
  improvisatory approach, 85–86
  intermediality, 83–84, 94–95
  literary techniques, 83
  as unconventional in form and content, 83
  "Up the Junction," 85–86
  working-class Battersea, 81–82, 83
  working-class women, 81–82, 90–91
  See also Dunn, Nell; *Up the Junction*: comparison between Collinson and Loach's adaptations
Up the Junction: Collinson's adaptation (film 1968), 7–8, 81–82
  conventional narrative, 87, 93–94
  homage to Loach's version, 87–89, 94–95
  intermediality, 87–89
  narrator, 87
  relationship with Dunn's stories, 87
  self-reflexiveness, 88–89
  social commentary, 87, 89–90
  technology (colour and widescreen), 87–88, 89–90, 90*f*, 93–95
  See also Collinson, Peter; *Up the Junction*: comparison between Collinson and Loach's adaptations
Up the Junction: comparison between Collinson and Loach's adaptations, 94–95
  approach to characters, 87, 94–95
  "Gold Blouse" incident, 90–95
  intermediality, 81–82, 87, 90–95
  reflexivity, 94–95
  relationship with Dunn's original stories, 81–82, 87
  social change, 89–90, 94–95
  technological change and aesthetic experiment, 88–89, 94–95
  technological features, 87–88, 89–90, 94–95
  See also *Up the Junction*: Collinson's adaptation; *Up the Junction*: Loach's adaptation
Up the Junction: Loach's adaptation (TV play, 1965), 7–8, 81–82, 85*f*
  aural properties, 85–86, 92, 94–95
  "Bad Girl" (song), 86
  BBC *Wednesday Play*, 81–82
  closeness to Dunn's narrative and sensibility, 81–82, 83–84, 85–86, 87, 94–95
  documentary elements, 83–84, 89
  Dunn/Loach collaboration, 81–82, 83–84, 86, 94–95
  elliptical editing, 86
  exterior locations, 89, 94–95
  Garnett, Tony (story editor), 81–82, 83
  improvisational techniques, 85–86
  intermediality, 82, 86
  as milestone in British TV drama, 85–86, 89
  music, 86
  realism, 85–86, 88–89, 92, 94–95
  screenplay by Dunn, 81–82
  See also Loach, Ken; *Up the Junction*: comparison between Collinson and Loach's adaptations
Uroskie, Andrew V., 79n.13

Valentino, Rudolph, 157, 162
Varda, Agnès, 31–32
Vertov, Dziga, 38–39

Vila, Eva, 174
  Bajarí: Històries de la Barcelona gitana, 174–75
  See also *Bajarí*
Visconti, Luchino: *Death in Venice* (*Morte a Venezia*, 1971), 18
viuvinha do cinema, A (*The Little Widow of the Cinema*, play), 153–54, 155, 165n.6
  censorship, 154
  Companhia Leopoldo Froes, 153–54
  filmic prologue, 154, 155
  plot, 153–54
  See also Brazil's light theatre/*teatro de revista*
voice/human voice, 253–54, 262
  AMY!, 248, 254–61, 262
  "causal listening," 253–54
  FIG: voice/vocal sounds, 252, 253–54, 262
  as intermedial act, 247
  recorded voice, 247, 248, 253–54
  voice-over, 120, 210, 242–43, 253–54, 257, 259–61, 285–86
  See also sound/soundtrack
Voigts-Virchow, Eckart, 50–51
Vona Michell, Tris: *Finding Chopin: Dans l'Essex* (slides, 2014), 78n.2
von Moltke, Johannes, 205–6, 216–17, 218

Wagner, Richard, 9, 16, 25
  Gesamtkunstwerk/totalisation of the arts, 9, 16, 23, 34–35
  Meistersingers, The, 16
  Valkyries, The, 16
Walden (Daniel Zimmerman, 2018), 121–22
  cover of, 126–27, 127f
  Documentary Special Jury Prize, 121–22
  Earth, 116–17
  experimental documentary work, 8–9
  film festivals, 121–22
  forests: vegetal world seen from an insider's perspective, 124, 125f
  gallery installation, 116–17, 121–22, 127–28, 128f
  intermediality, 116–17, 121–22
  locations, 121–22, 123

  mapping out globalisation, 121–28
  moving panorama, 125–26
  panoramic shot (circular/half circular), 8–9, 113, 116–17, 121–22, 125–27
  as structural film, 123
  Walden (title), 124
  wood planks trade route, 122–24, 125–27
  world-encompassing ambitions, 126–27, 127f
  See also Zimmerman, Daniel
Walley, Jonathan, 135–36
Wardle, Irving, 270
Warhol, Andy, 227
Web 2.0, 7, 40
Weidner, Tina, 78n.3
Welsby, Chris: *Weather Vane* (1972), 144n.4
Werner, Michael, and Bénédicte Zimmermann, 277–78
West, Jennifer: *Pink Beach Red Desert Dream Sand Film* (2017), 133
Whiting, John, 270
Williams, Raymond, 276, 277–78
Wolf, Werner, 50–51, 53–54, 204
Wollen, Peter. See *AMY!*; Mulvey, Laura and Peter Wollen
Women's Aid, 263n.12
Women's Liberation movement, 247–48
Woods Peiró, Eva, 170–71
World War II, 4–5, 255, 281–82
Wright, Katherine, 259–60
Wyler, William, 268
  Desperate Hours, The (1955), 271–72

Xavier, Ismail, 4, 8–9
X-Ray Spex, 255–56, 257, 260–61

Yacavone, Daniel, 293–94
YouTube, 7, 38–39
  Lizzie Bennet Diaries, The (YouTube vlog series, 2012–2013), 37–38

Zanger, Anat, 51, 54
Zhong Dafeng, 186–87
Zielinski, Siegfried, 135–36
Zimmerman, Daniel, 121–22, 124, 126–27
  See also *Walden*